Critical Essays on

JANE AUSTEN

CRITICAL ESSAYS
ON
BRITISH LITERATURE

Zack Bowen, General Editor
University of Miami

◆

Critical Essays on
JANE AUSTEN

◆

edited by

LAURA MOONEYHAM WHITE

G. K. Hall & Co.
An Imprint of Simon & Schuster Macmillan
New York

Prentice Hall International
London   Mexico City   New Delhi   Singapore   Sydney   Toronto

G. K. Hall & Co.
An Imprint of Simon & Schuster Macmillan
1633 Broadway
New York, NY 10019

Library of Congress Cataloging-in-Publication Data

Critical essays on Jane Austen / edited by Laura Mooneyham White.
    p.   cm.—(Critical essays on British literature)
    Includes bibliographical references and index.
    ISBN 0-7838-0093-2 (alk. paper)
    1. Austen, Jane, 1775–1817—Criticism and interpretation.
    2. Women and literature—England—History—19th century. I. White,
Laura Mooneyham. II. Series.
PR4037.C75   1998
8239.7—dc21   98-22545
                                                          CIP

This paper meets the requirements of ANSI/NISO Z3948–1992 (Permanence of Paper).

10 9 8 7 6 5

Printed in the United States of America

To John and Louise Garrigues

Contents

◆

General Editor's Note

♦

The Critical Essays on British Literature series provides a variety of approaches to both classical and contemporary writers of Britain and Ireland. The formats of the volumes in the series vary with the thematic designs of individual editors and with the amount and nature of existing reviews and criticism, augmented, where appropriate, by original essays by recognized authorities. It is hoped that each volume will be unique in developing a new overall perspective on its particular subject.

Laura Mooneyham White's introduction covers Austen's critical and popular reception for most of the last two centuries, from the early praise of Sir Walter Scott and the commentary of major nineteenth-century novelists, through new critical analyses, to the rebirth of her work in contemporary film and television, and the emerging critical emphasis on new historicism and feminism/gender issues. She focuses throughout on the dual roles of popular culture and audiences whose interest is principally enjoyment, and critics' professional and ideological concerns, each viewing Austen's gentility and concern with upper-class values and life, with an eye that reflects their own fantasies or politics.

White's selections, all written in the last 15 years, cover larger issues and commentary on multiple works, as well as essays that address an individual novel. Two original essays written especially for this volume include one by Devoney Looser and another by White herself.

ZACK BOWEN
University of Miami

Publisher's Note

◆

Producing a volume that contains both newly commissioned and reprinted material presents the publisher with the challenge of balancing the desire to achieve stylistic consistency with the need to preserve the integrity of works first published elsewhere. In the Critical Essays series, essays commissioned especially for a particular volume are edited to be consistent with G. K. Hall's house style; reprinted essays appear in the style in which they were first published, with only typographical errors corrected. Consequently, shifts in style from one essay to another are the result of our efforts to be faithful to each text as it was originally published.

Introduction

Laura Mooneyham White

"Jane Austen"—the woman, the writer, the cultural icon—has been a contested figure among her various publics for almost 200 years. Since at least 1822, when Sir Walter Scott praised Austen's novels by contrasting them with his own "Big Bow-wow strain," Austen's advocates—as much as her detractors—have tended to judge her worth on such highly charged grounds as scale, "artfulness," realism, morality, and a wide field of interconnected sociocultural values, especially those related to class, politics, gender, and sexuality.[1] The most recent renegotiation about "Jane Austen," one that has occurred in the last three years, has taken place on the very limits of her reading public, as film after film based on Austen's novels has swept into British and American middlebrow culture.[2] Suburban bookstores have fresh stocks of the novels now in place, several with covers graced by the movie stars (Gwyneth Paltrow, Emma Thompson) who portray Austen's heroines. There is little to indicate, however, a genuine explosion in the reading of Austen's novels beyond the three general sets of people who have been her largest public for at least half a century: middle-class aficionados (this a mostly female group), university students, and professional scholars.

One curiosity—perhaps to be expected—is the enormous gap between the "Jane Austen" presented in these new films that have occasioned such significant public pleasure and attention and the Jane Austen the contemporary academy finds of equal interest. Scholarly interest in Austen has been high since the 1940s, and especially since the mid-1970s, which saw an explosion of feminist depreciations—or qualified appreciations—of Austen's marriage plots. The most important strain of Austen criticism in the last two decades has been historicist. This historicism has had a particular bent, however, for although Austen's critics have asked a series of connected historical questions about class relations, colonialism, economics, gender, and sexuality, they have attended much less often to the historical dimensions of religion, music, art, the natural world, or philosophy (with the exception of political philosophy).[3] Feminist critics in particular have worked through—it seems—all the conceivable inadequacies of the marriage plot in Austen's work, and in that of other eighteenth- and nineteenth-century authors. The new films, however, proceed as if no voice had ever been raised to interrogate romance plots, or as if the rapid social and political changes of the Regency period had no particular place in presentations of Austen's plots. It may be unfair to charge, as has Louis Menand, that the films proceed "without a shadow of an idea in sight," but it cannot be too far off the mark.[4]

The films, indeed, recapitulate the oldest strains of Austen appreciation—the pleasure taken in a love story, the enjoyment of humorous characters, and the nostalgia that had attached itself to the Regency period even by the mid-nineteenth century. As Lindsay Duguin has noted,

> Regency England, with its curricles and pelisses, its comfortable country seats and its roaming strangers, has long been the place for romance. Frances Burney invented it; Georgette Heyer capitalized on it, now Hollywood is capitalizing on it. That Jane Austen was doing something altogether different seems not to matter to the filmmakers.[5]

This is a difficulty admitted but not necessarily overcome by the filmmakers themselves (vide the admission made by Andrew Davies, the screenwriter of the BBC *Pride and Prejudice* and the Arts and Entertainment *Emma*, "Most Jane Austen adaptations seem to drown in social comedy and costumery— the men trapped in their buttons and stocks and jackets and boots").[6] The films tend to be lavish in their use of woolly sheep, children, and puppies; further, as many scenes as can be moved from indoors to out are so transported to render any possible sweeping panoramas or, at the very least, broad sweeps of lawn (for instance, in the McGrath *Emma*, Emma talks Harriet into refusing Robert Martin under a striped awning set amid Hartfield's pastoral greenway; later Emma attempts to console Harriet in her "loss" of Mr. Elton by showing her a litter of puppies).

The films capitalize on "character," a long-standing preoccupation in Austen appreciation that was immortalized in Kipling's short story "The Janeites" (1924). In "The Janeites," a British artillery company in World War I mitigates the horrors of trench warfare by creating a secret society based on its love of Austen's characters and of the details of her Regency world.[7] The films continue this tradition by emphasizing and in some cases overdrawing character, as in the Langton *Pride and Prejudice*. As Louis Menand complains,

> the most irritating thing about [this production] is [that] whenever a character says something silly or stupid, another character smirks or snickers . . . or in some similar fashion signals to us that a fatuity has been uttered, [a practice that defeats] the famous Austenian irony [that] what is funny or absurd to us is not funny and absurd [to her characters]. (Menand, 13)

By broadening and flattening character, the films thus accentuate each character as a "character," or humor, and thus become part of the long stream of Janeite fashion—in vogue since Kipling's artillery officers and current to this day in the doings at Jane Austen Society meetings—of treating Austen's characters as if they were separable from the novels in which they appear (as Claudia Johnson notes, one entertainment at the Jane Austen Societies is to "imagine together how a character in one novel might behave towards a character from another" [Johnson, 20]).

The most significant divergence from contemporary critical understandings of Austen is, however, seen in the films' unproblematic treatment of the romance plots. But these adaptations go further, relying on the presumption that Austen's film audience is hungry for even more romance than Austen herself provided. Critics have struggled for many decades over the adequacy of Austen's romantic plots, over her capacity for representing passion or the emotional life, and over the degrees to which the movement to marriage in the novels operates as the primary structural device through which her heroines undergo their emotional, moral, and intellectual development. The films reveal few qualms on these scores. The poster advertising the McGrath *Emma,* for instance, shows the heroine brandishing bow and arrow, and blares, "Cupid is armed and dangerous!" The Lee *Sense and Sensibility* begins by establishing a witty, charming, and handsome Edward Ferrars (portrayed by the actor Hugh Grant) and ends with a double wedding, beflowered village children much in evidence; the final gesture is that of a jubilant Colonel Brandon throwing coins in the air for the children to gather. The Michell *Persuasion,* although generally more serious in its treatment, nonetheless incorporates *both* of the proposal scenes Austen wrote for the novel: first, the rather strained version she put aside—which has Wentworth sent on the uncomfortable errand of determining whether Anne intends to marry Mr. Elliot—and, second, the more nuanced and powerful version with which the romance plot comes to its resolution. In general, the films reinforce the erotic by continually emphasizing the body: in Langton's *Pride and Prejudice,* Darcy practices fencing and even swims in a lake; Emma and Mr. Knightley share archery practice in McGrath's *Emma;* and the continual disarrangement of clothes and hair—by wind, exercise, or passion—in the Michell *Persuasion* insists upon the physical selves of the hero and heroine.

The presentation of the erotic, the passionate, and the bodily in these recent films operates as a kind of restitution, an answer to those of Austen's readers (from Charlotte Brontë to George Eliot, from Mark Twain to Marvin Mudrick) who have faulted her for her presumably inadequate commitment to romance. Charlotte Brontë complained to George Henry Lewes, the eminent scholar and critic, that "Miss Austen is only shrewd and observant." Brontë had read Austen at Lewes's instigation, for Lewes was a rabid enthusiast for Jane Austen. In an 1853 issue of his magazine, the *Westminster Review,* he wrote, "[She is] the greatest artist that has ever written, using the term to signify the most perfect mastery over the means to her end."[8] But Brontë demurred, on grounds well in keeping with the sensibilities of Austen's current interpreters in popular culture; in *Pride and Prejudice,* she found only a carefully fenced, highly cultivated garden, with neat borders and delicate flowers; but no glance of a bright, vivid physiognomy, no open country, no blue hill, no bonny beck. I should hardly like to live with her ladies and gentlemen, in their elegant but confined houses. (Southam, 126)

It seems the current middlebrow cultural project is to reinstate the "blue hill" and "bright, vivid physiognomy" into Austen's works.

Brontë was not the only one to take issue with Lewes's inordinate enthusiasm for Austen; his partner, George Eliot, also found Austen inadequate, and for reasons very similar to Brontë's. From January 1857 on, Eliot and Lewes together read aloud all the novels of Jane Austen (with the exception of *Pride and Prejudice,* which Eliot had read previously).[9] Though not widely known, it is thus a curious fact of literary history that Eliot's second attempt at fiction, "Mr. Gilfil's Love Story," was written as Eliot received nightly visitations from Jane Austen's voice. This reading program was almost certainly proposed by Lewes, who wished Eliot to know Austen's work better. However, Lewes's enthusiasm for Austen was not (seemingly) matched by Eliot herself, who had written four years earlier, in 1853, of Austen's limitations:

[She] shows[s] us too much of the littlenesses and trivialities of life, and limit[s] [herself] so scrupulously of the sayings and doings of dull, ignorant, and disagreeable people that their very truthfulness makes us yawn. They fall short of fulfilling the objects . . . of Fiction in its highest aspect, . . . to "take man from the low passions and miserable troubles of life into a higher region, . . . to excite a generous sorrow at vicissitudes not his own, to raise the passions into sympathy with heroic troubles, and to admit the soul into that serener atmosphere from which it rarely returns to ordinary existence without some memory . . . which ought to enlarge the domain of thought, and exalt the motives of action." (qtd. in Southam, 145–46)[10]

Eliot quotes in the second half of this passage from that now-ridiculed Victorian novelist, Bulwer-Lytton (remembered chiefly for his "It was a dark and stormy night" and the tumultuous *The Last Days of Pompeii* [1834]).[11] Rebuking Austen by means of—surprisingly—Bulwer-Lytton, Eliot shows her allegiance to "raising the passions into sympathy with heroic troubles" and her concomitant dismissal of Austen's presumed "littlenesses" and "trivialities." Emerson joined Eliot and Brontë in depreciation: "I am at a loss to understand why people hold Miss Austen's novels at so high a rate, which seem to me vulgar in tone, sterile in artistic invention, [and] imprisoned in the wretched conventions of English society. . . . Never was life so pinched and narrow" (qtd. in Southam, 28).[12] And Mark Twain was equally brutal: "Whenever I take up *Pride and Prejudice* or *Sense and Sensibility,* I feel like a barkeeper entering the Kingdom of Heaven."[13]

Ian Watt has characterized this line of eminent sniping as springing from "the encounter of . . . poetic, idealistic temper[s] with an alien mode of imagination" (Watt, 28). But Austen's supporters, from the mid-Victorian period to the present, have also tended to have temperamental and cultural reasons for their advocacy. Watt argues, "Just as the dislike of Jane Austen's detractors springs from their sense that she is coolly indifferent to the forward or the upward or the inward look which they favor, so her most uncritical devotees, the 'Janeites,' find in her a fortifying occasion for looking backward, or down their noses" (Watt, 10). This "Janeite" tradition, reinforced by nostalgia and gentrified class consciousness, has been at its weakest a relatively uncritical and self-serving proposition.

There have been, however, as Johnson has delineated, at least two distinct strands of early-twentieth-century Janeitism. The first, described in the previous paragraph, was also the target of Henry James's complaint in 1905 that Austen had been overwhelmingly appropriated by the tea-and-doily set eager to assert its gentility. Serving this set, James argues, is a group of middle-class publishers, anxious to commodify Austen along demure lines for their own commercial benefit, "who have [thus] found their 'dear,' our dear, everybody's dear, Jane so infinitely to their material purpose."[14]

The terms of James's assault on the genteel Austen constructed by those eager to claim their "dear Jane," however, work at the same time to place him within the second strand of Janeitism: the belletristic tradition, that of the "scholar-gentlemen at play" (Johnson, 10). For though James is at pains to unravel the idea that Austen worked her narrative art through a kind of inspired amateurism, he is nonetheless equally willing to knit together a claim that her artistry repels critical analysis. As B. C. Southam argues, James is "ready to usher in a . . . Jane Austen who defies or evades the embrace of the 'critical spirit' ":

> James speaks of "her little touches of human truth, little glimpses of steady vision, little master-strokes of imagination"; yet all this is managed with a "light felicity" that leaves us incurious of "her process or of the experience in her that fed it." (Southam, 31–32)

In describing Austen thus, James enters into a long line of argument that debates whether Austen herself was much aware of the artistry of her effects, an argument surely laid abed by the treatment of scholars and researchers of the latter twentieth century. In displaying such incuriosity about Austen's artistry, James thus becomes—despite himself—a participant in the belletristic tradition of Austen appreciation, a tradition more interested in the charming contents of Austen's novels than in the formal artistry that constructed them.

This tradition was strongly established by the late nineteenth century and has had a continuous history since then. Claudia Johnson describes the high tide (in the 1910s, 1920s, and 1930s) of this brand of Janeitism as a mostly male enthusiasm shared among an elite corps of publishers, professors and literati such as Montague Summers, A. C. Bradley, Lord David Cecil, . . . R. W. Chapman, and E. M. Forster. At the Royal Society in particular Austen's genius was celebrated with a militantly dotty enthusiasm. (Johnson, 8)

It is in keeping with this tradition that the English gentleman's reply to the question of whether he ever read novels—"Certainly, all six of them every year"—may best be understood.

What these two strains of Janeitism—the genteel ladies and the effete scholars—shared was a pleasure in the seemingly cozy world and humorous characters Austen produced; they differ, however, in their interest in the courtship plots that structure the novels. The genteel ladies James attacks valued—and commonly exaggerated—the romance elements of the novels, whereas the "scholar-gentlemen at play" undervalued the same out of a thoroughgoing suspicion of women and domesticity (Johnson, 9–10). And though the recent films furnish enough attention to "character" to satisfy the latter group, it seems that the genteel ladies have won out on the much larger question of how to treat the romance plots; that is, that the love stories of the novels should be emphasized and expanded as much as possible.

In roughly midcentury, however, the academy, strongly influenced by New Criticism, began to make a rival claim upon the field of Austen interpretation. Though the genteel ladies were left to their own devices, unmindful, by and large, of developments in critical approaches, the upper-class male devotees found themselves superseded by "a middle-class professoriate . . . [as] the disciplined study of the novel was being founded" (Johnson, 4). The profusion of New Critical approaches included D. W. Harding's "Regulated Hatred: An Aspect of the Work of Jane Austen" (1940).[15] Harding's concern was to demolish the practice of reading Austen as an act of sensitivity and culture; he ruthlessly charged that Austen is "read and enjoyed by precisely the sort of people whom she disliked" (Harding, 342). Even as middle-class academicians took over Austen criticism, however, Austen remained something of an anomaly, included only as "Jane Austen" rather than, say, "Dickens" or "Fielding." As John Bender argued, in the 1930s, Austen joined that

> small group of women allowed into the canon of great writers on the condition that her given and family name remain inseparably fused, presumably as a sign that professional scholars would treat her differently from the enthusiasts who called her "Jane" or the belletrists who called her "Miss Austen."[16]

Despite the steady production of Austen criticism between 1940 and 1970, scholars were nonetheless slow to address Austen as a historical figure, a woman writing in and about her time. Kingsley Amis certainly was moving against the grain, for instance, when he described Austen as a "war novelist."

By 1971, matters were such that the eminent Austen scholar B. C. Southam complained of what was then modern criticism's tendency "to treat Jane Austen as an ahistorical novelist": "[It is said] that in taking her own society for the stage and setting for the novels . . . she was merely turning to the material at hand [to reveal her] concern . . . with human nature and human values [that] are timeless."[17]

That deficiency, that gap in our collective understanding of Austen's work as a product of a particular historical and cultural moment, has certainly been redressed in the last two decades. It cannot be particularly controversial to claim that the most exciting developments in Austen criticism in the last 20 years have been in two large and commonly connected venues: historicism ("new" or otherwise) and feminism (see, for instance, in this volume, the essay by Devoney Looser on Austen's own understanding of "history," an essay that links feminist analysis with both literary and social history). The first historicist analyses of Austen emerged in the 1940s as a by-product of the academy's partial attention to Marxist thought, in studies by (among others) David Daiches, Arnold Kettle, and Mark Shorer.[18] However, political analysis of Austen became full-blown only after the mid-1970s. We can identify the advent of the last two decades' wave of political criticism with the publication of two works: Alistair Duckworth's *The Improvement of the Estate* (1971) and Marilyn Butler's *Jane Austen and the War of Ideas* (1975).[19] Duckworth's study places Austen within a conservative tradition; he argues that "her novels . . . uncovered the threats posed by false improvers and materialists to the transmission of a worthy social heritage" (Duckworth 1971, xv). (In "Austen's Accommodations," reprinted in the present volume, Duckworth extends his historicist analysis of the novels to the particulars of pounds, shillings, and pence.) Butler's work situated Austen as a conservative and read Austen's novels as continuing the tradition of the polemical fiction of Maria Edgeworth. In Butler's account, Austen's novels are a field on which conservative political values duel against progressive ideas, undoing the latter's lures of moral relativism, subjectivity, and emotionalism. Despite Butler's narrow judgments of the novels themselves (e.g., of *Pride and Prejudice*, that "it does not read like satire at all" [Butler, 219]) and her general proclivity for seeing the novels as propagandistic devices rather than creations of art, she nonetheless usefully gives weight to the arguments for Austen's essentially anti-Jacobin position, one aligned with the interests of landed Tories. Read in concert with Duckworth, Butler establishes a strong case for Austen as political conservative. Butler and Duckworth were answered in 1983 by Margaret Kirkham, whose *Jane Austen, Feminism, and Fiction* argues that Austen is better understood as an exemplar of Enlightenment feminism, in a more or less direct line from Mary Wollstonecraft; by defining feminism as a position that favors women's moral and intellectual growth as well as growth toward rational self-control,

Kirkham can readily include Austen in the line of protofeminists that led to Eliot, Woolf, and beyond.[20]

As the previous paragraph suggests, the rehistoricized understanding of Austen's novels in several cases subsumes feminist criticism, in that much of the best of Austen studies informed by feminism, from those of Kirkham to Mary Poovey to Nancy Armstrong to Claudia Johnson to Deborah Kaplan, rely on a careful placement of Austen within the surging developments—political, economic, and cultural—of the late eighteenth and early nineteenth century. (The current volume includes representative essays from the last four of the five critics mentioned.) This linking of historical analysis with feminist argument, however, is less present in what is perhaps the locus classicus of feminist evaluations of nineteenth-century women's fiction (including Austen's): Gilbert and Gubar's *The Madwoman in the Attic* (1979).[21] In it, Gilbert and Gubar continue the train of argument begun by Harding and also by Marvin Mudrick, whose *Jane Austen: Irony as Defense and Discovery* explored a "subversive" Austen, a second self writing against her culture.[22] Gilbert and Gubar posit the existence of a cover story in Austen's fiction, a surface plot in each of her novels that requires young women to acquiesce to the submission and stasis of marriage after an adolescence as relatively free agents. Under this cover story lies, presumably, insurrection. Austen's heroines survive, Gilbert and Gubar claim, by only "seeming to submit"; Austen herself thus succeeds in maintaining a double consciousness "that proclaims its docility and restraint even as it uncovers the delights of assertion and rebellion" (Gilbert and Gubar, 174–75).

The debate about the nature and degree of Austen's feminism is one of the most salient features of Austen criticism in the past 20 years. The debate only begins with arguments about Austen's inheritance from Mary Wollstonecraft and other progressives, for there is wide agreement that Austen at the very least shared with Wollstonecraft a belief in women's moral equality with men, as well as Wollstonecraft's subversive dream that women can be trained to think rationally.[23] Agreement falters, however, in the face of the unalterable fact that each of Austen's novels relies on the marriage plot as its central structuring device. Feminist critics often wish that novels written by women in the eighteenth and nineteenth centuries were not ended so automatically by marriage or death for the heroine, the choice depending on whether the particular novel's vision is comic or tragic. But, as Nancy K. Miller has pointed out, "the novel, more than any other form of art, is forced by the contract of the genre to negotiate with social realities in order to remain legible."[24] For this reason, it is probably unreasonable to wish that Austen had depicted happy, fulfilled unmarried women or to revile her for her failure to imagine a rosier future for women outside of marriage. Nonetheless, Austen's reliance on the marriage plot has inevitably led many critics to express a wide range of demurrals with Austen's cultural values as they seem to be expressed by the novels. Such demurrals include some straightforward attacks, perhaps the most striking of which has been Nina Auerbach's characterization of Fanny Price as a second Grendel, Frankenstein's monster, or Dracula, and even the even-tempered Wayne Booth has put forward provisionally the proposition that *Emma* may be a "dangerous work to put in the hands of the young."[25]

Feminist analyses have also contributed to debates about Austen's sexuality, or rather, about the sexuality expressed by her values and narrative designs. The longstanding issue of her putative coldness or queerness has led some critics to question heterosexual normative ways of reading her novels (see, for instance, this volume's essay by D. A. Miller). Claudia Johnson describes this normative view and suggests its limitations:

> In her novels, men are gentlemen, women are ladies, and the desires of gentlemen and ladies for each other are intelligible, complementary, mutually fulfilling, and above all *inevitable*. Not that such assumptions are articulated. The whole point is that they do not have to be, but that they must never be; as David Halperin has suggested, heterosexuality is the love that dares not speak its name, and argument would denaturalize and *out* it. (Johnson, 2)[26]

The question of Austen's sexual values rose to the status of a cause célèbre with the appearance in the *London Review of Books* in 1995 of a review article headlined (not by the author) "Sister-Sister." The author, Terry Castle, had meant to raise the question of Austen's homosocial and homoerotic dimensions, not to suggest, for instance, that Austen and her sister were practicing incestuous lesbians. Nonetheless, the following months saw wave upon wave of popular and scholarly disapproval descend upon Professor Castle's head.[27]

The other historical strand of Austen criticism, following Marxist lines of argument, has focused on economics, and, most recently, on colonialism and imperialism as unconscious or barely represented pressures in Austen's fictional world. That line of analysis has been put forward most famously by Edward Said, who analyzes *Mansfield Park* in terms of its relation to slave owning (see also the essay by Moira Ferguson, in the present volume, on the historical substrates of *Mansfield Park* and colonialism).[28] Continually at issue in such analyses is the question of moral autonomy: even Raymond Williams claimed in *The Country and the City* (1973) that "what happens in *Emma*, in *Persuasion*, in *Mansfield Park* is the development of an everyday, uncompromising morality which is in the end separable from its social basis and which, in other hands, can be turned against it."[29] For Said, this separation is not really possible; rather "morality in fact is not separable from its social basis: right up to the last sentence, Austen affirms and repeats the geographical process of expansion involving trade, production, and consumption that predates, underlies, and guarantees the morality" (Said, 92–93). This interpenetration of morality by society means for Said that the reader is left in an uncomfortable position regarding Austen (one familiar to feminists), for if one endorses her moral views, one is by extension endorsing her ideology, an ideology that among other things is relatively uncritical of the class system and of British imperialism. Such a view, of course, implies that Austen's moral views—as articulated from novel to novel, from character to character—have a monolithic quality about them that is organically connected to the presiding social understanding of her day, and argues that neither reader nor characters have much moral freedom.

The power of new historicist and/or feminist views in scholarly domains has been considerable. The ahistorical view of Austen that B. C. Southam fretted over in 1971 has indeed been routed from the scene. However, Austen seems to have fallen into a welter of conflicting histories. Not only do different critics have widely divergent views about Austen's political values (compare Butler's and Duckworth's work to Kirkham's, for instance), but further, what counts as a historical understanding varies enormously. As James Thompson has noted, "what passes under the name of history [in Austen studies] ranges from explorations of class conflict [and gender relations] on down to the more ordinary annotation [of] obscure social details."[30]

And, of course, as the recent films make plain, the popular conception of Austen rolls along in general oblivion of the efforts and debates of the critics. Still there *are* some nods to history in this current rash of films. For instance, the 1995 *Persuasion* begins with Admiral Croft toasting his sailors on the occasion of Napoléon's first imprisonment, so that when we learn later in the film of his escape we are thus made aware that Wentworth will have to return to active duty. Further, almost every one of these films acknowledges the class system in some way, particularly by showing the working poor and servants who make Austen's genteel world possible, a portrayal that goes beyond Austen's slight treatment of the lower classes. Nonetheless, the films reveal the continuing divide between popular and professional understandings of Austen. Like Shakespeare, Jane Austen has an enduring and contested role to play in British and American culture—both for academics and for more general members of her audience (readers and nonreaders alike). That current scholarly preoccupations mirror the moral and cultural issues that beset contemporary life (class and gender, in particular) cannot surprise us much, nor can it much surprise us that a popular audience might wish to escape these issues by relaxing in an Austenian world of stately homes and quaintly dressed maidens. There is however an asymmetry, for although the film public will remain blissfully unaware of academic contestations, the scholars do go to films—and take their enjoyments as other mortals do. At best, critics and readers of Austen can aim to be aware of the complexities of their responses to Austen, her world, and her implied values, even as we aim to be aware of the complexities in our own culture and time.

Notes

1. "Scott on Jane Austen," *Jane Austen: The Critical Heritage,* ed. B. C. Southam (London: Routledge & Kegan Paul, 1968), 106; hereafter cited in text. The long train of Austen's reception has been most usefully canvased by Southam's introduction, 1–33, and by Claudia Johnson, "The Divine Jane Austen: Jane Austen, Janeites, and the Discipline of Novel Studies" (to appear in *boundary* 2 [Fall 1998]); hereafter cited in text. Southam is strongest on the reception history of the nineteenth century, Johnson strongest on the first half of the twentieth century, though each have important things to say about the whole range of Austen's reception.

2. There have been five important Austen films appearing on either the screen or television between 1995 and 1997: *Persuasion,* dir. Roger Michell, perf. Amanda Root and Ciaran Hinds, British Broadcasting Company Films, 1995; *Sense and Sensibility,* dir. Ang Lee, perf. Emma Thompson, Hugh Grant, and Kate Winslet, Columbia Pictures, 1996; *Pride and Prejudice,* dir. Simon Langton, perf. Jennifer Ehlo and Colin Firth, British Broadcasting Company, 1995; *Emma,* dir. Douglas McGrath, perf. Gwyneth Paltrow, Buena Vista, 1996; and *Jane Austen's Emma,* dir. Diarmuid Lawrence, perf. Kate Beckinsale, A&E, 1997. There has also been a very loose Hollywood adaptation of *Emma* in *Clueless,* which replaces Highbury with a San Fernando Valley high school (dir. Amy Heckerling, perf. Alicia Silverstone, Paramount Studios, 1995). For sheer improbability, one has to prefer the 1940 Hollywood version of *Pride and Prejudice,* which gives Lady Catherine de Bourgh a heart of gold (she'd been scheming to get Elizabeth and Darcy together, one understands, even as she seemed to stand in opposition) and provides an entirely superfluous carriage race between Mrs. Bennet and Mrs. Lucas (dir. Robert Leonard, perf. Lawrence Olivier and Greer Garson, Hunt Stromburg, 1940).

3. For instance, Robert K. Wallace's *Jane Austen and Mozart: Classical Equilibrium in Fiction and Music* (Athens: University of Georgia Press, 1983) is one of the few explorations of the relationship between Austen's formal elements and those of the classical music with which she would have been most familiar, though Austen was a devoted amateur pianist and though critics no less eminent as Virginia Woolf and Lionel Trilling have thought the affinity worth the mention (from Trilling: "one understands very easily why many readers are moved to explain their pleasure in [*Pride and Prejudice*] by reference to Mozart, especially *The Marriage of Figaro*").

4. Louis Menand, "What Jane Austen Doesn't Tell Us," *The New York Review of Books* 43 (February 1, 1996): 13; hereafter cited in text.

5. Lindsay Duguin, "*Emma,*" *Times Literary Supplement,* September 27, 1996, 19. Nostalgia for the two decades of the nineteenth century was well in place by the time the beginning writer George Eliot invoked these past days as a simpler, more innocent past in her first three short stories, collected as *Scenes of Clerical Life* (1858). The modern edition is edited by David Lodge (Harmondsworth: Penguin, 1973).

6. Andrew Davies, "Picture the Scene," *Times Educational Supplement,* September 15, 1995, 10.

7. Rudyard Kipling, "The Janeites," in *Debits and Credits,* ed. Sandra Kemp (Harmondsworth: Penguin, 1987), 99–128. See Johnson's excellent explication of the sexual and cultural ideology expressed by Kipling's Janeites, 9–14.

8. George H. Lewes, "The Lady Novelists," *Westminster Review* 58 (1952): 134.

9. Gordon Haight, *George Eliot: A Biography* (New York: Oxford University Press, 1968), 225.

10. This passage from an unsigned review in Lewes's *Westminster Review* was, in the opinion of Gordon Haight, Eliot's preeminent biographer and critic, almost certainly written by George Eliot. See Southam, 145. Eliot's opinion here was based on her reading of *Pride and Prejudice,* the only Austen novel she'd read by this point.

11. Bulwer-Lytton, preface to *Night and Day* (Edinburgh: W. Blackwood, 1841), 2.

12. Southam quotes Ralph Waldo Emerson, *The Journals of Ralph Waldo Emerson: 1856–1863,* ed. E. W. Emerson and W. E. Forbes, vol. 9 (Boston: Houghton Mifflin, 1913), 336–37.

13.   Mark Twain, quoted in Ian Watt, introduction to *Jane Austen: A Collection of Critical Essays*, ed. Ian Watt (Englewood Cliffs, N.J.: Prentice-Hall, 1963), 7; Watt hereafter cited in text.

14.   James made these points about Austen in a 1905 lecture entitled "The Lessons of Balzac." The lecture is reprinted in *The House of Fiction: Essays on the Novel*, ed. Leon Edel (London: R. Hart-Davis, 1957), 61–63.

15.   D. W. Harding, "Regulated Hatred: An Aspect of the Work of Jane Austen," *Scrutiny* 8 (1940): 342–62; reprinted in *Jane Austen: A Collection of Critical Essays*, ed. Ian Watt (Englewood Cliffs, N.J.: Prentice-Hall, 1963), 166–79; citations to the former will be included hereafter in text.

16.   John Bender, "In the Public Domain," *Times Literary Supplement*, August 10–16, 1990, 854.

17.   B. C. Southam, "General Tilney's Hot-Houses: Some Recent Jane Austen Studies and Texts," *Ariel* 2, no. 4 (1971): 57.

18.   See David Daiches, "Jane Austen, Karl Marx, and the Aristocratic Dance," *American Scholar* 17 (1947–1948): 289–96; Arnold Kettle, *An Introduction to the English Novel*, vol. 1 (London: Hutchinson's University Library, 1951), 90–104; and Mark Shorer, "Fiction and the 'Matrix of Analogy,' " *Kenyon Review* 11 (1949): 539–60.

19.   Alistair Duckworth, *The Improvement of the Estate* (Baltimore: The Johns Hopkins University Press, 1971); Marilyn Butler, *Jane Austen and the War of Ideas* (Oxford: Clarendon Press, 1975); both hereafter cited in text.

20.   Margaret Kirkham, *Jane Austen, Feminism, and Fiction* (Totowa, N.J.: Barnes and Noble, 1983).

21.   Sandra M. Gilbert and Susan Gubar, *The Madwoman in the Attic: The Woman Writer and the Nineteenth-Century Literary Imagination* (New Haven: Yale University Press, 1979), hereafter cited in text.

22.   Marvin Mudrick, *Jane Austen: Irony as Defense and Discovery* (Princeton: University of Princeton Press, 1952).

23.   See, for instance, Alison G. Sulloway, "Emma Woodhouse and *A Vindication of the Rights of Women*," *The Wordsworth Circle* 7 (1976): 320.

24.   Nancy K. Miller, *The Heroine's Text: Readings in the French and English Novel, 1722–1782* (New York: Columbia University Press, 1980), 157–58.

25.   Nina Auerbach, "Jane Austen's Dangerous Charm: Feeling as One Ought about Fanny Price," *Women and Literature* 3 (1983): 208ff; Wayne Booth, *The Company We Keep: An Ethics of Fiction* (Berkeley: University of California Press, 1988), 430.

26.   Johnson is referring to David M. Halperin, *Saint Foucault: Towards a Gay Hagiography* (New York and Oxford: Oxford University Press, 1995), 48.

27.   Terry Castle, "Sister-Sister," *The London Review of Books*, August 3, 1995, 3–6.

28.   Edward Said, *Culture and Imperialism* (New York: Alfred A. Knopf, 1993); hereafter cited in text.

29.   Raymond Williams, *The Country and the City* (New York: Oxford University Press, 1973), 145. Williams's discussion of Austen, 108–19, is also one of the more salient Marxist readings of her work, despite his willingness to separate Austen's moral vision from her social and economic condition. See, however, one of his concluding gestures: "All her discrimination is, understandably, internal and exclusive. She is concerned with the conduct of people who, in the complications of improvement, are repeatedly trying to make themselves into a class. But where only one class is seen, no classes are seen" (117). For an examination of the question of the possible division between ethics and social forces in Austen, particularly in *Mansfield Park*, see Allen Dunn, "The Ethics of *Mansfield Park*: MacIntyre, Said, and Social Context," *Soundings* 78, nos. 3–4 (1995): 483–500.

30.   James Thompson, "Jane Austen and History," *Review* 8 (1986): 21–32.

Circles of Support

DEBORAH KAPLAN

I

Jane Austen became a novelist, so many biographers have told us, because she was a genius. That explanation first appeared in postromantic nineteenth-century narratives of the writer's life, but it has received the most play in twentieth-century biographies as diverse as those by Jane Aiken Hodge, David Cecil, and John Halperin.[1] In their renderings, genius is part of Austen's "double life." She is both artistic genius *and* ordinary woman, two strikingly discrete identities. Indeed, in Cecil's *Portrait of Jane Austen,* which offers the most elaborated account of the so-called double life, artist and woman inhabit entirely different realms. Only Austen's life as a woman is subject to empirical investigation; the artist is, by contrast, "a detached invisible figure, observant to gather the fuel that might one day kindle her imaginative spark to flame."

The Austen of Cecil's *Portrait* does not require an encouraging social context in order to realize her talent. Indeed, his vision of the double life suggests that Austen found novel-writing possible only by removing herself from social experience. Although Cecil refers to her as an artist and a woman, he implies that she had to be an artist *or* a woman. The "detached, invisible figure" of genius must have no gender because he identifies women only with their procreative potential. Austen, we are told, "differed from most women. The creative impulse which in them fulfilled itself as a wife and mother in her fulfilled itself as an artist."[2]

This explanation is simplistic, not because it attributes to Austen's innate talent—surely she had that—but because it renounces any influence whatever of social life on that talent. Because it is so simplistic, however, Cecil's perception of a double life for Austen makes especially apparent the problem that confronts all who attempt to explain how Austen came to be a writer: her sexual identity. Given her community's adherence to the ideology of domesticity, given that Austen *was* expected to fulfill herself "as a wife and

Deborah Kaplan, "Circles of Support," in *Jane Austen among Women* (Baltimore: The Johns Hopkins University Press, 1992), 89–108. © 1992 by The Johns Hopkins University Press; reprinted by permission.

mother," where did she meet with encouragement for writing? The double-life explanation acknowledges (and endorses) the feminine identity that the ideology constructs but gets around it by exempting the presumably rare genius from that identity. Still, there are other, less extreme explanations that do acknowledge social influences on Austen's achievement; how do they treat the issue of her gender?

The most widely recognized influence has been Jane Austen's family. Biographers have credited her relatives with supporting and inspiring her to write. Even biographers who have proffered the view of double life have, despite the incompatibility, advanced this explanation as well. "Family influence" does not, as does Cecil's "double life," overtly reject the impact of domestic femininity on the extraordinary woman artist, but it is still problematic. Evincing its own patriarchal perspective, the explanation is simply oblivious to the role played by Austen's gender. Because it doesn't consider what it meant to be female in Jane Austen's community, the "family influence" explanation cannot, then, adequately account for Austen's achievement, either.

Drawing on the framework of Austen's dual cultures—gentry and women's—this chapter points to the limitations of the "family influence" explanation for different stages in Austen's literary development. In the process, it also reperceives the customary biographical representation of the novelist's family. To be sure, it is easier to review than to revise the conventional story of Austen's literary development. Biographers have been handicapped by the small number of surviving primary documents. The internal evidence of Austen's letters indicates that she had several correspondents and that she wrote frequently to Cassandra in particular, when they were apart. But only just over 150 of her letters have survived, all of them written between 1796 and the year of her death, 1817.[3] Her sister destroyed many of the novelist's letters after she died, as did her brother Henry and probably others of her relatives. Contemporary testimonies are also sparse. Most, by nieces and nephews, describe her only in the last decades of her life. But the framework of gentry and women's cultures enables us to see some of this evidence differently and, in some instances, to couple or contextualize some of the usual materials with additional and previously ignored sources—the writings of Austen's neighbors and kin, for example.

By situating Austen's family in the context of their community's cultural affiliations and expressions, this chapter shows that biographers usually portray it as an insular and unchanging unit. What they have labeled "family" might be seen more precisely as a shifting circle of supporters over the course of Austen's life. She was born not just into a family but into a community whose culture fostered wide reading and playful writing—rich exercises in literacy that we should not overlook. As Austen matured and encountered the inhibiting pressures of the community's domestic ideology, however, she found still another supportive culture generated by a small group of female kin and friends within her wider community. In this female circle Austen was able to develop her creative voice and a professional writer's identity.

At different moments in her life Austen benefited from encouragements offered by the gentry's and women's cultures. But if it is simplistic to suggest that only an abstract quality of genius made Austen the novelist she became, it is equally simplistic to maintain that her dual cultures alone made her a writer. We might say, rather, that part of Austen's undeniably great talent consisted in recognizing the cultural resources of her social world and in learning how to make use of them.

II

Jane Austen's first extant literary compositions date from 1787, the year in which she was eleven years old, but she may have started writing fiction even earlier. Her spectacularly precocious beginning, recorded in her witty juvenilia, testifies not only to her talent but also to those social circumstances that enabled its expression. Two of her earliest biographers, themselves kin to the novelist, have praised her family and especially some Austen men for motivating her to write. Her brother Henry Austen, whose 1818 "Biographical Notice of the Author" provided the public with the first history of Jane Austen, singled out the impact of their father, the Reverend George Austen: "Being not only a profound scholar, but possessing a most exquisite taste in every species of literature, it is not wonderful that his daughter Jane should, at a very early age, have become sensible to the charms of style, and enthusiastic in the cultivation of her own language."[4] Austen's nephew James Edward Austen-Leigh, whose *Memoir of Jane Austen* appeared in 1870, called attention to the father-figure role of Jane Austen's brother (Austen-Leigh's own father) James: "He was more than ten years older than Jane, and had, I believe, a large share in directing her reading and forming her taste."[5]

Following these precedents, subsequent biographers and critics have acknowledged the influence of her father and oldest brother but have credited, too, the literary atmosphere generated by the whole family. They have been portrayed as lovers of wit, who play-acted and read novels. They are said to have thought and talked critically about contemporary literary tastes and conventions and to have formed an enthusiastic audience for any clever, homemade entertainments.[6] Moreover, many family members, not just the young Jane, are shown to have enjoyed composing. Her mother and sister wrote poems and riddles, and some of her brothers were, as literary critic B. C. Southam has put it, "minor versifiers and essayists."[7] James was particularly and consistently prolific; his numerous surviving poems (including prologues and epilogues for plays performed at Steventon) span a period of almost forty years, from the early 1780s to his death in 1819.[8] As a young man, he also produced a periodical, *The Loiterer,* to which he and Henry Austen contributed more than half the essays. Surrounded by these affectionate and highly receptive scribblers, Jane Austen was apparently prompted to write also.

The Austens *were* unusually literary and did provide a stimulating setting for Jane Austen's girlhood writing. Biographers generally have not acknowledged, however, that the Austens were part of a broader context of encouragement: their genteel community. James Edward Austen-Leigh, for example, does briefly concede the "good taste and cultivated minds" of some Austen neighbors, but family pride and a strong belief in progress led this influential Victorian biographer to look back on late eighteenth- and early nineteenth-century Hampshire and see a shining cluster of talented Austens surrounded by the dull and uneducated. In the world in which his aunt was born, Austen-Leigh tells his readers, "ignorance and coarseness of language . . . were still lingering even upon higher levels of society than might have been expected to retain such mists." To prove his point, he relates the story of "a neighbouring squire, a man of many acres," who "referred the following difficulty to Mr. Austen's decision: 'You know all about these sort of things. Do tell us. Is Paris in France, or France in Paris? for my wife has been disputing with me about it.' "[9] Austen's family members, as biographer David Cecil has suggested, may have been "cleverer" than their neighbors.[10] But the surviving nonvocational writings of even just that segment of Austen's community living in the immediate vicinity of the Steventon parsonage, where Austen grew up, suggest that her Hampshire neighbors were in fact highly— we might almost say hyper—literate, intellectually curious, and playful.[11]

Their letters and diaries offer brief but intriguing references to their wide and varied reading. Mary Bramston of Oakley Hall, for example, had strikingly broad tastes, recommending in her letters to a close friend histories and gothic novels, the works of William Wilberforce and of Lord Byron. Elizabeth Chute of the Vyne had a particular fondness for French literature, and, although she had not read it (as of the summer of 1800), she was interested in what people were saying about radical William Godwin's novel *Caleb Williams.* "In morals, in religion & politics, everyone allows it to be very faulty," she wrote to a friend.[12] As one of Jane Austen's own playful letters informs us, her friends at Manydown, Elizabeth Heathcote and Alethea Bigg, liked "enormous great stupid thick quarto volumes."[13]

The letters and diaries written by members of Austen's Hampshire neighbors, of course, testify not only to their reading but to their writing habits. As we have seen in previous chapters, they were prolific correspondents and diarists. Women more often than men wrote letters of family and personal news and probably kept more of the diaries that functioned partly as social calendars. Men often composed detailed accounts of travel and hunting adventures, though, and both sexes penned family histories, making notes for future generations, and kept logs of daily and monthly expenditures.

Austen's neighbors were capable of a pious, sometimes more formal prose as well. Although not a few gentlemen in the community, having entered the Church, routinely drafted sermons, nonprofessionals devoted their pens to religious concerns too. Lady Frances Heathcote, wife of the third baronet of Hursley and mother-in-law of Austen's friend Elizabeth Heathcote, wrote at least one long sermon in verse, probably for her own private instruction;[14] others wrote prayers.

They also frequently produced and delighted in lighthearted, fanciful compositions. In a world without Hallmark greeting cards they responded to one another's birthdays, weddings, anniversaries, and childbearing with their own homemade, cheerful doggerel. J. H. George Lefroy, oldest son of Jane Austen's friend Anne Lefroy, sent poems to one of his younger brothers in honor of the boy's birthday, incorporating in one of them a fairly realistic assessment of his poetic talents:

> Again, Dear Boy, Novembers blast
>   Bids me my tribute pay
> And joyous I resume my task
>   And greet thy natal day.
>
> What tho' in me no vivid rays
>   Hath Genius bade to glow
> Despise not thou these simple lays
>   Affection bids them flow.[15]

Austen's neighbors broke into verse even when not marking the key events of personal life. Wither Bramston of Oakley Hall wrote ten stanzas for his aunt in 1782, describing his efforts to buy her some oranges:

> . . . Stop'd at Cooks, tasted some, but alas! cou'd get none,
>   Till I reached Botolph Lane in the City,
> Where I picked up a Chest, that seem'd of the Best,
>   If they do not succeed, 'tis a Pity. . . .[16]

Stephen Terry of Dummer wrote poetry about his hunting escapades. And even the commonplace scene of boys playing outdoors could put Anne Lefroy into a rhyming mood. The neighbors also produced numerous charades very like the one *Emma*'s Mr. Elton contributes to Harriet Smith's lavishly ornamented album.

A playful spirit found its way into more extended endeavors. Jane Austen was not the only member of her community to try parody. Elizabeth Heathcote's eleven-year-old son, for example, created "The Mirror," a mock newspaper filled with parodies of international and local events. It reported the loss of Bonaparte's nose, for instance, and the marriage of Miss Blachford (one of Heathcote's cousins) "to John Prion aged 70—the Beauty of her spouse (it is generally believed) is the reason of the Lady's choice being Captivated by him one day as he was cutting wood & sporting off a new pair of hedging gloves & an old wig."[17]

The neighbors also liked and sometimes wrote songs. As county elections neared, many new lyrics set to familiar tunes were produced, describing and lampooning the candidates and their competitions. If Austen's neighbors did not write them (many were published anonymously or under pseudonyms) they certainly relished them. In 1790, for example, "Nurse Jervoise's Lullaby to Lord Jacky" appeared, mocking Lord John Russell, one of Heathcote and Chute's opponents in the Hampshire contest for Parliament. "Jacky shall ride round the County," charged one of its stanzas, "And pop in at every door'a, / Take care it dont miss its way, / it ne'er was in Hampshire before'a."- Mary Bramston so enjoyed the verses that she made a copy for her invalid mother-in-law, residing in Bath, who had her daughter Augusta copy them over and send them to her niece.[18] Wars also inspired song. Perhaps because she believed that there was "nothing more useful in exciting & keeping up the spirit of a nation than popular songs," Anne Lefroy supplied new patriotic words to a Robert Burns poem sung to the tune of "Hey Tittie Tattie."[19] She adapted it to suit a corps of Newport Volunteers, formed in the Isle of Wight to defend the inhabitants in case of an invasion by the French. Finally, gentlemen wrote songs in celebration of sports and fellowship. Charles Powlett's uncle, the Rector of Itchen Abbas, achieved a local reputation as "the Laureate of the Hunt" with rousing verses sung at the Hampshire Hunt dinners.[20]

None of this work, of course, approaches the brilliance of Jane Austen's early writings, "Love and Freindship" in particular, but these widespread, albeit unremarkable, literary undertakings form the broad context for Austen's juvenilia. They also provide the context for many of the other compositions Austen produced over the course of her life—her numerous poems and charades and her household prayers. All these works, as well as those by other Austen family members, expressed and contributed to the wider community's patterns of reading and writing, were part of its culture.

Although some of the writings of members of the Austen family and their community (some personal diaries, for instance) were kept utterly private and some, such as songs, were often offered to the public, many of these works, especially letters and poems, were neither very private nor very public. They were instead the products of domesticity and kinship, written by one family member for others. If these family writings were like today's greeting cards, they were also gifts, offered for the pleasure and sometimes the entertainment of loved ones. The dedications attached to the majority of Jane Austen's childhood parodies make their domestic and familial identity especially clear and closely associate them with the other genteel home productions of her community, such as poems marking birthdays and anniversaries.

Indeed, it is *because* many of these works were expressions of family feeling that they were sometimes preserved. Some of the extant letters of Austen's friends and neighbors have notations on the outside, added by the letter recipient several years after they were received. These notations constitute, in effect, an emotional index, listing the family member who wrote the particular letter, sometimes its date, and its especially meaningful topics. After their author had died, letters and other domestic writings were also handed on by their original recipient, given to surviving family members as mementos of the deceased. Cassandra Austen's treatment of her sister's letters was typical behavior within her community. She withheld a relatively small number of Jane Austen's letters from the fireplace, probably not because she thought their charm and wit ought to be saved for posterity but because she wanted to give her relatives tokens, not unlike a lock of hair, of the dead. She treated the juvenilia as tokens too, giving sections to three members of the family.

III

Biographers and critics, in stressing the role of Austen's kin, have ignored the general impact of their community's culture while insisting that the influence of the novelist's family, after getting her started as a writer, continued unchanging. Throughout her life her family is said to have stimulated and supported her talent.[21] "Her novels remained to the last a kind of family entertainment," according to Mary Lascelles.[22] Mary Poovey concurs with Lascelles's representation of Austen's relatives: "Jane Austen wrote her first stories of the amusement of her family. . . . Austen's first longer works . . . were also apparently family entertainments, and, even after she became a published author, she continued to solicit and value the response of her family as she composed and revised her novels."[23] But just as the family's influence was permeated by the culture of Austen's community in her childhood, so that influence was reshaped by the community's values in Austen's adulthood. "Family" became a smaller circle in Austen's adult life, but that group, though private and exclusive, was still not disconnected from the community and patriarchal culture surrounding it.

The literary interests and pursuits of Jane Austen's family *and* community explain how, as a young girl, she came to be interested in literature and to try imaginative writing, but they cannot account for Austen's mature writing. In the second half of the 1790s Austen was becoming a serious, committed writer. We can follow the transformation by considering her productions. The majority of her juvenilia, like the works of her family and neighbors, are very brief; some mere fragments or, as she called one selection of them, "Scraps." Most of the longer pieces are unfinished. *Lady Susan,* the first composition written after the juvenilia in 1793–94, while not incomplete, is brought to a quick finish with a short, tacked-on conclusion. But beginning in 1795, Austen wrote and completed three extended manuscripts: "First Impressions," "Elinor and Marianne," and "Susan," and those efforts changed the nature of Austen's creative life, differentiating it both from her work on her earlier fictions and from the leisure-time composing of other members of the gentry. The manuscripts required sustained concentration. They took time.

We have only to remember the dictums of the widespread ideology of domesticity to appreciate the potential subversiveness of that writing. The ideal woman was to engage in activities that served her family, contributing either to the pleasures of her husband or to the education of her children. Certainly, a young girl or even an adult woman who whiled away an occasional solitary afternoon by composing a poem or by writing brief parodies could not be accused of putting herself first in an "unfeminine" way. But to write three books in four years? Although biographers and critics have routinely portrayed the charming family context for Austen's girlhood precociousness, they have not provided a persuasive rendering of that context for the novelist's difficult transition from play to professionalism, a transition that began in the second half of the 1790s and extended into the second decade of the nineteenth century. They have not been able to do so because they have ignored the increasing cultural pressures on females in Jane Austen's community who were becoming adult women.

Was the Austen family somehow indifferent to their culture's domestic ideology? The little surviving evidence of their responses to Austen's novel-writing suggests that they may have been, but only to a degree. Certainly, her father's effort to find a publisher for "First Impressions" in 1797 indicates that he knew and approved of his daughter's work. Nor was he naive or inattentive to the implications of his action: in his letter to publisher Thomas Cadell he compared his daughter's manuscript to Frances Burney's *Evelina*.[24] Her brother Henry often negotiated with her publishers after their father's death, and he proudly blurted out the secret of her authorship to his acquaintances. But some of the novelist's other male kin expressed ambivalence, if not over the novels then over their sister's being known as the author of them. Frank was in favor of maintaining secrecy. James's discomforts with his sister's work are expressed in "Venta," a poem that he composed after she died. It acknowledges an Austen family "prejudice" against "fair female fame," referring to family members who "Maintain that literary taste / In womans mind is much misplaced, / Inflames their vanity & pride, / And draws from useful works aside." And it defends her against this prejudice: although she was a novelist, she was "ready still to share / The labours of domestic care."[25] This defense, however, does not refute the "prejudice." Instead, the elegy's praise sounds like an apology for Jane Austen's literary career.

The novelist's own behavior provides richer evidence, suggesting that she understood that her devotion to writing could create at least tension in some of her family relationships and that she wished to avoid such tension. She attempted to keep her novel-writing and eventually her publishing a secret from her reading public as well as her neighbors. Although she didn't hide the fact of her writing from her male family members, she did keep her time-consuming and self-absorbing labors out of their view.

Some biographers have found these efforts peculiar. The "obsessive secrecy about her writing," claims David Cecil in *A Portrait of Jane Austen*, "is the nearest thing to an eccentricity in her otherwise well-balanced character."[26] According to John Halperin's *Life of Jane Austen*, "her passion for secrecy came close to being a mania."[27] Yet Austen was part of a community in which the guarding of secrets was a common practice, particularly among women who needed to hide desires, interests, and activities not sanctioned by the domestic ideology. And women writers of her day, in general, often resorted to anonymity or pseudonyms when publishing.

Literary critics have studied the strategies for self-effacement practiced by eighteenth- and nineteenth-century British women writers from a variety of cultural milieux.[28] But the letters of Jane Austen's neighbors offer us a very local example. In November 1802, Austen's friend Anne Lefroy announced to her son Christopher Edward that she had recently published an "Explanation of the little horn mentioned in the 7th chapter of the prophet Daniel" anonymously in the *Gentleman's Magazine*. But she quickly added, "You will, of course, not mention who put it in."[29] No such secrecy surrounded the publications of her brother, Egerton Brydges, however. She sent her son his new novel, *Le Forester*, in the same month, "which," she assured him, "you are at perfect liberty to mention as your Uncle's writing."[30]

For the second half of the 1790s it is difficult to determine precisely who knew Austen was writing and when they knew it. The testimony of Austen's niece Anna Austen Lefroy gives some indication of the secret's boundaries, but there are two versions of her story. One comes directly from Anna in her "Reminiscences of Aunt Jane," though she wasn't remembering in this case; she was reporting what her older relatives had told her about her early years. Austen's "earliest Novels," Anna noted, "certainly P. & P were read aloud in the Parsonage at Dean." When the very young Anna began talking about the characters, "it was resolved for prudence sake to read no more of the story aloud in my hearing."[31] Since the manuscripts were read in James and Mary Austen's home, presumably her female and male kin were "in" while servants, neighbors, and children were "out."

The second version appears in *Jane Austen: Her Life and Letters*, a 1913 biography published by W. and R. A. Austen-Leigh, the novelist's grand-nephew and great-grandnephew, respectively.[32] Sometime after Anna's mother died, according to this account, the little girl was staying at Steventon, where she was admitted to her aunts' "chocolate-carpeted dressing-room, which was now becoming a place of eager authorship. Anna was a very intelligent, quick-witted child, and, hearing the original draft of *Pride and*

Prejudice read aloud by its youthful writer to her sister, she caught up the names of the characters and repeated them so much downstairs that she had to be checked; for the composition of the story was still a secret kept from the knowledge of the elders."[33] This rendering indicates that Cassandra was privy to Jane Austen's work while she was writing and that other family members were being told about or shown the fiction after she was finished. We can infer that some of the Austen family's members were becoming liminal figures, standing between her intimates and members of the community outside the home. They knew less of Austen's work than Austen's confidante, Cassandra, but presumably more than the neighbors.

Austen's letters suggest that by the end of the 1790s she had a small inner circle of enthusiastic female supporters. Only two references to readers of her manuscripts appear in her letters from the period, but we can conclude from them that her writing was a source of entertainment to which those to whom she was closest returned frequently. In 1799 Austen's mocking responses to Cassandra and Martha Lloyd's requests to read one of her manuscripts suggest that both had already done so several times. "I do not wonder," she tells her sister in what must be a sarcastic tone, "at your wanting to read 'First Impressions' again, so seldom as you have gone through it, and that so long ago."[34] Martha's petition she pretends to mistrust: "I would not let Martha read 'First Impressions' again upon any account, and am very glad that I did not leave it in your power. She is very cunning, but I saw through her design; she means to publish it from memory, and one more perusal must enable her to do it."[35]

Although Austen joked about Cassandra and Martha's requests, she was also expressing self-confidence in her response to Martha. Such expressions were not consistent with domestic femininity, though they were typically encouraged by the women's culture. The audience for some of Austen's responses to her own work, however playful, was shifting in the late 1790s. Austen's writing and her consciousness of that effort were becoming part of the distinct culture of her female friendships. To be sure, most of these ties, particularly in future years, were to be to female kin, but "family" nonetheless was beginning to have a meaning different from that evident during Austen's youth and early adolescence.

IV

The shift toward a circle of female supporters is much more apparent during Austen's most productive period, beginning in 1809. Between 1800 and 1808 Austen, as far as we know, wrote a portion of a work subsequently titled "The Watsons" and made substantial revisions to "Susan." She may also have done revisions on her other full-length manuscripts, as well. Moreover, she made a second unsuccessful effort to publish. When in 1797 her father offered "First Impressions" on her behalf to Cadell, the publisher had refused to consider it. But in 1803 Henry Austen (through his business associate, Mr. Seymour) submitted "Susan" for her to publisher Richard Crosby, who purchased it but did not bring it out.

That is where matters stood when in 1809 Jane Austen aggressively renewed her attempts to publish and began to revise old works and to write new ones in rapid succession. She wrote to Crosby under the assumed name of "Mrs. Ashton Dennis" or "M. A. D.," as she actually signed the letter. She offered to send him another copy of the manuscript, supposing the original lost, and threatened to seek another publisher. "Should no notice be taken of this address," she insisted, "I shall feel myself at liberty to secure the publication of my work, by applying elsewhere."[36] Crosby's response was not ideal. He was willing only to sell the manuscript to Austen for the ten pounds he had paid for it. Disheartened or, perhaps, unable to spare the money, Austen let the matter drop until 1816, when she finally did buy "Susan" back. Nevertheless, at the same time, she embarked on another, more successful attempt. She turned to "Elinor and Marianne," which she had first written in 1795 or 1796. Austen had already revised it once in 1797, renaming it at that time *Sense and Sensibility*. Now she rewrote it again and, with her brother Henry as the intermediary, sold it to the firm of Thomas Egerton. She became, finally, a published writer when it appeared in 1811. That publication was followed in 1813 by *Pride and Prejudice,* a revision of another early manuscript, "First Impressions"; in 1814 by *Mansfield Park;* and in 1816 by *Emma.* Austen finished *Persuasion* in 1816 but died in 1817, a year before it and her revision of "Susan," retitled *Northanger Abbey,* appeared.[37]

Those biographers who have specifically commented on the context enabling this wave of creativity and publishing success have made of it an opportunity to reinvoke Austen's earliest family context. Following the example of W. and R. A. Austen-Leigh, they have generally attributed the literary work of this period to the intervention of one of her elder brothers. In the fall of 1808, in the wake of his wife's shockingly sudden death, Edward Austen offered his mother a house on one of his estates. Mrs. Austen, her daughters, and Martha Lloyd chose to settle in a cottage at Chawton. According to W. and R. A. Austen-Leigh's *Jane Austen: Her Life and Letters,* the removal to a country cottage, so remote from the bustle of Bath and Southampton (where Austen had lived since 1801), made possible Austen's series of publications: "She was no doubt aided by the quiet of her home and its friendly surroundings. In this tranquil spot, where the past and present even now join peaceful hands, she found happy leisure, repose of mind, and absence of distraction, such as any sustained creative effort demands."[38] Austen, in this version, owed the work that she did beginning in 1809 to the literal and metaphoric shelter that Edward provided.

The explanation of Edward's patronage in 1808 makes claims for a patriarchal family influence on the career of the novelist, but it has only symbolic weight in W. and R. A. Austen-Leigh's *Life and Letters*. It stands for a family circle that had altered radically since the late 1780s and early 1790s. In 1809 Austen's father had been dead for four years. Her brothers were preoccupied with careers and families of their own—all except George, who had not, in any case, whether because of illness or disability, lived among the family since he was a child.[39] Although Frank and his new wife, Mary, lived with the Austen women in Southampton from the fall of 1806 to 1808, Mary was the more long-term housemate, for Frank was at sea from April 1807 to June 1808. Martha Lloyd had also set up housekeeping with Mrs. Austen and her daughters beginning in 1805. The four people who moved to Chawton Cottage in the spring of 1809, then, constituted a considerably altered, all-female version of the Austen "family." Austen's housemates had a more sustained and immediate effect on her writing than her brother's gift of the cottage.

In these later years Austen continued to try to restrict knowledge of her writing. She signed the first edition of *Sense and Sensibility* "By a Lady" and her subsequent novels "By the Author of," listing some of her earlier works. Family and close friends knew; neighbors and acquaintances she tried to keep in the dark. The Middletons, who leased Chawton Manor from 1808 to 1813, were unaware of the writing going on in the cottage across the road.[40] And one of her letters from January, 1813, shows Austen and her mother trying to keep the authorship of the just-published *Pride and Prejudice* a secret from their houseguest, Miss Benn—even as they read the novel aloud to her.[41] Jane or Cassandra also habitually enjoined family members to be discreet. The September 28, 1811, entry in the diary of her niece Fanny reads, "Another letter from Aunt Cassandra to beg we would not mention that Aunt Jane Austen wrote 'Sense & Sensibility.' "[42] As late as 1817, the year she died, the novelist wrote to Fanny, "I have a something ready for Publication, which may perhaps appear about a twelve-month hence." She followed this announcement with a warning to her niece *not* to pass the news on to her Kent acquaintances: "This is for yourself alone. Neither Mr. Salusbury nor Mr. Wildman are to know of it."[43]

The female *and* male members of her immediate family knew of her work, of course, but because over time her family had not only changed but grown, adding a new generation, Austen's reliance on the support of women is even more visible in this period. Her niece Fanny became part of the inner circle of confidantes, as did Fanny's sister Lizzy. James's daughter, Anna, also probably had intimate knowledge of her aunt's writing when they became quite close in the last four or five years of the novelist's life.[44] The younger nieces and nephews were locked out of the secret, presumably until they were old enough to control their tongues.

Only Anna could report anything of her aunt's years at Steventon, but others of Austen's nieces and nephews were able to remember something of her years at Chawton. Their testimonies inadvertently help to reveal her choice of confidantes. What is striking about their descriptions of their aunt as a writer is how little some of them had to remember. They knew retrospectively that she was beginning a career as a novelist, but they saw very few signs of that career when they called up their memories.

Austen did no fiction writing while fulfilling her domestic duties, even when that meant no more than entertaining young relatives. We know that she did, however, write letters within gatherings, at least of family members, because part or all of her letters voiced their concerns and interests. As Caroline Austen half recalls and half guesses, "My Aunt must have spent much time in writing—her desk lived in the drawing room. I often saw her writing letters on it, and I believe she wrote much of her Novels in the same way—sitting with her family, when they were quite alone; but I never saw any manuscript of *that* sort, in progress."[45] James Edward Austen-Leigh, who had read Austen's first two novels before he learned that they were written by his aunt, can only assume in his *Memoir* that Austen wrote in the company of just the women closest to her at Chawton: her sister, mother, and Martha Lloyd. But he *knows* that she put the duties enumerated by the domestic ideology before her writing and never revealed any hesitancy to do so. Or, rather, she never revealed any reluctance to him and other kin who were outside her circle of confidantes:

> In that well occupied female party there must have been many precious hours of silence during which the pen was busy at the little mahogany writing-desk, while Fanny Price, or Emma Woodhouse, or Anne Elliot was growing into beauty and interest. I have no doubt that I, and my sisters and cousins, in our visits to Chawton, frequently disturbed this mystic process, without having any idea of the mischief that we were doing; certainly we never should have guessed it by any signs of impatience or irritability in the writer.[46]

One of Austen's nieces, however, was able to recall Austen's writing with more certainty and specificity because older sisters of hers were allowed to hear works in progress. Marianne Knight advanced the "behind shut doors" imagery about her family's estate at Godmersham, which, along with the stories of the squeaky door and the blotting paper at Chawton, biographers have often evoked in order to describe Austen's working conditions. According to Marianne's reminiscence, when Austen stayed with the Knights in Kent, she shared her manuscripts with Fanny, Marianne's eldest sisters, and probably with Lizzy, the next eldest sister, but only with them. As Marianne tells it, "I remember that when Aunt Jane came to us at Godmersham she used to bring the MS. of whatever novel she was writing with her, and would shut herself up with my elder sisters in one of the bedrooms to read them aloud. I and the younger ones used to hear peals of laughter through the door, and thought it very hard that we should be shut out from what was so delightful."[47]

In such restricted gatherings Austen received affirmation of her work as a writer. In accordance with feminine dutifulness and deference, she generally hid her work and kept silent about it. Even to show the pages of a manuscript, then, and to read from them was a striking, liberating change. Moreover, by sharing work in progress, she was not only acknowledging the fact of her products but the labor of creating them, and she was welcoming her female audience's participation in that labor. They laughed, but they also offered suggestions and criticisms. One of the youngest of her nieces, Louisa Knight, though no doubt excluded from Austen's private readings, later remembered—perhaps one of her older sisters, Fanny or Lizzy, told her—that Cassandra Austen tried to persuade her sister to change the ending of *Mansfield Park* by allowing Mr. Crawford to marry Fanny Price.[48] And one of Austen's letters to Fanny Knight suggests that they had debated the traits desirable for heroines.[49]

Because Austen's brothers did know that she was writing and publishing, we can compare the ways in which she represented her work to them and to contributors to her women's culture. A few of the remarks Austen made about her writing to female kin and friends and to her brothers were the same. She talked freely to them all about the financial arrangements she had with her publishers (Henry, of course, made many of them for her) and about her desire to make money from her books. She informed her brother Frank in 1813, for example, "You will be glad to hear that every Copy of S. & S. is sold & that it has brought me £140 besides the Copyright, if that shd ever be of any value.—I have now therefore written myself into £250—which only makes me long for more."[50] In response to an inquiry of her niece Fanny's in 1814, she expressed a similar sentiment, "It is not settled yet whether I *do* hazard a 2d Edition [of *Mansfield Park*]. We are to see Egerton today, when it will probably be determined.—People are more ready to borrow & praise, than to buy—which I cannot wonder at;—but tho' I like praise as well as anybody, I like what Edward calls *Pewter* too."[51]

But Austen volunteered less information to the male members of her family than she offered to her small female circle about works in progress, about what and when she was writing. Her allusion to a scene in *Mansfield Park* in a January 1813 letter that she wrote her sister indicates that Cassandra was very familiar with that still unfinished manuscript. By contrast, Austen mentioned it to Frank in July of 1813, when she had already completed the manuscript, telling him simply that a novel was "in hand."[52] And Henry embarked on his first reading of the completed novel in March, 1814, without any prior information on its plot or characters.[53] In a letter to Fanny Knight, written in 1817, we find more evidence that, despite his help with the business of publishing, Henry was—perhaps because he was not discreet enough to suit his sister—generally one of the last to learn of Austen's manuscripts. "Do not be surprised at finding Uncle Henry acquainted with my having another ready for publication," Austen wrote. "I could not say No when he asked me, but he knows nothing more of it."[54]

We can see an even more dramatic difference between what Austen said to contributors to her women's culture and what she said to her brothers and other members of her wider community in the way she represented herself as a writer and assessed her novels. Her biography-writing male relatives, beginning with Henry Austen, have insisted that she had little confidence in her work and was meekness itself in discussions of her writing.[55] More recently, literary critics Susan Gubar and Sandra Gilbert have radically altered this vision of the novelist by arguing that Austen consciously crafted modest, even self-abasing images of herself and her work: "With her self-deprecatory remarks about her inability to join 'strong manly, spirited sketches, full of Variety and Glow' with her 'little bit (two Inches wide) of Ivory,' Jane Austen perpetuated the belief among her friends that her art was just an accomplishment 'by a lady,' if anything 'rather too light and bright and sparkling.' "[56]

Austen's letters suggest that Gilbert and Gubar, though closer to the truth than biographers such as Henry Austen, are still only partially correct. Austen did indeed consciously construct self-deprecating images. She contributed them, however, only to the culture of the gentry. It was to her nephew James Edward that Austen represented her work as "the little bit (two Inches wide) of Ivory on which I work with so fine a Brush, as produces little effect after much labour."[57] To the Prince Regent's Librarian, J. S. Clarke, she offered a similarly self-deprecating pose: "I think I may boast myself to be, with all possible vanity, the most unlearned and uninformed female who ever dared to be an authoress."[58] Austen advanced such humble, albeit witty, self-representations with the intent, no doubt, of countering her society's general distrust of the femininity and gentility of women with public reputations as writers. She was always conscious of how she might appear to others if she were known as a writer. After the publication of *Pride and Prejudice*, a Miss Burdett expressed the desire to meet Austen. "I am rather frightened by hearing that she wishes to be introduced to *me*," Austen wrote her sister in dread of becoming a very unladylike public spectacle. "If I *am* a wild Beast, I cannot help it."[59]

In the discourse of her women's culture, Austen did not similarly depict herself as barely competent. Since her close friends generally promoted female assertiveness and pride in accomplishments, Austen could be sure of appreciative support when she announced to them the success of a dinner, a charitable act, some fine handiwork—or a piece of fiction. Thus, in her private discourse with female friends, Austen was able to develop a self-assured, even professionalized persona as a writer, a self-image that surely helped her to write. She was sometimes critical of or, to be more exact, sometimes a critic of her own writing but hardly in a self-demeaning way. When she told Cassandra that *Pride and Prejudice* was "too light, and bright, and sparkling," she was wondering if "the playfulness and epigrammatism of the general style" would be fully appreciated without "something unconnected with the story; an essay on writing, a critique on Walter Scott, or the history of Buonaparté, or anything that would form a contrast."[60]

She was also proud of her work. She spoke triumphantly to Cassandra, for example, about Elizabeth Bennet and the novel in which she figures, declaring her own superiority over those who either would not like or would not understand *Pride and Prejudice:* "I must confess that I think her as delightful a creature as ever appeared in print, and how I shall be able to tolerate those who do not like *her* at least I do not know. There are a few typical errors; and a 'said he,' or a 'said she,' would sometimes make the dialogue more immediately clear; but," Austen continued, adapting a passage from Scott's *Marmion,* no less, " 'I do not write for such dull elves / As have not a great deal of ingenuity themselves.' "[61]

Only to women did she reveal the power she felt as an author. She may have pretended to a trivial "feminine" art before her nephew, but she was quite in earnest when she told her niece Anna about one of her manuscripts: "I *do* think you had better omit Lady Helena's postscript;—to those who are acquainted with P. & P. it will seem an Imitation."[62] Mine is the originating and original work, she was, in effect, declaring. She also admitted to Cassandra her enjoyment of her second publisher's deferential treatment. After complaining to John Murray, "a rogue of course," about the delays in the publication of *Emma,* she was "soothed & complimented" and happily enumerated Murray's gestures of respect: "He has lent us *Miss Williams* & *Scott,* & says that any book of his will always be at *my* service. . . . We are not to have the trouble of returning the sheets to Mr. Murray any longer, the Printer's boys bring & carry."[63]

Only with women friends did she bask in the compliments she received, knowing that they would share her pleasure. We know the names of some of those who admired her work, because she told them to Cassandra and Fanny. In a letter of 1813 she reported to her sister about *Pride and Prejudice:* "Lady Robert [Kerr] is delighted with P. and P., and really *was* so, as I understand, before she knew who wrote it. . . . And Mr. [Warren] Hastings! I am quite delighted with what such a man writes about it. Henry sent him the books after his return from Daylesford, but you will hear the letter too."[64] As she explained to Cassandra after describing in considerable detail Henry's enthusiastic response to *Mansfield Park:* "I tell you all the good I can, as I know how much you will enjoy it."[65] After mentioning the possibility of putting out a second edition of *Mansfield Park,* she similarly noted to Fanny: "I am very greedy & want to make the most of it;—but as you are much above caring about money, I shall not plague you with any particulars.—The pleasures of Vanity are more within your comprehension, & you will enter into mine, at receiving the *praise* which every now & then comes to me, through some channel or other."[66]

The Austen life-writing tradition has not utterly ignored the women to whom Austen was particularly close while she produced her six novels. Park Honan's recent *Jane Austen: Her Life* is the only work, however, to call attention repeatedly and appreciatively to Austen's close female friends, when she was living at Chawton and earlier.[67] It also singles out Cassandra's support, emotional *and* intellectual.[68] Indeed, describing life at the cottage, Honan suggests that Jane Austen was "actively helped by" the "critical opinions" of Martha Lloyd as well as Cassandra.[69] But *Jane Austen: Her Life* does not situate these female bonds in the more general context of a women's culture. Thus it cannot do more than hint, and then only in descriptions of Jane and Cassandra's interactions, that such ties permitted greater freedom in behavior and discourse than did the community's overall culture.[70] Other biographies give considerably less credit to Austen's female ties, even at Chawton. Because these studies have generally overlooked the difficulties for women who wished to write in a community committed to the domestic ideology, they have missed the significance of female ties for Austen's career. They have carefully mapped the Chawton Cottage inmates' daily activities—the gardening, the household chores, the reading, sewing, and walking. They have even asserted the compatibility of Austen's writing and relationships with women. But they have understood compatibility to mean simply that Austen was able to work because her female relations and friends didn't disturb her.

James Edward Austen-Leigh first put forward this vision when he described "that well occupied female party" at Chawton in which "there must have been many precious hours of silence" during which Austen composed.[71] While emphasizing Edward Austen's gift of Chawton Cottage, W. and R. A. Austen-Leigh also noted "the quiet of her home" and the "absence of distraction."[72] Elizabeth Jenkins, in her *Jane Austen,* has elaborated on references to the quiet home, imagining a society very like a nunnery: "The many long spells of quiet when the others had walked out, her mother was in the garden and she had the room to herself; or when the domestic party was assembled, sewing and reading, with nothing but the soft stir of utterly familiar sounds and no tones but the low, infrequent ones of beloved, familiar voices—these were the conditions in which she created *Mansfield Park, Emma,* and *Persuasion."*[73]

Biographers have made the women so quiet and static that when chroniclers discuss Austen's writing, her companions sometimes seem to disappear. Life-writers, in fact, often invoke visions of Austen as a solitary genius or even of her double life at this point in their narratives. For James Edward Austen-Leigh, the quiet of Austen's female household enabled the "mystic process" of creation.[74] To David Cecil, whose vision of the female society at Chawton is a good deal less reverent than Elizabeth Jenkins's, Austen's life there "apparently so stagnant, served rather to provide the needed time and incentive for her genius to operate."[75] Because none of them supposes that Austen had a community at Chawton worthy of or necessary to her talents, many life-writers have insisted, as John Halperin does, on Austen's "loneliness" as a writer.[76] Even Jane Aiken Hodge, whose biography, *Only a Novel: The Double Life of Jane Austen,* shows a good deal more interest in Austen's relationships with women, has maintained that "the artist is inevitably alone" when describing Austen during this period.[77]

It was not her housemates' quiet or apparent capacity for invisibility that enabled Austen to write her novels. Before and after she moved to Chawton, her all-female "family" served as the crucial bridge between modest, self-effacing femininity and the self-assertion and self-expression of authoring. They formed a social circle among whom she could produce fiction and to whom she could talk—easily, confidently—about that work. We may never know the specific catalyst for the novels on which Austen embarked in 1809, but this much is clear: Had she only devoted herself to the interests of male and female neighbors and kin, had she always spoken a discourse filled up with their voices and concerns, she could not have become a novelist. Thus her alternative culture enabled her to do something for which the gentry's culture alone did not prepare her and to diverge considerably from the domestic ideal of womanhood without coming into conflict with it.

Notes

The following manuscript collections have been abbreviated.

A-L	Austen-Leigh
CKS U624	Harris (Centre for Kentish Studies, Maidstone)
CKS U951	Knatchbull (Centre for Kentish Studies, Maidstone)
CKS U1015	Papillon (Centre for Kentish Studies, Maidstone)
HRO 20M64	Bramston, Hicks, Beach, and Chute (Hampshire Record Office, Winchester)
HRO 31M57	Chute (Hampshire Record Office, Winchester)
HRO 63M84	Heathcote (Hampshire Record Office, Winchester)
JAH	Caroline Gore Diaries (Jane Austen's House, Chawton)
LF	Lefroy
NMM AUS/101–9	Charles John Austen, Journals and Diaries (National Maritime Museum, Greenwich)
PL	Powlett
PML MA4500	Gordon N. Ray (Fanny Palmer Austen Letters) (Pierpont Morgan Library, New York)

I have retained spelling and punctuation as they appear in these unpublished sources.

Two published sources cited in this text have also been given abbreviations:

AP   *Austen Papers, 1704–1856,* ed. R. A. Austen-Leigh (Colchester: Ballantine Press, 1942)

JAL   *Jane Austen's Letters to Her Sister Cassandra and Others,* ed. R. W. Chapman, 2nd ed. (1952; rpt. Oxford Univ. Press, 1979)

1.   Jane Aiken Hodge, *Only a Novel: The Double Life of Jane Austen* (New York: Coward, McCann, & Geoghegan, 1972); David Cecil, *A Portrait of Jane Austen* (New York: Hill and Wang, 1978); John Halperin, *The Life of Jane Austen* (Baltimore: Johns Hopkins Univ. Press, 1984).

2.   Cecil, *A Portrait,* 141.

3.   What I refer to as Austen's extant letters are in some cases only copies. The originals of approximately thirty letters have not been found. In addition, a few of the letters are

brief fragments. See *Jane Austen's Manuscript Letters in Facsimile,* ed. Jo Modert (Carbondale: Southern Illinois Univ. Press, 1990).

4. Henry Austen, "Biographical Notice of the Author," in *Northanger Abbey: and Persuasion,* vol. 1 (London: John Murray, 1818); rpt. in *The Novels of Jane Austen,* ed. R. W. Chapman, 3rd ed. (Oxford: Clarendon Press, 1933), 5:3.

5. J. E. Austen-Leigh, *Memoir of Jane Austen,* 2nd ed., ed. R. W. Chapman, (1871; rpt. Oxford: Clarendon Press, 1926), 12.

6. See, for example, B. C. Southam, *Jane Austen's Literary Manuscripts: A Study of the Novelist's Development through the Surviving Papers* (Oxford: Clarendon Press, 1964), 4–5, 8; A. Walton Litz, *Jane Austen: A Study of Her Artistic Development* (New York: Oxford Univ. Press, 1965), 14–15, 17; and Jane Aiken Hodge, *Only a Novel,* 34.

7. Southam, *Jane Austen's Literary Manuscripts,* 4–5. Southam names James, Henry, and Charles, but I have found no evidence of Charles's penchant for literary writing.

8. A collection of James Austen's poetry and a few prose pieces is located at Jane Austen's house at Chawton. For a discussion of his writings, see George Holbert Tucker, *A Goodly Heritage: A History of Jane Austen's Family* (Manchester: Carcanet New Press, 1983), 99–114.

9. Austen-Leigh, *Memoir,* 9.

10. Cecil, *A Portrait,* 35.

11. Austen's knowable community was very literate; the general adult population of England was not. See Roger S. Schofield, "Dimensions of Illiteracy in England 1750–1850," in *Literacy and Social Development in the West: A Reader,* ed. Harvey J. Graff (Cambridge: Cambridge Univ. Press, 1981), 201–13. According to Schofield, "long before the mid eighteenth century the subculture of the social elite presupposed literacy, and literacy was also essential to the economic functions of men in the professions and official positions" (210). By contrast, in the late eighteenth and early nineteenth centuries male illiteracy in the general population hovered at about 40 percent and female illiteracy was between 50 and 60 percent. This larger context should remind us of Austen's good fortune in being born to parents who were part of a genteel community.

12. Elizabeth Chute to Elizabeth Gosling, 16 Aug. 1800, A-L.

13. "To Cassandra Austen," 9 Feb. 1813, Letter 78, *JAL,* 304.

14. Lady Frances Heathcote, HRO 63M84/233/56.

15. J. E. George Lefroy to Christopher Edward Lefroy, Nov. 1801, LF.

16. Wither Bramston to Mrs. Beach, 3 March 1782, HRO 20M64/1.

17. William Heathcote, HRO 63M84/234/7.

18. Augusta Bramston to Mrs. Hicks, 20 Jan. 1790, HRO 20M64/8.

19. Anne Lefroy to Christopher Edward Lefroy, 1 Aug. 1803, LF. The poem was "The Address of Robert Bruce to his Soldiers on the Eve of the Battle of Bannockburn" ("Scots, Wha Hae"). The Scottish Burns's nationalistic poem, written in 1793, was partly inspired by the French Revolution. When Lefroy transformed it into a pro-English, anti-French poem, she showed no awareness of the irony of her undertaking.

20. "Old Hampshire Hunt Songs," Jan. 1880, 31. This article, in the possession of the Hampshire Record Office and cited with permission, bears no accession number. See also *The Diaries of Dummer,* ed. A. M. W. Stirling (London: Unicorn Press, 1934), 78.

21. Park Honan provides the most elaborated version of this view in *Jane Austen: Her Life* (New York: St. Martin's Press, 1987) and in his subsequent article, "The Austen Brothers and Sisters," *Persuasions,* no. 10 (1988): 59–64.

22. Mary Lascelles, *Jane Austen and Her Art* (1939; rpt. London: Oxford Univ. Press, 1963), 146, 32.

23. Mary Poovey, *The Proper Lady and the Woman Writer: Ideology as Style in the Works of Mary Wollstonecraft, Mary Shelley, and Jane Austen* (Chicago: Univ. of Chicago Press, 1984), 202. See also Alison Sulloway, *Jane Austen and the Province of Womanhood* (Philadelphia: Univ. of Penn-

sylvania Press, 1989), 86, 87, 92. Sulloway stresses the lifelong role of the family, particularly Austen's father and her brother Henry. She also singles out Austen's mother and sister as decidedly unsupportive and unhelpful.

24.   "George Austen to Mr. Cadell," 1 Nov. 1797, in W. and R. A. Austen-Leigh, *Jane Austen: Her Life and Letters,* 2nd ed. (London, 1913; rpt. New York: Russell and Russell, 1965), 97–98.

25.   Quoted in Tucker, *A Goodly Heritage,* 113.

26.   Cecil, *A Portrait,* 142.

27.   Halperin, *The Life of Jane Austen,* 189.

28.   See, for example, J. M. S. Tompkins, *The Popular Novel in England: 1770–1800* (1932; rpt. Lincoln: Univ. of Nebraska Press, 1961), 116–22; and Elaine Showalter, *A Literature of Their Own: British Women Novelists from Brontë to Lessing* (Princeton: Princeton Univ. Press, 1977).

29.   Anne Lefroy to Christopher Edward Lefroy, 3 Nov. 1802, LF.

30.   Ibid., 9 Nov. 1802, LF.

31.   Anna Austen Lefroy, *Jane Austen's Sanditon: A Continuation by her Niece Together with "Reminiscences of Aunt Jane,"* ed. Mary Gaither Marshall (Chicago: Chiron Press, 1983), 106. Anna Lefroy remembers the manuscript as "P & P" [*Pride and Prejudice*] in retrospect; in the late 1790s it was called "First Impressions."

32.   W. and R. A. Austen-Leigh probably adapted the story from the account given by Anna's daughter, Fanny C. Lefroy, in her "Family History," A-L.

33.   W. and R. A. Austen-Leigh, *Her Life and Letters,* 73.

34.   "To Cassandra Austen," 8 Jan. 1799, Letter 17, *JAL,* 52.

35.   Ibid., 11 June 1799, Letter 21, *JAL,* 67.

36.   "To Crosbie & Co.," 5 April 1809, Letter 67, *JAL,* 263.

37.   *Emma* actually appeared in December 1815, but its title page is dated 1816. Similarly, *Persuasion* and *Northanger Abbey* were published in December 1817, but their title pages are dated 1818.

38.   W. and R. A. Austen-Leigh, *Life and Letters,* 236.

39.   For a comprehensive review of the information that has survived about Austen's older brother George, see George Holbert Tucker, *A Goodly Heritage,* 115–17.

40.   This information appears in a letter of reminiscence written by one of the Middleton children more than fifty years later, probably in the 1870s. Two of her letters were published in "Recollections of Chawton," *Times Literary Supplement,* 3 May 1985, 495, col. 2–3.

41.   "To Cassandra Austen," 29 Jan. 1813, Letter 76, *JAL,* 297. Despite her efforts, word of her authorship trickled out among some of her neighbors and acquaintants. Austen's collections, "Opinions of *Mansfield Park*" and "Opinions of *Emma,*" in *The Works of Jane Austen,* 6:431–39, provide the names of some of those who knew her secret by 1814.

42.   Quoted in Deirdre Le Faye, "Fanny Knight's Diaries: Jane Austen Through her Niece's Eyes," in *Persuasions: Occasional Papers,* no. 2 (1986), Jane Austen Society of North America, 1986, 15.

43.   "To Fanny Knight," 13 March 1817, Letter 141, *JAL,* 484.

44.   Anna Austen Lefroy, *"Reminiscences,"* 160.

45.   Caroline Austen, *My Aunt Jane Austen: A Memoir* (Alton: Jane Austen Society, 1952), 9.

46.   J. E. Austen-Leigh, *Memoir,* 102–3.

47.   Constance Hill, *Jane Austen: Her Home & Her Friends* (1901; rpt. Folcroft: Folcroft Library Editions, 1977), 202.

48.   Elizabeth Jenkins, "Some Notes on Background," in Jane Austen Society, *Report for the Year 1980* (Alton: Jane Austen Society, 1981), 26.

49.   "To Fanny Knight," 23 March 1817, Letter 142, *JAL,* 486–87. For other evidence that Austen's confidantes discussed her writing with her, see William Austen-Leigh and

Richard Arthur Austen-Leigh, *Jane Austen: A Family Record,* revised and enlarged by Deirdre Le Faye (London: The British Library, 1989), 214, 219.

50. "To Francis Austen," 3 July 1813, Letter 81, *JAL,* 317.

51. "To Fanny Knight," 30 Nov. 1814, Letter 106, *JAL,* 419–20.

52. "To Francis Austen," 3 July 1813, Letter 81, *JAL,* 317.

53. Jane Austen described his reading experience to her sister in Letters 92, 93, and 94 of *JAL.*

54. "To Fanny Knight," 23 March 1817, Letter 142, *JAL,* 487.

55. See, for example, Henry Austen, "Biographical Notice," 6–7.

56. Sandra Gilbert and Susan Gubar, *The Madwoman in the Attic: The Woman Writer and the Nineteenth-Century Literary Imagination* (New Haven: Yale Univ. Press, 1979), 108.

57. "To J. Edward Austen," 16 Dec. 1816, Letter 134, *JAL,* 469.

58. "To James Stanier Clarke," 11 Dec. 1815, Letter 120, *JAL,* 443.

59. "To Cassandra Austen," 24 May 1813, Letter 80, *JAL,* 311.

60. Ibid., 4 Feb. 1813, Letter 77, *JAL,* 299–300.

61. Ibid., 29 Jan. 1813, Letter 76, *JAL,* 297–98.

62. "To Anna Austen," 10 Aug. 1814, Letter 98, *JAL,* 394.

63. "To Cassandra Austen," 17 Oct. 1815, Letter 111, *JAL,* 425; and ibid., 24 Nov. 1815, Letter 116, *JAL,* 433, 435.

64. Ibid., 15 Sept. 1813, Letter 82, *JAL,* 320.

65. Ibid., 2 March 1814, Letter 92, *JAL,* 378.

66. "To Fanny Knight," 18 Nov. 1814, Letter 103, *JAL,* 411.

67. See, for example, Honan, *Jane Austen: Her Life,* 156, 175, and 205.

68. See, for example, ibid., 403.

69. Ibid., 351; see also 251. But elsewhere in the biography Honan stresses the impact of Austen's brothers on her writing and downplays the influence of Martha or other female friends; see, for example, 62.

70. See, for example, ibid., 27 and 119.

71. J. E. Austen-Leigh, *Memoir,* 102.

72. W. and R. A. Austen-Leigh, *Life and Letters,* 236.

73. Elizabeth Jenkins, *Jane Austen* (London: Victor Gollancz, 1938), 181.

74. J. E. Austen-Leigh, *Memoir,* 103.

75. Cecil, *A Portrait,* 141.

76. Halperin, *The Life of Jane Austen,* 190.

77. Hodge, *Only a Novel,* 116.

Reading Jane Austen
and Rewriting "Herstory"

DEVONEY LOOSER

Arguments linking Jane Austen and history were once critical oddities. Seeing Austen's writing as limited to a "little bit (two Inches wide) of Ivory"[1] and to the milieu of "3 or 4 families in a Country Village" (*Letters,* 275) was firmly entrenched and frequently juxtaposed to the "Big Bow-wow strain" of Sir Walter Scott's historical novels.[2] Scott was believed to have cornered the market on the weighty worldly matters and Austen the quaint quotidian ones. Biographical details, too, were marshaled in to argue that a country spinster would not have had knowledge of—or perhaps even interest in— events beyond her own sphere. Austen was often not purposefully denigrated in such accounts. She and her writings were placed outside of mainstream national history because received wisdom deemed her a genius of the minute human universal, just not the political or the historical, realm. As Raymond Williams facetiously put it, "It is a truth universally acknowledged that Jane Austen chose to ignore the decisive historical events of her time."[3]

The critical heyday of Austen's ahistoricism is now happily behind us, and myths of Jane Austen's "extrahistoricity" or "subhistoricity" appear to have been debunked.[4] The new historicism of the last decades brought attention to all texts as potential forces of cultural change. This wider theoretical interest, coupled with the significant work of feminist literary critics, resulted in the emergence of Austen and history as a viable area of study.[5] Attention to Austen as a woman writer, as James Thompson has argued, "contributed to the more pervasive trend toward historicizing her novels."[6] Scholarship appeared on Austen's relationship to such matters as the French and American Revolutions, the industrial revolution, the economics of the marriage market, and the literary marketplace.[7] The political implications of Austen's writings, once seen as either a nonquestion or as tacitly Tory (following her family), provoked new debates.[8] Critics argued about Austen's progressiveness or conservatism on such matters as gender, class, and race. Studies of Austen's

This essay was written specifically for this volume and is published for the first time by permission of the author.

relationship to feminism flooded the field, showing the ways in which her texts participated in discussions about women's rights and roles.[9] More recently, Austen's positions vis-à-vis British imperialism, the military, and the clergy have been studied. Austen as a writer concerned with history has arrived.[10]

Despite this emergence of scholarship on Austen and history, she remains, in Nancy Armstrong's words, "a particularly hard nut for historical critics to crack."[11] Some who nonetheless have taken a crack at studying Austen's writings in a historical frame have done so in the form of commenting on the sparse textual references to "great events" or by ferreting out between-the-lines historical implications. Setting up Austen's use of history as a critical curio, interpretations of historical minutiae—although not without merit—rarely go far enough.[12] What is meant by "history" or "historical context" in Austen studies remains "as vague and various as ever," as James Thompson has maintained ("History," 1986, 24).[13] History has too often been defined narrowly where Austen is concerned, remaining a fuzzy, critically unrealized term. This does not do justice to Austen herself or her writings.

Marilyn Butler has argued that "by placing Jane Austen within her genre, we help define her meaning," but one way to see history more widely in Austen's writings is to consider its definitions in a wider frame of reference, one that falls outside "her genre" of the novel.[14] In what follows, I am concerned with history primarily as a kind of writing—as a changing genre in the eighteenth-century field of letters. Recovering the forces that formed and informed Austen's relationship to literary (and nonliterary) genres gives us crucial material to understand her authorship. In addition, it provides information to explain why, for all of those years, arguments about Austen's connection to matters historical were viewed as untenable. Considering Austen's letters and a piece from her juvenilia, the *History of England,* I examine how Austen positioned her texts in relation to historiographical trends and to historical novels. Finally, I discuss *Northanger Abbey,* arguably the most fruitful text for discerning Austen's understanding of history. *Northanger Abbey* has been perceived by many critics as a response and a corrective to the sentimental or Gothic novels flourishing in the 1790s. Other critics have viewed *Northanger Abbey* as Austen's plea for the need to add women to historical accounts. As I argue, there was more at stake than either of these accounts allow. Austen's writings were involved in a struggle for gaining readers at a time when novels were not yet considered a polite form. Austen made light of histories and defended novels in *Northanger Abbey,* usurping certain elements from historical discourses while making romance probable. She was defining her writing not simply against other kinds of novels or novelists but against other kinds of writing, including histories. In effect, Austen combined genres said to be "masculine" or "feminine" into something that was both—or neither. Austen did not avoid history. On the contrary, as I will show, she engaged it directly, grappled with it, and refashioned it for her own purposes.

GENRE IN THE EIGHTEENTH CENTURY

Austen uses the words *history* and *historian* a mere 66 times in her published writings, usually to mean *narrative,* though not necessarily narratives of national import or of the distant past.[15] For example, in *Pride and Prejudice* and *Northanger Abbey* we are offered a "history of . . . acquaintance." Catherine Morland gives "her own history" to Eleanor Tilney three times. *Mansfield Park* presents the "history of [Mr. Yates's] disappointment" in not getting to play the character he wanted to in the private theatricals at Ecclesford. In *Lady Susan,* Manwaring tells his wife's history; recent visits are often deemed worthy of "histories," and accounts of "history and character" abound. *Mansfield Park's* modest Fanny Price has a history, as does *Emma's* more colorful Jane Fairfax. Mr. Weston gives his audience a "history of engagements" in the neighborhood. In almost all of these references, history is not political history (not an account of past "great" events) but something we might call history-as-fiction—that is, "history" as the account of the minutiae of a character's life. Even in *Northanger Abbey,* in which history is commented on directly as a written form (as we shall see later), there are few explicit references to historical events.

The meanings of *history* that Austen employs in her novels have largely dropped out of common parlance. "Let me tell you my history" has become today's "story." As the *Oxford English Dictionary* notes, *history* once signified "a relation of incidents (in early uses, either true or imaginary; later only those professedly true); a narrative, tale or story," and the *OED* shows the word used in this way from 1390 to 1834. Other definitions of *history,* most now obsolete, implied "a story represented dramatically" (examples from 1596 to 1877) or "a pictorial representation" (primarily an eighteenth-century meaning), in addition to what we now consider *history* to mean—a branch of knowledge recording past events, often in writing—for which *Northanger Abbey's* "real solemn history" is used as an *OED* example. Raymond Williams builds on these definitions, concluding that *history* was used in a new sense in the eighteenth century. According to Williams, "past events are seen not as specific histories but as a continuous and connected process. . . . history . . . becomes connected not only to the present but to the future."[16] In other words, *history* in the eighteenth century comes to be associated with contemporary characteristics said to make up "human nature," intimately connected with new notions of progress and development.[17] Those who study historiography have seen this change as part and parcel of the advent of providential Whig histories.[18] Such understandings of *history* as present-day progress are common in eighteenth-century novels as well, beginning on title pages and traveling through the narrative in content and form, as critics from Leo Braudy to John Bender have shown.[19] Some scholars have argued it was the novel's eighteenth-century "rise" that provided the major textual vehicle for promoting this sense of *history* as chronicle of human development and subjectivity.[20]

Some of these arguments, however, may have given us misleading impressions about the position of the novel in the eighteenth century—both in terms of its status and its popularity. Market demands were for leisure reading, but as John Feather notes, this did not mean light reading: "Indeed, the largest single category of books produced by British publishers in the eighteenth century was in the field of religion. . . . books of voyages and travels were among the most popular of the century, and . . . history, both domestic and foreign, was also in heavy demand."[21] Historical works, in fact, enjoyed a revival from 1791 to 1800, with the percentage of such works doubling from the (already significant) number published in the 1780s (Feather 1986, 43). In the eighteenth century, 10,000 books were published on British history alone, as compared to 3,000 novels (Feather 1986, 42–43). In the category of what we would now call literature, poetry was by far the most popular genre, making up almost half of the publications in that group (Feather 1986, 42). Novels were frequently seen as impolite—even dangerous—before and during Austen's lifetime, though they increased greatly after 1750, ultimately constituting 11 percent of the "literature" published during the century (Feather 1986, 41–42).[22] It should be of little surprise, then, that many who wrote novels wanted to label them something else. The issue goes beyond mere labeling, however. "History," as the *OED* reminds us, was understood as an account that could be true or false. Though histories and novels may appear to be discrete entities to us now, the word *history* was used interchangeably with novel and romance during much of the eighteenth century.

The contingency of history and literature in this period—especially in regard to the distinction between fact and fiction—has been widely discussed.[23] Ian Haywood's *Making History* charts the interconnections and ambiguities of history and literature from the time of the Chatterton forgeries until the period of Scott's historical novels.[24] In a study of the early modern period, Michel De Certeau has suggested that fiction and history were "quasi-identical."[25] Michael McKeon has argued that in the seventeenth and early eighteenth centuries the words *romance, history,* and *novel* were used interchangeably.[26] Lionel Gossman has claimed that "as late as the eighteenth century, and probably beyond, history was still a literary genre."[27] Though most of these scholars are concerned with writings that circulated before Austen's day, these studies provide a crucial context to understand the conditions that led to Austen's authorial milieu. In order to juxtapose Austen's *history* to what we might now call, following the lead of Christopher Kent, "schoolroom history," we must ask further questions about how Austen envisioned herself as an author in gendered and disciplinary terms.

Austen's Letters, Gender, and Genre

Various (and contradictory) self-understandings of Austen's authorship appear in her collected *Letters*. Austen reveals an interest in her own social circle, but she also demonstrates that she was well aware of the wider literary marketplace; that she read the writings of her contemporaries; and that she puzzled over the best way to construct her own books in order to appeal to an audience. These letters have been mentioned in many studies of Austen, but it is useful to reevaluate them in the context of genre and authorship. In a famous letter of 1813, Jane Austen wrote to her sister Cassandra that she felt *Pride and Prejudice* was "too light & bright & sparkling;—it wants shade" (*Letters*, 203). The way Austen contemplated achieving that shade illustrates the kinds of writing that she believed readers wanted "mixed" with their fiction:

> [*Pride and Prejudice*] wants to be stretched out here & there with a long Chapter—of sense if it could be had, if not of solemn specious nonsense—about something unconnected with the story; an Essay on Writing, a critique on Walter Scott, or the history of Buonaparte—anything that would form a contrast & bring the reader with increased delight to the playfulness & Epigrammatism of the general stile.—I doubt your quite agreeing with me here—I know your starched Notions. (*Letters*, 203)

Austen's account of what her novel should be to please readers focuses here almost exclusively on history and literary criticism, which, she implies, range in value from "sense" to "solemn specious nonsense." She considers adding an essay on writing, a critique of Scott (whose popularity was then better established as a poet), or an account of Napoléon.[28] Austen considers these additions to add weight and historical depth to her prose and to increase the pleasing jocularity and pithy phrases throughout. Austen is perhaps teasing when she notes that adding these historical and critical digressions will, by contrast, remind readers how much fun they are having otherwise. Regardless of her level of sincerity in this letter, Austen demonstrates her awareness that she is competing for readers with histories and historical novels, though she seems unwilling to modify her prose to resemble them. Subsequent letters shed some additional light on her reasons why.

A year later, in 1814, Austen expresses her anxiety that Sir Walter Scott's historical novels will challenge the success of her own. In another frequently quoted letter to her niece Anna Austen, Jane Austen writes: "Walter Scott has no business to write novels, especially good ones.—It is not fair.—He has Fame & Profit enough as a Poet, and should not be taking the bread out of other people's mouths.—I do not like him, & do not mean to like Waverly if I can help it—but fear I must. . . . I have made up my mind to like no Novels, really, but Miss Edgeworth's, Yours [Anna's], & my own" (*Letters*, 277–78). We might ask why Austen expresses worry about Scott's novels but not Edgeworth's. Edgeworth's earnings on one book often rivaled the amount that Austen made during her entire lifetime.[29] It is possible that Austen sees Scott as a threat to her potential "market share." It is possible that Scott, whose *Waverly* differed in kind from Austen's works, is viewed as a rival, whereas Edgeworth (whose writings Austen may have seen as more similar to her own) is not.[30] The position that Scott might carve out for himself as a novelist could force out domestic novelists like Austen, unless they followed his generic lead into fictional historical material.

In the eighteenth century, novels were seen as something to be borrowed rather than bought. In addition, the war with France caused a jump in the price of new books and, though libraries continued to purchase books, the smaller libraries were at risk.[31] The circulating libraries established at the end of the century (which, in effect, "rented" books) helped the market for novels but did little to establish most novels as "classics" to be purchased and added to one's personal library (Feather 1988, 97, 99). As Feather notes, "From the trade's point of view, the significance of the novel lay not in its literary merit but in its essential triviality. It was seen as an ephemeral production to be read once and then forgotten. This meant that, once the demand had been created, a continuous supply of new novels was needed to fill it. Waves of fashion swept over the novel" (Feather 1988, 97). Austen's concerns about Scott's success might have arisen from more than a desire for sales or "bread," however. Austen may have feared that Scott, as an author who was already established in a more respected genre (poetry), could carry over his authorial respectability only to historical novels rather than to all types of fiction. Furthermore, historical novels, if they became the ruling fashion, might, as I have suggested, diminish the potential future popular demand for novels like Austen's. Finally, riding the coattails of well-regarded and popular histories, historical novels might become a more exalted and acceptable form than domestic novels, which had long been denigrated as feminine "trash." Austen must have preferred a situation in which her own novels would be seen as not trivial and not ephemeral, though at the same time not historical—in either a factual or romantic strain.

From what source did her skeptical stance toward historical novels (and perhaps history, too) arise? There are no easy answers.[32] Austen's letters show her grappling with historical writing, especially in her oft-cited correspondence with James Stanier Clarke, the librarian and chaplain of the Prince Regent (later George IV) and subsequently of Prince Leopold of Saxe-Cobourg (who became the husband of the Prince Regent's daughter Charlotte). Clarke and Austen exchanged letters about her willingness to dedicate a novel to the Prince Regent, which she did with *Emma* in 1816. Along the way, however, Clarke made free with suggestions for topics he believed Austen should pursue in her writings, including his insistence that she should write about a clergyman. Clarke even went so far as to suggest material from his own life on which she might build a plot. Austen's responses, couched as modesty rather than outright refusal, need not be taken at face value. Austen tells Clarke she will not write about a clergyman because she is "the most unlearned, & uninformed Female who ever dared to be an Authoress"—presumably a polite plea to be released from Clarke's unwelcome ideas (*Letters,* 306).

Clarke's suggestions continued in subsequent letters. Later that year, Clarke asked that Austen consider dedicating her next work to Prince Leopold and that it might be "any Historical Romance illustrative of the History of the august house of Cobourg," which Clarke claimed would "just now be very interesting" (*Letters,* 311). Austen's response to him was, again, a pointed refusal:

> You are very, very kind in your hints as to the sort of Composition which might recommend me at present, & I am fully sensible that a Historical Romance, founded on the House of Saxe Cobourg might be much more to the purpose of Profit or Popularity, than such pictures of domestic Life in Country Villages as I deal in—but I could no more write a Romance than an Epic Poem.—I could not sit seriously down to write a serious Romance under any other motive than to save my Life, & if it were indispensable for me to keep it up & never relax into laughing at myself or other people, I am sure I should be hung before I had finished the first Chapter.—No—I must keep to my own style & go in my own Way; And though I may never succeed again in that, I am convinced that I should totally fail in any other. (*Letters,* 312)

It is difficult to know how much of this letter to Clarke (like her last) is deliberate posturing and how much true confession. I agree with Donald Greene who detects "no sense of real limitation in [Austen's] expression of inability" in this letter.[33] It is important to note, however, that Austen does not explain her distaste for writing historical fiction out of an ignorance of history, as she implied before. Austen's refusal to undertake historical fiction or romance resulted from her wish not to be "serious," if this letter is to be believed. Clarke's proposal would have involved Austen's pleasing royal personages with her characterizations—likely at penalty of her life and livelihood. If she followed Clarke's suggestions in choosing a new genre, Austen would have been unable to tell many "truths" about her subjects. She would have had to paint these Saxe-Cobourg characters, regardless of their shortcomings, in high heroic fashion. Oddly enough, then, in her comic, ironic style, Austen was better able to get at the kind of truths she wanted to tell (truths about "human nature") than she would have been able to do in a fictional "History," as Clarke envisioned it.

Austen initially pleads her sex as a reason why she should not tackle historical fiction, implying that "unlearned" female authors must not dare to attempt such work. This was simply not the case. Austen was well aware of the earlier Gothic historical fiction of Charlotte Smith and Harriet Lee, for example. Most importantly, Austen herself was by no means uninformed when it came to history. Though her letters may suggest otherwise, we know that

Austen must have engaged questions of history. Her complex relationship to history arose from more than her predilection for comic forms. We need to turn to her earlier writings to understand the way Austen opposed her novels to histories, because, as Clifford Siskin has argued, Austen "poses not just an individual enigma but a disciplinary one."[34]

HISTORY AND AUSTEN'S JUVENILIA

More than 20 years before Austen wrote the letters quoted in the previous section, she dabbled in history and historical fiction. Though that may once have constituted a little-known fact about Austen, today's scholars have gone a good distance toward making it widely appreciated. Austen's "History of England from the Reign of Henry the Fourth to the Death of Charles the First"—a burlesque composed when she was just 15 years old—has enjoyed reprinting on three occasions in the 1990s and was adapted for and performed on the stage in 1996.[35] That is a significant amount of attention for a slight work of 34 manuscript pages that included illustrations added by Austen's sister Cassandra. Jane and Cassandra's "rowdy mock-history" has long charmed readers for its humorous wit, its wry intelligence, and its incisive characterizations, displaying Jane's promise as a writer long before her novels appeared in print.[36] What the *History of England* has that Austen's novels, for the most part, do not is a "wild early irony" or a "saucy disrespect" for English political history, as well as a display of fierce royal loyalties.[37] Austen's reverence and irreverence flip-flop from one phrase to the next in the *History*. Although she claims at the outset that she is a "partial, prejudiced, & ignorant Historian" and that her history will include "very few Dates," her wide reading is implicitly and explicitly on display throughout the text (*HE*, 1).[38]

Austen's *History of England* begins "Henry the 4th ascended the throne of England much to his satisfaction in the year 1399, after having prevailed on his cousin & predecessor Richard the 2nd to resign it to him, & to retire for the rest of his Life to Pomfret Castle, where he happened to be murdered" (*HE*, 2). Austen thus sets the tone for the rest of the work—mocking, sarcastic, and light in the face of far more serious charges and events. Austen then moves from monarch to monarch, as Cassandra provides a picture of most of the personalities involved. "Personalities" is an apt characterization of Austen's historical portraits, because we get an immediate sense of their humanity and their foibles, with little reverence to their royal personages. Henry V "grew reformed and amiable, forsaking all his dissipated Companions" (*HE*, 4). Henry VI's entry gives Austen the opportunity to express her pro-York and anti-Lancaster sentiments: "I suppose you know all about the Wars between him & the Duke of York who was of the right side; if you do not, you had better read some other History" (HE, 5). Austen makes it clear to her readers that she intends in her history to "vent . . . Spleen," to "shew . . . Hatred," and "not to give information" (HE, 5).

When she arrives at Edward IV's biography, she remarks his beauty and courage and concentrates on his romantic entanglements. Austen writes, "One of Edward's Mistresses was Jane Shore, who has had a play written about her, but it is a tragedy & therefore not worth reading" (HE, 7). She concludes by noting ironically that after all of these "noble actions," Edward IV died, and his son was crowned. By the time, several pages later, Austen arrives at Henry VIII, she again illustrates that she has placed her historical readers' needs (though not their expectations) at the forefront: "It would be an affront to my Readers were I to suppose that they were not as well acquainted with the particulars of this King's reign as I am myself" (HE, 11). Austen goes on to give four pages of her partialities and prejudices in his case.

The most extensive account, however, is reserved for Queen Elizabeth I, whose treatment of her cousin, Mary Stuart, Queen of Scotland, provokes Austen's wrath. Elizabeth is accused of many crimes, including ordering Mary's execution, but the first of Elizabeth's shortcomings outlined is her having had "bad Ministers" (HE, 20). This is one of many descriptions purportedly of Elizabeth that turns out to be about other people. Much of this section focuses on redeeming Mary, who was "entirely Innocent," (HE, 23). Austen concludes: "Having I trust by this assurance entirely done away every Suspicion & every doubt which might have arisen in the Reader's mind, from what other Historians have written of her, I shall proceed to mention the remaining Events that marked Elizabeth's reign" (HE, 24). Her bravado here is somewhat less comic in nature than what we find in other sections of the History, but the mocking extravagance continues until the end of the History, which notes that because Charles I was a Stuart, he must have been a better ruler than many believed. As Austen notes, "The Events of this Monarch's reign are too numerous for my pen, and indeed the recital of any Events (except what I make myself) is uninteresting to me; my principal reason for undertaking the History of England being to prove the innocence of the Queen of Scotland, which I flatter myself with having effectually done, and to abuse Elizabeth, tho' I am rather fearful of having fallen short in the latter part of my Scheme" (HE, 33–34). Her History, she claims, invents her own version of events, sticks to what is interesting, and deals exclusively in justifying or damning royal personalities, both of whom happen to be women.

As a piece of writing, the History of England may be considered engaging, like other Austen texts, but it is by no means as accomplished. It would be foolish to see this short piece—undertaken apparently to amuse and entertain family members—as the groundwork for the rest of her fiction. Nevertheless, there are issues dealt with in the History of England that reappear in altered forms in later work. Austen defines herself as a "Historian" in this piece, but she produces something that looks like neither political history nor domestic fiction. In effect she produces comic domestic historical fiction; implicitly disavows schoolroom history; and draws heavily on (what we would now call) literary sources in constructing her account of England from the reign of Henry IV to the death of Charles I. The latter point—on Austen's use of and commentary on fictional historical texts—is one that deserves further scholarly exploration.

Those who have written about Austen's *History of England* examine how her *History* parodies Oliver Goldsmith's *History of England in a Series of Letters from a Nobleman to His Son* (1764). Austen's comments in the margins of her family's copy of that book, read when she was 12 or 13 years old, have been frequently mentioned.[39] Goldsmith's epistolary history, as well as his four-volume *History of England from the Earliest Times to the Death of George III* (1771) and subsequent abridgments, were often used to educate children.[40] Goldsmith would therefore have been an easy target for Austen's early burlesque. Much has also been made of Austen's Stuart allegiances in her *History* (especially as a correction to Goldsmith's anti-Stuart bias) and what they might tell us about her politics. Brigid Brophy sees the *History of England* as Austen family history writ large.[41] Critics have long traced Austen's preference for the Stuarts to the Leighs' (Austen's mother's family) assistance to Charles I during the Civil War, but Brophy further speculates on the ways in which the Austen family may have considered itself similarly dispossessed a century later. In Brophy's reading, the *History of England* is reduced to autobiography, revealing the young Austen's psychological state. According to Brophy, "Jane Austen was simultaneously writing, in metaphor, a history of her family and a history of herself to date."[42] Though Brophy's reading is provocative, it verges on repeating the myth of Austen's ahistoricism. In Brophy's account, Austen is again stealthily writing about her own small sphere, rather than about the wider world. To consider the *History* in what is virtually a first-person frame prevents us from asking important questions about Austen and history.

Fortunately, such psychological readings have not held sway in discussions of Austen's juvenilia, which have long been discussed as allusive texts (especially of novels) that go beyond Austen's own sphere. Seeing Austen's juvenilia as the most feminist and radical of her writings is a relatively new critical phenomenon.[43] The *History of England* has been part of this critical trend, used as evidence of Austen's commitment to the stories of real as well as fictional women, particularly Mary, Queen of Scots. Seventeen women are featured in Austen's history, as are 26 men—a high proportion, as Jan Fergus notes.[44] Not all of these women are queens or wives and daughters of monarchs; three women—Joan of Arc, Jane Shore, and Lady Jane Grey also grace this "parade of female characters"; Oliver Goldsmith's history, by contrast, mentions "just four women and twenty men . . . in the reign of Henry VII."[45]

Although Austen's choice to jettison many important events of political and military history may have been unusual for schoolroom histories of the time, her inclusion of women was not revolutionary. Several histories with precisely this goal had appeared in the decades before Austen wrote. Charlotte Cowley's *The Ladies History of England; from the Descent of Julius Caesar, to the Summer of 1780* (1780) set out "to convey to posterity a faithful picture of the characters of our most illustrious women for a long series of ages," in addition to relating standard historical fare. A "History of England, by Question and Answer," by "Jasper Goodwill," was published in the *Ladies' Magazine* in 1749 and included accounts of celebrated queens. A spate of works that dealt solely in the characters of celebrated women (many of them royal) appeared, including George Ballard's *Memoirs of Several Ladies of Great Britain* (1752); *Biographium Faemineum. The Female Worthies* (1766); Thomas Amory's *Memoirs Containing the Lives of Several Ladies of Great Britain: A History of Antiquities, Productions of Nature, and Monuments of Art* (1769); William Alexander's *The History of Women, from the Earliest Antiquity to the Present Time* (1779), and others. Few of these efforts can be called explicitly feminist, unless feminist is defined as simply giving attention to female worthies, regardless of the stance taken on their cultural position.

Several recent critics have viewed Austen's *History* as an explicitly feminist text, citing its historically revisionist tendencies, for one, as constituting a feminist impulse. It would be easy and even self-evident, as Antoinette Burton notes, "to argue that part of what makes this history 'feminist' is that it insists on placing a wronged woman at its center," in the form of Mary, Queen of Scots.[46] Burton shows that Austen's feminism goes beyond this, especially in the courageous choice to highlight how women, too, can be implicated in "the operations of patriarchy," rather than opting to present an easy (and disingenuous) historical "sisterhood" (Burton, 44). Both Burton and Jan Fergus are convincing in their arguments that Jane and Cassandra Austen created a collaborative feminist text in the *History*, one that was "questioning conventional notions of history and revising history itself."[47] As Burton concludes, Austen's *History* "testifies to the power of history to allow women to reinvent the past and so too perhaps to differently imagine their own future" (Burton, 46). Such arguments have paved the way for further exploration of Austen's *History*, as well as of eighteenth-century women's historical education and historiographical practices.

However, to deem Austen's *History* a feminist parody and close the book on it risks missing related and crucial elements at play. The aim of Austen's juvenilia, as Claudia Johnson has contended, "is demystification: making customary forms subject to doubt by flaunting their conventionality."[48] This "flaunting" has been discussed primarily as Austen's send-up of sentimental novels. When conventions are discussed in relation to Austen's *History*, they are frequently historiographical conventions. Austen's burlesque is identified as "revenge on history—on schoolroom history—a species of history as subject, still very much with us, that was largely a creation of the eighteenth century" (Kent 1989, 60). Schoolroom history "was reduced for childhood consumption into facts and dates," as Christopher Kent has shown, and was considered "a particularly appropriate subject for girls" (Kent 1989, 61). Boys studied the classics, so English history was believed too lightweight for their education (Kent 1989, 60). This did not change until well into the nineteenth century, when history was professionalized. As Kent argues: "History's weakness as a discipline was bound up in its weakness as a profession. A man might *make* history as a soldier or a statesman. He might also *write* history as a participant . . . But to *study* history in our sense of doing historical research, that was pedantry . . . To write history was essentially a literary activity aimed at capturing the interest of the general reader" (Kent 1989, 60–61).

Schoolroom history was an appropriate subject for females because it allowed them to be entertained and educated at the same time. As Kent explains, "The entertainment lay in the excitement, the danger, the glamour of court, battlefield, and bedroom—all the staples of traditional 'high' history. The improvement lay in the fact that it all happened, that it was true, not invented" (Kent 1989, 61). These qualities in "histories" were important for women as a substitute for direct experience—to make up for those parts of the world they should not see. Reading schoolroom history provided a way for women to gain all of the benefits of understanding—but encounter none of the problems of decorum in "experiencing"—aspects of life to which they were not supposed to have access. Young women were to read schoolroom history so that they "may learn that love is not the only, nor always the predominant, principle in the hearts of man," according to Reverend Broadhurst's 1810 treatise.[49] Similar dictates excluded untruths as well as limited acceptable themes: "Throughout the eighteenth century, educational theory remained absolutely firm on this point . . . 'Use no Monstrous, Unnatural, or Preposterous Fictions to divert her with, but either ingenious fables, or real histories.' "[50] Schoolroom history played an integral part in women's education (such as it was), but history also had an essential role in the drawing room. Classed as "polite knowledge," histories gave women material for acceptable conversation. We can see evidence of this emphasis on girls knowing history in *Mansfield Park,* in which the more accomplished (though less likable) Bertram sisters gracelessly complain of their cousin Fanny Price's ignorance, because she does not yet "repeat the chronological order of the kings of England, with the dates of their accession, and most of the principal events of their reigns," though she is 10 years old.[51]

It is quite possible, then, that Austen's early burlesque on history is more than a feminist attack on the way the past is textualized and more than a paean to the Stuarts—and even more than a clever pupil's attack on schoolroom history. The significance of Austen's allusions may be plainer once we integrate an oft-noted element of the *History*—Austen's trafficking in the Gothic—with the understanding of the *History* we have gained so far. that must be seen alongside the aforementioned understandings. Brophy's psychological reading of the *History of England* also offers some keen parenthetical insights about genre. Austen's *History of England* models itself heavily on "goth-ick novelists," as Brophy argues (31). By using a vaguely dated costume-drama historical form, Austen shows in her *History* that she was "thoroughly conversant with the gothick metaphor" (Brophy, 31). That may seem only natural; Gothic novels, with their centuries-old foreign settings, labyrinthine castles, supernatural occurrences, villainous men, and innocent heroines (who were often alone or orphaned) were, after all, popular reading material and would become even more fashionable as the 1790s progressed. But why would they play a part in a burlesque of history?

In his study of Austen's literary manuscripts, B. C. Southam speculates that Austen's treatment of the Duke of Norfolk is indebted to Sophia Lee's immensely popular "gothic-historical" novel *The Recess* (1783–1785) and that Delamere's appearance in Austen's *History* is courtesy of Charlotte Smith's novel *Emmeline* (1788).[52] Both Lee's and Smith's texts have been referred to in the notes to Austen's *History* by A. S. Byatt, Jan Fergus, and Margaret Doody and Douglas Murray, all of whom find the connections significant but do not elaborate on them.[53] Though the references to Smith and Lee are only implied, there are in fact direct references to other fictional texts in Austen's *History*. Richard Sheridan's play *The Critic* (1781) and Nicholas Rowe's *The Tragedy of Jane Shore* (1714) secure a mention, as do several of Shakespeare's plays, including *Henry IV, Part 2* and *Henry V.* Austen's direct citations are not primarily to what we would now consider historical sources; she mentions only what we perceive as "literary" ones.

What we can infer from these allusions is that, in Austen's literary world, history is believed to owe its color and life to fictional, imaginative texts, not to supposedly objective, impartial reconstructions of the past. The *History*'s pronouncement that it will have "very few dates" (*HE,* 1) is not just Austen's joke, as many have noted; it is a textual cue taken from Goldsmith, whose history eschewed dates, mentioning only May 6. Austen may use her lack of dates for more than parodic purposes. Goldsmith claims in his *History* that filling minds "with little more than dates, names, and events" constitutes "uselessness."[54] He otherwise assumes that his readers must start with the basics in terms of historical narrative and recorded anecdotes. Austen, on the other hand, suggests that it would be foolish for her to repeat in her *History* those details that her readers must already know, whether dates, names, events, or anecdotes (*HE,* 11–12). Goldsmith assumes that he must present certain kinds of historical information to his novice readers, who will not know it. He envisions them as historical tabula rasas needing to be filled with his own ideas of what is historically significant. Austen's imagined audience (again, likely a family one) is educated, and so her *History* (like her novels) be-gins in media res, rather than at some imagined origin. Her texts are not aimed at readers who are "dull elves"; Austen does not instruct tyros. Her *History* usurps historical material in a fictional mold, claiming with tongue in cheek that truth is "very excusable in an Historian" (*HE,* 27). We might add that, for Austen, truthfulness (i.e., telling it like it is) appears not to be optional for a good novelist.

Austen's truths are of a distinctive cast. They are present-day truths, as we will also see in *Northanger Abbey*. In the *History* Austen ties her anecdotes to the present, mentioning herself, her neighbors, and other living persons, (*HE*, 22). The portraits Cassandra provided also depict historical figures in present-day dress and manner.[55] Austen treats historical events as "the occurrences of everyday life" and historical personages "as if their characters and feelings were fully known."[56] Austen's concentration throughout the *History* is on romantic affairs of state, rather than the "prominent features of war and turbulence" that Goldsmith sees as constitutive of history.[57] Though these characteristics may be viewed as evidence of a feminist or a female concern, we should also entertain the possibility that they are novelistic concerns. Christopher Kent believes that Austen does not present herself as a rival to historians in the *History,* but I believe it is possible that she was doing just that (Kent 1981, 94, 102). Novels dealing directly with war and political turbulence became a feature of nineteenth-century literary history to a degree that was unrealized in the eighteenth.[58] Austen may be said not merely to be interested as a student and reader but also self-interested as a budding late-eighteenth-century novelist in the relative merits of history writing (and reading).

NORTHANGER ABBEY: NOVEL APPROACHES TO HISTORY

Because her name has long been synonymous with restraint, Jane Austen is rarely thought of as combative, but in *Northanger Abbey*—even more so than in the *History of England*—we glimpse Austen as she engages in written warfare. The stakes might be seen as very high indeed: success or failure as a writer. Austen's place in the literary market, and ultimately in the history of letters, hung in the balance. Although this description gives the situation perhaps too melodramatic a turn, we have the ability to read back from the outcome as Austen did not.[59] *Northanger Abbey* has gained a reputation as the definitive commentary on the history of late-eighteenth-century fiction, as A. Walton Litz has put it.[60] However, Austen's comments go beyond the realm of fiction writing. Austen's first completed novel (and her last published) shows most directly how she understood her relation to history writing and how she distanced herself from that genre.[61] Viewing this in the context of late-eighteenth-century writings in toto allows us to speculate about some potential reasons why.

The question of whether or not schoolroom history helped to mold sensible and qualified females—perhaps implicit in the *History of England*—is taken up directly in *Northanger Abbey*. Though it has received more attention as a result of today's renewed critical interest in Gothic and sentimental novels, *Northanger Abbey*'s relationship to Austen's oeuvre remains somewhat unstable.[62] In relation to the Gothic tradition, *Northanger Abbey* has been extricated from it as parody and implicated in it as imitator.[63] It has been called the "most political of Jane Austen's novels," as well as the "shortest and lightest" and "most trivially entertaining."[64] On the level of character, Catherine Morland has been alternately defined as a self-actualized heroine and as a colonized protagonist and Henry, in turn, as a benevolent mentor and a bullying monster.[65] Though these critical debates tell us more about today's literary criticism than about Austen, there are parallels to be noted. Austen, too, was involved in labeling and classifying her work as a particular kind of writing—a task that involved making differentiations between her own novel and other kinds of texts, notably history.

The plot of *Northanger Abbey* presents a relatively uncomplicated story: a young woman (Catherine Morland) is taken by chaperones to Bath, where (unbeknownst to her and to the reader) she is mistakenly thought to be wealthy. Her initial circle of acquaintance forms a significant subplot, but the Thorpes serve to prevent rather than to forward the advancement of the novel's most significant romance. Catherine meets a rich and eligible man (Henry Tilney) whose father (General Tilney) promotes the match and invites her to stay at their home (Northanger Abbey). When the General finds out that Catherine is of much more modest means than he was led to believe, he rudely sends her packing, much to the horror of his son and his admirable daughter (Eleanor Tilney). Eventually all is forgiven, Catherine is deemed morally exemplary, and she and Henry are wed, having secured the blessings of both families. What makes this novel a far more entertaining one than this sketch suggests is Catherine's unworthiness as a heroine and her misguided penchant for seeing the world as a Gothic novel. As a quixotic woman, Catherine is oddly lovable like Charlotte Lennox's Arabella in *The Female Quixote* (1752), though Catherine has neither the panache nor the fortune that Arabella has.[66] Austen's use of the eerie Gothic as Catherine's false reality is in some ways a more colorful foil than Arabella's chivalric French romances, however. At issue in both novels is the question of what constitutes dangerous reading for young women—and what does not—though Lennox and Austen encountered different contexts for the reception of their fiction. *Northanger Abbey* is, as a result, "structured like a Chinese box of fiction within fictions within fictions," as Laura Mooneyham has argued.[67]

By the late eighteenth century, the caveat against women reading fiction—prevalent in earlier decades—had softened to some degree. Even if in 1798 Austen did not have the same struggle for legitimation as did earlier fiction writers, novels did not yet enjoy stable ground. What a novel included, how it was to be defined, and how it should be valued among other kinds of writing were still being negotiated. Austen attempted to convince readers that fiction could be authoritative and educational, rather than just trivial, entertaining, or morally dangerous. In *Northanger Abbey,* the narrator several times justifies her undertaking—defining the elements of good and bad reading and writing. Austen reveals through this defense that novels were not established to the degree she would have liked at the time she wrote. Rather, she participated in changes in what would come to be understood as educational, as well as "literary" and "historical."

The famous justification of the novel in *Northanger Abbey*'s chapter 5 has been a favorite with critics, most of whom recognize that "In writing her first novel, Jane Austen was . . . concerned to stake out her literary territory."[68] Austen's narrator suggests there that when any narrator or heroine disparages novels, the authors who express (and the readers who embrace) this opinion necessarily become ludicrous:

> Yes, novels;—for I will not adopt that ungenerous and impolitic custom so common with novel writers, of degrading by their contemptuous censure the very performances, to the number of which they are themselves adding—joining with their greatest enemies in bestowing the harshest epithets on such works, and scarcely ever permitting them to be read by their own heroine, who, if she accidentally take up a novel, is sure to turn over its insipid pages with disgust. Alas, if the heroine of one novel be not patronized by the heroine of another, from whom can she expect protection and regard? I cannot approve of it. Let us leave it to the Reviewers to abuse such effusions of fancy at their leisure, and over every new novel to talk in threadbare strains of the trash with which the press now groans. Let us not desert one another; we are an injured body. Although our productions have afforded more . . . pleasure than those of any other literary corporation in the world, no species of composition has been so much decried. From pride, ignorance, or fashion, our foes are almost as many as our readers.[69]

This amusing passage also engages serious matters, as most readers agree.[70] By calling on her audience to join her in healing the injured and unfashionable body of her text—to take pride in the purveyed intelligence and pleasing form she implies that her novel offers—Austen argues that her writing provides readers the same benefits formerly believed the provenance of other kinds of texts.

When interpreting this passage, some critics have been quick to claim this injured body is an injured female body. They point to Austen's subsequent statement—" 'Oh! it is only a novel!' "—in which the narrator proclaims: " 'It is only Cecilia, or Camilla, or Belinda;' or, in short, only some work in which the greatest powers of the mind are displayed, in which the most thorough knowledge of human nature, the happiest delineation of its varieties, the liveliest effusions of wit and humour are conveyed to the world in the best chosen language" (*NA,* 38). This section, with its references to the writings of Frances Burney and Maria Edgeworth, has been used by some to argue that Austen invokes a women's literary tradition, creating a bond with her sister authors. As I have stated elsewhere, however, it is also entirely possible that Austen is using Burney and Edgeworth for her own purposes.[71] Austen's literary "sisters" did not label their productions novels. Edgeworth called *Belinda* (1801) "a moral tale" because she considered novels immoral.[72] Burney, too, insisted that *Camilla* (1796) was a "work" and not a novel. Rather than simply embracing these female authors as comrades, Austen may have co-opted them in order to advance her own classificatory cause. This is not to say that Austen meant Edgeworth or Burney any harm. It shows, however, that Austen preferred to forge a relationship to these authors on her own terms rather than on theirs.

In delineating what reviewers should applaud in novels, Austen mocks the "abilities of the nine-hundredth abridger of the *History of England*" and "the man who collects and publishes in a volume some dozen lines of Milton, Pope and Prior with a paper from the Spectator and a chapter from Sterne" (*NA*, 37) as garnering too much praise. Margaret Kirkham argues for this section as Austen's feminist critique, claiming that each of the works chastised here is to some degree sexist in tone: "Jane Austen's skepticism about 'History' is a feminist skepticism in which she anticipates a later age . . . The 'man' of whom she speaks contemptuously is a miscellanist and incurs scorn because he lacks the original creative gifts of the novelist, but his choice of authors also has a feminist point. Milton, Prior, and Pope had all written works to which a feminist might take exception."[73] This is a possible and provocative reading, but equally as convincing is the idea that putting together scraps of "classics," as the writings of Milton, Pope, and Prior would have been considered, is a worthless authorial act that Austen believes doesn't deserve kudos (or, it might be added, purchase). This section may simply be a sign of the first part of Kirkham's argument—Austen's dislike for anything but original work.

After holding the novel above history and poetry (and above collections of excerpts of "great works"), the narrator describes a mock female reader who would not be afraid to show people that she was reading something like the *Spectator.* The narrator concludes that this reader is foolish because the *Spectator* does not show good taste. If we take the narrator's word, the "greatest powers of the mind" and "thorough knowledge of human nature" are no longer to be found in past accounts, like the abridger's or the *Spectator*'s: "the substance of [the *Spectator*'s] papers so often consisting in the statement of improbable circumstances, unnatural characters, and topics of conversation, which no longer concern any one living; and their language, too, frequently so coarse as to give no very favorable idea of the age that could endure it" (*NA*, 38). By devaluing the writings and opinions of the past, Austen's narrator claims for the emerging novel the primary connection to current events and opinions—things that concern those "now living." The *Spectator* is faulted because its subject and its diction—its old-fashioned qualities and improprieties—will reflect poorly on the current age. Instead of a concentration on past history, or even on Whig histories illustrating how the present is shaped by lessons learned from the past, *Northanger Abbey* implies that reading present-tense "histories" (presumably in the form of the novel of manners) offers readers the best option.

As Jocelyn Harris has convincingly argued, "In *Northanger Abbey*, Jane Austen transforms philosophy into fiction, but what she attacks in that fiction is history. Her defence of the novel, like other famous defences of the imagination, claims superiority to them both."[74] Harris's argument opens up crucial questions similar to those I have been discussing here by comparing and contrasting *Northanger Abbey*, John Locke's *Essay concerning Human Understanding*, and Sir Philip Sidney's *Apology for Poetry*. In making these important comparisons, however, Harris necessarily brackets off the question of whether Austen's novel might be gauged against a larger field of writings. *Northanger Abbey* must be viewed within the wider disciplinary context in which Austen wrote.

The discourse of history takes a beating once again in *Northanger Abbey*, through the commentary of the well-meaning, naive Catherine Morland. Catherine thinks the world operates in the same manner as her favorite Gothic novels, which are rife with haunted abbeys, kidnappings, suspected murders, and other dark deeds. In addition to being a devotee of Gothic novels, Catherine professes a hatred for reading history. She disparages historical writings for their lack of entertainment value, not primarily for their lack of probability or contemporary relevance, though these issues also arise. In chapter 14, when Catherine is on a walk at Beechen Cliff with her soon-to-be "hero," Henry Tilney, and his worthy sister, Eleanor, the conversation turns to the premier gothic novelist, Ann Radcliffe, and her *Mysteries of Udolpho* (1794), which each of them has read and enjoyed. Catherine tells Eleanor that she does "not much like any other" reading than novels, except perhaps poetry, plays, and travels. "History," she says, "real solemn history, I cannot be interested in" (*NA*, 108). This might remind us of Jane Austen's later comment about "solemn specious nonsense" in her letter to Cassandra, but "real solemn history" would seem to signify "schoolroom history" for Catherine Morland.

Eleanor counters that she enjoys reading history, and Catherine launches into a critique of that genre:

> I read it a little as a duty, but it tells me nothing that does not either vex or weary me. The quarrels of popes and kings, with wars or pestilences, in every page; the men all so good for nothing, and hardly any women at all—it is very tiresome; and yet I think it very odd that it should be so dull, for a great deal of it must be invention . . . [which] is what delights me in other books. (*NA*, 108)

Eleanor responds that she finds history to be good reading and that she believes it is as true or as false as anything that one does not observe oneself. Interestingly, Eleanor likes in history what Catherine does not find there: imaginative speeches, whether or not they are produced by Hume and Robertson instead of Caractacus, Agricola, or Alfred the Great (*NA*, 109). In effect, Eleanor (who has previously been characterized as more educated and wiser than Catherine) reads history to be entertained by human nature—the things for which novels would become valued. Even while reading schoolroom history, Eleanor envisions herself as a reader of what we might call history-as-fiction, whereas Catherine understands schoolroom history to be the furthest thing from the Gothic novels she enjoys reading. It seems plausible, as Christopher Kent has argued, that Eleanor, rather than Catherine, is the character whose views the novel endorses.[75] Eleanor does not criticize histories or historians. Instead she consumes their words for her own use—uses them on her own terms. Eleanor seeks not dates or events but insights into the "history and character" of important personalities. In short, Eleanor reads histories as if they were novels.

The conversation of Catherine, Eleanor, and Henry turns to the role history has traditionally played in educating young people. Catherine responds that she knows only men who read history by choice. She says that she will take Eleanor's case in reading history and no longer feel sorry for the writers of history: "If people like to read [histories], it is all very well, but to be at so much trouble in filling great volumes, which, as I used to think, nobody would ever willingly look into . . . always struck me as a hard fate, and though I know it is all very right and necessary, I have often wondered at the person's courage that could sit down on purpose to do it" (*NA*, 109). Catherine does not merely question the historian's "courage." She criticizes both the messenger and the message. History is a necessary cultural evil, she implies, but it is so boring that its practitioners deserve pity as much as praise. Henry suggests that the historian has a higher aim than Catherine assigns him—to instruct and not to torment himself or his readers. At issue is what kind of reading is frivolous and what edifying, as well as what kind is best used in educating the young. Catherine's point is not fully articulated, however, and the conversation moves to matters of taste about which Catherine "had nothing to say" (*NA*, 110). Henry has the upper hand and influences both women to come around to his point of view on these matters (*NA*, 110–11).

Shortly following this discussion and another on the picturesque, the conversation devolves once again from a comment that Catherine makes about hearing that "something very shocking indeed, will soon come out in London" (*NA*, 112). Catherine is referring to a Gothic novel, but Eleanor mistakes her meaning, believing that she is describing a "dreadful riot" in the making (*NA*, 112). Henry serves as the all-knowing buffer, clearing up the misunderstanding between the two with his characteristically pompous explanation:

My dear Eleanor, the riot is only in your own brain. . . . Miss Morland has been talking of nothing more dreadful than a new publication which is shortly to come out, in three duodecimo volumes. . . . And you, Miss Morland, my stupid sister has mistaken all your clearest expressions. You talked of expected horrors in London—and instead of instantly conceiving, as any rational creature would have done, that such words could relate only to a circulating library, she immediately pictured to herself a mob of three thousand men assembling in St. George's Fields; the Bank attacked, the Tower threatened, the streets of London flowing with blood. . . . Forgive her stupidity. (*NA,* 113)

This passage has become a favorite with critics of *Northanger Abbey* and history, who have tried to decide precisely which riot Austen alluded to. The anti-Catholic Gordon Riots of 1780, in which widespread destruction was caused and 300 people were killed, have been raised as a possibility, as have subsequent riots in the 1790s in which St. George's Fields were a central location.[76] The conclusion I draw from this section, however, is the one Nancy Armstrong comes to in her fine discussion of *Northanger Abbey;* this conversation among Catherine and the Tilneys "takes place against a landscape where fiction displaces history" (Armstrong 1990, 235). After beginning with a discussion of novels and moving on to history and the picturesque (landscape), chapter 14 displaces history two times (once in the form of "real solemn history" and once in the form of "riots"), only to return us on each occasion to the topic of fiction, as well as to the fiction we continue to read—the second half of *Northanger Abbey.*[77] Armstrong sees that displacement in Austen's writings as a whole as a "narrowing down" of history (1990, 236–37).

Austen and "Herstory"

Northanger Abbey pokes fun at more than Gothic conventions. At the least, it pokes fun at histories, too, perhaps going so far as to oppose itself to them.[78] Many have viewed this novel-as-opposed-to-history maneuver as Austen's attempt to change the status of women in standard historical accounts. The dialogue in which Catherine's disinclination for history (with "men all so good for nothing," with "hardly any women at all") is revealed has been quoted far and wide in the last two decades of feminist scholarship. Some have used this section to suggest that Austen was making a prescient call for "herstory," for historical accounts that—as a corrective—centered on women rather than on men.[79] In such arguments Catherine's pronunciations on history are taken to be Austen's own, and those pronunciations are deemed a novelistic crystal ball that sees into a feminist future.

Austen is then implicitly or explicitly congratulated for realizing before her time that women were excluded from histories. To accept this formulation, however, is to miss a much more complex relationship between women and history. As I indicated earlier, histories by, about, and for women were not unheard of in the decades before Austen wrote these lines, though they by no means dominated the field. This history of history has been neglected, by and large, thanks in part to the powers of writers like Jane Austen. By the late twentieth century, women's relationship to the discourse was believed to resemble Catherine Morland's picture of it, however ironically Austen may have meant to render it when she wrote *Northanger Abbey*.

Contemporary feminist critics have used Catherine's conclusions about history, literature, and women toward a variety of ends. Cataloging these uses of Catherine's pronouncements provides an interesting glimpse into how feminists in recent decades have appropriated Austen on the subject of history and gender. Educator Lyn Reese begins her Women in the World Curriculum Resources workshops for teachers by citing Catherine as an authority on both history and women.[80] In *The Women's History of the World*, Rosalind Miles uses Austen as an authority to ground her own authorial undertaking, putting Catherine Morland's words directly into Austen's mouth. Miles writes, "As Jane Austen demurely remarked, 'I often think it odd that history should be so dull, for a great deal of it must be invention.' "[81] In chapter 7, "Woman's Work," Miles takes Catherine's "real solemn history" speech as its first epigraph.[82]

Even writers who address a scholarly audience have similarly mischaracterized Austen's *Northanger Abbey*. In their far-ranging and useful multivolume study, *A History of Women in the West*, Michelle Perrot and Georges Duby sum up their introduction with Catherine Morland's words, professing a hope that Jane Austen would find their own efforts less tiresome.[83] Duby and Perrot begin their study with conclusions similar to Catherine's: that history and women were, and had long been, categories that did not overlap. Karen Offen and Susan Groag Bell's collection of eighteenth- and nineteenth-century historical writings, *Women, the Family and Freedom: The Debate in Documents*, on the other hand, takes this section of *Northanger Abbey* for its epigraph, partially to argue against it:

> The omission of women from the histories discussed by Jane Austen's characters is misleading. The debate about women was unmistakably present in the dialogues of popes and kings, and in the consideration of wars and natural disasters, even though the chroniclers did not refer to it. Indeed, the "woman question" may be the most central, yet overlooked, "quarrel" in the political and intellectual history of Western nations. It became an issue precisely because it challenged long-standing ideas of male dominance, which had remained implicit in Western political and social thought—published by men—until the seventeenth century.[84]

Bell and Offen rightly conclude that Catherine's claims about the omission of "women" from history are misleading because "the woman question" has in fact received a good deal of unacknowledged historical attention. At the end of this section, however, they claim of their own anthology, "Here, in contrast to the books read by Jane Austen and her contemporaries, women are on every page."[85] Thus they present a contradictory tension: Austen misleads us by suggesting that "the woman question" was not present in the chronicles of history, but, in the case of "the books read by Austen and her contemporaries," women were indeed often absent. That statement seems to take Catherine Morland at her word once again, mistaking her for an authority on books.

The most extreme—and certainly the most influential—example of Austen as herstorical critic can be found in Sandra Gilbert and Susan Gubar's *The Madwoman in the Attic,* a one-time Goliath in feminist literary criticism that has been both appreciatively cited and widely criticized in the nearly two decades since its publication. Though I think Gilbert and Gubar are right that "Austen attempted through self-imposed novelistic limitations to define a secure place," they make the suspect claim that Jane Austen's writings "imply a criticism, even a rejection, of the world at large."[86] Furthermore, Gilbert and Gubar equate Austen with Catherine, arguing that "both Catherine and Austen realize that history and politics . . . have been completely beyond the reach of women's experience" (Gilbert and Gubar, 134). For Gilbert and Gubar, Austen shows "sympathy and identification with Catherine Morland's ignorance" (133). Although they recognize that Catherine's views are raised only to be criticized within the novel, Gilbert and Gubar determine that Catherine "is, after all, correct, for the knowledge conferred by historians does seem irrelevant to the private lives of most women" (132).

We might add that, using that standard, history is irrelevant to the lives of most men as well, but that is to digress. Gilbert and Gubar make a final, incredible argument about Austen and history that sums up their views: "Ignoring the political and economic activity of men throughout history, Austen implies that history may very well be a uniform drama of masculine posturing that is no less a fiction (and a potentially pernicious one) than gothic romance. She suggests, too, that this fiction of history is finally a matter of indifference to women, who never participate in it and are almost completely absent from its pages" (Gilbert and Gubar, 134). Gilbert and Gubar attribute Austen's supposed motives to feminist anger, even going so far as to comment that the novel is "not unfittingly pronounced North/Anger" (135). As the previous section of this essay argues, however, Austen's anger may well have been an authorial anger, a generic anger—the anger of an author who was competing for readers with historical forms—both "real solemn" histories and historical gothic novels. To suggest that, in Austen, history is a "matter of indifference to women" seems patently untrue. As Christopher Kent has claimed, "Sandra Gilbert and Susan Gubar have recently attempted to 'dehistoricize' Austen in the name of feminist literary criticism. They choose to identify her with Catherine Morland and maintain that she 'refused to take historical "reality" seriously.' . . . This feminist version of history is the mirror image of the conventional chauvinistic view of history as a men's club. Happily, this gender stereotyping of history as a subject (one which, if it existed in Austen's time, was if anything reversed) is currently dissolving" (Kent 1989, 69).

Recent feminist scholarship has theorized British women's writings to better effect, primarily because an abundance of previously little-known and unknown texts have now come to light and because theories of women's writing have begun to address historical and cultural differences among women. In a discussion of women's historical writings, for example, Isobel Grundy alludes to Catherine Morland's characterizations of history. Grundy recognizes that Austen's Catherine is not a precocious expert on women and history:

> Women's history before the nineteenth century—history written about, or by, or for women—is generally assumed to be non-existent, a classic absence or silence. Examination, however, shows that the presumed absence is merely an absence of what we have mistakenly expected to find. Fully-fledged female writers of mainstream, national political history emerged late: Catherine Macaulay in Britain, 1763, and Mercy Otis Warren in the USA, 1805. The differences of these women from their male peers (though they exist and merit attention) are less immediately striking than their likenesses. Their great works fall under the stricture of Jane Austen's Catherine Morland about history writing.[87]

Grundy's astute reading shows Catherine to be correct in her assumptions not only about histories written by men but about also those written by women. That Macaulay and Warren produced similar histories to those of their male contemporaries is a correct but, in some circles, potentially unpopular feminist critical claim.[88] If we agree with Grundy, Catherine cannot be seen as disparaging only male writers of history; she must necessarily be seen as criticizing women writers, too. This alone should give pause to those who look for Austen the herstorian. Perhaps the point is not that Austen's *Northanger Abbey* presents us with a male versus female issue in its comments on history, but that it is a matter of stereotypically masculine versus feminine discourses in Austen's time. History was never completely "male" in its production or content, just as novels were not wholly "female." Each, however, had aspects of femininity and masculinity grafted onto it. In her writing, Austen did not replicate these assumed gender divisions, nor did she necessarily seek to overturn them. Instead, it appears that she attempted to integrate them. Austen took the "masculine" benefits that were said to accrue to female readers of experiential, true genres (like history) and grafted them onto the "feminine" novel to create something that was, at the moment of its combination at least, not so easy to classify in terms of gender.[89]

The strongest argument against viewing *Northanger Abbey* as a call for "herstory" involves a return to the novel. Until the end of *Northanger Abbey*, when Catherine is lectured by Henry and cured of her Gothic predilections, Catherine can hardly be mistaken for a trustworthy authority on most matters. Upon closer reading of chapter 14, we must conclude that the novel cannot be seen as a text that empowers women to make their voices heard. At the end of her critique of history, Catherine is silenced by Henry, and the narrator ironically suggests that those unfortunate women who know anything should keep their mouths shut (*NA,* 111). That sentence puzzles critics, who either take the sentiment at face value and see Austen's conservatism or who believe this is evidence of her sarcastic anger. Whether this aside is meant to instruct the naive Catherine, the more accomplished Eleanor, or Austen's readers remains unclear. Whether it is meant as a critique of society, of Henry, or of assertive, intelligent women cannot be easily determined. What is clear is that Austen is once again letting us in on the joke. We are encouraged to laugh at the characters, at society, and at ourselves. In Austen's fictional world, novels (as opposed to "shaded," dry histories) just want to poke fun, but "fun" involves didactic benefits, too. Novels teach what history cannot— how to (and how not to) function in the present. Novels offer all of the edifying pleasure with none of the haughty, didactic pain.

Walter Anderson is surely right when he claims that in *Northanger Abbey* "Austen intends her work, through its superiority in reality and substance, to compete with and ultimately to outstrip Gothic Romances," but there were more competitors to be faced.[90] Austen opposed her novel to history as well, when the boundaries of what both might be (or become) were themselves shifting. *Northanger Abbey* may be said to suggest leaving behind the pedantry of schoolroom history while keeping its supposedly good qualities of probable events and natural behavior. These were factors often considered missing from history-as-fiction (especially gothic-historical fiction), which was put down for its fancifulness. Austen gives her history-as-fiction a more substantive turn. In taking certain elements from schoolroom history and historical fiction and in making romance probable, Austen offers us a reconciliation in her own writings. *Northanger Abbey* is hardly the sole textual revolving door through which history exits and literature enters as the more edifying reading material. But Austen's novel is an important artifact in that shift, complicitous in change that we might now be tempted to see as inevitable.

Austen lived and wrote at the threshold of a new era of and for history, as Christopher Kent has suggested (1989, 59). For Austen, novels and histories seemed to be competitors more often than bedfellows. Though Austen has a legitimate place in the pantheon of feminist writers, she should no longer uncomplicatedly prop up arguments about the absence of women in mainstream national histories during the eighteenth and early nineteenth century. Catherine's views of history must not be uncomplicatedly grafted onto Austen, and Austen's views of history (as illustrated in *Northanger Abbey*'s chapter 5, in the *History of England,* and in her *Letters*) must continue to be examined in a broader disciplinary context. Unlike many of her predecessors and contemporaries, male and female, Austen positioned her writings in a way that gave them extraordinary posthumous staying power in literary history. To attribute that to the universality of her subject matter or only to her genius is to ignore her professional savvy and ultimate disciplinary good fortune, as well as to imply that the now-forgotten writers of her time have deserved the attention they did not or do not receive. It is possible that, rather than standing before us as a founder of "herstory," Austen's effect on feminist literary history has had quite the opposite effect. Jane Austen's nineteenth-century literary success and twentieth-century lionization may have inadvertently propelled forces that prevented women's history from emerging as a widespread scholarly concern for more than a century and a half.

Notes

1. Jane Austen, *Jane Austen's Letters,* ed. Deirdre Le Faye, new ed. (Oxford: Oxford University Press, 1995), 323; hereafter cited in text as *Letters.*

2. B. C. Southam, ed., *Jane Austen: The Critical Heritage,* (London: Routledge & Kegan Paul, 1968), 106. Christopher Kent illustrates that this critical trend in Austen studies "opened in the mid-Victorian period" when, in 1870, Richard Simpson "cast doubt upon the historicity of the novels." See Kent, " 'Real Solemn History' and Social History," in *Jane Austen in a Social Context,* ed. David Monaghan (London: Macmillan, 1981), 87; hereafter cited in text.

3. Raymond Williams, *The Country and the City* (New York: Oxford University Press, 1973), 113. Williams goes on to describe the ways in which Austen's writings are implicated in history. For a recent study of Austen's writings in relation to Regency England, one which goes much further than Williams's, see Roger Sales, *Jane Austen and Representations of Regency England* (London: Routledge, 1994).

4. Christopher Kent, "Learning History with, and from, Jane Austen," in *Jane Austen's Beginnings: The Juvenilia and* Lady Susan, ed. J. David Grey (Ann Arbor: University of Michigan Press, 1989), 59; hereafter cited in text.

5. On new historicism, see H. Aram Veeser, ed., *The New Historicism,* (New York: Routledge, 1989). As Stuart Tave has put it, in Jane Austen's novels "there are passing allusions to a contemporary history that included the flogging of soldiers, the slave trade, the enclosure of commons, new seed drills, émigrés eking out livings in London, bloody political riots, major and minor battles on land and sea, including privateering, even the American War of 1812." See Stuart Tave, "Jane Austen and One of Her Contemporaries," in *Jane Austen: Bicentenary Essays,* ed. John Halperin (Cambridge: Cambridge University Press, 1975), 61.

For early studies of Austen's relationship to history, debunking her supposed "limitations," see Donald Greene, "The Myth of Limitation," in *Jane Austen Today,* ed. Joel Weinsheimer (Athens: University of Georgia Press, 1975), 142–75; Joseph Wiesenfarth, "Austen and Apollo," in *Jane Austen Today,* ed. Joel Weinsheimer, 46–63 (especially 46–47 and 59–63); Joseph Wiesenfarth, "History and Myth in Jane Austen's *Persuasion,*" *Literary Criterion* 11 (1974): 76–85; B. C. Southam, ed., " 'Regulated Hatred' Revisited," in *Jane Austen:* Northanger Abbey *and* Persuasion: *A Casebook* (London: Macmillan, 1976), 122–27; and Robert Hopkins, "General Tilney and Affairs of State: The Political Gothic of *Northanger Abbey,*" *Philological Quarterly* 57 (1978): 213–24.

6. See James Thompson, "Jane Austen and History," *Review* 8 (1986): 23; hereafter cited in text. Not all feminist critics have been interested in Austen's writings. Mary Evans argues that "For many contemporary feminists Jane Austen's novels have neither interest nor a place in the feminist tradition. It is enough to note that Austen accepts heterosexual marriage for her to be condemned and crossed off the list of feminism's leading figures." See Mary

Evans, *Jane Austen and the State* (London: Tavistock, 1987), 43. This is not true, by and large, of feminist critics who study eighteenth-century and Romantic women writers.

7.   See Warren Roberts, *Jane Austen and the French Revolution* (New York: St. Martin's, 1979); Jan Fergus, *Jane Austen: A Literary Life* (New York: St. Martin's, 1991); Marilyn Butler, *Jane Austen and the War of Ideas* (Oxford: Clarendon, 1975); and Williams, *Country and the City*. Warren writes that "Thus far historians have only added to the misunderstanding of Austen by perpetuating the myth of her remaining aloof from the great events of her day" (4).

On Austen as a historical novelist, see Karl Kroeber, "Jane Austen as an Historical Novelist: *Sense and Sensibility." Persuasions* 12 (1990): 10–18. For a full-length account on Austen by a historian who argues that Austen presents "access to the felt reality" and is the first and finest "historian's novelist," see Oliver MacDonagh, *Jane Austen: Real and Imagined Worlds* (New Haven: Yale University Press, 1991), ix.

8.   For an engaging article that deems Austen a Tory but takes issue with the ways that *Tory* has been defined by today's critics, see Edward Neill, "The Politics of 'Jane Austen,' " *English: The Journal of the English Association* 40, no. 168 (1991): 205–13. Neill refers to Austen as having been "Bastilled for life" by critics who view her as ahistorical or anti-Jacobin (207). He argues that Austen's novels are politically "contradictory amalgams" (211).

9.   For a summary of this criticism, see David Monaghan, *Jane Austen in a Social Context* (New York: Macmillan, 1981), especially 1–8, and Claudia L. Johnson, *Jane Austen: Women, Politics, and the Novel* (Chicago: University of Chicago Press, 1988), especially xxiv–xxv, 48. For arguments claiming a feminist Austen, see Margaret Kirkham, *Jane Austen, Feminism, and Fiction* (Sussex: Harvester, 1983) and Leroy W. Smith, *Jane Austen and the Drama of Womanhood* (New York: St. Martin's, 1983). For an account that distances Austen from feminism, see Butler, *Jane Austen*. As Butler claims, "Jane Austen's novels belong decisively to one class of partisan novels, the conservative" (3).

10.   On Austen and imperialism/slavery, see Edward Said, *Culture and Imperialism* (New York: Vintage, 1993), and Susan Fraiman, "Jane Austen and Edward Said: Gender, Culture, and Imperialism," *Critical Inquiry* 21 (1995): 805–21. Alistair Duckworth's *The Improvement of the Estate: A Study of Jane Austen's Novels* (Baltimore: Johns Hopkins University Press, 1971) is largely credited with transforming Austen studies by its infusion of careful historicizing. A second edition of this book was published in 1994.

11.   Nancy Armstrong, "The Nineteenth-Century Jane Austen: A Turning Point in the History of Fear," *Genre* 23 (1990): 227; hereafter cited in text. Armstrong persuasively argues, "That we tend to see the Austen text as a limited one ultimately says more about the limits of our notion of history, then, than about the limits of her world" (237).

12.   For an insightful account of this criticism on historical and ahistorical Austens, see Kent 1981, especially 86–93.

13.   Thompson concludes, "Despite its mass Austen studies still have a long way to go before we can begin to restore and uncover the repressed history embodied in the novels," noting that what passes for history in Austen studies is often conventional background or annotation ("History," 1986, 30).

14.   Butler, *Jane Austen*, 4. Tara Ghoshal Wallace's interesting article on *Northanger Abbey*'s "collision of genres" also focuses only on fiction (parody, romance, and the realistic novel), though Wallace's use of Mikhail Bakhtin's theories of the novel takes the discussion to a more sophisticated level. See Tara Ghoshal Wallace, "*Northanger Abbey* and the Limits of Parody," *Studies in the Novel* 20, no. 3 (1988): 262–73. A similar argument is put forward by Frank J. Kearful, who suggests that "Austen is writing what is not simply a novel of satire, a burlesque or a parody, a comedy or a tragedy, a romance or an anti-romance. She is, rather, combining elements of all of these in such a fashion as to make us aware of the paradoxical nature of all illusion—even those illusions by which we master illusions." See Frank J. Kearful, "Satire and the Form of the Novel: The Problem of Aesthetic Unity in *Northanger Abbey*," *ELH* 32 (1965): 527. Even Edward Neill, in his correct claim that the label "novelist" has limited our

range of comparisons for Austen's work, restricts his call for further comparison to "radical male poets" (Neill, "Politics," 212). Most critics see *Northanger Abbey* and works in the juvenilia as combining literary genres and subgenres, but few look to other kinds of writing.

15. Peter L. De Rose and S. W. McGuire, *A Concordance to the Works of Jane Austen*, vol. 3 (New York: Garland, 1982), 516.

16. Raymond Williams, *Keywords: A Vocabulary of Culture and Society*, rev. ed. (New York: Oxford University Press, 1983), 146–47.

17. Williams, *Keywords*, 147. Although Williams notes that this shift occurs in the early eighteenth century with Vico, others have suggested that progress and self-development come into being through the novel after Richardson or as late as Austen. See Clifford Siskin, *The Historicity of Romantic Discourse* (Oxford: Oxford University Press, 1988).

18. On Whig history in Austen's writing, see Kent 1989, 64.

19. See John Bender, *Imagining the Penitentiary: Fiction and the Architecture of Mind in Eighteenth-Century England* (Chicago: University of Chicago Press, 1987) and Leo Braudy, *Narrative Form in History and Fiction* (Princeton: Princeton University Press, 1970).

20. See Nancy Armstrong, *Desire and Domestic Fiction: A Political History of the Novel* (New York: Oxford University Press, 1987) and Clifford Siskin, *The Historicity of Romantic Discourse* (Oxford: Oxford University Press, 1988).

21. John Feather, *A History of British Publishing* (London: Routledge, 1988), 96; hereafter cited in text. As Feather notes elsewhere, however, "the classification of knowledge has become more complex since the eighteenth century" because "our understanding and interpretation of the relationship between different fields of knowledge has changed." See John Feather, "British Publishing in the Eighteenth Century: A Preliminary Subject Analysis," *The Library* 8 (1986): 32–46; hereafter cited in text.

22. For an excellent discussion of conditions of authorship for women and of the cultural position of novels, see Fergus, *Jane Austen*, especially 1–27.

23. On fact and fiction as blurred features in eighteenth-century writings, see Lennard J. Davis, *Factual Fictions: The Origins of the English Novel* (New York: Columbia University Press, 1983).

24. Ian Haywood, *The Making of History: A Study of the Literary Forgeries of James MacPherson and Thomas Chatterton in Relation to Eighteenth-Century Ideas of History and Fiction* (Rutherford, N.J.: Fairleigh Dickinson University Press, 1986), 11–12.

25. Michel De Certeau, *Writing of History*, trans. Tom Conley (New York: Columbia University Press, 1988), xi.

26. Michael McKeon, *The Origins of the English Novel: 1600–1740* (Baltimore: Johns Hopkins University Press, 1987), 25. McKeon's version of generic mixing is worth noting: "Typologies of fiction, romance, history, and novel are posited, take root, sprout subcategories, and quickly send out feelers that intersect with one another whose very existence finally must vitiate the discriminatory function of the original taxonomy. It is easy enough to see why this happens. The common understanding that the novel 'rose' around 1740 provides a terminus ad quem which appears to organize all that follows within the ample boundaries of the great modern form, but which also requires that what precedes this founding act will resemble chaos" (25).

27. Lionel Gossman, *Between History and Literature* (Cambridge, Mass.: Harvard University Press, 1990), 3.

28. On Scott's career as it compares with Austen's, see Jane Millgate, "Prudential Lovers and Lost Heirs: *Persuasion* and the Presence of Scott," in *Jane Austen's Business: Her World and Her Profession*, ed. Juliet McMaster and Bruce Stovel (New York: St. Martin's, 1996), 109–23.

29. Jane Austen, during her lifetime, made £685 from her writing. On Austen and Edgeworth, see Jane Aiken Hodge, "Jane Austen and Her Publishers," in *Jane Austen: Bicentenary Essays*, 84.

30.   On Edgeworth and Austen, see Butler, *Jane Austen,* especially chapter 5. Edgeworth also wrote historical novels, "broad and much more masculine sketches of national life," some of which were said to have influenced Scott, including *Ennui, The Absentee,* and *Ormond* (Butler, *Jane Austen,* 132). The Edgeworth novels that Austen values most appear, from other references, to have been her "philosophical novels," including *Belinda* and *Tales from a Fashionable Life.*

31.   Hodge, "Jane Austen and Her Publishers," 75.

32.   John Dussinger has suggested three possible answers: "Austen's silence about such momentous historical happenings may be attributed to one or more of the following causes: 1) a provincial's indifference toward the public world in general; 2) a comic novelist's aesthetic distancing of her story from local history; and (3) a late eighteenth-century woman writer's reluctance, or inability, to enter into the discourse of patriarchal politics." See John Dussinger, "Jane Austen's Political Silence," *Dolphin* 19 (Autumn 1990): 33. I hope that this essay and future work on Austen will add possibilities to this list.

33.   Greene, "Myth of Limitation," 152.

34.   Clifford Siskin, "Jane Austen and the Engendering of Disciplinarity," in *Jane Austen and Discourses of Feminism,* ed. Devoney Looser (New York: St. Martin's, 1995), 52.

35.   See Jane Austen, *History of England,* ed. A. S. Byatt and Deirdre Le Faye (Chapel Hill: Algonquin, 1993); Jane Austen, *History of England,* ed. Jan Fergus et al. (Edmonton: University of Alberta, 1995); and Jane Austen, *Catharine and Other Writings,* ed. Margaret Doody and Douglas Murray (Oxford: Oxford University Press, 1993). In the edition of Austen's early writings published prior to these, the *History of England* was not even included. See Jane Austen and Charlotte Brontë, *Juvenilia of Jane Austen and Charlotte Brontë,* ed. Frances Beer (Harmondsworth: Penguin, 1986). The 50-minute play based on Austen's *History of England* was adapted and directed by Tim Heath and performed by Rebecca Blech at the Theatre Royal, Bath, at the Cannizaro House, Wimbledon, and at Chawton in the summer of 1996. Subsequent references to Austen's *History of England* are from Byatt and Le Faye's edition, hereafter cited as *HE.*

Though most critics comfortably label Austen's *History of England* a burlesque, Butler disagrees. See *Jane Austen,* 168. At the same time, few see in Oliver Goldsmith's *History* anything other than "real solemn" historiography. *Northanger Abbey* took certain elements from historical discourses and made romance probable. Marvin Mudrick departs from this view, distancing Goldsmith's text from history, calling it a "potboiler" and "gossip masquerading as history." See Marvin Mudrick, *Jane Austen: Irony as Defense and Discovery* (Princeton: Princeton University Press, 1952), 23.

36.   Admirers of Austen's juvenilia in general and the *History* in particular go back as far as the text was known. See Jane Austen, *Love and Freindship* and Other Early Works, ed. G. K. Chesterton (London: Chatto & Windus, 1922) and B. C. Southam, *Jane Austen's Literary Manuscripts* (Oxford: Oxford University Press, 1964). On Austen's text as "rowdy mock-history," see Mary Lascelles, *Jane Austen and Her Art* (Oxford: Oxford University Press, 1939), 9.

37.   The phrase "wild early irony" is Byatt's. See *HE,* vi. The phrase "saucy disrespect" is Kent's (1981, 93).

38.   As Mary Lascelles argues, Austen's *Volume the Second* (of juvenilia) is "evidently allusive, sprinkled with references to which a list of the books that were then in the Steventon rectory would be a key" (Lascelles, *Jane Austen,* 9–10).

39.   On these marginal comments, see Mary Augusta Austen-Leigh, *Personal Aspects of Jane Austen* (New York: E. P. Dutton, 1920), especially 26–28, 33. These comments include the following: on Cromwell and his men, "Oh! Oh! The Wretches!" (26); on the verdict against the Stuart family, "A family who were always ill-used, BETRAYED OR NEGLECTED, whose virtues are seldom allowed, while their errors are never forgotten" (27); on Charles I being called unworthy, "Unworthy, because he was a Stuart, I suppose—unhappy family!" (27); and on Anne forsaking her father's cause for her brother-in-law, "Anne should not have done so, in-

deed I do not believe she did" (28). Austen did not always disagree with Goldsmith, as can be seen in her agreement with him on the destitution of the poor after the revolution: "How much are the poor to be pitied, and the Rich to be Blamed!" (33). Park Honan reprints some of this marginalia in *Jane Austen: Her Life* (London: Weidenfeld and Nicholson, 1987), 74–75.

40. Kent writes that Goldsmith's *History* went through 50 editions in the 100 years after it was published. See Kent 1989, 63.

41. B. C. Southam argues alternatively that the *History of England* is "not a sufficient vehicle for [Austen's] view of life." See *Jane Austen's Literary Manuscripts*, 3.

42. Brigid Brophy, "Jane Austen and the Stuarts," in *Critical Essays on Jane Austen*, ed. B. C. Southam (London: Routledge, 1968), 31; hereafter cited in text.

43. See Doody in Austen, *Catharine*, ix–xxxviii.

44. Fergus et al., *History*, iv. Christopher Kent sees the proportions as closer to half and half: "Nearly half its characters are women, and half its space is devoted to their exploits" (1989, 67). Kent also notes that "a third of the people Austen chose to mention in her history met violent deaths—mostly beheadings" (1989, 66).

45. Fergus et al., *History*, iv.

46. Antoinette Burton, " 'Invention Is What Delights Me': Jane Austen's Remaking of 'English' History," in *Jane Austen and Discourses of Feminism*, ed. Devoney Looser (New York: St. Martin's, 1995), 43; hereafter cited in text.

47. Fergus et al., *History*, i.

48. Claudia L. Johnson, " 'The Kingdom at Sixes and Sevens': Politics and the Juvenilia," in *Jane Austen's Beginnings*, ed. J. David Grey, 48. As Julia Epstein points out, Jane Austen's juvenilia "reveals her comprehensive knowledge of eighteenth-century prose traditions, her interest in the nature of women's voices in eighteenth-century narrative, and her sense of how those traditions and voices might be recast." See Julia L. Epstein, "Jane Austen's Juvenilia and the Female Epistolary Tradition," *Papers on Language and Literature* 21 (1985): 401.

49 Reverend Broadhurst, quoted in Armstrong, *Desire*, 104.

50. Armstrong, *Desire*, 104.

51. Jane Austen, *Mansfield Park*, vol. 3 of *The Novels of Jane Austen*, ed. R. W. Chapman, 3d ed. (Oxford: Oxford University Press, 1966), 18.

52. Jane Austen, *Volume the Second*, ed. B. C. Southam (Oxford: Clarendon, 1963), 215. Southam argues that "Charlotte Smith is the only contemporary novelist whose works are referred to in the juvenilia," in *Catharine*, though he's counting only direct references. See Southam, *Jane Austen's Literary Manuscripts*, 10. Indirect references would increase this number. On Austen and Smith, see Anne Ehrenpreis, "*Northanger Abbey:* Jane Austen and Charlotte Smith," *Nineteenth-Century Fiction* 25 (1970): 343–48.

53. Doody notes that "Jane Austen sustains the use of dramas as sources for history" and that "once again, Jane Austen cites drama rather than history." See Doody in Austen, *Catharine*, 329, 332.

54. Oliver Goldsmith, *History of England, in a Series of Letters from a Nobleman to His Son*, 2 vols. (London: J. Newberry, 1764), 3.

55. Though this feature of the *History*'s illustrations has been noticed by many critics, the edition by Fergus et al. is the first to identify the source of two of the portraits. A 1780 engraving by W. H. Bunbury provided the model for Cassandra's illustrations of Henry V and Edward IV. See Fergus et al., *History*, ii–iii.

56. Southam, *Jane Austen*, 28. As Ellen Martin puts it, "The whole notion of a great narrative of causation linking events is regarded as inadequate by an artist devoted to sapping what passes for consequence and celebrating the connections made by the private, eclectic fancy." See Ellen E. Martin, "The Madness of Jane Austen: Metonymic Style and Literature's Resistance to Interpretation," in *Jane Austen's Beginnings*, ed. J. David Grey, 93.

57. Goldsmith, *History*, 403.

58.   Of course, Jacobin and anti-Jacobin novels dealt to some degree with such militaristic fare in their accounts of the French Revolution. See Butler, *Jane Austen*. Furthermore, eighteenth-century novels such as *Tom Jones* or *Tristram Shandy* certainly used war as a narrative (though not *the* central narrative) feature or backdrop. Seventeenth- and eighteenth-century writings about war—by men and by women—seem to have come to us more often as memoir than as fiction.

59.   Language that is as melodramatic as my own can be found in Katrin Ristkok Burlin's " 'The Pen of the Contriver': The Four Fictions of *Northanger Abbey*." Burlin writes, "Jane Austen's motive is to fight for her craft, to prove that it is the responsible novelist who protects us by teaching us through his art to recognize and discriminate among the fictions of life and art alike." See *Jane Austen: Bicentenary Essays*, 89–90.

60.   A. Walton Litz, *Jane Austen: A Study of Her Artistic Development* (New York: Oxford University Press, 1965), 19.

61.   On the dates of composition of *Northanger Abbey* (which are not easy to fix), see Leslie F. Chard II, "Jane Austen and the Obituaries: The Names of *Northanger Abbey*," *Studies in the Novel* 7 (1975): 133–36.; Cecil S. Emden, "The Composition of Northanger Abbey," *Review of English Studies* 19, no. 75 (1968): 279–87; Darrel Mansell, "The Date of Jane Austen's Revision of *Northanger Abbey*," *English Language Notes* 7 (1969): 40–41; and B. C. Southam, *"Sanditon:* The Seventh Novel," in *Jane Austen's Achievement*, ed. Juliet McMaster (New York: Barnes & Noble, 1975), 4. On the questionable claim that the Bath section and the Abbey section were written at different times, see Kenneth L. Moler, *Jane Austen's Art of Allusion* (Lincoln: University of Nebraska Press, 1968), 31.

Cassandra Austen, who is responsible for naming the novel *Northanger Abbey,* dates the novel 1798. Austen had titled the novel *Susan* when she sold it to a publisher in 1803. Crosby, the publisher, did not publish it, and Austen eventually bought it back from him in 1816 for the price he had paid—£10. Austen referred to it at this time as *Miss Catherine*. Internal evidence proves revisions must have been made after 1798, though to what degree the novel was revised is subject to debate. The novel was published posthumously, with *Persuasion,* in 1818. Although Meenakshi Mukherjee speculates that Austen's "playful subversion of some of the conventions of the popular novel in *Northanger Abbey* resulted in the non-publication of the manuscript in her lifetime, even though a publisher had paid [for] it," the reasons for its non-publication have not been substantiated. See Meenakshi Mukherjee, *Jane Austen* (New York: Macmillan, 1991), 31. B. C. Southam suggests that Crosby may have "thought that the Gothic market was over-crowded." See Southam, *"Sanditon:* The Seventh Novel," 4.

62.   In 1976, B. C. Southam wrote that "While each of the other novels has attracted a substantial body of critical writing and possesses its own individual critical tradition, *Northanger Abbey* has inspired rather little, the unstated implication being that [it is] . . . the least in need of commentary." See his introduction to *Jane Austen:* Northanger Abbey *and* Persuasion: *A Casebook,* 20. Twenty years later, this can no longer be convincing, though *Northanger Abbey* has never received the unequivocal critical praise that the other novels have. Typical is Joan Aiken Hodge's assessment that *Northanger Abbey* is an "exuberant, faulty masterpiece," in her "How Might Jane Austen Have Revised *Northanger Abbey*?" *Persuasions* 7 (1985): 54.

63.   Michael Williams offers an account of *Northanger Abbey* as extricated from the Gothic tradition because it is parody. See *Jane Austen: Six Novels and Their Methods* (New York: St. Martin's, 1985), 10–30. For an argument that labels Austen as a Gothic imitator, see Judith Wilt, *Ghosts of the Gothic* (Princeton: Princeton University Press, 1980), 121–72. Amy Elizabeth Smith argues that readings of *Northanger Abbey* to date have been "somewhat lopsided" in their consideration of gothic novels and lack of focus on the reverberations with the sentimental genre. See her " 'Julias and Louisas': Austen's *Northanger Abbey* and the Sentimental Novel," *English Language Notes* 30 (1992): 33–43.

64.   The "most political" comment is from Robert Hopkins, "General Tilney and Affairs of State," 213–24. The "shortest and lightest" assessment is from Walter E. Anderson, "From Northanger to Woodston: Catherine's Education to Common Life," *Philological Quarterly* 63 (1984): 493–509. George Levine considers *Northanger Abbey* to be Austen's "most trivially entertaining novel," in "Translating the Monstrous: *Northanger Abbey*," *Nineteenth-Century Fiction* 30 (1975): 335–50. For a helpful summary of critical debates on *Northanger Abbey*, see Jan S. Fergus, *Jane Austen and the Didactic Novel:* Northanger Abbey, Sense and Sensibility, *and* Pride and Prejudice (Totowa, N.J.: Barnes & Noble, 1983), 12–14.

65.   T. V. Reddy dubs Catherine "self-actualized," a position also intimated by Susan Morgan in "Guessing for Ourselves in *Northanger Abbey*." Daniel Cottom alternatively labels Catherine "colonized." See Daniel Cottom, *The Civilized Imagination: A Study of Ann Radcliffe, Jane Austen, and Sir Walter Scott* (Cambridge: Cambridge University Press, 1985), 21; Susan Morgan, "Guessing for Ourselves in *Northanger Abbey*," in *Jane Austen: Modern Critical Views*, ed. Harold Bloom (New York: Chelsea, 1986), 109–28; and T. Vasudeva Reddy, *Jane Austen: The Dialectics of Self-Actualization in Her Novels* (London: Oriental University Press, 1987). In this section, I borrow ideas and arguments from my article, "(Re)Making History and Philosophy: Austen's *Northanger Abbey*," *European Romantic Review* 4, no. 1 (1993): 34–56.

66.   George Whalley believes that "At best Northanger Abbey is a sort of *Donna Quixote*." See George Whalley, "Jane Austen: Poet," in *Jane Austen's Achievement*, 127. See also Elaine M. Kauvar, "Jane Austen and *The Female Quixote*," *Studies in the Novel* 2 (1970): 211–21.

67.   Laura G. Mooneyham, *Romance, Language, and Education in Jane Austen's Novels* (New York: St. Martin's, 1988), 1.

68.   David Monaghan, *Jane Austen: Structure and Social Vision* (London: Macmillan, 1980), 16.

69.   Jane Austen, *Northanger Abbey and Persuasion*, vol. 5 of *The Novels of Jane Austen*, 37; hereafter cited in text as *NA*.

70.   Everett Zimmerman writes, "In her juvenilia Jane Austen burlesqued these failings of popular fiction; in *Northanger Abbey* she attempts to resuscitate the fiction and certain values on which it is based." See Zimmerman, "The Function of Parody in *Northanger Abbey*," *Modern Language Quarterly* 30 (1969): 62.

71.   See my introduction to *Jane Austen and Discourses of Feminism*, especially 8–9. Without engaging issues of feminist criticism, Frank Bradbrook remarks on this reference to Edgeworth as a possible reproach. See his *Jane Austen and Her Predecessors* (Cambridge: Cambridge University Press, 1966), 113. Bradbrook points to an even earlier source for this reading: C. Linklater Thompson, *Jane Austen: A Survey* (London: H. Marshall and Son, 1929), 45–46.

72.   Edgeworth, too, wanted to change the way novels were labeled, expressing a wish that a name ought to be devised to distinguish "philosophical novels" from "trifling, silly productions." See Butler, *Jane Austen*, 131.

73.   Margaret Kirkham, *Jane Austen, Feminism, and Fiction* (Sussex: Harvester, 1983), 69.

74.   Jocelyn Harris, *Jane Austen's Art of Memory* (Cambridge: Cambridge University Press, 1989), 26. Harris makes the provocative argument that in chapter 5 of *Northanger Abbey* Jane Austen implies that "historical writing soon looks out-of-date" (27) and that it is "in effect the essay that she said she omitted from *Pride and Prejudice*" (30). Harris further argues, "The upstart novelist challenges the philosopher and the historian, standing (as Sidney said of the poet) between the precepts of one and the examples of the other. . . . she stakes the bold claim that fiction usurps poetry as well" (32–33). Harris's argument has been important in formulating my own.

75.   As Kent writes, "There is every reason to believe that Eleanor Tilney, who was 'fond of history,' better represented Jane Austen's own mature views than did Catherine Morland." See Kent 1989, 68. On Eleanor, Catherine, and imagination in the Beechen Cliff episode, see Susan Morgan, "Guessing for Ourselves in *Northanger Abbey*," 117–18.

In Frans De Bruyn's interesting article "Edmund Burke's Gothic Romance: The Portrayal of Warren Hastings in Burke's Writings and Speeches on India," these insights are given to Catherine. De Bruyn argues that Catherine Morland "acknowledges a close generic kinship between histories and novels and pertinently questions the consistency of her own taste, given her avowed love of fiction." See *Criticism* 29, no. 4 (1987): 415. Some of De Bruyn's arguments, including that "the stated aims of historians and novelists often converged remarkably in the period" and that Austen belongs to a tradition of " 'historical' novel-writing," overlap with my own (415).

76. On the "something shocking" passage as a historical reference, see Litz, *Jane Austen,* 64; B. C. Southam, " 'Regulated Hatred' Revisited," 124–26; Robert Hopkins, "General Tilney and Affairs of State," especially 216–17; Eric Rothstein, "The Lessons of *Northanger Abbey,*" *University of Toronto Quarterly* 44, no. 1 (1974): 29; Ronald Paulson, *Representations of Revolution (1790–1820)* (New Haven: Yale University Press, 1983), 216; and Mark Loveridge, "*Northanger Abbey;* or, Nature and Probability," *Nineteenth-Century Literature* 56, no. 1 (1991): 4. Rothstein notes that "St. George's Fields were the common gathering ground of any riotous mob from the early seventeenth century on" (29).

77. In Eric Rothstein's view, the Beechen Cliff conversation is not about the triumph of fiction over history but about the components of gothic fiction: "one can see that the subjects discussed are really an analysis of the Gothic novel into components: words, pleasure for readers, history, didacticism, picturesque scenery, and the violence of life which it professes to imitate" (18–19). See Rothstein, "The Lessons of *Northanger Abbey,*" 14–30.

78. As Ronald Paulson has suggested, however, the Gothic and history should not be strictly opposed: "We notice the difference between gothic fiction and history, but also the similarity. . . . The gothic did in fact serve as a metaphor with which some contemporaries in England tried to understand what was happening across the channel in the 1790s." See Paulson, *Representations,* 217.

79. In the *Dictionary of Feminist Theory, herstory* is defined as "Women's history. The theory of, and documentation about, past and contemporary lives, groups, language and experience of women." See Maggie Humm, *The Dictionary of Feminist Theory* (Columbus: Ohio University Press, 1990), 94. Women's history is not always in the "herstorical" mode, however. "Herstory" might be defined, twisting Catherine Morland's words, as accounts in which there are gestures toward "men all so good for nothing" and hardly any women who aren't worthy of celebration and commemoration.

80. Lyn Reese and Jean Wilkinson, eds., *Women in the World: Annotated History Resources for the Secondary Student* (Metuchen, N.J.: Scarecrow, 1987).

81. Rosalind Miles, *The Women's History of the World.* (New York: Harper and Row, 1990), xii.

82. Miles, *Women's History,* 117.

83. Georges Duby and Michelle Perrot, eds., "Writing the History of Women," in *A History of Women in the West* (Cambridge, Mass.: Harvard University Press, 1992), ix–xxiii.

84. Susan Groag Bell and Karen M. Offen, eds., *Women, the Family and Freedom: The Debate in Documents,* vol. 1, *1750–1880* (Palo Alto: Stanford University Press, 1983), 1.

85. Bell and Offen, *Women,* 1. For another account that understands Catherine's complaint as anticipating today's feminist criticism, see Tony Tanner, *Jane Austen* (Cambridge, Mass.: Harvard University Press, 1986), 44.

86. Sandra M. Gilbert and Susan Gubar, *Madwoman in the Attic: The Woman Writer and the Nineteenth-Century Literary Imagination* (New Haven: Yale University Press, 1979), 108; hereafter cited in text.

87. Isobel Grundy, "Women's History?: Writing by English Nuns," in *Women, Writing, History: 1640–1740,* ed. Isobel Grundy and Susan Wiseman (Athens: University of Georgia Press, 1992), 126.

88. Grundy finds Macaulay's predecessors most worthy of further feminist study. As Grundy suggests, much of women's historical writing before the late eighteenth century included epic or fictionalized history, biography, scandalous court memoirs, and family history— a claim that is central to this study as well. Grundy argues that these women's historical writings provide "a history of a whole female culture. Together they make up one of those barely explored subgenres which are now emerging in such numbers among works written by women" (Grundy, "Women's History?" 126). She locates a pre-nineteenth-century "feminine" relationship to "history proper" that women enacted. Here I depart from Grundy's views, in that I don't believe there was such a feminine relationship but instead that there were various, often competing, relationships.

89. Ina Ferris has made a similar but opposite claim—that Sir Walter Scott incorporated the masculine world of political or public history into the form of the novel, a largely female domain, thus changing the ground on which the novel was classified. See Ina Ferris, *The Achievement of Literary Authority: Gender, History, and the Waverly Novels* (Ithaca: Cornell University Press, 1991). That Scott's novels have been subsumed by Austen's in the canon tells us more about the twentieth century than the nineteenth.

90. Anderson, "From Northanger to Woodston," 495. As Mark Loveridge has argued in his important article, *Northanger Abbey* "has recently come to be recognized as a transitional work in a much wider sense: as a work highly suggestive of changes in novelistic technique that were taking place between the eighteenth and nineteenth centuries" ("*Northanger Abbey*," 2). I would suggest, however, that Loveridge's "wider sense" could be even wider still. On possible "wider senses" beyond the scope of this argument, see Armstrong's *Desire;* Armstrong 1990; Siskin's *Historicity;* and Bender's *Imagining.* See also James Thompson, "Jane Austen," in *The Columbia History of the British Novel,* ed. John Richetti, (New York: Columbia University Press, 1986), 275–99; and Paul Morrison, "Enclosed in Openness: Northanger Abbey and the Domestic Carceral," *Texas Studies in Literature and Language* 33, no. 1 (1991): 1–23.

Ideological Contradictions
and the Consolations of Form:
The Case of Jane Austen

Mary Poovey

Reading Jane Austen's novels in the context of the works of Mary Woll-stonecraft and Mary Shelley reminds us that Austen also lived through and wrote about the crisis of values that dominated late eighteenth- and early nineteenth-century English society. Austen's perspective on this crisis was, of course, markedly different from those of the other two women, for whereas both the lower middle-class Wollstonecraft and the emigrée Shelley witnessed the radicals' challenge to propriety from outside its eminent domain, Austen spent her entire life in the very heart of propriety. Austen never traveled as widely as either Wollstonecraft or Shelley, she never flamboyantly defied propriety, and she never wrote to support herself or anyone else. Perhaps partly as a consequence of her limited experience, Austen did not choose to write about politics, nature, or metaphysics, and she assiduously avoided the highly imaginative, melodramatic incidents that so fascinated her contemporaries.

Yet for all the obvious differences between her life and aesthetic interests and theirs, Jane Austen did concern herself with many of the same issues as Wollstonecraft and Shelley—with the process of a young girl's maturation, for example, and, more important, with the complex relationship between a woman's desires and the imperatives of propriety. Considering Austen's novels from the perspective of these issues and in terms of the debate already set out in the works of Wollstonecraft and Shelley enables us to recognize what the challenge to traditional values looked like from the inside and how an artistic style could constitute part of a defense against this challenge. As we will see, Austen's class position placed her firmly in the middle of the crisis of values we have been examining. As with Wollstonecraft and Shelley, Austen's gender and her decision to write professionally focused the contradictions inherent in this crisis. What is new is that Austen's aesthetic choices—her style

Mary Poovey, "Ideological Contradictions and the Consolations of Form: The Case of Jane Austen," in *The Proper Lady and the Woman Writer: Ideology as Style in the Works of Mary Wollstonecraft, Mary Shelley, and Jane Austen* (Chicago: University of Chicago Press, 1984), 172–207. © 1984 by The University of Chicago Press; reprinted by permission.

and her subject matter—can be seen as "solutions" to some of the problems that neither Wollstonecraft or Shelley could solve. My analysis of Austen's work therefore comes last not because this order is faithful to chronology but because her novels culminate a sequence of stages of female insight and artistic achievement. We can never fully "explain" genius, but in considering the ways in which Austen both completes Wollstonecraft's analysis of female inhibition and perfects Shelley's attempt to make propriety accommodate female desire, we can better understand her accomplishment and some of the functions her artistic strategies served.[1]

Our access to Jane Austen's personal attitudes to historical events and to propriety will always be blocked by her sister Cassandra, who destroyed many of Austen's letters and censored numerous others; moreover, the letters that did survive at times convey contradictory opinions and, what is perhaps even more confusing, almost always employ a decidedly ambiguous tone.[2] When an individual work by Wollstonecraft or Shelley seems morally or stylistically ambiguous, surviving letters or journals help provide a background for interpretation; and the psychological or aesthetic complexities that appear in their fiction and nonfiction alike can be clarified in the same way. But the incompleteness and opacity of Austen's personal record often compound the notorious instability of her novelistic irony, thus leading us further into confusing (if delightful) ambiguity. When Austen tells the obsequious James Stanier Clarke, for example, that "I think I may boast myself to be, with all possible vanity, the most unlearned and uninformed female who ever dared to be an authoress" (*JAL*, 2:443; 11 December 1815), we feel certain that she pretends to diminish herself at her silly correspondent's expense. But when she tells her nephew that she cannot manage his "strong, manly, spirited Sketches" upon the canvas of her art—"the little bit (two Inches wide) of Ivory on which I work with so fine a Brush, as produces little effect after much labour" (*JAL*, 2:468–69; 16 December 1816)—it is difficult to determine exactly how much of her self-depreciation is genuine, how much is simply encouragement for the young writer, and how much is the mock vanity of a self-confident miniaturist. The Austen legacy has been further complicated, of course, by the officious concern of her relatives. In addition to Cassandra's excessive concern for propriety, the efforts of her brother and nephews to beatify "Aunt Jane" for Victorian readers has also blurred our hindsight and has no doubt generated, in some cases, as much overcompensation as accurate evaluation.

LADY SUSAN

In the absence of extensive biographical documentation, then, Austen's juvenilia provide a logical point of departure. Indeed, her most extended early work, *Lady Susan* (composed c. 1793–94),[3] places her precisely "between" Wollstonecraft and Shelley and broadly establishes the aesthetic and ethical issues that were to occupy her for the remainder of her career. *Lady Susan* is an epistolary satire that takes to task both the ideal of "natural" propriety, which Mary Wollstonecraft also challenged, and the suggestion, similarly rejected by Mary Shelley, that individual desire is, automatically, socially constructive. In the course of *Lady Susan,* Austen seems to agree with *both* Wollstonecraft and Shelley; for, like Shelley, she insists on the destructive potential of individual desire, and, like Wollstonecraft, she points to the way in which the contradictions of social manners may distort the constructive energies women do possess. Because of the hypocrisy implicit in propriety, Austen suggests, there can be no victors: society cannot afford to unleash the energy inherent in female desire, yet the morality by which society controls desire destroys the individual and threatens society itself. In many ways the "heroine" of *Lady Susan* is Austen's version of the energy that Shelley was to call a "monster"; but because Lady Susan's society is almost as repressive and barren as the one depicted in Wollstonecraft's *Maria,* Austen's presentation of this creature is even more ambiguous than Shelley's dramatization of the monster in 1818.

The first two letters that appear in *Lady Susan* establish the unmistakable tone and range of the heroine's voice. Recently widowed, immediately ejected from her "particular" friend's house for her outrageous flirtations, Lady Susan Vernon writes first to her brother, Charles Vernon, to whom she displays only her "winningly mild" countenance. "My kind friends here are most affectionately urgent with me to prolong my stay," she assures him, "but their hospitable & chearful dispositions lead them too much into society for my present situation & state of mind."[4] She is looking forward, she says, to meeting her new "Sister" in the "delightful retirement" of the country. But the reader, more privileged than Mr. Vernon, immediately receives another version of these "facts." In the next letter, addressed to her confidential friend, Alicia Johnson, Lady Susan explains that "the Females of the Family are united against me"; "the whole family are at war" (pp. 244, 245). "Charles Vernon is my aversion, & I am afraid of his wife," she acknowledges; nevertheless, out of necessity, she is off to visit them in "that insupportable spot, a country Village" (pp. 246, 245–46). Already we see that Lady Susan uses her letters to manipulate reality—to create it, in fact; for we can assume that she plays on Mr. Johnson's prejudices against propriety almost as consistently as she plays on her brother's simpleminded belief that "truth" has only one face and a single voice.

In Lady Susan's adroit manipulation of "truth" Austen is dramatizing the way that the gap between appearance and reality, which is intrinsic to the paradoxical configuration of propriety, generates a crisis of moral authority. And the remarkable success Susan enjoys with most of her audience for most of the novel suggests the gravity of this crisis. Because her retreat to the country enhances the impression she cultivates of being both virtuous and unavailable, Susan sustains the interest of both of her town admirers and adds to them Reginald De Courcy, Mrs. Vernon's brother and the heir to his family's estate. Susan is able to manipulate others chiefly because she knows that the use of language is an art capable of generating plausible, internally consistent, but wholly malleable fictions—just as the manners of propriety can. Thus she reverses Reginald's initial prejudices against her simply by revising the "facts" on which her notoriety is based, and she prejudices the Vernons against her own daughter Frederica so as better to control the child and then almost manages to make this timid daughter marry the man she herself has chosen for her—her own cast-off suitor, Sir James Martin. Lady Susan freely admits to the pleasure her quick wit and creative pen afford: "If I am vain of anything," she preens, "it is of my eloquence. Consideration & Esteem as surely follow command of Language, as Admiration waits on Beauty" (p. 268). In the end she fails to control reality completely only because the people she has successfully duped—Mrs. Manwaring and Reginald, Frederica and Mrs. Vernon—escape the closed system of her rhetoric by talking to each other. "Horrid" facts obtrude, and her victims conspire to drive Susan out of both family circles. Ultimately, Susan without a pen or audience, has no influence because she has no vehicle or context by which to create her "self."

Throughout the novel, Lady Susan also aspires to maintain a related but equally precarious balance: she wants to retain the power to exercise her aggressive energies and, at the same time, the reputation for propriety that gives her that power. "Those women are inexcusable," she scoffs, "who forget what is due to themselves & the opinion of the World" (p. 269). The principle that Lady Susan overlooks but that Jane Austen underscores is that, given the nature of female desire, these two "dues" are incompatible. Susan's fidelity to herself would entail indulging her apparently insatiable appetite for attention; yet the "World" will not grant that appetite free expression or substantial gratification. Lady Susan, in other words, is trapped in the very paradox of propriety that she thought she could exploit; because it demands indirection, propriety effectively distorts the desires it seemed to accommodate.

Despite her apparently indomitable wit, Lady Susan also finds herself thwarted by another irony of the female situation. She seems to be a woman of the mind and to pride herself on her ability to dominate not only other people and their perceptions of reality but emotion itself. Susan's sharpest comments are reserved for women who, like her own daughter and Mrs. Manwaring, experience and express strong feeling without inhibition or art. Of her daughter Susan despairs: "I never saw a girl of her age, bid fairer to be the sport of Mankind. Her feelings are tolerably lively & she is so charmingly artless in their display, as to afford the most reasonable hope of her being ridiculed & despised by every Man who sees her." "Artlessness will never do in Love matters," she continues, "& that girl is born a simpleton who has it either by nature or affectation" (p. 274). Yet despite her professed preference for art over spontaneity, Austen hints that Susan yearns for a genuine contest—perhaps even for defeat by an emotion that prudence cannot master. She will not marry the "contemptibly weak" Sir James, she vows, for all his wealth: "I must own myself rather romantic in that respect, & that Riches only, will not satisfy me" (p. 245). Initially she is aroused by Reginald precisely because he seems a worthy antagonist. "There is something about him that rather interests me," she admits; "a sort of sauciness, of familiarity which I shall teach him to correct. . . . There is exquisite pleasure in subduing an insolent spirit, in making a person predetermined to dislike, acknowledge one's superiority" (p. 254). The problem here is that even though Susan insists that power resides in the mind, she fears that it may actually originate in emotion. Noting the perceptible increase in Frederica's affection for Reginald, Susan admits to "not feeling perfectly secure that a knowledge of *that* affection might not in the end awaken a return. Contemptible as a regard founded only on compassion, must make them both, in my eyes, I [feel] by no means assured that such might not be the consequence" (p. 280).

Beneath Lady Susan's artful self-presentation, then, lurk fears and desires she can neither conceal nor acknowledge. Her boasts of the power of art belie a fascination not only with the "romantic" love that drives her daughter to defy her but even with the fear that compels Frederica to run away from Sir James. Similarly, Susan's need to be flattered hides her persistent anxiety that neither she nor the "World" is as admirable as she wants to believe, and her impatience with spontaneity cloaks her fear that its real liability is just what she says it is: if one is not loved in return, the lover may ridicule, despise, and make sport of a woman's heart.

Despite her aggressive hostility to feminine stereotypes, Lady Susan conforms precisely to the typical female the mid-eighteenth-century moralists described: she is vain, obsessed by men, dominated by her appetites, and, finally, incapable of creating any identity independent of the one she tries to denounce.[5] Ironically, her aggressiveness only affirms the vulnerability she prides herself on having overcome, and she is finally caught in the most fatal paradox of female feeling: to express love is to risk rejection, yet never to acknowledge feeling is to court isolation and the hollow victory of having successfully repressed desire.

Part of the problem, Austen implies, is that society fails to provide any power adequate to Lady Susan. Even in this patriarchal society there are simply no men strong enough either to engage or resist her irrepressible energy. The novel is consistently dominated by women, despite Susan's preoccupation with men. Mr. Vernon seems oblivious to what is happening beneath his roof; Reginald's father, even when told of Susan's plot, refuses to believe that such women exist; Sir James, Mr. Manwaring, and Reginald are simply dupes of Susan's wiles. Only the women are capable of grasping the implications of her exuberance or of doing anything about it. Even timid Frederica three times defies her mother; Mrs. Manwaring finally overthrows Susan by pursuing her husband to London; and Mrs. Vernon consistently proves herself capable not only of understanding Susan's art but of matching it with machinations of her own. As Lloyd W. Brown has noted, the only real contest in *Lady Susan* is between the heroine and Mrs. Vernon; Reginald and Frederica constitute the pawns and the spoils. Like Lady Susan, Mrs. Vernon seeks to control the emotions and the futures of these two young people; both women are egotists, who use their epistolary art to manipulate "reality," and only they can fully comprehend any desire other than avarice.[6]

By the end of the story, the failure of every moral authority in Susan's society threatens to subvert any didactic effect this novel might have seemed to promise. On the one hand, *Lady Susan* constitutes an attack on propriety, which, paradoxically, Austen presents as both restrictive and permissive. Such morality, Austen suggests, is inadequate not because it has misrepresented female nature but because its attempt to control desire has served only to distort this powerful force, to drive it into artful wiles and stratagems that are often both socially destructive and personally debilitating. On the other hand, because the world Austen depicts contains neither adequate outlets for this energy nor a paternal authority capable of mastering it, we cannot imagine what constructive form Susan's exuberance could take—or, for that matter, what social or moral institution could control it. Because Susan's energy exceeds the capacity of the world she inhabits, it is necessarily destructive—not only of the foolish men but of innocent young persons like Frederica and, ultimately, of Lady Susan herself.[7]

Despite its destructive tendencies and effects, however, Lady Susan's energy—like that of Shelley's monster—remains the most attractive force in this novel. And, as in *Frankenstein,* the power of this attraction is reinforced by the epistolary form, which allows us not only to engage ourselves with Lady Susan's intellect but to sympathize with her conflicting feelings as well. Even though the letters Mrs. Vernon writes supply another perspective on Susan's schemes, her judgments are no more "objective" or authoritative than Susan's whims—especially given her personal grudge against Susan. Similarly, the final agent of "justice"—Mrs. Manwaring—comes from the household that was, initially, so easily duped, and she too, like Mrs. Vernon, retaliates from personal motives, not to save some absolute system of disinterested values. In a novel that lacks a spokesperson for such values, the epistolary form generates moral anarchy; Austen does not establish a genuinely critical position within the fiction but depends instead on an implicit contrast between the values presented and those the satire presumes but does not formulate. Within the moral consensus of a family such allusiveness might well suffice, and we can imagine Austen reading *Lady Susan* to her amused family circle. But without this consensus there is no moral authority because there is no narrative authority. In the laissez-faire competition the epistolary *Lady Susan* permits, the reader will identify with whatever character dominates the narration or most completely gratifies the appetite for entertainment. In *Lady Susan* this character is, of course, the dangerous heroine.

So compelling and so complete is this heroine's artful power that the only way Austen can effectively censure her is to impose punishment by narrative fiat. Predictably, this entails disrupting the epistolary narrative and ridiculing not just the correspondents but the morally anarchic epistolary form itself. "This Correspondence," Austen playfully announces in the "Conclusion," ". . . could not, to the great detriment of the Post office Revenue, be continued longer. Very little assistance to the State could be derived from the Epistolary Intercourse of Mrs. Vernon & her niece" (p. 311). She then abruptly summarizes the fate of the characters: Mrs. Vernon and Mrs. Manwaring triumph, and Frederica and her mother reverse positions in almost every important respect: the daughter marries Reginald, and Lady Susan is reduced to marrying the suitor whom Frederica has now cast off, Sir James Martin. But Austen will not allow even this summary to have final authority, for in her final reference to Lady Susan she leaves her in exactly the same moral vacuum in which we found her: "Whether Lady Susan was, or was not happy in her second Choice—I do not see how it can ever be ascertained—for who would take her assurance of it, on either side of the question?" (p. 313).

Austen's final ambivalence here suggests an attempt to accomplish the same feat to which Lady Susan aspired: to obtain both "what is due to [herself] & the opinion of the World." What is due to herself as an artist is uninhibited self-expression; the "opinion of the World" requires conclusive moral order. Austen seems reluctant to deny the power or attraction of female energy, perhaps because it is too close to the creative impulse of her own wit; nor does she fully condone the indulgence of that energy, for its destructive potential is undeniable. By allowing herself and her reader imaginative engagement with her heroine, Austen seems to satisfy the prerogatives of desire; by abruptly severing that engagement, she aspires to reassert the system of social principles whose authority Lady Susan has so effectively challenged.

The narrative impasse at the conclusion of *Lady Susan* is in many ways reminiscent of the problems that beset Wollstonecraft's *Maria:* the appeal of female feeling competes with Austen's reservations about it almost as dramatically as Wollstonecraft's attraction to "romantic expectations" jeopardizes her critique of sentimentalism. In both cases, one consequence of this aesthetic ambiguity is uncertainty for the reader as to the moral ground of the novels. Just as *Maria* seems to hover between irony and wholehearted sentimentalism, so *Lady Susan* occupies the gray area between satire and direct social criticism. But the intervention of the unmistakable narrative voice at the end of *Lady Susan,* while necessitated by a version of *Maria's* tonal uncertainty, points to one essential difference between these two writers—a difference that becomes more marked during Austen's subsequent career. The "solution" Wollstonecraft offers in *Maria* involves two extreme gestures: on the one hand, she rejects social institutions that inhibit individual feeling; on the other hand, she redefines human emotions so that they transcend social institutions altogether. By contrast, Austen brings individual desire into confrontation with social institutions in order first to discipline anarchic passion and then to expand the capacity of such institutions to accommodate educated needs and desires. One reason *Maria*'s conclusion remains blocked is that everything in the sections Wollstonecraft finished suggests her desire to segregate the realistic depictions of corrupt society from her romantic effusions of passion. The conclusion of *Lady Susan,* on the other hand, for all its contrivance, suggests an impulse to contain even momentary fantasies of unmitigated power within the twin controls of aesthetic closure and social propriety. In this sense, Jane Austen resembles Mary Shelley more than Mary Wollstonecraft. But the balance of her sympathies, along with the aesthetic solutions she developed to convey them, take her beyond the artistic achievement of either of the other two.

The division of sympathies we see in *Lady Susan* bears a particularly interesting relationship to Jane Austen's complex social and economic position during this period of change. As we have already seen, the period between 1775 and 1817, the years of Austen's life, was punctuated by challenges to the traditional hierarchy of English class society and, as a consequence, to conventional social roles and responsibilities. William Wordsworth's 1817 survey of the preceding thirty years summarizes the chaotic impact of these changes:

> I see clearly that the principal ties which kept the different classes of society in a vital and harmonious dependence upon each other have, within these 30 years, either been greatly impaired or wholly dissolved. Everything has been put up to market and sold for the highest price it would buy. . . . All moral cement is dissolved, habits and prejudices are broken and rooted up, nothing being substituted in their place but a quickened self-interest.[8]

In England, the decisive agent of this change was not just the French Revolution but the more subtle, more gradual, dissemination of the values and behavior associated with capitalism—first, agrarian capitalism in the mid- and late eighteenth century, then, in the early nineteenth century, industrial capitalism, as money made itself felt in investment and capital return. As we have seen, by the first decades of the nineteenth century, birth into a particular class no longer exclusively determined one's future social or economic status, the vertical relationships of patronage no longer guaranteed either privileges or obedience, and the traditional authority of the gentry, and of the values associated with their life-style, was a subject under general debate. In the midst of such changes, the assumptions that had theoretically been shared by eighteenth-century moralists and their audiences seemed increasingly problematic, requiring refinement and defense if not radical change. As the literature and political debates of this period unmistakably reveal, the crisis in imaginative and moral authority was pervasive and severe; even conservative writers generally abandoned arguments about absolute truths in favor of discussions in which one set of principles was defended against a contrary but equally coherent system of values.[9]

As the daughter of a country clergyman with numerous and strong ties to the landed upper gentry, Jane Austen was involved in this crisis of authority in an immediate and particularly complex way. As Donald J. Greene has conclusively demonstrated, Jane Austen was acutely aware of her kinship to several prominent families, among them the Brydges, who were earls and lords of Chandos, and the lords Leigh of Stoneleigh.[10] More immediately, as a clergyman Austen's father belonged to the lesser realms of the gentry, and Jane and her siblings all benefited more or less directly from the patronage that traditionally reinforced the gentry's hegemony. One of Austen's brothers, Edward, was adopted by the wealthy Knight family, of Kent, and, as heir to the valuable estate of Godmersham, he was eventually able to provide a home at Chawton Cottage for Jane, her mother, her sister, and their friend Martha Lloyd. Two of Austen's other brothers, James and Henry, became clergymen, and her two youngest brothers, Francis and Charles, entered the British navy and eventually became admirals; Francis in fact became a knight. Thus Jane Austen was raised in the heart of middle-class society; she shared its values, and she owed her own position to the bonds of patronage that cemented traditional society, even though her immediate resources never permitted her fully to emulate the gentry's life-style.

In keeping with this class affiliation, Jane Austen's fundamental ideological position was conservative; her political sympathies were generally Tory, and her religion was officially Anglican; overall, she was a "conservative Christian moralist," supportive of Evangelical ethical rigor even before she explicitly admitted admiring the Evangelicals themselves.[11]

But neither the external evidence of Austen's social position nor the internal evidence of her novels supports so strict a delineation of her sympathies. In the first place, even the traditional practices of paternalism were influenced during this period by the rhetoric and practices of individualism. (To give but one relevant example: promotion in such prestigious professions as the navy could result from individual effort and merit [as *Persuasion* indicates]; at other times it depended on the interest of a patron [as William Price learns in *Mansfield Park*]). In the second place, the role played by Austen's class in the rise of capitalism was particularly complicated; for the agricultural improvements that preceded and paved the way for early industrial capitalism were financed and initiated in many cases by the landowning gentry, yet the legal provisions of strict settlement and entail were expressly designed to prohibit land from becoming a commodity susceptible to promiscuous transfer or easy liquidation. Despite the fact that the landowning gentry participated in the expansion of agrarian capitalism, their role was passive, not active; as a consequence, their values and life-style were not extensively altered until the more radical and rapid expansion of industrial capitalism began in the first decades of the nineteenth century. When that occurred, the gentry were suddenly awakened to the implications of the changes to which their patterns of expenditure had contributed.[12] From the more vulnerable position of the lower levels of the gentry, Jane Austen was able to see with particular clarity the marked differences between the two components of the middle class: the landed gentry and the new urban capitalist class.[13] The division of sympathies that occurs in her novels when middle-class daughters get rewarded with the sons of landed families emanates at least partly from Austen's being both involved in and detached from these two middle-class groups at a moment when they were implicitly competing with each other.

In Austen's very early works, like *Lady Susan,* this division of sympathies characteristically leads either to broad farce or to the tonal uncertainties of parody.[14] As her career progresses, however, we see Austen gradually develop aesthetic strategies capable of balancing her attraction to exuberant but potentially anarchic feeling with her investment in traditional social institutions. This balance is embodied in the thematic material she chooses and the rhetorical stance she adopts. At their most sophisticated, Austen's rhetorical strategies harness the imaginative energy of her readers to a moral design; she thus manages to satisfy both the individual reader's desire for emotional gratification and the program of education prescribed by traditional moral aestheticians.

To understand why Austen assumed that a novel could simultaneously gratify the cravings of the imagination and provide oral instruction, it is useful to turn to Samuel Johnson, Austen's favorite eighteenth-century essayist. According to Johnson, novel-reading is an active, not passive, enterprise, for it aggressively engages the imagination of its young reader. Novels, Johnson explains,

> are the entertainment of minds unfurnished with ideas, and therefore easily susceptible of impressions; not fixed by principles, and therefore easily following the current of fancy; not informed by experience, and consequently open to every false suggestion and partial account. . . . If the power of example is so great, as to take possession of the memory by a kind of violence, and produce effects almost without the intervention of the will, care ought to be taken that, when the choice is unrestrained, the best examples only should be exhibited; and that which is likely to operate so strongly, should not be mischievous or uncertain in its effects.[15]

Johnson's wariness about the power of the imagination should remind us of Mary Shelley; for, as different as these two writers were, they shared a profound anxiety about the insatiable hunger of the imagination. Johnson's answer to this anxiety was to compose not novels but moral essays that were characterized by a tremendous respect for reason's antagonist. Mary Shelley's solution, as we have seen, was simultaneously less evasive and less effective.

In fact, her novels represent the two dangers to which imaginative engagement might lead. At one extreme, as the 1818 *Frankenstein* proves, a "romantic" novel might so thoroughly activate the imagination as to undermine all moral authority; at the other extreme, as in *Falkner,* the moral novel might so dogmatically focus the imagination that all subversive exuberance would be driven into the background of the fiction, only to return to the forefront in troubling reminders of what cannot be contained.

To a certain extent, Jane Austen shared this ambivalence with regard to the imagination. When Anne Elliot advises Captain Benwick in *Persuasion* to admit "a larger allowance of prose in his daily study" so as to "rouse and fortify" a mind made "tremulous" by immersion in Romantic poetry, she is warning against the "susceptibility" of the indulged imagination.[16] But while Austen might well agree with Johnson that novels should "serve as lectures of conduct, and introductions into life," her major works are not as defensive as either his *Rasselas* or Shelley's *Falkner;* they do not, that is, "initiate youth by mock encounters in the art of necessary defence."[17] Instead, Austen attempts to convert the pleasure generated by imaginative engagement into a didactic tool. As the "productions" that provide "more extensive and unaffected pleasure than those of any other literary corporation in the world," novels are best suited for such education. For in the best novels, Austen continues in *Northanger Abbey,* "the greatest powers of the mind are displayed, . . . the most thorough knowledge of human nature, the happiest delineation of its varieties, the liveliest effusions of wit and humour are conveyed to the world in the best chosen language."[18]

SENSE AND SENSIBILITY

The narrative impasse reached in Wollstonecraft's *Maria* and the Scylla and Charybdis of Shelley's aesthetic choices remind us that achieving such a balance was not easy. Jane Austen's first published novel, *Sense and Sensibility* (1811), suggests how persistent this problem proved to be for her early in her career.[19] *Sense and Sensibility* is a much darker novel than any of the juvenilia or the parodic *Northanger Abbey* (1818), and we might speculate that one origin of its somber tone and the eruptions of anarchic feeling that punctuate it lies in the anxiety with which Austen viewed individualism's challenge to paternalism. For in *Sense and Sensibility,* as, in a slightly different way, in *Lady Susan* and *Northanger Abbey,* the most fundamental conflict is between Austen's own imaginative engagement with her self-assertive characters and the moral code necessary to control their anarchic desires.

In the greater part of *Sense and Sensibility,* Austen's aesthetic strategies endorse the traditional values associated with her "sensible" heroine, Elinor Dashwood. One of these strategies consists in measuring all of the characters (including Elinor) against an implicit, but presumably authoritative, moral norm. As early as the second chapter, in that free, indirect discourse that is the hallmark of her mature style, Austen shadows the opinion of a single fallible character with this implicit moral standard.[20] Irony in *Sense and Sensibility* arises for the most part from the novel's action; the dialogue between Mr. and Mrs. John Dashwood points up as surely as any overt narrative commentary the parsimony behind their dwindling good will. But our response to this dialogue is initially shaped by such sentences as the following: "To take three thousand pounds from the fortune of their dear little boy, would be impoverishing him to the most dreadful degree"; "How could he answer it to himself to rob his child, and his only child too, of so large a sum?"[21] The hyperbole expressed in the words "impoverishing," "dreadful," and "rob" conveys both the strategy of Mrs. Dashwood's rhetoric and its absurdity, and the repeated use of the word "child" suggests how effective she is in manipulating John Dashwood's generosity. Because these sentences belong to the narrative and not to direct dialogue, they mimetically convey the tone of the conversation and simultaneously judge it by reference to an implicit system of more humane values—the undeniably Christian values that one should love one's neighbor as one's self and that the man who hoards treasures in this world (or the woman who encourages him to do so) will never get into the kingdom of heaven.

But despite this ground of Christian principles, nearly everything in the plot of *Sense and Sensibility* undermines the complacent assumption that they are principles generally held or practically effective. Almost every action in the novel suggests that, more often than not, individual will triumphs over principle and individual desire proves more compelling than moral law. Even the narrator, the apparent voice of these absolute values, reveals that moral principles are qualified in practice. The narrator's prefatory evaluation of John Dashwood, for example—"he was not an ill-disposed young man, unless to be rather cold hearted, and rather selfish, is to be ill-disposed" (p. 5)—directs our attention most specifically to the way in which what should, in theory, be moral absolutes can, and in practice do, shade off into infinite gradations and convenient exceptions. Is it always morally wrong to be "rather" selfish, especially in a society in which such selfishness is the necessary basis for material prosperity? What efficacy will moral absolutes have in such a society? How could Elinor's patient, principled fidelity win the passive, principled Edward if it were not, finally, for Lucy Steele's avarice?

A second strategy that is apparently designed to forestall such questions by aligning the reader's sympathies with Elinor's "sense" involves the juxtaposition of Elinor and her sister Marianne at nearly every critical juncture in the novel. Consistently, Elinor makes the prudent choice, even when doing so is painful; almost as consistently, Marianne's decisions are self-indulgent and harmful, either to herself or to someone else. But this neat design is less stable than an absolute and authoritative moral system would seem to require.

Many readers have found Marianne's "spirit" more appealing than Elinor's cautious, prim, and even repressive reserve, and they have found Marianne's passionate romance with Willoughby more attractive than the prolonged frustration to which Elinor submits. That such preferences may be in keeping with at least one countercurrent of the novel is suggested by the fact that whenever Austen herself explicitly compares the two putative heroes—Colonel Brandon and Edward Ferrars—with the less moral, more passionate Willoughby, it is Willoughby who is appealing. On two occasions when Willoughby is expected but one of the more subdued lovers appears instead, the disappointment is unmistakable; and when the reverse situation occurs, in the climactic final encounter between Elinor and Willoughby, Elinor is aroused to a pitch of complex emotion we never see Edward inspire in anyone. Moreover, Willoughby repeatedly bursts into the narrative with "manly beauty and more than common gracefulness," but Edward and Brandon seem inert fixtures of the plot, incapable of energetic gallantry and attractive only to the most generous observer. The initial description of each of them is dominated by negative constructions and qualifying phrases, and even Elinor cannot unreservedly praise the man she wants to marry. "At first sight," she admits, "his address is certainly not striking; and his person can hardly be called handsome, till the expression of his eyes, which are uncommonly good, and the general sweetness of his countenance, is perceived. At present, I know him so well, that I think him really handsome; or, at least, almost so" (p. 20). Colonel Brandon, "neither very young nor very gay," is "silent and grave" much of the time (p. 34), and his "oppression of spirits," like Edward's chronic depression, can scarcely compete with Willoughby's charm.

The most telling dramatization of the contest between the potentially anarchic power of feeling and the restraint that moral principles require takes the form of a conflict within Elinor herself. This scene, in the final volume, owes much to conventional eighteenth-century didactic novels, but Austen's placing it at a moment when the generally self-disciplined Elinor is unusually susceptible to emotion gives it a particularly complicated effect. Colonel Brandon has presented a living to Edward Ferrars, and Elinor is finally, but sadly, reconciled to the fact that her lover will marry someone else. In the midst of this personal disappointment, she is also particularly sensitive to her sister's condition, for Marianne, whose own romantic disappointment had sent her into a dangerous decline, has just been declared out of danger. Elinor's "fervent gratitude" for this news is especially great because of the joy and relief it will bring to her mother, whose arrival is expected at any moment. It is this hectic peace—as Marianne sleeps quietly upstairs and a violent storm assaults the house—that Willoughby invades when he melodramatically steps into the drawing room.

Elinor's first response is "horror" at his audacious intrusion; but before she can leave the room, Willoughby appeals to something even more powerful than Elinor's "honour": her curiosity. Elinor is momentarily captivated by

Willoughby's "serious energy" and "warmth," and she listens "in spite of her-self" to the story he unfolds—the chronicle of his passions, both honorable and base. At the end of his dramatic recital, Willoughby asks Elinor for pity, and, even though she feels it is her "duty" to check his outburst, she cannot repress her "compassionate emotion." It is this emotion that governs her judgment of Willoughby—a judgment that verges disconcertingly on ratio-nalization:

> Elinor made no answer. Her thoughts were silently fixed on the irreparable in-jury which too early an independence and its consequent habits of idleness, dis-sipation, and luxury, had made in the mind, the character, the happiness, of a man who, to every advantage of person and talents, united a disposition natu-rally open and honest, and a feeling, affectionate temper. The world had made him extravagant and vain—Extravagance and vanity had made him cold-hearted and selfish. [p. 331]

When Willoughby departs, he leaves Elinor in an even greater "agitation" of spirits, "too much oppressed by a croud of ideas . . . to think even of her sister."

> Willoughby, in spite of all his faults, excited a degree of commiseration for the sufferings produced by them, which made her think of him as now separated for ever from her family with a tenderness, a regret, rather in proportion, as she soon acknowledged within herself—to his wishes than to his merits. She felt that his influence over her mind was heightened by circumstances which ought not in reason to have weight; by that person of uncommon attraction, that open, affectionate, and lively manner which it was no merit to possess; and by that still ardent love for Marianne, which it was not even innocent to indulge. But she felt that it was so, long, long before she could feel his influence less. [p. 333]

One purpose of this episode is clearly to dramatize the odds against which Elinor's "sense," or reason, ultimately triumphs and therefore to in-crease, not undermine, our admiration for that faculty. But a second effect of the passage is to subject the reader to the same temptation that assails Elinor. Because the presentation is dramatic and because, for a moment at least, the character whose judgment has thus far directed our own hesitates in her moral evaluation, the reader is invited to judge Willoughby not by reference to an objective standard but by his immediate appeal to our imaginative, sympathetic engagement. As Elinor temporizes, the moral principle for which she otherwise speaks seems dangerously susceptible to circumstances, to the appeal of "lively manners," and to the special pleading of aroused female emotion.

Jane Austen seems anxious to control the moral anarchy that strong ap-peals to feeling can unleash; yet, significantly, she does not exclude passion from the novel, nor does she so completely qualify it as to undermine its power. Instead, Austen attempts to bend the imaginative engagement it elicits in the reader to the service of moral education. To do so, she restricts the reader's access to the romantic plot by conveying its details and its emotional affect only through indirect narration. At the beginning of the novel, for example, the incident in which Willoughby rescues Marianne is summarized by the dispassionate narrative persona, who supplies sentimental clichés but *not* Marianne's response to her rescue: "The gentleman offered his services, and perceiving that her modesty declined what her situation rendered necessary, took her up in his arms without farther delay" (p. 42). Similarly, the episode in which Willoughby cuts and kisses a lock of Marianne's hair is given to Margaret to relate (p. 60), and the emotional specifics of Willoughby's farewell at Barton Cottage can be deduced only from their aftermath (p. 82). Most of Marianne's outbursts of passion to Willoughby are confined to letters, which are concealed from the reader until after Willoughby has snubbed Marianne. In fact, the only emotionally charged encounter between the lovers that Austen presents dramatically is their final meeting at the London ball, and there Marianne's passion is transmuted by Willoughby's silence into the terrible muffled scream that both voices and symbolizes her thwarted love. So careful is Austen to keep the reader on the outside of such "dangerous" material that she embeds the most passionate episodes within other, less emotionally volatile stories. Thus the story of the two Elizas—related, as we will see, by a character whose relationship to the tale immediately activates our judgment—is contained within the story of Marianne's passion for Willoughby— a relationship whose emotional content is conveyed to the reader more by innuendo, summary, and indirection than by dramatic presentation. And this second story, in turn, is contained within the story of the relationship that opens and closes the novel—Elinor's considerably less demonstrative affection for Edward. By embedding these stories in this way, Austen seeks to defuse their imaginative affect and increase their power to educate the reader: from the fates of the two Elizas we learn to be wary of Marianne's quick feelings, and from the consequences of Marianne's self-indulgent passion we learn to value Elinor's reserve.

Instead of being allowed to identify with Marianne, then, for most of the novel we are restricted to Elinor's emotional struggles. This enables Austen to dramatize the complexities of what might otherwise seem an unattractive and unyielding obsession with propriety; it also permits her to filter the two stories of illicit passion through a character whose judgment generally masters emotion. That the passion bleeds from the narrators of these two tales into Elinor's "sense" attests to the power of this force and to the dangerous susceptibility that, without proper control, might undermine the judgment of even the most rational reader.

Austen also attempts to control the allure of Marianne's romantic desires by refusing to consider seriously either their social origin or their philosophical implications. As Tony Tanner has pointed out, Austen really avoids the systematic examination of "sensibility" that the novel seems to promise.[22] The novel begins like a novel of social realism. In the first paragraphs the narrator sounds like a lawyer or a banker; family alliances, the estate that is the heart of paternalistic society, even the deaths of loved ones, are all ruthlessly subordinated to the economic facts. Given this introduction, the reader has every reason to believe that the most important fact—that Mrs. Dashwood will have only five hundred pounds a year with which to raise and dower her daughters—will govern the futures of Elinor, Marianne, and Margaret. And given this probable development, the reader can understand why romantic fantasies are appealing. It is no wonder that Marianne—facing a life of poverty, the spiritual banality of relatives like the John Dashwoods, and the superficial urbanities of a neighborhood composed only of the Middletons and Mrs. Jennings—turns to Cowper for imaginative compensation; nor is it surprising that she fancies (in accordance with the promise of romantic novels) that her beauty will win the heart and hand of an errant knight. Beneath Marianne's effusions on nature and her passionate yearning for a hero lies the same "hunger of imagination" that Mary Wollstonecraft tried and failed to analyze in *Maria*. But to take Marianne's passions and longings seriously on their own terms would be to call into question the basis of Christian moral authority, the social order that ideally institutionalizes that authority, and, finally, the capacity of orthodox religion or society to gratify imaginative desires.[23] Elinor's sense, despite its admirable capacity to discipline and protect the self, cannot begin to satisfy this appetite, and no other social institution in the novel does any better. Instead of taking this implicit criticism to its logical conclusion, as Wollstonecraft tried to do, Jane Austen defuses its threat by directing our judgment away from bourgeois society and toward the self-indulgent individual. Austen caricatures just enough of Marianne's responses to nature and love to make her seem intermittently ridiculous, and when her desires finally explode all social conventions, Austen stifles her with an illness that is not only a result but also a purgation of her passion. At the end of the novel, Austen ushers Marianne into Brandon's world of diminished desires in such a way as to make Marianne herself negate everything she has previously wanted to have and to be.

> Marianne Dashwood was born to an extraordinary fate. She was born to discover the falsehood of her own opinions, and to counteract, by her conduct, her most favorite maxims. She was born to overcome an affection formed so late in life as at seventeen, and with no sentiment superior to strong esteem and lively friendship, voluntarily to give her hand to another! . . . Marianne could never love by halves; and her whole heart became, in time, as much devoted to her husband, as it had once been to Willoughby. [pp. 378–79]

To further defuse the questions raised by Marianne's assertive subjectivity, Austen seconds the opinion of eighteenth-century moralists that women's appetites are particularly dangerous and more akin to inexplicable natural forces than to socialized—hence socializable—responses. Except for Elinor, nearly all of the women in *Sense and Sensibility* are given to one kind of excess or another. Mrs. John Dashwood and her mother, Mrs. Ferrars, attempt to dominate the opinions, the professions, and even the emotions of the men who are closest to them; Willoughby's aunt, who is empowered by money and age, is even more tyrannical; and Sophia Grey, Willoughby's fiancée, enacts her passion and her will when she commands Willoughby to copy her cruel letter for Marianne. Austen implies that these women are exceptional only in the extent of their power, not in the force of their desires. The narrator describes a "fond mother," for example, as "the most rapacious of human beings" (p. 120)—a description borne out by the monomaniacal Lady Middleton—and she refers lightly to the "suffering" endured by every lady who has the "insatiable appetite of fifteen" (p. 33). Until her compassion is necessary to the plot, even Mrs. Jennings seems dominated by a single uncontrollable desire, the hunger to live vicariously through the romantic attachments of her young friends.

Austen's female characters certainly do not monopolize passion, nor are their little contrivances finally more destructive than Willoughby's deceit. But the implications of her characterizations of such women can be identified by contrasting them with her presentation of male characters. Austen consistently provides men's behavior with a realistic explanation by describing the social or psychological contexts that shaped it. Mr. Palmer's general contempt, Elinor concludes (without any narrative qualification), "was the desire of appearing superior to other people" (p. 112)—a desire that is an understandable compensation for Palmer's initial error: "his temper might perhaps be a little soured by finding, like many others of his sex, that through some unaccountable bias in favour of beauty, he was the husband of a very silly woman" (p. 112). Austen's comparable references to Mrs. Palmer's history are both cursory and curt: her mantelpiece, the narrator informs us, is adorned with "a landscape in colored silks of her performance, in proof of her having spent seven years at a great school in town to some effect" (p. 160). Austen also more extensively explains the differences between the Ferrars brothers than between the oldest Dashwood sisters; she makes no attempt to account for the temperamental contrast between Elinor and Marianne but carefully attributes the differences between Robert and Edward to their education. The only female character Austen appears to explain is Lucy Steele. Initially, Lucy's "deficiency of all mental improvement" seems to be the effect of her neglected education: "Lucy was naturally clever; her remarks were often just and amusing . . . but her powers had received no aid from education, she was ignorant and illiterate, and her deficiency of mental improvement could not be concealed from Miss Dashwood" (p. 127). Soon we discover, however, that this "explanation" is really only Elinor's generous and erroneous first impression. Austen explicitly ridicules the notion that Lucy's "want of liberality"

could be "due to her want of education" by having Edward cling to this ratio-
nalization to the end. But in jilting Edward for his brother Robert, Lucy conclusively proves herself inherently flawed. Like Shelley's 1831 characterization of Frankenstein, and like both portrayals of the monster, female nature
appears to be fated, fixed. Austen's final comments on Lucy are decisive: her
behavior exposes "a wanton ill-nature" (p. 366), characterized by "an earnest,
an unceasing attention to self-interest" (p. 376).

The harshness with which Austen disposes of Lucy Steele exceeds the ne-
cessities of the plot but it is perfectly in keeping with her moral design. For,
like Shelley, Austen wants to convince the reader that female nature is simply
inexplicable and that propriety must restrain this natural, amoral force. At
least one other set of female characters also supports this argument, but,
paradoxically, the episode in which they appear alludes not to an innate female nature but to the constraints imposed on women by patriarchal society.
Because of this, the episode threatens to subvert the argument for propriety it
theoretically should support. The characters are the two Elizas, and their
story belongs to Colonel Brandon.

Colonel Brandon relates the story of the two Elizas to Elinor ostensibly
to persuade her to warn Marianne about Willoughby. But both the hesita-
tions with which he interrupts his narrative and the fact that he focuses not
on the second Eliza (Willoughby's victim) but on her mother ("his" Eliza)
suggest that Brandon does not fully recognize his own motives for telling the
story. As the tale unfolds, it becomes clear that Brandon's deepest intention is
to warn Marianne about the dangerous nature of her own passion; paradoxically, however, the overall effect of the episode is to reveal to the reader the
depth—and consequences—of *Brandon's* sexual anxiety.[24] This anxiety, initially aroused by the first Eliza, is now being reactivated by Marianne. But
there is one critical difference between the two situations: unlike the first
Eliza, Marianne's passion is not for Brandon but for Willoughby. Thus Brandon's anxiety is doubly displaced: it is a past fear of too much emotion *and* a
present fear of too little love. The first Eliza *did* love him, Brandon asserts, as
if to enhance his own appeal, but she could not withstand her guardian's
pressure to marry Brandon's older brother, heir to the family's encumbered
estate. As he tells the story, Brandon stumbles over the details that wounded
him most:

> "My brother did not deserve her; he did not even love her. I had hoped that her
> regard for me would support her under any difficulty, and for some time it did;
> but at last the misery of her situation, for she experienced great unkindness,
> overcame all her resolution, and though she had promised me that nothing—
> —but how blindly I relate! I have never told you how this was brought on. We
> were within a few hours of eloping together for Scotland. The treachery, or the
> folly, of my cousin's maid betrayed us. I was banished and she was allowed no
> liberty, no society, no amusement, till my father's point was gained. I had de-

pended on her fortitude too far, . . . —but had her marriage been happy, . . . a few months must have reconciled me to it. . . . This however was not the case. My brother had no regard for her. . . . The consequence of this, upon a mind so young, so lively, so inexperienced as Mrs. Brandon's, was but too natural. . . . Can we wonder that with such a husband to provoke inconstancy, and without a friend to advise or restrain her . . . she should fall? Had I remained in England, perhaps—but I meant to promote the happiness of both by removing from her for years. . . . The shock which her marriage had given me," he continued, in a voice of great agitation, "was of trifling weight—was nothing—to what I felt when I heard, about two years afterwards, of her divorce. It was *that* which drew this gloom, even now the recollection of what I suffered—". . . . [pp. 205–06; ellipses added]

The story begins and ends in Eliza's infidelity to Brandon; only as an extension of this does her infidelity to her husband matter, only as the origin of his pain does Eliza's unhappiness figure. The weakness of this woman—and her sexual abandon—are "natural," according to Brandon; only the presence of a male guardian could have protected her from herself. Once Eliza has fallen, her fate is so predictable (and disturbing) that it warrants only summary description—except in regard to Brandon's own misery:

So altered—so faded—worn down by acute suffering of every kind! hardly could I believe the melancholy and sickly figure before me, to be the remains of the lovely, blooming, healthful girl, on whom I had once doated. What I endured in so beholding her—but I have no right to wound your feelings by attempting to describe it—I have pained you too much already. [p. 207]

Given the fate of the mother, Brandon is not surprised at the fall of the second Eliza, the daughter, who has been bequeathed to his protection. At seventeen, her mother's fatal year and Marianne's current age, she too evaded her male guardian and ran away with Willoughby. Now pregnant, abandoned, poor, and miserable, this Eliza is a second monument to the passionate excesses of women.

The intense anxiety that Brandon betrays here is produced by his fear of female sexual appetite. If female sexuality had caused the first Eliza to betray him, how vulnerable might the excitable Marianne be to Willoughby, who had seduced the second Eliza? Yet Brandon expressly admires Marianne for the very passion that occasioned the downfall of the two Elizas. Brandon wants Marianne to be emotionally responsive, but he wants her sexuality to answer only to his command. When Elinor wishes that Marianne would renounce sentimental prejudices, Brandon's response is swift: "No, no, do not desire it,—for when the romantic refinements of a young mind are obliged to give way, how frequently are they succeeded by such opinions as are but too common, and too dangerous! I speak from experience" (pp. 56–57). The allusion is clearly to the first Eliza; Brandon fears that beneath the "romantic refinements" of the girl lurks a woman's sexual appetite, which is both "common" and "dangerous." Better far to keep women innocent, to protect them from themselves—and to protect men from their "natural" volatility.

The anxieties Brandon unwittingly reveals suggest that Austen at least intuits the twin imperatives that anchor patriarchal society: men want women to be passionate, but, because they fear the consequences of this appetite, they want to retain control over its expression. This anxiety explains why women in this society must experience so problematic a relation to their own desire. In order to win the husband necessary to their social position, women must gratify both of men's desires by concealing whatever genuine emotions they feel so as to allow men to believe that *they* have all the power. Women must use indirection, in other words, the allure of "romantic refinements," and the subterfuges of manners and modesty in order to arouse male desires and assuage male anxieties.

The implications of this passage are very close to those Mary Wollstonecraft specifically addresses in both *The Rights of Woman* and *Maria*. But in *Sense and Sensibility* Jane Austen will no more pursue the criticism of patriarchy that is inherent in this insight than she will pursue the grim reality that is implicit in the narrator's account of the Dashwoods' economic situation. Despite its gestures toward realism, *Sense and Sensibility* repeatedly dismisses the analysis of society that realism might imply and instead embraces the idealism of romance. But Austen's idealism never completely banishes her realistic impulse either. Instead, Austen retains both "principles" and romance. Thus Marianne debunks her own youthful romance, and the novel as a whole endorses the "heroism" (the word itself appears on pp. 242 and 265) of Elinor's self-denial. Nevertheless, Austen rewards both characters at the conclusion of the novel precisely in terms of romantic love and of lives lived happily ever after.

Some of the tensions that we finally feel in *Sense and Sensibility* emerge, then, from the conflict between the realism in which the action is anchored and the romantic element that Austen harnesses to this realism. Throughout, she attempts to use realism to control the imaginative excesses that romances both encourage and depict: not only does the point of view repress the romantic plot, but Austen also suggests that Elinor's self-denial—her refusal to reveal Lucy Steele's secret and her willingness to help Edward even to her own disadvantage—ultimately contribute to her own happiness as well as to the happiness of others. The prerogatives of society, Austen suggests, sometimes make secrecy and repression necessary; but if one submits to society, every dream will come true. The last part of this formulation reminds us, of course, that, just as Austen uses realism to control the irresponsible and morally anarchic imagination, she also enlists the power of the reader's wishes to buttress her moral design. Theoretically, if her readers will submit to a version of the frustration Elinor suffers or even the compromise to which Marianne grows accustomed, their wish for a happy ending will be legitimized and gratified. This fusion of realism and romance in the service of aesthetic closure decisively distinguishes between Wollstonecraft's *Maria* and Austen's early novels. For notwithstanding her imaginative engagement in "romantic expectations," Wollstonecraft's persistent goal is to criticize the social institutions that seem to her to thwart female feeling. Jane Austen, on the other hand, despite her recognition of the limitations of social institutions, is more concerned with correcting the dangerous excesses of female feeling than with liberating this anarchic energy. Her turn to aesthetic closure enables her to dismiss many of the problems her own divided sympathies have introduced. That the need for such closure grows out of society's inability to grant happiness to everyone in the terms it promises is a problem that can remain unexamined because it is, ideally, irrelevant to this fiction. The most troubling aspect of *Sense and Sensibility* is Austen's inability to establish narrative authority because she is ambivalent toward both realism and romance. Her inability to establish moral authority is clearly related to this ambivalence. But its complexities and implications are more clearly apparent in her next novel, *Pride and Prejudice*.

PRIDE AND PREJUDICE

In *Pride and Prejudice* (1813) the challenge that feeling and imaginative energy offer to moral authority is particularly persistent and problematic, for it is posed by the heroine herself. As the outspoken champion of the prerogatives of individual desire, Elizabeth Bennet should jeopardize both the social order, which demands self-denial, and the moral order, which is based on absolute Christian principles. Yet, despite the dangers she seems to embody, Elizabeth Bennet was Jane Austen's special favorite. "I think her as delightful a creature as ever appeared in print," she wrote to Cassandra (*JAL*, 2:297; 29 January 1813). And, as a favorite, Elizabeth is handsomely rewarded: she marries the richest man in all of Jane Austen's novels and is established as mistress of Pemberley, one of those great country estates that superintend and stabilize patriarchal society. In fact, Elizabeth's triumph signals the achievement of the balance that characterizes Austen's mature novels, for it is the result, on the one hand, of the gradual transformation of social and psychological realism into romance and, on the other, of a redefinition of romance. Essentially, Austen legitimizes romance by making it seem the corrective— not the origin or the product—of individualism. By such narrative magic, Austen is able to defuse the thematic conflict between sense and sensibility— or reason and feeling, or realism and romance—that troubled her earlier works. What is more, by forcing her reader to participate in creating the moral order that governs the novel's conclusion, Austen is able to make this aesthetic "solution" seem, at least momentarily, both natural and right.

Pride and Prejudice depicts a world driven by ethical relativity, a fact that both mocks any pretense to absolute moral standards and enhances the quality of everyday life in a small country village. "The country," Darcy remarks, "can in general supply but few subjects for such a study. In a country neighbourhood you move in a very confined and unvarying society." "But people themselves alter so much," pert Elizabeth responds, "that there is something new to be observed in them for ever."[25] This principle of infinite variety within apparent unity extends from the object of study to the observer, of course; the fact that Elizabeth can praise Bingley for his compliance when he offers to remain at Netherfield and call that same trait weakness when he stays away (pp. 50, 135) tells us more about Elizabeth's desires than the principle of tractability. And the fact that Elizabeth can excuse Wickham for preferring a practical marriage when she will forever blame Charlotte for making the same choice reveals more about Elizabeth's personal investment in these two situations than Jane Austen's views on matrimony or money. Judgment is always inflected—modulated—by personal desire, Austen suggests, just as vision is always governed by perspective. "Principles" are often merely prejudice, and prejudices simply project one's own interests onto the shifting scene outside so as to defend and reinforce the self.

Ideally, in such a world, conventions of propriety and morality make living together possible by compensating for the competing desires of individuals and by stabilizing standards of judgment and value. But in *Pride and Prejudice,* as in Austen's other novels and, presumably, in her society as well, social conventions no longer necessarily serve this end; instead, as Wollstonecraft complained, social institutions have ossified until they threaten to crush the desire from which they theoretically grew and which they ought to accommodate. Beside the arrogant Miss Bingley, parading around the drawing room in hopes of catching Darcy's eye, or Mr. Collins, pompous embodiment of unyielding propriety itself, Elizabeth's impulsiveness, outspokenness, and generosity seem admirable and necessary correctives. When she bursts into Netherfield to see her sick sister, for example, the mud on her skirts becomes completely irrelevant beside the healthiness of her unself-conscious concern for Jane. That Miss Bingley despises Elizabeth for what she calls "conceited independence" simply enhances our sympathy for conceit and independence, if these are the traits Elizabeth embodies. And when Elizabeth refuses to be subdued by Lady Catherine, whether on the subject of her music or her marriage, we feel nothing but admiration for her "impertinence"—if this is what her energy really is.

Yet the juxtaposition of Elizabeth's lively wit with this pretentious and repressive society cuts both ways; for if the vacuity of her surroundings highlights her energy, it also encourages her to cultivate her natural vivacity beyond its legitimate bounds. As the novel unfolds, we begin to recognize that Elizabeth's charming wit is another incarnation of willful desire, which, by rendering judgment unstable, contributes to moral relativity. As Elizabeth embellishes her surroundings with imaginative flourishes, we begin to see that indulging the imagination can harm others and that it in fact serves as a defense against emotional involvement. Through this juxtaposition, then, Austen is able to enlist the reader's initial imaginative engagement with Elizabeth in the service of moral education—an education for the reader, which shadows (but does not correspond precisely to) Elizabeth's own education, and which schools the imagination by means of its own irrepressible energy.

One of the first indications that Elizabeth's quick wit and powerful feelings may be unreliable moral guides emerges in her initial conversation with George Wickham. Until this moment, Elizabeth's companions and the settings in which she had appeared have enhanced her charm and appeal. But as soon as Elizabeth enters into her intimate conversation with Wickham, Austen encourages us to recognize that something is wrong. The problem here is not that a responsive young woman is attracted to a handsome young militia man; instead, the problem is that Elizabeth is unconsciously using Wickham to reinforce her prejudice against Darcy and is, as a consequence, allowing herself to be used by Wickham to reinforce his own false position. There are no disinterested or straightforward emotions in this scene; what appears to be Elizabeth's simple response to Wickham's physical and emotional charm is actually being fed by the subterranean force of her anger at Darcy. Elizabeth is flattered by Wickham's particular attention to her, but she is equally aroused by the fact that his story justifies her anger at Darcy. As a consequence of this double flattery, Elizabeth is blinded to the impropriety of this stranger's intimacy, she is seduced into judging on the grounds of Wickham's "countenance" rather than some less arbitrary principle, and she is encouraged to credit her feelings instead of testing her perceptions against reality.

The action of *Pride and Prejudice* generally reveals that, despite what looks like a generous overflow of irrepressible energy, Elizabeth's "liveliness" is primarily defensive.[26] More specifically, her "impertinence" is a psychological defense against the vulnerability to which her situation as a dependent woman exposes her. Elizabeth's prejudice against Darcy is so quickly formed and so persistent because, at the first assembly, he unthinkingly confronts her with the very facts that it is most in her interest to deny. "She is tolerable," Darcy concedes, rejecting Bingley's overtures on Elizabeth's behalf, "but not handsome enough to tempt *me;* and I am in no humour at present to give consequence to young ladies who are slighted by other men" (p. 12).

Despite the fact that Elizabeth's "playful disposition" enables her to turn this "ridiculous" remark against Darcy, his cool observation continues to vex and haunt her for much of the novel and to govern not only her anger toward Darcy but also her "mortification" at the antics of her family. It has this effect for two closely related reasons. First of all, in spite of her professed unconcern, Elizabeth, like everyone else, is immediately attracted to this handsome, eminently eligible bachelor, and, if only for a short time, he engages her natural romantic fantasies. We discover this later, when Darcy offers to make her dream come true and Elizabeth retorts by acknowledging that, though she once considered him as a possible husband, she no longer does so: "I had not known you a month," she exults, inadvertently acknowledging the longevity of her fantasy, "before I felt that you were the last man in the world whom I could ever be prevailed on to marry" (p. 193). But, given Elizabeth's social position and economic situation, even to dream of marrying Darcy is an act of imaginative presumption. The second reason for her lingering pain, then, is that Darcy's rejection deflates not only her romantic fantasies of marriage to a handsome aristocrat but, more important, the image of herself upon which such fantasies are based.

Darcy's casual remark suggests that the fact that Elizabeth is momentarily without a partner indicates that she will always be so "slighted," that her "tolerable" beauty will never attract the permanent partner she desires. And this remark strikes very close to home. For the inevitable result of an entail in a household more blessed with daughters than frugality is, at best, a limited choice of suitors; at worst, the Bennets' shortage of money for dowries and their equivocal social position foretell spinsterhood, dependence on a generous relative, or, most ominous of all, work as a governess or lady's companion. Austen never lets the reader or Elizabeth forget how very likely such a future is. Darcy lays the groundwork for this scenario when, alluding to their uncles in trade and law, he remarks that such connections "must very materially lessen [the sisters'] chance of marrying men of any consideration in the world" (p. 37). Even closer to home, when Charlotte Lucas rejects romance, she does so for its opposite, the matter-of-fact assessment that a "comfortable home" is more substantial than romantic fantasies. Elizabeth's mother is even more brutally frank. "If you take it into your head," she warns Elizabeth, "to go on refusing every offer of marriage in this way, you will never get a husband at all—and I am sure I do not know who is to maintain you when your father is dead" (p. 113). In the context of such dark realism, even Mr. Collins's compensatory retaliation sounds ominously like a self-evident truth. "Your portion is unhappily so small," he smugly informs Elizabeth, "that it will in all likelihood undo the effects of your loveliness and amiable qualifications" (p. 108).

Elizabeth chooses to ignore all of these warnings, of course, because, with the arrogance born of youth, natural high spirits, and intellectual superiority, she believes herself too good for such a fate. But Darcy challenges her self-confidence, and, in the disappointment he indirectly inflicts on Jane, he proves himself capable of bringing the Bennet family face to face with undeniable reality. In the face of real dependence and practical powerlessness, Elizabeth grasps at any possible source of power or distinction. As she confides to Jane in a moment of telling self-awareness, wit and prejudice have been her two sources of power, two means of distinguishing herself:

I meant to be uncommonly clever in taking so decided a dislike to him, without any reason. It is such a spur to one's genius, such an opening for wit to have a dislike of that kind. One may be continually abusive without saying any thing just; but one cannot be always laughing at a man without now and then stumbling on something witty. [pp. 225–26]

From this statement, Elizabeth's psychological economy is clear: she directs her intelligence toward defending herself against emotional vulnerability; she bases her moral judgments at least partially on her defensiveness; and she rationalizes both the romantic fantasies with which she consoles herself and the forays of wit with which she protects herself as spontaneous effusions of a lively and superior mind.

Such criticism of Elizabeth's "liveliness" is elaborated by Austen's characterizations of both Mr. Bennet and Lydia. Elizabeth is her father's favorite daughter, and Mr. Bennet's witty intelligence clearly reinforces and feeds off Elizabeth's superiority. But Mr. Bennet is finally a failure, for he is lax when it comes to the social duties that are most important to the Bennet family as a whole and to Elizabeth in particular. Like Elizabeth's society in general, Mr. Bennet's character is a moral vacuum; his "indolence and the little attention he has [given] to what was going forward in his family" (p. 283) finally permit, if they do not encourage, Lydia's rebellion. Mr. Bennet tries to make light of his moral irresponsibility by describing social relations as an amusing game. "For what do we live," he asks rhetorically, "but to make sport for our neighbours, and laugh at them in our turn?" (p. 364). But the pain that unthinking Lydia visits on the rest of the family proves conclusively how serious—and how selfish—his evasion really is.

Just as her father's defensive intelligence refracts and exaggerates Elizabeth's intellectual "liveliness," so Lydia's wild, noisy laughter helps clarify Elizabeth's "impertinence." But perhaps the most important function of Lydia's story derives from its placement. For Austen positions the announcement of Lydia's elopement so as to precipitate the second, and most important, stage of Elizabeth's education. Through Darcy's letters, Elizabeth has already learned that she was wrong about both Wickham and Darcy, but Darcy's proposal and her angry rejection have, if anything, increased, not lessened, her pride and sense of superiority. "Vanity, not love, has been my folly," Elizabeth exclaims at the moment of this first "humiliation" (p. 208); but, on second thought, she is deeply flattered by the great man's attentions, and, since she does not regret her decision, she is free to bask in the triumph his proposal gives her over his "pride," over his "prejudices," and over Lady Catherine and Miss Bingley as well. Thus, even though she feels that her own "past behaviour" constitutes "a constant source of vexation and regret" (p. 212), Elizabeth visits Pemberley with her vanity very much intact: "at that moment she felt, that to be mistress of Pemberley might be something!"

(p. 245). This dream of what she might have been is jolted into the present and then into the future when Darcy suddenly appears, proves courteous to the very relatives he had previously slighted, and then invites Elizabeth back to Pemberley to meet his sister. At this moment, Elizabeth realizes that her "power" is even greater than she had dared imagine it to be.

> She respected, she esteemed, she was grateful to him, she felt a real interest in his welfare; and she only wanted to know how far she wished that welfare to depend upon herself, and how far it would be for the happiness of both that she should employ the power, which her fancy told her she still possessed, of bringing on the renewal of his addresses. [p. 266]

While this reflection is neither cool nor calculating, it does suggest that Elizabeth feels herself more superior than ever—not so much to Darcy as to love.

Jane's letter arrives when Elizabeth is basking in this self-confidence; its effect is to strip her of self-control, self-assurance, and her confident superiority over feeling. In Darcy's presence she bursts into tears and then, suddenly recognizing what she now believes she has lost, she realizes that true power belongs not to the imagination but to love: "Her power was sinking; every thing *must* sink under such a proof of family weakness. . . . The belief of his self-conquest . . . afforded no palliation of her distress. It was, on the contrary, exactly calculated to make her understand her own wishes; and never had she so honestly felt that she could have loved him, as now, when all love must be vain" (p. 278).

Elizabeth's fantasies no longer seem as wild or romantic as they once did, but, before her wish can be fulfilled, she must be "humbled" by her own sister—not only so that she (and the reader) will recognize the pernicious effects of Lydia's passionate self-indulgence, but so that Elizabeth herself will understand how intimately her own fate is bound up in the actions and characters of others. Individualism is not simply morally suspect, Austen suggests; it is also based on a naïve overestimation of personal autonomy and power. To pretend that one can transcend social categories or refuse a social role (as Mr. Bennet does) is not only irresponsible; it also reveals a radical misunderstanding of the fact that, for an individual living in society, every action is automatically linked to the actions of others. And to believe that one can exercise free will, even when parents do not intercede, is to mistake the complex nature of desire and the way in which social situation affects psychology and self-knowledge.

Yet, despite its sobering implications, the "mortification" of Elizabeth's vanity does not constitute a rebuke to the premises or promises of romance, as Marianne's illness does in *Sense and Sensibility*. Instead, in order to convert the power of romance into a legitimate corrective for harsh realism, Austen redeems romance by purging it of all traces of egotism. As we have already seen, to believe that one's beauty and wit will captivate a powerful lord is really a form of vanity. But Elizabeth's actual romantic fantasies about Darcy are short-lived; the only dashing young man she fantasizes extensively about is Wickham. Elizabeth's response to her aunt's query about Wickham may be only half serious, but her confusion does reveal the extent of her susceptibility.

> At present I am not in love with Mr. Wickham; no, I certainly am not. But he is, beyond all comparison, the most agreeable man I ever saw—and if he becomes really attached to me—I believe it will be better that he should not. I see the imprudence of it.—Oh! *that* abominable Mr. Darcy!—My father's opinion of me does me the greatest honor, and I should be miserable to forfeit it. My father, however, is partial to Mr. Wickham. In short, my dear aunt, I should be very sorry to be the means of making any of you unhappy; but since we see every day that where there is affection, young people are seldom withheld by immediate want of fortune from entering into engagements with each other, how can I promise to be wiser than so many of my fellow creatures if I am tempted, or how am I even to know that it would be wisdom to resist? All that I can promise you, therefore, is to not be in a hurry. I will not be in a hurry to believe myself his first object. When I am in company with him, I will not be wishing. In short, I will do my best. [pp. 144–45]

Just as Elizabeth's prejudice against Darcy originally fed her admiration for Wickham, now her attraction to the young soldier focuses her resentment against Darcy: if Wickham's story is true, after all, Darcy has been directly (although inadvertently) responsible for preventing a marriage between Elizabeth and Wickham. But Austen does not allow this or any other romance to develop or capture Elizabeth's imagination; indeed, when she dismisses this particular suitor, she does not ridicule either the claims or the attractions of romance. Instead, when Wickham declares for the wealthy Miss King, Elizabeth remains undisturbed, and the entire issue of romantic love is simply pushed to the periphery of the narrative. Wickham's decision to marry for money does, after all, leave Elizabeth's vanity intact. "His apparent partiality had subsided, his attentions were over, he was the admirer of some one else. Elizabeth was watchful enough to see it all, but she could see it and write of it without material pain. Her heart had been but slightly touched, and her vanity was satisfied with believing that *she* would have been his only choice, had fortune permitted it" (p. 149).

Elizabeth's eventual love for Darcy is legitimate because it springs not from the vanity we ordinarily associate with romantic expectations but precisely from the mortification of pride. Yet because Elizabeth only belatedly realizes that she loves Darcy, her humbling does not entail a rejection of romantic love. Indeed, unaccountable, uncontrollable romantic love continues to play a role in *Pride and Prejudice*—in *Darcy's* desire for Elizabeth. This passion, which Austen notes but does not dwell on, is the subtextual force behind much of the action. In response to love, Darcy overcomes his prejudices against Elizabeth's connections, proposes to her, returns to her even after hope seems gone, and eventually brings about the marriages of three of the Bennet daughters. The narrative does not focus on the development or pressures of this passion; even when Elizabeth playfully asks Darcy for an account of his love, her mocking celebration of "impertinence" deflects any explanation he might have given. Romantic love remains the unexamined and unaccountable source of power in a novel preoccupied with various forms of social and psychological power and powerlessness. It not only overcomes all obstacles; it brings about a perfect society at the end of the novel.

The romantic conclusion of *Pride and Prejudice* effectively dismisses the social and psychological realism with which the novel began. Elizabeth's "impertinence" may have originated in her need to dispel the vulnerability of her dependent situation, but when marriage with Darcy cancels all the gloomy forecasts about Elizabeth's future, Austen no longer suggests a possible relationship between social causes and psychological effects. Elizabeth's "liveliness" persists, of course, but it is purified of its defensiveness and its egotism. In essence, in awarding Elizabeth this handsome husband with ten thousand pounds a year, Austen is gratifying the reader's fantasy that such outspoken liveliness *will* be successful in material terms, but she earns the right to do so precisely because Elizabeth's first fantasy of personal power is *not* rewarded. *Pride and Prejudice,* in other words, legitimizes the reader's romantic wishes by humbling the heroine's vanity. At the level of the plot, power is taken from egotism and given to love; at the level of the reading experience, power seems miraculously both to emanate from and to reward individualistic desire.

Darcy and Elizabeth, then, learn complementary lessons: he recognizes that individual feelings outweigh conventional social distinctions; she realizes the nature of society's power. Their marriage purports to unite individual gratification with social responsibility, to overcome the class distinctions that elevated Lady Catherine over the worthy Gardiners, and to make of society one big happy family. The last pages of *Pride and Prejudice* describe family connections radiating throughout society, closing the gap between geographical locations, social classes, and temperamental differences. The union that concludes this novel reestablishes the ideal, paternalistic society that Mr. Bennet's irresponsibility and Wickham's insubordination once seemed to threaten. With Darcy at its head and Elizabeth at its heart, society will apparently be able to contain the anarchic impulses of individualism and humanize the rigidities of prejudice, and everyone—even Miss Bingley—will live more or less happily in the environs of Pemberley, the vast estate whose permanence, prominence, and unique and uniquely satisfying fusion of individual taste and utility, of nature and art, symbolize Jane Austen's ideal.[27]

Austen is able to effect an aesthetic resolution of what is essentially a moral dilemma partly because the realistic elements in her portrayal of the situation are so carefully contained. As in *Sense and Sensibility,* Austen simply does not explore to the full the social or psychological implications of her realism. Darcy, Charlotte Lucas, Mr. Collins, and Mrs. Bennet all warn Elizabeth that her impertinence will probably result in spinsterhood, but Austen does not imperil the integrity of the romantic ending by dramatizing the perils of such a future in a character like Jane Fairfax, Miss Bates, or Mrs. Smith. But even beyond curtailing the extent of her realism Austen controls the response of her readers by drawing them into a system of values that seems, by the end of the novel, both "natural" and right. She can generate this system of common values because one of the fundamental principles of her art is to assume that the relationship between an author and an audience is ideally (if not automatically) a version of the relationship she knew best: the family.

The model of the family governs Jane Austen's art in at least three important ways. To begin with, her own personal family served as her first and most appreciative audience. Like the Brontës after her, Jane Austen wrote her first stories for the amusement of her family; most of her surviving juvenilia are dedicated to her siblings or cousins, and it is easy to imagine these stories and plays being read in the family circle, with various members contributing jokes from time to time. Austen's first longer works—*First Impressions* (later *Pride and Prejudice*) and *Elinor and Marianne* (later *Sense and Sensibility*)—were also apparently family entertainments, and, even after she became a published author, she continued to solicit and value the responses of her family as she composed and revised her novels.[28] For Austen, the entire enterprise of writing was associated with hospitality and familial bonds. Her letters reveal that she sometimes half-jokingly talked of her novels as her "children" and of her characters as if they were family friends. She assured her sister, for instance, that she could "no more forget" *Sense and Sensibility* "than a mother can forget her sucking child" (*JAL*, 2:272; 25 April 1811); she referred to *Pride and Prejudice* as her "own child" (*JAL*, 2:297; 29 January 1813); and she pretended to find a portrait of Jane Bingley exhibited in Spring Gardens: "There never was a greater likeness," Austen playfully announced; "She is dressed in a white gown, with green ornaments, which convinces me of what I had always supposed, that green was a favourite colour with her" (*JAL*, 2:310; 24 May 1813).[29]

The fact that Austen's completed novels and the activity of writing itself were part of the fabric of her family relationships helps to explain why she was able to avoid both the aggressive polemicism that Mary Wollstonecraft employed and the enfeebling defensiveness to which Mary Shelley resorted. Austen actively wondered what her readers thought of her novels, and she regretted that her works did not receive adequate critical attention, but she never seems to have imagined an audience openly hostile to either her novels or herself, as both Wollstonecraft and Shelley did, for different reasons. But in addition to providing a hospitable transitional area between her private imagination and the public bookstall, Jane Austen's experience of a close and supportive family also provided models both for the way an individual's desires could be accommodated by social institutions and for the context of shared values that an author could ideally rely on to provide a moral basis for art.

The notion of the family that served Jane Austen as a model for the proper coexistence of the individual society was essentially patriarchal, supportive of, and supported by, the allegiances and hierarchy that feminine propriety implied. Its smallest unit—the marriage—embodied for Austen the ideal union of individual desire and social responsibility; if a woman could legitimately express herself *only* by choosing to marry and then by sustaining her marriage, Austen suggests, she *could,* through her marriage, not only satisfy her own needs but also influence society. For the most part, the culminating marriages in Austen's novels lack the undercurrents of ambivalence that characterize Shelley's depictions of even happy marriages. This is true in part because the energies of Austen's heroines are not so rigorously channeled by propriety into self-denial either before or after marriage. As *Sense and Sensibility* suggests, however, Austen does discipline female energies, but, increasingly, she also suggests that the psychological toll exacted by patriarchal society from women is too high. The fact that almost all of the peripheral marriages in her novels are dissatisfying in one way or another seems to indicate that Austen recognized both the social liabilities that Wollstonecraft identified and the psychological complexities that Shelley intuited. Nevertheless, and especially in *Pride and Prejudice,* the most idealistic of all of her novels, marriage remains for Austen the ideal paradigm of the most perfect fusion between the individual and society.

As the actual basis and ideal model of the contract between an author and an audience, the family also promised a context of shared experiences, assumptions, and values against which the writer could play and to which he or she could eventually return. And it is in this sense—and for this reason—that the moral relativism theoretically unleashed by individualism does not necessarily undermine Austen's conservative moral pattern or her didactic purpose. For if an author can assume a set of basic assumptions and values, such as family members share, then he or she can depend on the reader's returning with the narrator to that common ground, in spite of liberties to stray that have been permitted in the course of the fiction. In fact, given the common ground, these liberties often contribute to the didactic design of the novel, for they foster the illusion that challenges to ethical and aesthetic authority are actually being engaged and defeated in their own terms.

In *Pride and Prejudice* Austen tries to ensure that her readers will share a common ground by making them participate in constructing the value system that governs the novel. This participation is a necessary part of reading *Pride and Prejudice* because Austen combines a predominantly dramatic presentation of the action with an irony so persistent that it almost destroys narrative authority.[30] Even what looks like omniscient commentary often turns out, on closer inspection, to carry the accents of a single character. The famous first sentence of the novel, for example—"It is a truth universally acknowledged, that a single man in possession of a good fortune, must be in want of a wife"—points to the radical limitations of both "truth" and "universally." Masquerading as a statement of fact—if not about all unmarried men, then certainly about a community that collectively assumes it to be true—this sentence actually tells us more about Mrs. Bennet than anyone else. In such local instances, irony allows us a certain freedom of interpretation even when it teases us to test our "first impressions" against our developing understanding of individual characters and the priorities of the novel as a whole.

As Wayne Booth has noted, irony forces the reader not only to participate in interpretation and evaluation but to choose one *system* of values over another.[31] And it is through the value system developed in the overall action of the novel that Austen hopes to counter the relativism that the localized ironies might permit.[32] We can see this principle at work in Charlotte Lucas's argument about marriage. The narrator, conveying Charlotte's thoughts indirectly, takes no explicit stand on her position: "Without thinking highly either of men or of matrimony, marriage had always been her object; it was the only honourable provision for well-educated young women of small fortune, and however uncertain of giving happiness, must be their pleasantest preservative from want" (pp. 122–23). Certainly this statement illuminates the limitations of Charlotte's romantic expectations, but is it meant to be an authoritative assessment of reality? Or is Elizabeth's indignant rejoinder more authoritative? "You must feel, as well as I do," she exclaims to Jane, "that the woman who marries him, cannot have a proper way of thinking" (p. 135). Elsewhere Elizabeth's "proper way of thinking" has proved self-interested. Is this case any different? And how are we, finally, to decide?

In such passages, Austen is both permitting momentary freedom of choice and demonstrating the vertigo that accompanies it. But through the unfolding action of the novel she seems to qualify this freedom by endorsing one option over the other: Mr. Bingley and Mr. Darcy *do* both want and need wives; the love matches Elizabeth believed in *do* come about, despite all the odds against them. And, most important, the paternal order established at the end of the novel both embodies an authoritative system of values and abolishes the apparent discrepancy between individual desire and social responsibility. Jane Austen's irony, then, enables her to reproduce—without exposing in any systematic way—some of the contradictions inherent in bourgeois ideology; for by simultaneously dramatizing and rewarding individual desire *and* establishing a critical distance from individualism, she endorses both the individualistic perspective inherent in the bourgeois value system *and* the authoritarian hierarchy retained from traditional, paternalistic society. Moreover, by allowing her reader to exercise freedom of judgment in individual instances while controlling the final value system through the action as a whole, Austen replicates, at the level of the reading experience, the marriage of romantic desire and realistic necessity that she believed was capable of containing individualism's challenge to traditional authority.

In *Pride and Prejudice* this strategy effectively focuses what had remained two distinct narrative parts in *Lady Susan* and two competing centers of authority in *Northanger Abbey* and *Sense and Sensibility*. The closure of *Pride and Prejudice* is thus aesthetically successful, but whether it insures a comparable ideological resolution is doubtful. For at the level of the plot Austen can grant moral authority to feeling by stripping desire of egotism, but she cannot guarantee that every reader will be as educable as Elizabeth or that all expressions of feeling will be as socially constructive as Elizabeth's desire for Darcy. This problem is raised specifically in *Pride and Prejudice* by Lydia, and Austen never really dismisses this character or the unruly energy she embodies:

> Lydia was Lydia still; untamed, unabashed, wild, noisy, and fearless. She turned from sister to sister, demanding their congratulations, and when at length they all sat down, looked eagerly round the room, took notice of some little alteration in it, and observed, with a laugh, that it was a great while since she had been there. [p. 315]

Even Austen's concluding comment on Lydia acknowledges that she finally finds a place within the same society that Elizabeth superintends. "In spite of her youth and her manners," the narrator informs us, Lydia "retained all the claims to reputation which her marriage had given her" (p. 387).

Austen's tacit assumption that her readers will renounce the moral anarchy epitomized in Lydia and generated by the pattern of localized ironies would be accurate only if her audience already shared her own experiences and values. For the purposes of her art, Austen makes this assumption because it allows her to contain not only individual interpretations but also the social criticisms implicitly raised in the course of *Pride and Prejudice*. In fact, this assumption enables her to bring the real experiences of her readers to bear on her narrative in such a way as to underscore the necessity of the aesthetic solution, which pushes aside social realism and criticism. Austen's contemporary readers would no doubt have been all too familiar with the facts and pressures that made Charlotte Lucas's cool assessment of marriage reasonable, and, merely by alluding to this shared experience, Austen enhances the gratification that Elizabeth's improbable success provides. Thus she introduces the specters of spinsterhood, dependence, and compromise less to explore the social strictures of Elizabeth's situation than to invoke the reality that makes her own consoling art necessary. The inadequacy of the aesthetic solution to the social problems it supposedly answers remains implicit but unproblematic; for it is precisely the gap between imaginative desire and social reality—a gap that still exists—that makes the escape into romance attractive to all readers and probably made Austen's contemporaries, in particular, anxious to believe that Elizabeth's happiness was available to every daughter of the middle class.

The special resonance and impact that her contemporaries sensed in the statements and situations of Austen's novels are dim or absent altogether of twentieth-century readers. But even the experiences Austen's contemporaries shared with her, merely by virtue of their historical, geographical, and class proximity, would not have guaranteed a common set of values. For, as we have seen, in this period of social turmoil even the dominant system of values was characterized by internal tensions and contradictions—stresses that reflected the competition between bourgeois individualism and old patterns of patronage and also the inevitable gap between the promises of individualism and the general inequalities and personal repressions that bourgeois society requires. Given the structure of bourgeois society, the system of absolute Christian principles that is the foundation of Austen's novels necessarily had to have its everyday, functional version, which allowed one to be "rather" selfish in pursuit of material prosperity as long as one practiced charity and thought good thoughts. It is precisely the latitude of interpretations permitted by this compromise of ethical and moral absolutes that finally imperils the didactic design of *Pride and Prejudice*. For the family of readers that Austen posited did not necessarily exist; even in her own day, the consensus of values she needed to assume was as wishful a fiction as Elizabeth Bennet's marriage to Darcy.

Because of the sophistication of her narrative skills, the romance Austen dramatizes at the end of *Pride and Prejudice* seems not only right but plausible. But it is plausible only because, in this novel, Austen separates the power to gratify and discipline desire from the conditions that generate and frustrate that desire. The power moves from society to the realm of art; in *Pride and Prejudice* Austen substitutes aesthetic gratification—the pleasures of the "light and bright and sparkling" plays of wit—for the practical solutions that neither her society nor her art could provide. That we do not more often feel shortchanged by this sleight-of-hand attests to the power of her artistry and to the magnitude of our own desire to deny the disturbing ideological contradictions that have made such imaginative compensation necessary.

Notes

1. The most extensive discussion of Austen's treatment of propriety is Jane Nardin's *Those Elegant Decorums: The Concept of Propriety in Jane Austen's Novels* (Albany: State University of New York Press, 1973). Nardin's analysis is extremely perceptive and discriminating, but, finally, it cannot accept the degree of conscious intention she attributes to Austen (see pp. 10–11). The most telling recent analysis of the contradictions in Austen's novels, and thus a reading more in keeping with my own, is Igor Webb's *From Custom to Capital: The English Novel*

and the Industrial Revolution (Ithaca and London: Cornell University Press, 1981), pp. 49–70, 101–21, 158–61.

2. One example of Austen's apparent self-contradiction is evident in her opinions about Evangelicalism. On 24 January 1809 she told Cassandra: "You have by no means raised my curiosity after *Caleb* (Hannah More's *Coelebs in Search of a Wife*];—My disinclination for it before was affected, but now it is real; I do not like the Evangelicals." On 18 November 1814, however, she informed Fanny Knight that "I am by no means convinced that we ought not all to be Evangelicals, & am at least persuaded that they who are so from Reason and Feeling, must be happiest & safest" (*Jane Austen's Letters to Her Sister Cassandra and Others*, ed. R. W. Chapman, 2 vols. [Oxford: Clarendon Press, 1932], 1:256; 2:410; hereafter cited as *JAL*). Austen might simply have changed her opinion; on the other hand, she might have been making distinctions we can no longer confidently reconstruct.

3. The one extant copy of *Lady Susan* is a fair copy that bears the watermark 1805. Chapman acknowledges, however, that the transcription of the novel could easily have post-dated its composition by a number of years. B. C. Southam, in *Jane Austen's Literary Manuscripts: A Study of the Novelist's Development through the Surviving Papers* (London: Oxford University Press, 1964), pp. 45–62, presents a strong case for the earlier date.

4. *Lady Susan,* vol. 6 of *The Works of Jane Austen,* ed. R. W. Chapman (London: Oxford University Press, 1954), p. 243. (Volumes 1–5 appeared in the second edition of the *Works,* published in 1926.)

5. See Lloyd W. Brown, "Jane Austen and the Feminist Tradition," *Nineteenth-Century Fiction* 28 (1973): 334, and Sandra M. Gilbert and Susan Gubar, *The Madwoman in the Attic: The Woman Writer and the Nineteenth-Century Literary Imagination* (New Haven: Yale University Press, 1979), p. 118.

6. See Lloyd W. Brown, *Bits of Ivory: Narrative Techniques in Jane Austen's Fiction* (Baton Rouge: Louisiana State University Press, 1973), pp. 147–48, 153.

7. Gilbert and Gubar point out that one way in which Austen attempts to control our sympathy for Lady Susan is by making her cruelty to Frederica exceed the demands of the plot. See *Madwoman*, pp. 155–56.

8. William Wordsworth, letter to Daniel Stuart, 1817, quoted by Alistair M. Duckworth, *The Improvement of the Estate: A Study of Jane Austen's Novels* (Baltimore: Johns Hopkins University Press, 1971), p. 81.

9. For a discussion of the spirit of "party" and the "contrary systems of thought" typical of the literature of this period, see L. J. Swingle, "The Poets, the Novelists, and the English Romantic Situation," *Wordsworth Circle* 3 (1979): 218–28, and David Simpson, *Irony and Authority in Romantic Poetry* (Totowa, N.J.: Rowman & Littlefield, 1979).

10. Donald J. Greene, "Jane Austen and the Peerage," *PMLA* 68 (1953): 1017–31; reprinted in *Jane Austen: A Collection of Critical Essays,* ed. Ian Watt (Englewood Cliffs, N.J.: Prentice-Hall, 1963), pp. 156–57.

11. See Marilyn Butler, *Jane Austen and the War of Ideas* (Oxford: Clarendon Press, 1975), pp. 161–67, 284–85, and Duckworth, *The Improvement,* pp. 2–80. For another discussion of Jane Austen's religion, see Warren Roberts, *Jane Austen and the French Revolution* (New York: St. Martin's Press, 1979), pp. 109–54.

12. See Terry Lovell, "Jane Austen and the Gentry: A Study in Literature and Ideology," *The Sociology of Literature: Applied Studies,* ed. Diana Laurenson (Hanley, Eng.: Wood Mitchell & Co., 1978), pp. 20–21.

13. See ibid., p. 21.

14. For an excellent discussion of the complexities of parody, see George Levine, "Translating the Monstrous: *Northanger Abbey,*" *Nineteenth-Century Fiction* 30 (1975): 337.

15. Samuel Johnson, *Rambler* 4, in *The Yale Edition of the Works of Samuel Johnson,* ed. W. J. Bate and Albrecht B. Strauss, 14 vols. (New Haven: Yale University Press, 1969), 3:21, 22.

16. *Persuasion*, in *The Works of Jane Austen*, 5:101.

17. Johnson, *Rambler* 4, pp. 23, 21.

18. *Northanger Abbey*, in *The Works of Jane Austen*, 5:37, 38. Patricia Meyer Spacks also points out that education in an Austen novel requires imaginative engagement; see her "Muted Discord: Generational Conflict in Jane Austen," in *Jane Austen in a Social Context*, ed. David Monaghan (Totowa, N.J.: Barnes & Noble, 1981), pp. 170, 174, 177–78.

19. The precise order in which Austen composed her major works is unknown, but B. C. Southam, having consulted Cassandra's original memorandum and the surviving manuscripts, argues persuasively for the following chronology: *Elinor and Marianne*—completed before 1796; *First Impressions*—October 1796–August 1797; *Sense and Sensibility*, the revision of *Elinor and Marianne*—begun November 1797, revised again at Chawton 1809–10; *Northanger Abbey*, originally entitled *Susan*—c. 1798–99, never substantially revised; *Pride and Prejudice*, the revision of *First Impressions*—conducted in 1809–10 and 1812; *Mansfield Park*—February 1811–June 1813; *Emma*—21 January 1814–29 March 1815; *Persuasion*—8 August 1815–6 August 1816 (Southam, *Jane Austen's Literary Manuscripts*, pp. 52–58). The dates given in parentheses in my text are the publication dates.

20. For a discussion of Austen's "free, indirect speech," see Norman Page, *The Language of Jane Austen* (New York: Barnes & Noble, 1972), pp. 123 ff.

21. *Sense and Sensibility*, in *The Works of Jane Austen*, 1:8.

22. Tony Tanner, Introduction to the Penguin edition of *Sense and Sensibility* (Harmondsworth, Eng., 1969), p. 32.

23. See Tanner, ibid., p. 30.

24. I am indebted to Patricia Meyer Spacks and to her Yale College seminar on Jane Austen for many of the observations about this episode.

25. *Pride and Prejudice*, in *The Works of Jane Austen*, 2:42–43.

26. Bernard J. Paris makes this point in *Character and Conflict in Jane Austen's Novels: A Psychological Approach* (Detroit: Wayne State University Press, 1978), pp. 118–39. While many of my observations are consistent with Paris's reading, I disagree with his central thesis that Elizabeth can be treated as a "real" person throughout the novel. It is precisely Austen's aborting of psychological realism that interests me.

27. See Duckworth, *The Improvement of the Estate*, pp. 123–26 (see n. 8, above).

28. In 1799, for instance, Austen remarked to her sister Cassandra, "I do not wonder at your wanting to read 'First Impressions' again" (*JAL*, 1:52; 8 January 1799); her letters also show her sharing *Mansfield Park* with her brother Henry before its publication, and she kept a list of the responses her family and friends made to that novel and to *Emma*. See "Opinions of *Mansfield Park* and *Emma*" in *The Works of Jane Austen*, 6:431–39. For another discussion of the relationship between Austen's composition and her family, see Mary Lascelles, *Jane Austen and Her Art* (Oxford: Clarendon Press, 1939), pp. 4, 146.

29. Austen's niece Catherine Hubback commented that their aunt "always said her books were her children" (quoted by R. W. Chapman, *Jane Austen: Facts and Problems* [Oxford: Clarendon Press, 1948], p. 67), and from her nephews we learn that Austen supplied her family with information about her characters' "after-life": "In this tradition any way we learned that Miss Steele never succeeded in catching the Doctor; that Kitty Bennet was satisfactorily married to a clergyman near Pemberley, while Mary obtained nothing higher than one of her uncle Phillips' clerks, and was content to be considered a star in the society of Meriton; that the 'considerable sum' given by Mrs. Norris to William Price was one pound; that Mr. Woodhouse survived his daughter's marriage, and kept her and Mr. Knightley from settling at Donwell, about two years; and that the letters placed by Frank Churchill before Jane Fairfax, which she swept away unread, contained the word 'pardon' " (J. E. Austen-Leigh, *A Memoir of Jane Austen* [London: Macmillan, 1906], pp. 148–49). Julia Prewitt Brown also discusses the importance of the family for Austen; see her *Jane Austen's Novels: Social Change and Literary Form* (Cambridge, Mass.: Harvard University Press, 1979), p. 9.

30. One of the best discussions of this function of irony is in Nardin, *Those Elegant Decorums,* pp. 4–11.

31. See Wayne C. Booth, *A Rhetoric of Irony* (Chicago: University of Chicago Press, 1974), p. 44 and passim.

32. See A. Walton Litz, *Jane Austen: A Study of Her Artistic Development* (New York: Oxford University Press, 1965), p. 108.

Mansfield Park:
Slavery, Colonialism, and Gender

MOIRA FERGUSON

Mansfield Park (1814) is a eurocentric, post-abolition narrative that inter-twines with a critique of gender relations and posits a world of humanitarian interactions between slave-owners and slaves. As such, following the success-ful passage of the Abolition Bill in 1807, *Mansfield Park* initiates a new chap-ter in colonialist fiction. Nonetheless, although the novel works against the idea of the traditionally closed and brutal world of plantocratic relations, it entertains the option of emancipation—as opposed to abolition—only through the sound of muffled rebel voices. In order to stage a future society peaceably perpetuating British rule, Jane Austen transforms Sir Thomas Bertram of Mansfield Park—who is also a plantation-owner in Antigua—from a characteristically imperious "West Indian" planter—stock figure of ridicule in contemporary drama, poetry and novels—into a benevolent, re-forming land-owner.[1]

Given the state of agitation in the Caribbean in the early 1800s, the un-reality of this scenario forces textual contradictions and eruptions. No African-Caribbean people speak, no mention is ever made of slave plots or in-surrections, and even slaves' white counterparts—Anglo-Saxon women in re-bellion in one form or another—are assimilated or banished.[2] Thus gender re-lations at home parallel and echo traditional relationships of power between the colonialists and colonized peoples: European women visibly signify the most egregiously and invisibly repressed of the text—African-Caribbeans themselves. They mark silent African-Caribbean rebels as well as their own disenfranchisement, class and gender victimization.

Let me contextualize these remarks by noting that *Mansfield Park* was begun by Jane Austen in early 1811 and published in 1814, with its novelis-tic chronology extending from 1808 through 1809. As a result of the ener-getic abolition movement and parliamentary compromise with the West In-dia lobby in 1792, slaveowners' efforts to resist legal abolition, let alone emancipation, were notorious.[3]

Moira Ferguson, *"Mansfield Park:* Slavery, Colonialism, and Gender," *Oxford Literary Review* 13 (1991): 1–2, 118–39. © 1991 by Moira Ferguson; reprinted by permission.

A transatlantic land-owner, Sir Thomas Bertram is fictionally characterized as one of those members of parliament who defended plantocratic interests.[4] He belonged to the "outer ring" of absentee planters and merchants
who never, or rarely, visited the colonies, although their connections remained
solid.[5] In Raymond Williams' words:

> Important parts of the country-house system, from the sixteenth to the eigh-
> teenth centuries, were built on the profits of . . . trade [with the colonies].
> Spices, sugar, tea, coffee, tobacco, gold and silver: these fed, as mercantile prof-
> its, into an English social order, over and above the profits on English stock
> and crops. . . . The country-houses which were the apex of a local system of ex-
> ploitation then had many connections to these distant lands. . . . [Moreover],
> the new rural economy of the tropical plantations—sugar, coffee, cotton—was
> built by [the] trade in flesh, and once again the profits fed back into the coun-
> try-house system: not only the profits on the commodities but . . . the profits
> on slaves.[6]

After a brief, quiescent period following the passage of the bill, however,
fierce contestations over slavery began anew at home and abroad. As the
British press reported news of increasing atrocities in 1809, 1810, and 1811,
it became obvious that the abolitionists' utopian vision of a Caribbean plantocracy committed to ameliorating the conditions of their only remaining
slaves was palpably false.[7] This rise in atrocities, in addition to vigorous illicit
trading, spurred parliamentary proposals that all Caribbean slaves be regis-
tered.[8] Old colonial legislatures that included Antigua opposed slave reg-
istries on constitutional grounds because such a procedure violated their right
of internal taxation; not until 1820 did colonialists assent.

In fact, the time during which *Mansfield Park* was written marked a
turning point in the fortunes of the gentry, to which social class Sir Thomas,
as a baronet, arguably belonged.[9] In England the Luddite riots fomented un-
rest, the prime minister was assassinated, war was declared against the
United States, and the gentry endured a general economic crisis. Mrs Norris,
Sir Thomas' sister-in-law, informs us that Sir Thomas' financial stability depends on maintaining his Caribbean property:[10] his "means will be rather
straitened if the Antiguan estate is to make such poor returns."[11] Sir Thomas
needs his Caribbean profits to stay financially afloat in England; colonialism
underwrites his social and cultural position.

Thus, ongoing news of Caribbean economic crises exacerbates Sir
Thomas' already straitened circumstances. Sugar prices had plummeted as a
result of a major depression after 1807. The ensuing urgency to diversify the
imperiled sugar monoculture made the physical presence of customarily absentee landlords expedient, and so Sir Thomas was obliged "to go to Antigua
himself, for the better arrangement of his affairs."[12] The task at hand was to
maintain his estates at a profit and in the process, since trading was now ille-
gal, to ensure the survival of his slaves as steady, well-nourished workers.

Sadistic overseers, with whom Sir Thomas may have been content in the past, provided returns were satisfactory, would no longer do. His appearance when he returns to England suggests not only an exhausting engagement with his overseers and a severe reaction to noisome conditions, but through metonym it also emphasizes his affiliation with the Creole class. He "had the burnt, fagged, worn look of fatigue and a hot climate" (178).

The society to which Sir Thomas traveled was dominated by aggressive oppositional relations between colonialists and colonized people, although absentee landlordism was unusual on Antigua compared to its frequency on neighboring islands. As a near-noble landowner, Sir Thomas would socialize with the commander-in-chief of the Leeward Islands, the Right Honorable Ralph, Lord Lavington, who, in "real life," chose to set a constant pointed public example of desirable relations between colonizers and colonized:

> His Christmas balls and routs were upon the highest scale of magnificence; but he was a great stickler for etiquette, and a firm upholder of difference of rank and *colour* [Flanders' underlining]. . . . He would not upon any occasion, receive a letter or parcel from the fingers of a black or coloured man, and in order to guard against such *horrible* defilement, he had a golden instrument wrought something like a pair of sugar tongs, with which he was accustomed to hold the presented article.[13]

Back home, abolitionists contested the condoned maltreatment of slaves encapsulated in Lord Lavington's insidious public behaviour; they decried the atrocities that his cultural practice validated: violations of the Abolition Act, as well as individual cases of heinous maltreatment and murders of slaves by planters in 1810 and 1811.[14] Since the powerful proslavery lobby indefatigably suppressed these events as far as their power allowed, only those with access to ongoing revelations in the press and through rumor could stay abreast of daily developments. The centuries-long ideological battle over the humanity of Africans constantly and variously manifested itself.

PLANTOCRATIC PARADIGMS IN *MANSFIELD PARK*

Power relations within the community of Mansfield Park reenact and refashion plantocratic paradigms; those who work for Sir Thomas and his entourage both at home and abroad are locked into hierarchical and abusive patterns of behaviour, though under widely different circumstances. The cruel officiousness of protagonist Fanny Price's aunt, Mrs Norris, who is effectively Sir Thomas' overseer and lives in the suggestively named white house "across the park" from the Great House, underlines his plantocratic style of administration.

Mrs Norris' surname recalls John Norris, one of the most vile proslaveryites of the day. Austen was well aware of Norris' notoriety, having read

Thomas Clarkson's celebrated *History of the Abolition of the Slave Trade* in which Norris is categorically condemned. Clarkson's text was published in 1808 and read by Jane Austen while she was working out the plot of *Mansfield Park*.[15] Not only had Clarkson's history astounded her but she admitted to her sister Cassandra that she had once been "in love" with the famous abolitionist whose devotion, industry, and total lack of regard for his own life in the cause was legend.[16] Clarkson chronicles how Norris represented himself to Clarkson in Liverpool as an opponent of the slave trade, then arrived in London as a pro-slavery delegate representing Liverpool.[17] After contacting Norris for an explanation, Clarkson notes Norris' unctuously self-serving response:

> After having paid high compliments to the general force of my arguments, and the general justice and humanity of my sentiments on this great question, which had made a deep impression upon his mind, he had found occasion to differ from me, since we had last parted, on particular points, and that he had therefore less reluctantly yielded to the call of becoming a delegate,—though notwithstanding he would gladly have declined the office if he could have done it with propriety.[18]

Underscoring the intertextual designation of Mrs Norris as sadistic overseer, Sir Thomas himself is centerstaged as "master," especially in his treatment of niece Fanny Price. With very little ceremony and offering Fanny Price's family no say in the matter, Sir Thomas and Mrs Norris engineer the transference of this ten-year-old poor relation from her home in Portsmouth to Mansfield Park. A marginalized, near-despised family, the Prices lose one of their own to accommodate Mrs Norris' need to appear charitable; Sir Thomas eventually concurs in her decision although he reserves his judgment to return Fanny Price if she threatens domestic stability. Portsmouth, by this account, is the uncivilized other; its members overflow with energies that menace the security of Mansfield Park. Epitomizing the clash of epistemologies in the text, Portsmouth signifies a way of living that negates the tightly controlled social order and challenges the sovereign law embodied in Sir Thomas by ignoring it altogether. On the other hand, in a different way, since Portsmouth as a naval town serves to uphold Sir Thomas' position by enforcing British control of the West Indies, what might be more important is that in the domestic arena of England, the link between the two must be separated. The expropriated Fanny Price hails from the milieu of transgressors who always signify the target of their activities: kidnapped and captive slaves.

Young Fanny Price's removal from her family is described in terms often reserved for epiphanic moments in the narrative of slavery:

> The remembrance . . . of what she had suffered in being torn from them, came over her with renewed strength, and it seemed as if to be at home again, would heal every pain that had since grown out of the separation. (370)

This mercantilist attitude toward human relationships, represented as disinterested benevolence toward Fanny Price, invokes traditionally conservative rationales of the "trade-in-flesh." Family feeling or unity never becomes an issue, since proslaveryites do not recognize African and slave families as social formations. On the contrary, the West Indian lobby argued that bringing slaves to the Caribbean was a good deed, a way of civilizing those whose environment provided them with nothing but barbarism—precisely the same basis for the justification of bringing Fanny Price to Mansfield Park.

So, when Fanny arrives at Mansfield Park, she is closely watched for evidence of her uncouth otherness. She must accept Sir Thomas' authority unconditionally or she will be removed. Sir Thomas scrutinizes her "disposition," anticipating "gross ignorance, some meanness of opinions, and very distressing vulgarity of manner" (10–11). Eventually he decides she has a "tractable disposition, and seemed likely to give them little trouble" (18). She will acclimatize well. Nonetheless, his children "cannot be equals [with Fanny Price]. Their rank, fortune, rights, and expectations will always be different" (11).

Fanny herself begins to adapt to the value system at Mansfield, learning "to know their ways, and to catch the best manner of conforming to them." Fanny thinks "too lowly of her own claims" and "too lowly of her own situation" to challenge values that keep her low.[19] Underscoring class difference and alluding to the colonial-sexual nexus, profligate elder son Tom, the heir apparent to Sir Thomas' colonial enterprise, assures Fanny Price that she can be a "creepmouse" all she wants as long as she obeys his commands.

Just as markedly, when Fanny Price years later is deciding what to wear at the ball, the point of contention is whose chain (or necklace) she will wear. The lurking question is to whom will she subject herself or belong. To what extent has Mansfield Park and its values begun to construct her subjectivity? Gladly, she decides on the chain of her future husband, Sir Thomas' younger son, Edmund. Moreover, when Sir Thomas leaves for Antigua, she steps into his moral shoes; she opposes Mrs Norris' opportunism and informally assumes the role of the "good" overseer, her aunt's alter ego. Mimicking Sir Thomas, willingly cooperating in her own assimilation, she speaks for and through him. Fanny Price helps to foreshadow and map a new colonialist landscape that upholds the moral status quo but draws the line at arbitrary judgment and excessive indulgence. In the chapel scene at Sotherton, for instance, Fanny Price identifies herself as an opponent of change.[20] Edmund, on the other hand, underscores Fanny's complicity in her own assimilation when he confides—to her delight—as she leaves for Portsmouth that she will "belong to [them] almost as much as ever" (26–7).

Yet Fanny Price is still the daughter of Portsmouth—Mansfield Park's relegated other, reared to succeed pluckily against the odds. Her master-slave relationship with Sir Thomas operates on the register of two opposing discourses: complicity and rebellion. Her stalwart refusal to marry Henry Crawford and the punishment of summary banishment she incurs identifies Mansfield Park ideologically as an institution that rallies to disempower anyone who jeopardizes Sir Thomas' feudal reign. This is especially true in the case of the déclassé Fanny Price, to whom Mansfield Park has opened its portals. In return she opposes its patriarchal demands on females as property by claiming one form of autonomy, thereby rendering herself an unregenerate ingrate in ruling class eyes. Sir Thomas even describes her in language reserved for slave insurrectionaries:

> I had thought you peculiarly free from wilfulness of temper, self-conceit, and every tendency to that independence of spirit, which prevails so much in modern days, even in young women and which in young women is offensive and disgusting beyond all common offence. But you have now shewn me that you can be wilful and perverse. (318)

To Sir Thomas, Fanny Price's feelings are as irrelevant as slaves' feelings; she is his object. In Tzvetan Todorov's words, "those who are not subjects have no desires."[21]

Fanny Price responds to her natal family almost exclusively as an other, after Sir Thomas banishes her to Portsmouth. Such is the enormity of his ideological power. His risk in sending her to resist Portsmouth and embrace Mansfield Park values pays off. Her home is nothing but "noise, disorder, impropriety," her overworked impecunious mother pronounced "a dawdler and a slattern" (388, 390). Portsmouth reconstitutes Fanny Price as Sir Thomas' transformed daughter, no longer the exiled object; while at Portsmouth she barricades herself ideologically, as it were, inside Mansfield Park, functioning as its representative. Her mother's features that she has not seen in over a decade endear themselves to her—not because she has missed seeing them—but because they remind Fanny Price of Lady Bertram's, her mother's sister and Sir Thomas' wife: "they brought her Aunt Bertram's before her" (377). Fanny Price has come to resemble the eurocentrically conceived "grateful negro" in pre-abolition tales who collaborated with kind owners and discouraged disobedience among rebel slaves.[22] Her embrace of Mansfield Park's values dissolves any binding association with her family and her old life.

After leaving Portsmouth for the second time, Fanny "was beloved" by her adopted family in Mansfield Park, the passive tense affirming her surrender of agency. When Edmund decides she will make him an appropriate wife, her parents' response is not mentioned. We assume they are neither told nor invited to the wedding. The only Portsmouth members who textually reappear are conformists: sister Susan, coded as a second Fanny, ready to satisfy Lady Bertram's need for a round-the-clock assistant, and impeccable sailor-brother William, who exercised "continued good conduct" (462).

Sir Thomas' commercial approach to Fanny Price reformulates the treatment he previously accorded her mother, Frances Price, who "disoblig[ed]"

her family when she married a lieutenant of marines "without education, fortune, or connections"; as a result, the Mansfield Park inner circle acts almost
as if Frances Price senior did not exist; certainly she has no rights as a parent,
so her children can be more or less removed at will. The text hints, too, that
having ten babies in nine years is tantamount to a reprehensible lack of restraint. Neither Mrs Price's continuing independence in not seeking help nor
her maintenance of a large family on a pittance elicit textual approbation.
Rather, she is lucky, in the text's terms, to be the recipient of Sir Thomas'
charity. With almost all immediate family ties severed, her status, mutatis
mutandi, parallels that of her sister Lady Bertram, whose dowry has doomed
her to the borders in a different sense. Within a phallocratic economy, their
lives elicit contempt and condescension.

Lady Bertram, Mrs Norris, and Frances Price make up the trio of sisters
who collectively display the degradation of colonial-gender relations. In the
opening sentence of *Mansfield Park*, which highlights Sir Thomas' hegemonic
order, the trope of capture and control that infuses the text first appears:

> About thirty years ago Miss Maria Ward of Huntingdon, with only seven thou-
> sand pounds, had the good luck to captivate Sir Thomas Bertram, of Mansfield
> Park, in the county of Northampton, and to be thereby raised to the rank of a
> baronet's lady, with all the comforts and consequences of an handsome house
> and large income.

The text thus describes her alleged initial conquest of Sir Thomas in arrest-
ingly ironic tones and in doing so, as in the famous opening assertion in *Pride
and Prejudice, Mansfield Park*'s first sentence also celebrates its opposite: Sir
Thomas' acquisition of a desirable social object. Maria Ward instantly drops
out of sight, both in nomenclature and in self-led behaviour. Occupying the
role of a slatternly plantation mistress—"she never thought of being useful"
(179)—Lady Bertram's prominent class status through marriage collides with
the posture of an undermined female. The lap dog upon which she lavishes
attention—"no one is to tease my poor pug"—emblematizes her pathetically
protected status.[23] When Sir Thomas has to break news to her, he approaches
her as he would a child. During his absence, she rather tellingly works on
"yards of fringe"—appropriate for a marginalized wife—and when he returns, in recognition of her imposed vacuity, she waits to have "her whole
comprehension" filled by his narrative (196). She epitomizes emptiness, a vacant object-status, a slave or constructed subject who commits spiritual sui-
cide. Only once does a hint of spunky self-respect surface. On Sir Thomas' departure for Antigua when she comments that she does not fear for his safety, a
momentary ambiguity nags the text. Is she overly confident he will be safe
because she is oblivious to maritime danger due to the Napoleonic wars? Or
does she not care? Does her comment speak unconsciously about her recognition of powerlessness? Does it quietly express repressed anger?

Sir Thomas' behaviour on both sides of the Atlantic signals a planto-cratic mode of behaviour. Through the trope of his journey to Antigua, his long absence, and his sparing commentary about his experiences when he re-turns, Austen stresses his planter-like detachment from humanity, or his play-ing down of the facts, or both. One of the few things he did in Antigua—we learn—is attend a ball in the company of Creoles—as white planters were mockingly termed in the eighteenth and nineteenth centuries; culturally and economically, Sir Thomas is inextricably linked to his Antiguan counterparts. And given certain much-touted facts about planters, contemporaries could have amplified Sir Thomas' character in a way that would expressively inflect Lady Bertram's remark about not being concerned about his safety. Planters were infamous for taking slave mistresses and fathering children.

Edward Long, who wrote the immensely popular *History of Jamaica* (1774), describes Creole activities as follows:

> Creole men . . . are in general sensible, of quick apprehension, brave, good-na-tured, affable, generous, temperate, and sober; unsuspicious, lovers of freedom, fond of social enjoyments, tender fathers, humane and indulgent masters; firm and sincere friends, where they once repose a confidence; their tables are cov-ered with plenty of good cheer . . .; their hospitality is unlimited . . .; they af-fect gaiety and diversions, which in general are cards, billiards, backgammon, chess, horse-racing, hog-hunting, shooting, fishing, dancing, and music. . . . With a strong natural propensity to the other sex, they are not always the most chaste and faithful of husbands.[24]

Lowell Joseph Ragatz points out, furthermore, that from the mid-eighteenth century:

> private acts enabling white fathers to make generous provision for their illegit-imate half-breed children, despite existing laws prohibiting the transmission of extensive properties to blacks, were passed in all the island legislatures with painfully increasing regularity. The number of free persons of color in Barba-dos, largely recruited through illicit relations with white men and negresses, rose from 448 to 2,229 between 1768 and 1802, while the number in Do-minica soared from 600 in 1773 to more than 2,800 in 1804. This rapid growth of a mixed blood element in the British West Indies after 1750 arose chiefly from the Anglo-Saxon's now merely transitory residence there and the small number of white women remaining in the islands. Concubinage became well-nigh universal in the second half of the eighteenth century and the system pervaded all ranks of society. During the administration of Governor Ricketts in Barbados in the 1790s, a comely negress even reigned at government house, enjoying all a wife's privileges save presiding publicly at his table.[25]

According to August Kotzebue's well-known play that the characters in *Mansfield Park* choose to rehearse for their recreation, *Lovers' Vows,* no love/lust exists in England, only "in all barbarous countries."[26] Austen uses this play to intertextualize the characters' motives and interactions. A remark from the play's philandering Count Cassel that comments on sexual exploitation in the Caribbean matches contemporary accounts and illumines the character of Sir Thomas.[27]

Jane Austen was well aware of these infamous activities. She knew about the estate of the Nibbs family in Antigua because the Reverend George Austen, Jane Austen's father, was a trustee; she also knew of the Nibbs' "mulatto" relative.[28] As one critic concretely contends: "Jane Austen would certainly have been aware of the likelihood of a family such as her fictional Bertrams having numerous mulatto relatives in Antigua." Sir Thomas' condemnation of Mrs Price marrying low and his anger at Fanny Price's refusal to accommodate him by marrying Henry Crawford mocks planters' infamous, quotidian practices.

A question then crops up: Does Sir Thomas banish his daughter, Maria, and censure Henry Crawford because their sexual indulgences mirror his Antiguan conduct? Is one dimension of his behaviour a form of self-projection, an unconscious denial of his dual and contradictory relative in the Caribbean and Britain?

Another victim of Sir Thomas' mercantilist attitudes, elder daughter Maria refuses to be Lady Bertram's clone. Instead she stands with her exiled Aunt Frances and cousin Fanny in claiming sexual independence. Her actions are even more morally outré since she has already been manipulated into marriage with Rushworth, a man whom her father financially desires. For example in the gate scene at Sotherton, Maria symbolically and literally refuses to be imprisoned. Maria, that is, falls for the ideological trap that is set for her and is punished for trying to release herself.[29] Mary Crawford, who also disregards Sir Thomas' authority and is coded as a predator of sorts, similarly contests for personal autonomy and is configured as more evil because she disregards Sir Thomas' values. Linked by their given names, they are different versions of a gendered bid for identity.[30]

In the text's terms, none of these spirited acts by women in multiple postures of subjection can be vindicated except that of the conflicted Fanny Price. The Crawfords are reduced to the social margins, Henry for visible rakishness, Mary for "evil" and bold collaboration in her brother's escapades. The possibility smoulders that Sir Thomas cannot contain an English reflection of his Antiguan self. He represents men who control the general slave population and the female slave population in particular through varieties of abuse. When women like Frances and Fanny Price, Maria Bertram, and Mary Crawford articulate a counterdiscourse against their objectification, Sir Thomas stands firm. Insurgent women become deleted subjects, objects of his wrath who must be appropriately punished, usually for keeps. At the conscious and unconscious level, the text continually inscribes challenges to the assumed inferiority of women and the right of a hegemonic patriarch to use women as he pleases.

Most systematically of all, however, *Lovers' Vows* intertextualizes property-owning attitudes that characterize planter-slave relations, including Sir Thomas' flagrant neglect of female welfare.[31] At the same time, the dramatic resolution of these corrupt interrelationships appears to exonerate Sir Thomas and validate patriarchal rule. Clearly coded as Sir Thomas, the Baron is multiply conflicted. In former days, he had abandoned naive and pregnant Agnes, who bore Frederick. Like the "deserted and neglected negroes" of Antigua who will become a later focus of national concern, Agnes is now starving to death and homeless. Eventually, however, the Baron's callous desertion is mitigated by information that he has hired helpers to search constantly till they find her. In the end the Baron decides to marry Agnes though he fails to consult her about his plan. Like Maria Ward, she is assumed to desire such a splendid match.

In like manner, the Baron's efforts to marry off his daughter Amelia to silly Count Cassel are soon revealed as nonbinding. When he learns that Amelia loves Pastor Anhalt, the Baron readily consents, a scenario that comments on the marital imbroglio of Fanny Price, Henry Crawford, and Edmund Bertram. The case of Frederick, who strikes the Baron in the course of trying to save his mother's life, allusively invokes the nature of Sir Thomas' power: the Baron orders Frederick killed even though "a child might have overpowered him," for "to save him would set a bad example."[32] Only when the Baron discovers that Frederick is his son, does parental feeling induce him to relent. In doing so, the Baron earns permission to be readmitted to the human community. Feudal laws and relations in *Lovers' Vows* sign those of the plantocracy.

CONCLUSION

Mansfield Park initiated a new chapter in colonialist fiction as old and new abolitionists came to terms with the fact that the Abolition Bill did not fulfill its minimum requirement—amelioration of inhuman conditions. Jane Austen's repugnance toward the slave trade, moreover, is well documented— her brother Francis was a vigorous abolitionist—and by the time she writes *Emma* in 1816 her condemnation is forthright.[33] Hence Sir Thomas' chastening is one way of prescribing this letting-up process among a seemingly unregenerate plantocracy. He reconstitutes himself as a moral rather than a profit-oriented planter, a condition inveterately resisted among the colonial ruling class. Recent experience in the House of Commons as well as the Caribbean have persuaded Sir Thomas, Jane Austen subtly argues, that the old order may be doomed and disappearing. As a parliamentary member, Sir Thomas would have been witnessing at first hand the efforts of Wilberforce and his supporters to initiate corrective legislation. In admitting his errors and curbing his selfishness, Sir Thomas comes to represent the liberal-conservative ideal of humanitarian plantation ownership at a time when outright manumission is effectively a non-issue.

It hardly seems to be a coincidence that *Mansfield Park* echoes the name of Lord Chief Justice Mansfield, who wrote the legal decision for the James Somerset case in 1772, stipulating that no slaves could be forcibly returned from Britain to the Caribbean, which was widely interpreted to mean that slavery in Britain had been legally abolished.[34] Austen's invocation of Lord Mansfield's name suggests the novel's intrinsic engagement with slavery and a view of Sir Thomas' plantations as a place where feudal relations are beginning to dissolve.[35] To underscore that point, the word "plantation" is frequently used to denote Sir Thomas' property on both sides of the Atlantic.

At another level, the intertextualizing of Lord Mansfield's ruling warns and censures all those who try to further impose their will on the already subjugated, in Sir Thomas' case, Fanny Price and by extension his Antiguan slaves. The choice of Mansfield for the title underscores the idea of property in the hands of a patriarch—one man's plantations—and in its compression of several frames of meaning and reference, it connects the Caribbean plantation system and its master-slave relationships to tyrannical gender relations at home and abroad.

Jane Austen's recommendations for a kinder, gentler plantocracy, however, do anything but confront that institution head on. Not to put too fine a point on it, the opposite is virtually true. En route to the new dispensation, Sir Thomas' change of heart is accompanied and contradicted by his challenge to the heterogeneous utterances of those who flout his power. Hence paradoxically, his moral reformation reconfirms his control. With unruly elements purged or contained and his unitary discourse intact though refashioned, the same power relations persist in slightly different guise between the ruling class elite and dominated people, between male and female. Thus to read *Mansfield Park* as a text with closures that favour more benevolent socio-political relationships only serves to mask textual undercurrents that threaten to explode its tightly controlled bourgeois framework.

Let me briefly recite some of these closures that purport to foretell future felicity and a more uniform culture groping toward harmony. First, *Lovers' Vows* is intended to demonstrate how well the Baron (Sir Thomas) suppresses anarchic expression and restores peace after learning his lesson. Second, protagonist Fanny Price, despite announcing her right to autonomy, attains the status of an insider because she mirrors Sir Thomas' values and rather coldly rejects her origins. She embraces an imposed identity as a bona fide member of the Mansfield Park community. Sir Thomas, in turn, offers himself as a father: "Fanny was indeed the daughter that he wanted. His charitable kindness had been rearing a prime comfort for himself" (472). Third, the Price family in Portsmouth is exposed as decisively inferior except for those who agreeably adapt. Disobedience and heady self-determination are penalized by lifetime expulsion from the old order: Maria Bertram and Mary Crawford are excluded from the ruling class coterie while younger daughter Julia's repentance and her more accommodating disposition gain her a second chance.

Also to the point is Lady Bertram's languid life, which is criticized yet accepted as a familiar though inconsequential existence while the mettlesome spirit of the Price survivors goes unapplauded. That is, although Lady Bertram may draw sympathetic attention as a witless figure, the necessity for a social appendage in female form to round out plantocratic control is never gainsaid. But perhaps the most orally ambiguous textual judgment concerns Mrs Norris herself whose windfall is treated as her just deserts. Former overseer and exposed renegade, she is banished for good, like her sister Frances, from the family circle. That she encourages Maria Bertram to claim a certain kind of freedom is sweepingly condemned. The text obliterates the fact that she represents Sir Thomas' interests, but in excess of how the text wants him portrayed.[36] She is his avatar, Sir Thomas at his most acquisitive and self-indulgent. He cannot countenance the reflection of himself in Mrs Norris, who represents his displaced tacit approval of heinous cruelties and ensuing reduced profits. When he rejects her, he rejects part of his former self and life; he becomes part of the new order that seeks more wholesome relations at home and abroad. Since his regeneration cannot mean that he continues to treat people unfeelingly, Mrs Norris has to be reconstructed as a villain, tidily demolished, and eliminated as a speaking subject.

These methodical but artificial closures, however, in their blanket effort to smother opposition, only highlight ideological antagonisms that decentre Sir Thomas' power and question its validity. They elicit an insistent counter-discourse. His posture also underwrites a certain anxiety about outsiders, regardless of former familial or friendly relationships. Human connections count for naught compared to the obsession with control.

Most ironically, textual imbeddings surface in the person of Sir Thomas' major vindicator, the Baron, who turns out in one sense to be his most damning accuser. As Sir Thomas' autocratic counterpart, the medieval Baron has no compunction about killing an innocent man who defies his authority. Similarly, Sir Thomas himself can order severe punishment, if not death, against slaves he arbitrarily deems insubordinate. Such was the authority of planters. And not uncoincidentally, the Baron is execrating Frederick in *Lovers' Vows* while that other Baron, Sir Thomas, administers the Antiguan plantations, by implication in the same way. The Baron denies Frederick's humanity as planters deny the humanity of slaves, relenting only when he discovers Frederick is his son. In a remarkably unconscious self-projection, the Baron commands Frederick in words that would make more sense in reverse: "Desist—barbarian, savage, stop!!" (526). Moreover, by summarily terminating the theatricals, Sir Thomas reestablishes his authority over a symbolically uncontrollable situation.[37]

Most materially, the sparse counterdiscourse concerning slaves pinpoints a fundamental textual repression. Having affirmed her pleasure in Sir

Thomas' stories of his Caribbean visit, Fanny inquires about the slave trade. After absorbing her uncle's answer—significantly unreported—she expresses amazement to Edmund about the ensuing "dead silence" (198), a phrase that requires careful unpacking. Let me back up for a moment.

In this transitional post-abolitionist period that features a shaky British-Caribbean economy and multiple slave insurrections, no safe space, from a eurocentric perspective, is available for colonized others as speaking subjects, let alone as self-determining agents. Put baldly, slave subjectivity has to be effaced. As the oppressed daughter of an exigent family, Fanny Price becomes the appropriate mediator or representative of slaves' silenced existence and constant insurrectionary potential. In her role as a marginalized other (though in a vastly different cultural context), Fanny Price can project and displace personal-political anxieties and mimic her servile subject position.

As a brief for plantocratic gradual reform, the text disintegrates at "dead silence," a phrase that ironically speaks important debarred and smothered voices. As Mansfield Park's unofficial spokesman for Antiguan society, the beleaguered Sir Thomas has cut slaves off from representation. Lovers' Vows, besides, has already voiced and even accentuated the major topoi of a muzzled colonialist discourse: brutality, fractured families, and the violated bodies and psyches of innocent people. Thus the conceptualizations of "dead"' and "silence" that parallel the play's metonyms of bondage further indict the gaps in Sir Thomas' discourse. Beyond that, these loaded inscriptions of death and muteness accost the taboo enforced on dissent in the colonies. "Dead silence" affirms Sir Thomas' seeming pretence that power relations are stable in Antigua. For what other than dissimulation of some sort—most likely an obfuscation or omission—could explain Fanny Price's ready acceptance of his lengthy speech on the slave trade. "Dead" and "silence," in other words, forswear the reality of ubiquitous slave insurrections. For example, plots were organized and carried out in Jamaica, Tobago, and especially in Dominica, where the second maroon war was led by Quashie, Apollo, Jacko, and others.[38] Uncontainable conflicts are further unmasked by textual allusions to several issues of the Quarterly Review, which carried many troublesome facts about slavery in 1811:[39] for one, the periodical reported that the progressive diminution in slave population levels persisted, despite abolition of the trade, a fact that threw doubt on promises made by planters and colonial legislatures to ameliorate conditions. Old planters in Jamaica and Antigua were in the news, too, as zealous competitors of the "new" planters. The Quarterly Review also confirmed that the bottom had dropped out of the sugar market by 1808, that estates were in disrepair, and growers could not be indemnified.[40] What's more, the seemingly univocal colonial discourse of Mansfield Park that upholds a singular view of slavery as "working" belies domestic agitation inside and outside parliament for improved conditions.[41]

Antigua, then, tropes an anxiety-creating unknown venue, falsely coded as a run-down locale in need of an individual planter's semi-altruistic, definitively ethnocentric intervention. Profits are down, but workers and administrators suffer too. Antigua also correlates with Portsmouth, both being symbolic sites of indeterminacy near water and places where the allegedly uncivilized cluster. As a port and an island intimately involved with slavery, Portsmouth and Antigua witness slave ships arriving and departing; scenes involving the sale of people and naval engagements are in constant view. Sir Thomas may subsume Antigua within his monocular vision and Fanny Price may fail to see (or evade) Portsmouth's obvious immersion in the slave trade as she gazes at the sights of the town, but their buried knowledge and realities intertextually circulate nonetheless. Like the Orient in Edward Said's formulation, Antigua and Portsmouth are Mansfield Park's wild, colonized others, signs of potential disruption and sexual conflict.[42] They signal that the women of Mansfield Park are ideologically absorbed or unceremoniously expelled—or even obliterated (as the slavewomen of Antigua are) as autonomous beings.

In this space as Mansfield Park's other, Antigua satirizes Sir Thomas' authority. He may conduct his relationships in a recognizably plantocratic mode that solidifies his power, but both vocal and mute suppressions are evident. Sir Thomas' return assumes that he leaves behind a certain order, even harmony, on his plantations. He controls superficially obedient slaves, but that illusion will soon be fractured. By implication, other apparent fixtures might also turn out to be less enduring.

This is not to argue that the possibility of slave emancipation in *Mansfield Park* parallels a potential liberation for Anglo-Saxon women. But it is to posit that challenges to ossified thought and the received cultural representation of women are at least conceivable. Lady Bertram is comatose, but can that state last? The condition of indolent plantocratic wives is certainly coming to an end. Besides, the self-determining duo of Maria-Mary will not tolerate permanent disappearance. Their independent natures will soon reassert themselves, the text having forced them into a closure, demonstrably false. Fanny Price, however, the obedient daughter who replaces the ungovernable overseer, is pinioned in a conflict of searing and unresolvable tensions. So little room is available for repudiation of her place in Mansfield Park's social situation that it threatens to bind and fix her.[43] Ultimately the rebellious acts of Fanny Price and her ideological companions, Maria, Frances Price, and Frederick, are paradigmatic of slave resistance: Fanny Price signifies a bartered slave and the sign of the absent female slave. The deported Maria, in turn, is a variant of the marginalized Portsmouth family.

By contrast, Sir Thomas' authority is scarcely denied by the men of the text who fare somewhat differently. Each of them projects a part of that complex Sir Thomas, even the sybaritic Bishop Grant, symbolically linked to his malignant niece and nephew as Sir Thomas is linked to Mrs Norris. Despite debauchery, elder son Tom will take up his inheritance as does the foolish Rushworth, whose wealth and aristocratic status enable him to transcend a temporary setback. Henry Crawford continues to seduce women and Edmund settles down into married life.

Mansfield Park, then, I am arguing, is a post-abolition narrative that intertwines with a critique, conscious or unconscious, of gender relations. Although the text superficially presents itself at the end as an agreeable synthesis that has incorporated its contradictions—the hermeneutics of an attempted restoration of power—the text's relationship to emancipationist ideology creates the irrepressible contradictions and signals incompletion. As a colonialist script, it features epistemological ethnocentrism, blanks, ellipses, substitutions, and the homogenizing of silent slaves, occupying a space between old and new modes of discourse and agitation. It projects the end of an uncompromising proslavery lobby by fusing commentary on slaves and Anglo-Saxon women who are concurrently exhibiting forms of autonomy and powerlessness. Thus the reformed planter's voice in itself becomes a nullified force. His contradictory positions cancel themselves out. The indirectness of the commentary, moreover, indicates Jane Austen's temporary reluctance to sound the controversy over slavery into recognizable audibility. Not until *Emma* does she do so unmistakably.

As a quasi-allegory of colonial-gender relations, *Mansfield Park* offers itself as a blueprint for a new society of manners. Relationships in the colonies will match those at home, for domestic manners have been transformed for the better. But as we have seen, Sir Thomas' brand of eurocentric benevolence is dubious at best and the socio-political recommendations are decidedly and perhaps necessarily constrained. Nonetheless, the attempt to show the positive consequences of a kinder, gentler world in action, together with many potent silences and irruptions of nuanced subaltern voices, signifies the desirable, though possibly not attainable, transition to a new colonialist dispensation of gradualist politics at home and abroad. Despite this slow but positive evolution, however, emancipation still cannot be named.

Notes

1. Wylie Sypher, "The West-Indian as a 'Character' in the Eighteenth Century," in *Studies in Philology* vol. 36 (Chapel Hill: University of North Carolina Press, 1939), 504–5, 509.

2. Michael Craton, *Testing the Chains: Resistance to Slavery in the British West Indies* (Ithaca: Cornell University Press, 1982).

3. Elsa V. Goveia, *Slave Society in the British Leeward Islands at the End of the Eighteenth Century* (New Haven: Yale University Press, 1965). See also D. J. Murray, *The West Indies and the Development of Colonial Government 1801–1834* (Oxford: Clarendon Press, 1965); Dale Herbert Porter, *The Defense of the British Slave Trade, 1784–1807,* Dissertation, University of Oregon, June 1967, 25–166.

4. Mary Millard points out that Northampton squires were rarely sugar-planters and speculates that "an earlier Bertram married a lady who brought an estate in Antigua, as her dowry." Mary Millard, "1807 and All That," *Persuasions,* 50–1. I thank Professor Kenneth Moler for invaluable discussions on the question of Sir Thomas' slave-owning status.

5.   Sir Thomas probably belonged to the "outer ring" of absentee planters and merchants who had never visited the colonies. Between 1807 and 1833 forty-nine planters and twenty merchants belonged to this group. B. W. Higman, "The West India 'Interest' in Parliament 1807–1833," *Historical Studies* 13 (1967–69) 4, 1–19. See also Lowell Joseph Ragatz, *Absentee Landlordism in the British Caribbean, 1750–1833* (London: Bryan Edwards Press, n.d.), 1–19.

6.   Raymond Williams, *The Country and the City* (New York: Oxford University Press, 1973), 279–80.

7.   Sir George Stephen, *Anti-Slavery Recollections: in a Series of Letters Addressed to Mrs. Beecher Stowe, written by Sir George Stephen, at Her Request* (London: Frank Cass, 1971), 36–7. Note also that as a result of information about ongoing inhumane treatment, British abolitionists were shortly to publicize the condition of slaves in Antigua even more decisively in forming a committee for the "Neglected and Deserted Negroes" of that island. See John Rylands Memorial Library "The Case of the Neglected and Deserted Negroes in the Island of Antigua," pamphlet 21.5, pt. 8.

8.   Frank J. Klingberg, *The Anti-Slavery Movement in England. A Study in English Humanitarianism* (New Haven: Yale University Press, 1926), 131, 171–2. B. W. Higman, *Slave Populations of the British Caribbean, 1807–1834* (Baltimore: The Johns Hopkins University Press, 1984). See also James Walvin, "The rise of British popular sentiment for abolition 1787–1832," *Anti-Slavery, Religion, and Reform: Essays in Memory of Roger Anstey,* eds. Christine Bolt and Seymour Drescher (Folkestone: Dawson, 1980), 154 and *passim;* Sir George Stephen, *Anti-Slavery Recollections,* 25–27 and *passim.*

9.   Avrom Fleishman, *A Reading of Mansfield Park. An Essay in Critical Synthesis* (Minneapolis: University of Minnesota Press, 1967), 40–2.

10.   Fleishman, *A Reading of Mansfield Park,* 35–6.

11.   R. W. Chapman, *The Novels of Jane Austen. The Text based on Collation of the Early Editions,* vol. 3 (London: Oxford University Press, 1923), 30. Further references to *Mansfield Park* will be given in the text. The enormous chain of expenses that emanated from the Great House included a host of people from servants and overseers to waiters, "brownskin gals" of no official function, and the estate's managing attorney who received 60% of the gross. Michael Craton, *Sinews of Empire. A Short History of British Slavery* (New York: Anchor Books, 1974), 132–9.

12.   Fleishman, *A Reading of Mansfield Park,* 37. William B. Willcox touches briefly on the turmoil that would have precipitated Sir Thomas' decision, in *The Age of Aristocracy 1688–1830* (Lexington, MS: D. C. Heath and Company, 1971), 174–179. Willcox also points out that: "Though Miss Austen's two brothers were in the navy throughout the war, her world is untouched by anything outside itself; it is tranquil and timeless" (168). See also *Mansfield Park,* 65.

13.   With respect to Sir Thomas' "near-noble" status, Fleishman argues that "only some four hundred families could qualify for the higher class, and despite an economic fluidity which enabled some baronets and even commoners to enter it, this was an aristocracy composed mainly of noblemen" (40). Mrs. Flanders, *Antigua and the Antiguans: A Full Account of the Colony and its Inhabitants From the Time of the Caribs to the Present Day, Interspersed with Anecdotes and Legends. Also, an Impartial View of Slavery and the Free Labour Systems; the Statistics of the Island, and Biographical Notices of the Principal Families,* vol. 2 (London, 1844), 136.

14.   Sir George Stephen, *Anti-Slavery Recollections,* 8–19; Frank J. Klingberg, *The Anti-Slavery Movement in England,* 176–81.

15.   Chapman, *The Novels of Jane Austen,* 553–6.

16.   Frank Gibbon, "The Antiguan Connection: Some New Light on *Mansfield Park,*" in *The Cambridge Quarterly* 11 (1982), 303.

17.   Thomas Clarkson, *The History of the Rise, Progress, and Accomplishment of the Abolition of the African Slave-Trade by the British Parliament,* vol. 1 (London: 1808; rpt. Frank Cass, 1968),

378ff; 477ff. In reading Clarkson, Jane Austen would have been abreast of fierce abolitionist and pro-slavery infighting both inside and outside parliament and of the literature on the subject of the slave trade.

18. Clarkson, *History,* vol. 1, 479.

19. Johanna M. Smith, " 'My only sister now': Incest in *Mansfield Park,*" *Studies in the Novel* 19:1 (1987), 1–15.

20. Ruth Bernard Yeazell, "The Boundaries of Mansfield Park," in *Representations* 6 (1984), 133–152.

21. Tzvetan Todorov, *The Conquest of America. The Question of the Other,* trans. Richard Howard (New York: Harper & Row, 1982), 130.

22. In *Popular Tales* (1804) Maria Edgeworth, for example, has a story entitled "The Grateful Negro," that exemplifies exactly this familiar binary opposition. It is possible, given Jane Austen's admiration for Maria Edgeworth (Chapman, vol. 5, 299), that she had read some of Edgeworth's tales as well as her novels. Given the popularity of *The Farmer of Inglewood Forest* (1796) by Elizabeth Helme that also features a "grateful negro," Austen may well have read that novel or others featuring that motif.

23. *Mansfield Park,* 217. The connection of indolent house-mistresses despised by their authors frequently appears. Two examples are Lady Ellison in Sarah Robinson Scott's novel, *The History of George Ellison* (1766) and Mary Wollstonecraft's polemical attack on such practices in *A Vindication of the Rights of Woman* (1792).

24. Sypher, "The West Indian," 503, 506.

25. Ragatz, *Absentee Landlordism,* 1–21. Note also how Sir Thomas' "burnt, fagged, worn look" (178) matches signs of the contemporary West Indian in fiction. "A yellowish complexion, lassitude of body and mind, fitful spells of passion or energy, generosity bordering on improvidence, sentimentality combined with a streak of naughtiness and cruelty to subdeviates"; see also Sypher, *The West Indian,* 504.

26. *Lovers' Vows. A Play, in five acts. Performed at the Theatre Royal Covent-Garden. From the German of Kotzebue. by Mrs. Inchbald* (London, 1798) in Chapman, *The Novels of Jane Austen,* 475–538.

27. *Lovers' Vows,* 534.

28. Gibbon, "The Antiguan Connection," 298–305.

29. Gerald L. Gould, "The Gate Scene at Sotherton in *Mansfield Park,*" in *Literature and Psychology* 20:1 (1970), 75–8.

30. For the discussions of subjectivity and interpellation in ideology here and elsewhere in the essay, I am indebted to Michel Pêcheux, *Language, Semantics, and Ideology* (New York: St. Martin's Press, 1975).

31. I am assuming here and elsewhere in the text the reader's conversancy with *Lovers' Vows,* an assumption I think Jane Austen makes.

32. In *Discipline and Punish. The Birth of the Prison* (New York: Vintage Books, 1979), Michel Foucault argues that feudal torture of the criminal's body and subsequent death "made everyone aware . . . of the unrestrained presence [and power] of the sovereign. . . ." "The ceremony of the public torture and execution displayed for all to see the power relation that gave his force to the law. . . ." "We must regard the public execution, as it was still ritualized in the eighteenth century, as a political operation" (49–53).

33. Jane Austen, *Emma* (first published 1816) (Boston: The Riverside Press, 1933), 233.

34. See F. O. Shyllon, *Black Slaves in Britain* (London: Oxford University Press, 1974), especially 77–124 and 237–43. See also James Walvin, *The Black Presence. A documentary history on the negro in England, 1555–1860* (New York: Schocken Books, 1972), 95–114.

35. Margaret Krikham, *Jane Austen, Feminism and Fiction* (New York: Methuen, 1986), 116–119.

36.   I am indebted for the argument about the text's excess and unconsciousness to Pierre Macherey's *A Theory of Literary Production*, trans. Geoffrey Wall (London: Routledge & Kegan Paul, 1978), 75–97 and *passim*.

37.   Yeazell, "The Boundaries of *Mansfield Park*," 133.

38.   Craton, *Testing the Chains*, 337–8.

39.   *Mansfield Park*, 104. I would add data from the *Quarterly Review* to Chapman's list of sources for *Mansfield Park* and refashion his chronology of the novel from 1800–1809 accordingly.

40.   See *Quarterly Review*, 164.

41.   Pêcheux, *Language, Semantics and Ideology*, 13.

42.   I am thinking here of Edward Said's conceptualization of orientalizing in Chapter One, "The Scope of Orientalism," in *Orientalism* (New York: Vintage Books, 1979), and *passim*.

43.   Pêcheux, *Language, Semantics and Ideology*, 156–7.

The Self Contained: *Emma*

NANCY ARMSTRONG

In turning from *Pamela* to *Emma*, we turn from the expansive and heavily lit-
tered domain that Richardson carves out of the culture to the clean line of
Austen's minimalist art. Even though it conforms far more closely to what we
consider "the art of the novel," however, Austen's fiction is no less political for
achieving the self-enclosure that Richardson's writing lacks. It is clear that by
Austen's time, the female subject could step forth as an object of knowledge.
Unlike Richardson, who had to modify both fiction and conduct-book language to establish a category for domestic fiction, Austen was able to develop
finely nuanced differences within a stable framework of domestic relations.
Indeed, her novels bring to culmination a tradition of ladies fiction that con-
centrated on the finer points of conduct necessary to secure a good marriage—that is, on the minor indiscretions and good manners of respectable
people—rather than on the will and cunning it took to preserve one's chastity
from impending rape. Richardson used rape as the figure for an earlier class
sexuality. He contained it within his fiction where rape identified a self that
could not be violated. And by so doing, he used this woman to figure out a
new form of political resistance. Writing that posits such a distinctively modern notion of the self—Pamela's own record of the assaults on her sensibility—spells out the historical dilemma Richardson confronted as well. His
writing required the authorization of readers before it could lay claim to
truth. As if this authorization were one of the rites sanctifying Pamela's marriage into the gentry, Richardson has her walk among her husband's polite
circle of friends in the bizarre habit of a domestic saint. Bearing the letters
that tell the tale of her perseverance under the domination of a libertine master, she seeks public recognition as such a figure. Without it, the implication
is that her writing is nothing more than a record of subjective experience, a
thinly veiled wish (as indeed Fielding saw it) rather than an example that one
should use in negotiating reality. The woman is bound to her writing in a mutually authorizing relationship that awkwardly displays its circular nature in
the concluding episodes of the novel.

From *Desire and Domestic Fiction: A Political History of the Novel* by Nancy Armstrong. Copyright ©
1987 by Nancy Armstrong. Used by permission of Oxford University Press, Inc.

Much to Fielding's dismay, however, Richardson successfully introduced into fiction the highly fictional proposition that a prosperous man desired nothing so much as the woman who embodied domestic virtue. By Austen's time, this proposition had acquired the status of truth. It had usurped the body of rules as invoked by Mrs. Jewkes when rebuking Pamela for denying the master's natural dominion over the body of his servant girl. On this basis, it is fair to say that a novel like *Pride and Prejudice* began where *Pamela* ended, historically speaking, by opening with "a truth universally acknowledged, that a single man, in possession of a good fortune, must be in want of a wife." In representing the "wife" as a category that wanted to be filled rather than as a category of desire yet to be opened, fiction by definition no longer opposed truth, nor did it have to perform elaborate rites of self-authorization. For Austen obviously wrote to an audience who willingly granted fiction the status of a specialized kind of truth. The key to such authority was self-enclosure. Like Burney and the other lady novelists, Austen appeared more than willing to leave the rest of the world alone and deal only with matters of courtship and marriage. While Richardson introduced conduct-book materials into the novel as a strategy of conversion, then, novels of manners settled on various strategies of containment. They did not appear to work from inside the household to produce a text capable of revolutionizing its context. But by distinguishing her polite English from the linguistic materials that she inherited from earlier novelists, Austen's fiction achieved the same political objective even more effectively than Richardson's did.

Her novels deal with a closed community of polite country people who tend to be undistinguished by either great fortune or title. In such a community, social relations appear to be virtually the same thing as domestic relations. The community can therefore be represented in terms of a household and of a relationship among households in much the same manner as the graphic representation of various households offered by *The Compleat Servant*, a book of domestic economy written around the same time Austen was writing *Emma*.[1] As in the conduct books, the problems to be confronted in the world Austen depicts all have to do with the management of leisure time. Austen invariably resolves these problems by marrying off the eligible members within that community, which is to fix them to a role within a household among households, thereby stabilizing the community. She does this, furthermore, according to rules that are at least as rigorous, by psychological standards, as were the matters of dowry and family connections in determining marriages of convenience. She developed an intricately precise language for sexual relationships from the speech and behavior of polite country gentlefolk and did so, we should note, during the same period when the great migration to the cities was occurring. Thus it is a curious twist of cultural history that such a language as hers would help to create a standard for polite English that would be shared by the newly empowered groups who read novels. Only this specialized language, it appears, could set their particular kind of literacy apart from those above and below them on the social ladder and, at the same time, identify the particular interests of this class of people with those of the entire society. If one grants that Richardson's novel established a new role for literacy to play in constituting the individual, then we must see Austen's novels striving to empower a new class of people—not powerful people, but normal people—whose ability to interpret human behavior qualifies them to regulate the conduct of daily life and reproduce their form of individuality in and through writing.

In a manner unique to Richardson and the lady novelists of the late eighteenth century, Austen used fiction to create a community free of all traces of the regional, religious, social, or factional dialects that marked other kinds of writing.[2] At the beginning of the eighteenth century, Raymond Williams explains, the educational institutions for men were a very mixed lot, more so perhaps than at any other single moment in history. At the higher secondary or university-level schools established by Nonconformists after the Restoration, says Williams, "the curriculum begins to take its modern shape, with the addition of mathematics, geography, modern languages, and crucially, the physical sciences."[3] Of the nine grammar schools, "seven of them boarding institutions," he continues, all "kept mainly to the traditional curriculum of the classics, and, while less socially exclusive than they were to become, tended on the whole to serve the aristocracy and the squirarchy, on a national basis."[4] In addition to these schools, the upper classes observed the practice of tutoring at home, which was often followed by the Grand Tour of the Continent. According to Brian Simon, it was the mark of a gentleman "not to acquire any specialist knowledge; the aim was rather, acquaintance with polite literature through study of the classics."[5] The endowed grammar schools apparently varied according to locality, those in the urban areas showing some broadening of the curriculum toward practical disciplines under the influence of men in business and trade. "Of the three old professions, the clergy was still mainly served by the universities, while law and medicine were chiefly outside of them. Of the new professions, particularly in science, engineering, and arts," Williams concludes, "a majority of entrants were training outside the university as were most of the merchants and manufacturers."[6] Despite the signs of an increasingly practical curriculum at many levels of instruction and in different locales, the education of the middle ranks of early modern society appears to have comprised an extraordinarily heterogeneous field of learning. But what might strike us as a veritable babble of writing styles was probably, to the historically attuned ear, something more on the order of a finely graduated hierarchy of specialized languages.

These men were as distinguished from those who had a polite education as they were from the illiterate masses. At the same time, however, their learning served to mark differences among them rather than to create a coherent social character. If, as Williams claims, the point of educational institutions is always to train "the members of a group to the 'social character' or 'pattern of culture' which is dominant in the group or by which the group lives," then only the aristocracy and squirarchy could be said to possess such a character.[7] Through the eighteenth century and well into the nineteenth, the rest of the male population were not only set apart from the privileged group by what they knew, spoke, and wrote. They were set apart from one another as well. The language one used would have instantly identified him as a member of the Church of England or a Nonconformist, a student of the classical tradition of education as opposed to the practical curricula, or as part of the elite group of people who used polite English rather than some non-prestige dialect.

Austen follows the path cut through this tangle of speech patterns and writing styles by the female conduct books. At the same time, it must be said that Austen carries the project of creating the alternative standard of polite writing one step further. If Richardson uses Pamela's writing to transform the speech patterns of her community, then Austen gives writing a basis in the speech of polite country people. Her own prose displaces the mix of styles that would have more accurately represented society at large. For hers is a speech community that shares proper nouns but that, curiously enough, appears to be confused as to their relative value and the relations that should obtain among them. Thus she produces a prose style capable of displaying endless individual variants within polite spoken English. By means of conversation and gossip as well as the personal letter, such writing assigns motives and feelings to social behavior and, in this way, creates a psychological basis for its meaning. Such a prose style distinguishes one member of the speech community from another. At the same time, it places one individual in relation to another in terms of subjective features that are understood by the community as a whole. If this is to found a community on little else but a common language of the self, then language itself acquires unprecedented stability as Austen uses it to point to qualities inherent in the individual rather than to the accidents of fortune and birth.[8] Thus Austen's novels equate the formation of the ideal community with the formation of a new polite standard for English.

While Austen's fiction participates with earlier domestic novels in a single cultural project, we must still distinguish her work from earlier fiction because of the degree to which she grounds her ideal community upon communication.[9] Austen's objective is not to dispute the hierarchical principle underlying the old society, but to redefine wealth and status as so many signs that must then be read and evaluated in terms of the more fundamental currency of language: how much and how accurately do they communicate?[10] One finds that the major events in her novels are all based on faulty communication: Colonel Tilney's misreading of Catherine Morland's prospects as an heiress and her misreading of him as a husband and father; Darcy's first as opposed to his second letter to Elizabeth Bennet; the dramatic entertainments at Mansfield Park; and a series of such set pieces that make questions of conduct in *Emma* almost exclusively questions of interpretation. Consider, for instance, Emma's portrait of Harriet Smith, her interpretation of Mr. Elton's charade and of letters written by the other eligible young men in the novel, the defense of her misinterpretations in the face of Knightley's criticism, and her recognition of her true feelings for him. The procedures for reading and writing extend beyond the page to the dance floor and parlor. They suggest that sexual relations are, before anything else, a linguistic contract. And inasmuch as the novel confines its theater of action within a framework where social relations are determined by sexual relations, the linguistic contract is a social contract as well.

Austen's fiction plays out the Richardsonian thematics in which a female discourse struggles with that of the male for the power to represent individual identity. The heroine once again posits a notion of identity that is founded on gender differences rather than on the political distinctions to which men adhere and on which they base their authority. But several changes have occurred between the publication of *Pamela* and the writing of *Emma*. The gap between master and servant has narrowed down considerably to an elite group of individuals who are neither aristocrats nor laborers, nor even of the mercantile and industrial classes. At the same time, a whole spectrum of fine distinctions has opened up within this politically limited field. Among these are traditional political markers that designate one's source of income, the prestige of an estate and family name, one's future prospects, and the external signs of polish and education a person of means happens to display. Such social markings invoke the late eighteenth century country gentry which the previous century of economic fluctuation had made an extremely heterogeneous group. In such a group, an individual's social identity was no doubt very difficult to read. But in Austen one finds this situation complicated further; traditional status signs have been detached from their referent in some chain of economic dependency by a local communication system—gossip—which automatically converts this information into the stuff of subjective experience. On the basis of this information, for example, Mr. Knightley can say, " 'Elton is a very good sort of man, and a very respectable vicar of Highbury, but not at all likely to make an imprudent match. He knows the value of a good income as well as anybody. Elton may talk sentimentally, but he will act rationally.' " [11] Emma feels otherwise, and "more than a reasonable, becoming degree of prudence, she was very sure, did not belong to Mr. Elton" (p. 45).

Thus we see that—along with the social gap between male and female contenders—the differences in their manner of interpreting sexual behavior have dwindled considerably from those differentiating Mr. B's initial contract from Pamela's rejection and counter offer. Mr. Knightley and Emma differ only on the issue of the proportion of feeling to rationality that one should exercise in choosing a mate. Yet one feels great tension between the sexes in Austen's fiction all the same; her heroines are always seriously at odds with the men they eventually marry, and at stake in the conflict is always the basis for sexual exchange. In *Emma,* more so perhaps than in *Pride and Prejudice,* the struggle between male and female modes of representation is clearly not a struggle between two social classes. Of all the characters in this novel, Mr. Knightley and Emma are the most closely affiliated. And because they belong to the two oldest and best-propertied families in Highbury, their disagreement seems to be more a matter of personal differences—age, sex, and disposition—than one of politics. At the same time, they disagree about how individuals should find their appropriate place within the community, and their disagreement involves everyone in that community. Theirs is, in other words, precisely the issue distinguishing Tory from Whig during the eighteenth century. But when contained within a domestic framework and subjected to the outcome of courtship procedures, this political difference, as Austen imagines it, becomes one between the nineteenth century liberal and conservative positions.[12] No longer does the sexual contract constitute the terms for a conflict of classes so much as it identifies the poles of opinion within only one—literate—class. In contrast with Richardson who tends to obscure the difference between gentry and nobility, furthermore, Austen represents her elite group of country gentlefolk as one that adheres to domestic norms.

Of birth unknown and of subjective qualities as yet undecided, Harriet Smith offers the appropriate field for a debate that will determine the true signs of individual identity. The debate comprising the novel is set off, significantly, by two events that are both consequences of Emma's matchmaking. Her governess—a substitute for Emma's dead mother—takes up residence with her new husband, leaving Emma with unregulated leisure time on her hands and a supervisory position in her household to fill. The change gives her father cause to lament, " 'But my dear, pray do not make any more matches, they are silly things, and break up one's family circle grievously' " (p. 7). The terms of the debate are established as Emma prematurely takes on the role of domestic supervisor and turns to more matchmaking as the means by which to occupy her idle hours. She provides herself with a companion, Harriet Smith, whom she plans to educate:

> *She* would notice her; she would improve her; she would detach her from her bad acquaintance, and introduce her into good society; she would form her opinions and her manners. It would be an interesting, and certainly a very kind undertaking; highly becoming her own situation in life, her leisure, and powers. (p. 14)

Emma believes that education can make the woman by perfecting her manners and sensibility: " 'That she is a gentleman's daughter, is indubitable to me; that she associates with gentlemen's daughters, no one, I apprehend, will deny' " (p. 41). Mr. Knightley evaluates Harriet according to a male system of values: " 'She is the natural daughter of nobody knows whom, with probably no settled provision at all, and certainly no respectable relations' " (p. 40). Thus a struggle ensues to determine who—male or female—has the power to interpret the female accurately. Emma insists on the authority inhering in her gender: "She did not repent what she had done; she still thought herself a better judge of such a point of female right and refinement than he could be" (p. 43). In effect, she takes up the position of Pamela in arguing for Harriet's intrinsic worth, just as Knightley assumes Mr. B's role when he claims that people should marry at their own social level. He makes this claim on the basis of gender; he assumes that as a male he should establish the standard of reasonableness. When Emma questions this manly prerogative on grounds that men regard beauty and a pleasant disposition as " 'the highest claims a woman would possess,' " Knightley quickly seizes the logical advantage: " 'My word, Emma, to hear you abusing the reason you have, is almost enough to make me think so too. Better be without sense, than misapply it as you do' " (p. 42).

Richardson granted full authority to the female position in this debate, which allowed him to assert a new language of the self over and against a tradition of male writing that identified individuals first on the basis of their status. Austen qualifies the power Emma claims for language to constitute individuality, but in the conflict between male and female modes of interpretation, as Austen stages it, the female does not capitulate to the male code that authorizes social status. For her, status seems to matter as much as the essential qualities of a person. As a result, signs of political distinction are transformed to point not to the object represented so much as to the person who uses the signs. This may seem an overly subtle distinction, but it is nevertheless a profound one. By creating this distinction between representation and the object represented, Austen calls into being a set of rules—a grammar—that seems to be already there. The grammar is one she creates through usage which appears to violate the rules of grammar, but which she ultimately makes those rules contain.

Emma's failure to match Harriet Smith with Mr. Elton undermines the interpretive strategies of a male who attaches identity too firmly to social status. His rejection of Harriet on grounds of unknown lineage amounts to intolerable rudeness and places Elton among the characters who rank very low on Emma's scale of politeness. All by itself, Elton's concern for social status would not condemn him to such a position. Although Mr. Knightley's impeccable manners prevent him from endorsing a mix of what he calls "levels," this same notion of politeness requires him to tolerate such violations of traditional order when they occur. But in seeking a wife who enhances his status in the community, Elton does something a truly polite person would never do. He overvalues the income a woman will bring to a marriage and thus undervalues her as a woman. Although Emma believes that Harriet's sweetness of temper and ready compliance should be sufficient for someone of Elton's stature, Harriet has no value in his eyes if a gentle disposition and pleasant appearance are indeed all she offers. In his words, " 'Everyone has their level; but as for myself, I am not, I think, quite so much at a loss. I need not so totally despair of an equal alliance, as to be addressing myself to Miss Smith!' " (p. 151).

The apparent disparity between the social status and true value of an individual is no more disruptive than Emma's own abuse of language that misplaces the individual in the world of Highbury by undervaluing social status and endorsing the claims of desire over those of tradition and custom. For committing this female error of reading character, Emma must chastise herself:

> "Here have I," said she, "actually talked poor Harriet into being very much attached to this man. She might never have thought of him with hope, if I had not assured her of his attachment, for she is as modest and humble as I used to think him." (p. 155)

In this case, misreading entails a miswriting of sexual relations that misleads desire. More specifically, in representing Mr. Elton as a fit mate for Harriet, Emma has ignored their obvious social differences. As Austen was perfectly aware, this abuse of language was the vice for which novels, as well as the women who read them, were traditionally condemned. Ironically, too, it was to resist the tyranny of fixed social status signs that Richardson had Pamela steadfastly resist Mr. B's advances until he no longer lusted for her sensuous body and desired instead the qualities of mind that she displayed in her writing, writing, it should be noted, that she carefully concealed. Austen takes a critical stance toward just this kind of writing in order to produce a far more complicated situation in which representation constitutes a form of agency in its own right. In this way, she raises the question of how language may provide an accurate indication of an individual's value.

It is Emma's painting of Harriet rather than Harriet herself that attracts Mr. Elton to Emma, creating a triangulated situation where signs of the self have a seductive power independent of their author or referent. This is how Emma intends her painting to mediate relations between object and observer:

> The sitting was altogether very satisfactory; she was quite enough pleased with the first day's sketch to wish to go on. There was no want of likeness, she had been fortunate in the attitude, and as she meant to throw a little improvement into the figure, to give a little more height, and considerably more elegance, she had great confidence of its being in every way a pretty drawing at last, and of its filling its destined place with credit to them both—a standing memorial of the beauty of one, the skill of the other, and the friendship of both; with as many agreeable associations as Mr. Elton's very promising attachment was likely to add. (p. 30)

Elton values the portrait of Harriet, not because it is a portrait of Harriet, but because it embodies Emma's sense of elegant proportions, as well as her superior taste and eye. She uses representation to create the subject represented, but her power of representation gets out of control. It renders Harriet a life-less unlikeness while attracting the gaze to Emma herself: "he [Elton] was ready at the smallest intermission of the pencil, to jump up and see the progress, and be charmed" (p. 30). But a Pygmalion she is nevertheless, for Emma's use of language creates desire where none would otherwise have existed. Matchmaking is for Austen simply another word for fiction-making.

The addition of the element of language as an agent in its own right revises the struggle between male and female that one encounters in *Pamela*. Harriet has not only been led to misconstrue Mr. Elton's feelings, thanks to Emma's representation of their relationship. Mr. Elton has been inspired to misread Emma's feelings as well. He believes that though she is above him in the social register, her emotions incline her to value him as highly as if he were on a level with her. The problem in both instances of misreading is the same. It arises in Austen's fiction whenever desire overrules the dictates of one's relative social position, whenever, that is, the female mode of interpretation works in opposition to that of the male. Indeed, it is precisely as such a contradiction of gendered interpretations that Emma understands the moment of terrible stress and embarrassment when Elton proposes to her, his social superior, instead of to Harriet: "If *she* had so misinterpreted his feelings, she had little right to wonder that *he*, with self-interest to blind him, should have mistaken hers" (p. 93). It must be noted, however, that even though Austen exposes the fallacy in Richardson's egalitarian fantasy by having such fiction as his lead her heroine astray, she still carries forth the same project in which both he and the conduct books for women are implicated. True, the problem, as Emma ponders it, is a conflict between essential qualities of the self ("feelings") and traditional social signs (what Elton believes to be in his "self-interest"). What is more, Elton has erred, not only because he thought too much like a male, but also because he fell into female strategies that legit-imize feelings over and above one's social position. But Emma's fiction has, all the same, adopted these conflicting modes of interpretation and made them, as in Richardson's fiction, the basis for negotiating a contract in which gender ("his" and "hers") matters more than social signs of identity so long as social signs are designated as the domain of the male.

That Harriet Smith occasions all the semantic mismatching she does is due to the surplus of information generated by the debate over her character, which has become subject to the fictions of others. She is, like gossip itself, of anonymous origins. She has only natural beauty and a female education to recommend her. The narrator makes certain we know she comes from nowhere else but "an honest, old-fashioned boarding school, where a reason-able quantity of accomplishments were sold at a reasonable price, and where girls might be sent to be out of the way and scramble themselves into a little education, without any danger of coming back prodigies" (p. 13). In Harriet, Austen represents the woman of the conduct books whose value appears to be entirely self-generated. Like Pamela in this respect, Harriet provides the site for a mode of representation that disentangles the operations of love from relationships based on one's social station. In contrast with earlier authors of the domestic woman, however, Austen does not empower this woman to author herself. Harriet becomes the means of questioning the individual's power of writing in relation to conditions for speech that have been established by a community. She provides the means for calling attention both to the conventions that already define an individual's place in the community and to the changes that individuals may effect by making innovative use of those conventions.[13] She becomes, in other words, a way of introducing a paradox resembling the one that troubled Samuel Johnson as he pondered the relationship between grammar and usage within the speech community. Johnson claimed he was prompted to compile his *Dictionary* because English was changing so rapidly that, without some standardization of meaning, the writing of his day would be unintelligible to the next generation. But the attempt to standardize usage introduced risks of another kind. Ultimately, as Johnson conceded, the strength and longevity of a language resides in its ability to accommodate new uses in which it necessarily acquires new meaning.

Thus having raised this paradox by the insertion of extra information in the system, *Emma* proceeds to destabilize the language of the self by means of an entirely different strategy. Again, Austen disrupts communication by introducing an extra female of ambiguous status in the community. In the case of Jane Fairfax, however, it is a deficiency rather than a surplus of information that causes the problem. Jane's emotional life is contained within her impassive exterior rather than inscribed upon her appearance and behavior for others to read. It is this quality of Jane's for which "Emma could not forgive her. Wrapt up in a cloak of politeness, she seemed determined to hazard nothing. She was disgustingly, was suspiciously reserved" (p. 113). This particular imbalance in the composition of the sign produces the sense that there is much more happening beneath the surface of social identity than speech can adequately represent. This would seem to be the point of the triangulated desire of Emma, Frank Churchill, and Jane, where it is not an excess but a deprivation of signifiers that produces false desire. For sexual relations are declared by the slightest gesture or the briefest glance in such a communication situation, and the contention between the male and female modes of interpretation therefore assumes a very different form.

In the following exchange between Frank Churchill and Emma, the twin problems of suppression and disclosure overlap; there is at once too much and too little information revealed. His speech approaches the point of exposing his true feelings, whereupon hers intervenes and stifles his confession:

> He looked at her, as if wanting to read her thoughts. She hardly knew what to say. It seemed like the forerunner of something absolutely serious, which she did not wish. Forcing herself to speak, therefore, in the hope of putting it by, she calmly said. . . . (p. 265)

At this point, the problem with language in the novel, despite what Emma surmises, is not a matter of how to prevent the male in question from indiscriminate speech. The capacity to unleash asocial desire was, we should recall, the basis on which conduct books so strenuously objected to novels. It is therefore historically significant when a novel such as this no longer seeks authorization by opposing the seduction of other fiction, but calls upon fiction for a more complete representation of desire. Were Emma to let it happen in the instance cited above, the mediation of speech would provide an instrument for establishing polite relationships where they do not already exist. Where Frank Churchill is concerned, her moments of stress and embarrassment arise strictly out of her ignorance of his emotional attachment to Jane Fairfax, information that Emma suppresses by silencing him. It is as if, having condemned fiction-making as the source of unruly desire, Austen's novel can call upon fiction as a means of solving the problem that fiction itself has produced. Given its nature, this problem calls for linguistic reform.

It is worth noting how writing comes under suspicion in the process of such reform. Mr. Elton's preciously penned charade characterizes him as a man of class pretensions and mercenary concerns. To communicate love in highly figurative terms as he does is, in Austen's terms, to offer the signs of passion with a lack of emotional depth. Although Emma describes it as " 'a very proper compliment!,' " she does not concur with Harriet that Elton's poem is, " 'without exception, the best charade I ever read.' " Instead, she claims she " 'never read one more to the purpose, certainly' "(p. 51). In saying this, Emma contradicts herself, for she also confesses that she does " 'not consider its length as particularly in its favour. Such things in general cannot be too short' " (p. 52). I would like to take note of the procedures that, despite such observations, allow Emma so to misconstrue Mr. Elton's meaning, for these offer an important reversal of the sentimental translation of biblical verse I discussed in relation to *Pamela*. Emma interprets Elton's poem allegorically, creating a personal sentimental meaning to complement general political terms. Such an allegorical reading, we might recall, is perfectly in keeping with the conduct book's suggestions about the proper use of classical mythology and history within a female curriculum. But Elton's verse refuses to be nudged and coaxed into a sentimental meaning despite the fact the charade itself invites such usage. Although Emma confidently translates the first and second verses into "court" and "ship" respectively, these terms remain stubbornly affixed to a political motivation. To lend them any other meaning is to misconstrue not only the true object but also the very nature of Elton's desire:

To Miss
CHARADE

My first displays the wealth and pomp of kings,
Lords of the earth! their luxury and ease.

> Another view of man, my second brings,
> Behold him there, the monarch of seas!
>
> But, ah! united, what reverse we have!
> Man's boosted power and freedom, all are flown;
> Lord of the earth and sea, he bends a slave,
> And woman, lovely woman, reigns alone.
>
> (p. 48)

As a component of this novel, the poem is the more brilliant for being composed entirely of clichés. It represents sexual relations as a power struggle, and in claiming that "woman" makes of sovereign "man" a "slave," it dramatizes a refusal of meaning to be feminized. Although Emma considers herself to be "quite mistress of the lines," her sentimental interpretation simply conceals their meaning, which is all on the surface. Elton is hardly enthralled by the lowly Harriet but means to rise to the station of Emma herself. In the lines of this benighted man, sexual desire has not been sufficiently detached from power to be love, and no amount of interpretive ingenuity on Emma's part can make it so.

But this sentimental misreading of Elton's poem is one part of a twofold error that also entails her failure to understand the sincere feeling displayed in Robert Martin's letter. It is a mark of Emma's ignorance as a reader, then, that she fails to discern the superior self-worth in Robert Martin's plain style or to understand how its ability to communicate emotion so clearly to Harriet designates him as the right man for her to marry. For such writing suggests that it is Harriet herself—distinct and apart from any social identity—that he values. Again, the traditional categories of writing prove misleading, for just as men supposedly use grandiloquent expression to persuade, tradition would have it that they use the plain style for purposes of logical argument. Thus when Harriet asks if Robert's is " 'a good letter? or is it too short?,' " Emma replies "rather slowly,"

> "—so good a letter, Harriet, that every thing considered, I think one of his sisters must have helped him. I can hardly imagine the young man whom I saw talking with you the other day could express himself so well, if left quite to his own power, and yet it is not the style of a woman; no, certainly, it is too strong and concise; not diffuse enough for a woman. No doubt he is a sensible man, and I suppose may have a natural talent for—thinks strongly and clearly—and when he takes a pen in hand, his thoughts naturally find proper words." (p. 33)

I dwell on the analyses of style contained within Austen's novel because they are her means of raising the whole question of writing and what constitutes the polite style.

In his discussion of John Ward's lectures on rhetoric, Wilbur Howell calls attention to an interesting corruption of classical categories that occurred in many eighteenth century treatises on rhetoric. Of Ward's lectures on the plain, middle, and high styles, Howell contends, "These treatises intended the distinction to mean that different subjects require different treatments, and that true excellence in oratory consists not in cultivating the grand style at the expense of the plain but in being always able to command the three styles as the subjects demand." In borrowing the Ciceronian categories, however, rhetorical treatises such as Ward's—which grew rapidly in number along with female conduct books during the second half of the eighteenth century—adapted that "part of Latin rhetoric which gave the tropes and figures such an interminable emphasis as to discredit by implication the rhetorical function of plainness."[14] Without saying so explicitly, Howell's analysis demonstrates how the styles of oratory ranked writing according to its implicit familiarity with Latin texts; written usage of rhetoric maintained a political hierarchy, in other words, quite at odds with the classical principles of rhetoric as eighteenth century theory drew them from Cicero's *Orator.* According to Ward,

> Now each of these parts of an orator's province require [sic] a different stile. The low stile is most proper for proof and information. Because he has no other view here, but to represent things to the mind in the plainest light, as they really are in themselves, without coloring or ornament. The middle stile is most suited for pleasure and entertainment, because it consists of smooth and well turned periods, harmonious numbers, with florid and bright figures. But the sublime is necessary in order to sway and influence the passions.[15]

Thus it is highly significant that Austen should put the most admirable pen in the hand of a man of the "yeomanry," as Emma calls Robert Martin, rather than in that of a woman, as Richardson does. By means of Elton's charade, she declares the high style to be little more than pretension by attributing it to a man "without any alliances but in trade" (p. 93). But most telling of all in Austen's subtle critique is the failure of the high style of writing to translate into effective speech: "for with all his good and agreeable qualities, there was a sort of parade in his speeches which was very apt to incline her to laugh" (p. 56).

By means of Frank Churchill's letters, on the other hand, Austen introduces what Emma's former governess regards as "one of the best gentleman's hands I ever saw" (p. 202). In this case, Mr. Knightley proves a stern critic, however. He regards with suspicion the verbal decorum that comes from an elite education, since the man in question does not carry out his words in other forms of behavior. " 'It is Frank Churchill's duty to pay this attention to his father.' " Knightley argues, " 'He knows it to be so, by his promises and messages; but if he wished to do it, it might be done' " (p. 99). On another occasion, Knightley compares the gentleman's hand to "woman's writing," and only when Churchill's letter arrives to confess finally the extent of his in-

volvement with Jane Fairfax does this suspicion give way to qualified approbation. Knightley feels that at least the young man has begun to subordinate
style to truth in his writing: " 'Mystery; Finesse—how they pervert the understanding! My Emma, does not every thing serve to prove more and more
the beauty of truth and sincerity in all our dealings with each other?' " (p.
307). Writing has truth value in Knightley's critique only when it proves consistent with the other modes of an individual's behavior—particularly
speech—rather than with the class that individual comes from or aspires to.
Because Austen has introduced all this writing into *Emma* as an agent of social
disruption, we must regard such critical commentary as central to the strate-
gic intention of the novel. The novel contains other writing than fiction, I am
suggesting, to establish the novel as a new standard for writing. The preferred style of writing has its source in common English and derives its value
from its capacity to communicate the author's feelings without inflating or
concealing them; it has all the advantages of a stable currency. In terms of the
reigning system of values, however, Martin's writing ranks below the styles of
both Elton and Churchill. It ranks below theirs because male writing bears
the mark of the author's political position and indicates that Martin occupies
a lower place in the social world than either Elton or Churchill.

It is no wonder, then, that Austen turns away from writing and from the
materials of a male education in order to produce the linguistic reforms that
will eventually authorize Robert Martin's style of writing. Nor is it any wonder that she turns to gossip and conversation, which are speech modes identified with the female, when she wants to put forth a kind of writing that reveals the true qualities of the individual. It is important to mention that, in
addition to making fiction, Emma is less than conscientious in observing the
strictures of female education. As a girl, she drew up " 'a great many lists . . .
at various times of books that she meant to read regularly through—and very
good lists they were,' " according to Knightley, " 'very well chosen, and very
neatly arranged—sometimes alphabetically, and sometimes by some other
rule' " (p. 23). Like her inability to complete a painting, her failure to read
may be initially regarded as a flaw, but because of Austen's apparently critical
attitude toward written culture, Emma's lack of diligence in this respect
proves a virtue, a refusal to be written by culture.[16]

By the end of the novel, literacy is no longer represented in such (conduct-book) terms. It is not acquired from writing at all but through mastery
of the rules for polite speech. In renouncing the figures of fiction that invariably generate desire where none should be, Emma's speech acquires a kind of
politeness that represents emotional truth more accurately than writing presumably ever could. The model for this kind of speech is none other than that
which unfolds with the novel's first asseveration: "Emma Woodhouse, handsome, clever, and rich, with a comfortable house and happy disposition,
seemed to unite some of the best blessings of existence; and had lived nearly
twenty-one years in the world with very little to distress or vex her." Such a

statement appears to constitute writing that derives from speech rather than from writing. The speech is the speech of the parlor where behavior is observed and regulated, and the writing derived from that speech is a form of writing that uses gossip with all the force and precision of a diagnostic instrument. The novel's second major pronouncement on Emma's situation illustrates such use of this language: "The *real* evils indeed of Emma's situation were the power of having *rather too much* her own way, and a disposition to think *a little too well* of herself; these were disadvantages which threatened to alloy her many enjoyments" (p. 1, italics mine). How different these fine anomalies in an otherwise comfortable life are from the perils to body and soul which Pamela has to encounter.

If the hierarchy among styles of masculine writing creates a gap between writing and speech in this novel, then the hierarchy among styles of feminine speech effaces these differences between speech and writing. The writing that is closest to speech places an author low in a hierarchy of writing, but it is precisely the kind of English modeled on speech that identifies the well-educated woman. We might say that Austen attaches gender to writing in order to create a disjunction between writing and speech. Such disjunction always constitutes a serious crisis in the organization of her fictive communities. Producing this crisis allows her not only to valorize a new kind of writing based on polite speech, but also, and more importantly, it enables her to situate speech logically prior to writing. In this way, she uses speech to authorize her preferred style of writing on grounds that the source of speech, unlike that of writing, resides in the individual. And as she establishes this as the basis for the truth value of writing, Austen also grants priority to the verbal practices of women, women who may never carry out programs of reading literature, but who are nevertheless essential to maintaining polite relationships within the community.

To have the authority of language that comes straight from the heart, however, women's speech must be purified of all traces of writing. Thus it is early on in the novel that Austen has Emma renounce her novelistic practices:

> It was foolish, it was wrong to take so active a part in bringing any two people together. It was adventuring too far, assuming too much, making light of what ought to be serious, a trick of what ought to be simple. She [Emma] was quite concerned and ashamed, and resolved to do such things no more. (p. 83)

There is a special element of irony in this statement. For even as she has Emma renounce the strategies of fiction-making, Austen condemns her heroine to think out social relationships over and over again in terms of imaginary narratives. It is by this process that Emma develops a language that will enable her not only to express but also to know her own feelings, and such knowledge is the precondition for avoiding the pitfalls entailed in misrepresenting the feelings of others. Thus the novel produces a reliable language of the self by the curiously backward process of allowing its heroine to repeat her misreading of sexual relations until she knows her own feelings. Accordingly, Mr. Knightley recognizes two spirits in Emma, a " 'vain spirit' " that prompts her fiction-making and a " 'serious spirit' " that understands the violations of truth as they occur. " 'If one leads you wrong, I am sure the other tells you of it,' " he explains (p. 225). It is in such a dialectic with fiction-making that the self-regulating voice is produced, a voice, paradoxically, that becomes virtually indistinguishable from the voice of the novelist by the end of the novel.

In drawing this relationship between gender and truth, I want to isolate a political move that distinguishes Austen from Richardson. Like Richardson, Austen represents the struggle between various modes of representation as a struggle between male and female, but for Austen the female requires reform at least as much as—often more than—the male. In view of the fact that this struggle is all about language, it is fair to conclude that Austen is not out to seize cultural authority, as Richardson was when he put Pamela in charge of Mr. B's country estate. Emma is already too much in charge of the house when the novel opens. Left with too much leisure time on her hands, Emma naturally inclines toward matchmaking. With the influx of the Eltons and the Churchills and the decline of the Bates, the power to regulate sexual relations, Austen suggests, is quite as complex as it is powerful, and it requires a far more subtle means of standardization than Richardson offered by means of his dialogue between male and female. In those instances when fiction is allowed to proceed unrestrained, words behave promiscuously, and the power Emma inherits as the woman of the house proves disruptive. On the other hand, whenever she renounces the power of speech to constitute desire, she acquires another form of power, which influences even Mr. Knightley. Of Emma's long-withheld approval of Harriet's engagement to Robert Martin, he remarks, " 'You are materially changed since we last talked on this subject before.' " But upon Emma's admission, " 'I hope so—for at that time I was a fool,' " he accedes to her former interpretation of Harriet's character: " 'And I am changed also; for I am now very willing to grant you all Harriet's good qualities' " (p. 327). Thus, as in Pamela, male and female echo one another in a mutually authorizing relationship.

In *Emma*, however, the transformation is a double one whereby he acknowledges the value of an unextraordinary woman such as Harriet and she understands the uncommon value of the common man. The conflict between male and female did not require the conversion of the one to the other's system of values after all; it simply required finding the right kind of currency to represent what was in the interest of both. Knightley's speech is a renunciation of the conventional language of love: " 'I cannot make speeches, Emma,'—he soon resumed; and in a tone of such sincere, decided, intelligible tenderness as was tolerably convincing.—'If I loved you less, I might be able to talk about it more. But you know what I am.—You hear nothing but truth from me' " (p. 296). However faltering the terms in which she has Knightley confess his true feelings for Emma, Austen proves yet more withholding when it is Emma's turn to reply. On this occasion, the voice of the novelist completely supplants that of the lover: "she spoke then, on being so entreated.—What did she say?—Just what she ought, of course. A lady always does. She said enough to show there need not be despair—and to invite him to say more himself" (p. 297). At this moment in the novel when there seems to be an absence of words, one has the sense of language reborn, not borrowed and used, as it emerges directly from the individuals in question, word by word, each loaded at last with real meaning, because each is fixed to a feeling that already exists before the individual finds words and occasion to pronounce it. This is the language of pure desire uncolored by any form of value other than its own. It discloses the core of the individual, at least of individuals who have such a core, and the core of the novel as well, that is, the motivations that all along have been silently shaping behavior.

Although Austen suggests that writing should imitate speech because speech comes straight from the self, the novel itself operates according to an entirely different principle. To ground desire in a self that exists prior to language, Austen has to disclose areas in the self that have not yet been spoken. To be present before it is spoken, desire has to be inscribed within the individual. That is to say it has to be written.

As the reader first encounters her, Emma feels no sense of deficiency, even though, as the narrator says, she has "the power of having rather too much her own way, and a disposition to think a little too well of herself" (p. 1). The novelist grants Knightley authority to read the human character—authority that is nearly equal to her own—on grounds that he "was one of the few people who could see faults in Emma Woodhouse, and the only one who ever told her of them" (p. 5). But it is only the novelist who can turn Emma's self-sufficiency into a deficiency that instigates desire independent of a social origin. If early on Emma speaks of herself as a most complete individual, Austen writes this speech as the lack of a lack, the absence of Emma's awareness that she is missing something as a female. Austen situates the fact of gender prior to speech by making Emma's speech reveal as writing the very truth it denies as speech. As she confesses to Harriet,

> "I have *none* of the usual inducements of women to marry. Were I to fall in love, indeed, it would be a different thing! but I *never* have been in love; it is *not* my way, or my nature; and I do *not* think I ever shall. And, without love, I am sure I should be a fool to change such a situation as mine. Fortune *I do not want;* employment *I do not want;* consequence *I do not want;* I believe few married women are half as much mistress of their husband's house as I am of Hartfield; and so always first and always right in any man's eyes as I am in my father's."
> (p. 58, italics mine)

By giving her heroine such perfection through the possession of every material thing and every social prerogative that ever a polite person could want, Austen creates deficiency on another level. It is the same order of deficiency that prompts Emma to insult Miss Bates and thereby inspire Knightley's harshest indictment: " 'How could you be so unfeeling to Miss Bates?' " (p. 258). In similar fashion, Austen attributes the smallest lapse in social decorum to a failure within the individual, a flaw which she identifies as a defect of gender.

When understood as such, each lapse in turn gives rise to some form of subjectivity appropriate to a female. Thus it is by linking Harriet with Mr. Knightley in her most socially outrageous act of mismatching that Emma is finally shot through with genuinely monogamous desire. Again, it is by creating an absence that her fiction, like the novel itself, calls forth a desire that is gendered and that therefore, by implication, is genuine: "Til now that she was threatened with its loss, Emma had never known how much of her happiness depends on being *first* with Mr. Knightley, first in interest and affection" (p. 285). From this awareness come the first signs of utterly genuine feeling that establish relations between Emma and Knightley, a union that magically stabilizes the community. Why this depends on the production of female desire becomes clear when we examine the impact of such feeling. Emma's desire for Knightley manifests itself in two ways. She becomes her own disciplinarian—far less indulgent than the gently ironic novelist—as she subjects herself to Mr. Knightley's standard of conduct: "She was most sorrowfully indignant; ashamed of every sensation but the one revealed to her—her affection for Mr. Knightley—Every other part of her mind was disgusting" (p. 284). As she rises in her own esteem to meet this standard, however, she also grows far more tolerant (as the novelist is) of others' failings.

It is when she turns her critical eye on herself, not when she tries to regulate the feelings of others, that Emma becomes the very figure of politeness. As the essential quality of the new aristocrat—so closely akin to charity, on the one hand, and to condescension, on the other, yet utterly unlike them in the complex of emotions from which it springs—politeness hangs in the balance in Emma's gravest crime, a nearly imperceptible act of rudeness toward the tiresome Miss Bates. As Mr. Knightley explains the nature of this crime to Emma, politeness emerges as the model for feelings, speech, and social behavior:

> "Her situation should secure your compassion. It was badly done indeed—You, whom she had known from an infant, whom she had seen grow up from a period when her notice was an honour, to have you now, in thoughtless spirits, and the pride of the moment, laugh at her, humble her—and before her niece, too—and before others, many of whom (certainly *some*) would be entirely guided by *your* treatment of her." (p. 257)

It is more than a little interesting to note that in order to fill the model Mr. Knightley sketches out for her, Emma must not only learn that she desires, but must also suppress the aggravation she feels towards women she cannot absolutely control. That Emma is so transformed in the course of the novel suggests that the acquisition of this form of literacy is the same as the formation of a nineteenth century individual. The individual is, by her very nature, unformed and in want of perfection.

To work this modification upon the Richardsonian model is to put a double edge to the power of example. If to be real is to deviate from the type, then to perfect oneself is to modify the type in aspiring to fulfill it. For one can observe the shift in Austen's emphasis away from natural virtue as the quality a woman exemplifies to a more complex understanding of subjectivity and the part example plays in shaping it. Emma's problem, as the narrator notes in the second statement of the novel, originates in her absent mother. Because her "mother had died too long ago for her to have more than an indistinct remembrance of her caresses," she was raised by a woman who "had fallen little short of a mother in affection," but who allowed Emma to have "rather too much her own way" and "to think a little too well of herself" (p. 1). While there is no lack of nurturant figures in her world (if anything, there are too many), it is the self-regulatory function missing along with the mother that is significant, and it is this which Emma acquires in learning that she loves Mr. Knightley. It is also in taking on this particular feature of gender that her example will maintain polite relations within the community rather than breed disrespect and induce mutability.

Austen's novel castigates behavior that has been prompted by social motivation—Emma's low regard for Martin, Knightley's for Harriet, Elton's for Harriet, as well as Emma's for Miss Bates. It makes such motivation, which dominates the behavior of the new Mrs. Elton, into the distinctive feature of the nouveaux riches and a false basis, therefore for genteel behavior. By allowing the linguistic surface of relationships to be misread on repeated occasions, however, the novel inscribes the traditional signs of status within a domestic framework where they obey a new principle of political economy. That is, both men and women acquire status within an economy of conduct in which verbal behavior—their use of these signs—is paramount. The more prolifically they spend words, the less concealed and thus the less misinterpreted their feelings become, which is to say that the true nature of the self becomes more exposed. This is as true of Augusta Elton as it is of Harriet Smith and Miss Bates, even though the latter two ladies expose a self more benign and genial. Yet despite the sense of innocence generated by Miss Bates's redundancy, she is all on the surface, her meaning too readily apparent. That she leaves nothing for one to interpret is confirmed by a glance through any edition of *Emma*, which identifies the places seamlessly filled with her speech as pages one can afford to skim over quickly. The relative value of signified to signifier is just the reverse in the case of Jane Fairfax whose self-containment requires elaborate strategies of reading. On her behavior in respect to Frank Churchill, for example, Mr. Knightley muses,

> He could not understand it; but there were symptoms of intelligence between them—he thought so at least—symptoms of admiration on his side, which, having once observed, he could not persuade himself to think entirely void of meaning, however he might wish to escape any of Emma's errors of imagination. (p. 234)

For all the aesthetic value that seems to accompany the withholding of feelings, however, Jane's manner of conduct no more represents the ideal than Miss Bates's. " 'Jane Fairfax has feeling,' said Mr. Knightley—'I do not accuse her of want of feeling. Her sensibilities, I suspect, are strong—and her temper excellent in its power of . . . self control; but it wants openness' " (p. 195). Just because her true feelings are barely discernible, Jane, like Harriet, gives rise to impolite fictions. These narrative possibilities indeed break into the novel and destabilize the exchange of information that constitutes social relations themselves. Polite speech is not simply a psychological function—that point where candor meets discretion—but a medium of exchange, a form of currency that alone ensures a stable community.

I use these terms in an effort to lend the novel's self-enclosure a materiality it cannot achieve within conventional literary classifications. I use the notion of economic exchange to suggest that this novel dramatizes a linguistic exchange which it reproduces outside the framework of fiction as the conditions for reading the novel. Austen uses the traditional signs of social status to show how they wreak havoc among the members of her community if they have the power to define individuals. But communication is confused and the community disrupted just as surely when status signs are ignored. In this way, Austen demonstrates that these signs do not operate effectively within traditional rhetorical categories or within the reigning grammar of social identity. She slips signs of status into a new system of meaning, and by such usage, detaches them from a context. Through a plot consisting of repeated errors to the one (male) side and the other (female), Austen creates rules based on her usage. This grammar falls into place as such with the perfection of communication between Knightley and Emma:

> While he spoke, Emma's mind was most busy, and, with all the wonderful velocity of thought, had been able—and yet without losing a word—to catch and comprehend the exact truth of the whole; to see that Harriet's hopes had been entirely groundless, a mistake, a delusion, as complete a delusion of any of her own—that Harriet was nothing; that she was everything herself; that what she had been saying relative to Harriet had been all taken as the language of her own feelings. (p. 296)

Thus, one can argue, Austen allies herself more with Jeremy Bentham than with Samuel Johnson.

By saying this, I mean to refute the idea that Austen was an ardent little Tory who sought to make fiction justify a traditional notion of rank and status. But in opposing this position, I do not subscribe to the view of Austen as a proto-feminist rebel who thrashed against the constraints that bound an author of her sex unwillingly to convention. These, I would rather argue, are alternatives by which literary criticism rewrites the past because they are alternatives that authors such as Austen wrote into fiction, making it possible for fiction to do the work of modern culture. I have drawn upon the distinction between grammar and usage to represent the thematic opposition of personal desire to social constraint that criticism uses to figure out Austen's politics, and I have used the notion of economy, too, in an effort to lend Austen's writing a materiality it tends to lose in critical discussion. If nothing else, this chapter has attempted to demonstrate that writing, for Austen, was a form of power in its own right, which could displace the material body of the subject and the value of those objects constituting the household. In helping to establish the semiotic organization of nineteenth century England, in other words, the novel helped to create the conditions theorized by Bentham—a world largely written, one in which even the difference between words and things was ultimately a function of discourse.

My reading of *Emma* shows the degree to which Austen understood the power of usage to modify grammar or the rules governing usage. In this, her thinking resembles not only that of Samuel Johnson but that of Samuel Richardson as well. (What else is the last section of *Pamela* if not a demonstration of precisely this principle?) But unlike the eighteenth century intellectual, Austen also understood the principle underlying Bentham's theory of signs—that is, the degree to which words constitute the objects they represent. In putting forth his "entirely new system of logic," with its linguistic orientation rising out of the analysis and classification of fictions, Bentham insists on a certain economy of communication grounded in objects:

> Yonder stands a certain portion of matter. By that portion of matter feelings of a certain sort are produced in your mind: by that same portion of matter feelings of a sort, if not exactly the same, at least with reference to the purpose in question near enough to being the same, are produced at the same time in my mind. Here then is the channel of communication, and the only one. Of that channel language takes possession and employs it.[17]

Much the same communication model organizes the scene in which Emma paints Harriet's portrait. We could say, on the one hand, it is also possible to argue that the portrait, in Bentham's terms, transmits Emma's meaning quite effectively. Its attempt to enhance Harriet's figure bespeaks the lack of elegance Emma sees there. Austen not only understands the power of usage to transform the rules for usage, I am arguing, she also understands that real entities, when taken up by language, exist on a more or less equal footing with fictitious ones. Language constitutes a material reality in its own right as it displaces the world of things. In Bentham's words,

> as often as any object has been considered in the character of a subject of or for exposition, that object has been a word—the immediate subject of exposition has been a word; whatsoever else may have been brought to view, the signification of a *word*—of the word in question—has been brought to view: the word is not only a subject, but the only physically sensible subject, upon and in relation to which the *operation* called exposition has been performed. (p. 77)

Understanding full well the power of the word, Bentham asserts, in the chapter entitled "The Fiction of an Original Contract," that "the season of *Fiction* is now over: insomuch that what formerly might have been tolerated and countenanced under the name, would, if now attempted to be set on foot, be censured and stigmatized under the harsher appellations of *encroachment* or *imposture*" (p. 122). To put an end to the fictions on which he believed monarchy rested, however, required a new epoch of realism and a new language of truth, which did not so easily reveal its figurative power. His can be regarded as an early attempt in the great nineteenth century project to make language identical with truth, which did in fact initiate a new empire of signs.

With a kind of self-awareness rivaled, in my opinion, only by Jeremy Bentham, Austen proposes a form of authority—a form of political authority—that works through literacy rather than through traditional juridical means to maintain social relations. If, by Austen's time, sexual relations are assumed to be the specialized knowledge of the female, and if it is in female writing that the terms of such relationships are figured out, then fiction fulfills its discursive function by exemplifying the conduct of relationships between men and women. Novels do not have to launch elaborate self-defenses anymore, for they have appropriated the strategies of conduct books to such a degree that fiction—instead of conduct books—can claim the authority to regulate reading. More often than not, those conduct books that do not aim their wisdom specifically at children or members of the aspiring social groups turn a critical eye on the genre and deplore the limitations of educational programs meant only for women. I am suggesting that with Austen, if not with Burney before her, the novel supplants the conduct book as that writing which declares an alternative, female standard of polite writing.

Rather than perform the psychologizing function that conduct books by now presumed to be the purpose of female education, Austen's fiction set out to discover those same truths as the private reality underlying *all* social behavior, even that which belonged to the domain of the public and masculine, i.e., political, world. As architects of the new educational curriculum were also in the process of deciding, it was not enough to cultivate the hearts of women alone. It was now time to consider how social institutions might be changed. In the words of the Edgeworths:

> without depreciating or destroying the magnificence or establishments of universities, may not their institutions be improved? May not their splendid halls

echo with other sounds than the exploded metaphysics of the schools; and may not learning be as much rewarded and esteemed as pure *latinity.* [18]

So, too, on the fictional front, where the battle for representing the woman had already been won, one can see the entire matter of relative social position—or in other words, the ranking of men—undergoing translation into linguistic features. The Edgeworths' question of whether an aristocratic education provided the entire basis for male knowledge is simply recast to consider which style of writing best represented the relative value of men. No longer, by implication, was the aristocratic tradition of letters, or "latinity," necessarily privileged in this regard. To say this would seem to contradict the argument that identifies Austen's place in history with her formulation of strategies of containment.

To read *Emma,* we must not only equate language with power. We must also equate the language of power with prose that imitates the word spoken by an elite minority of country gentlefolk quite removed from the centers of power. And if it seems dangerous to make the first equation because it empowers the Eltons and the Churchills of the world and introduces a certain fluidity into the closed and stratified world of Austen's fiction, then the second of these equations offers a way of limiting the destabilizing effects of the first. This peculiar capability on the part of her communities to be both permeable and restrictive is one that also characterized the English country gentry at the turn of the century. How the fluidity of this membership, as described in my discussion of *Pamela,* translated into a question of language is explained in Lawrence and Jeanne Fawtier Stone's *An Open Elite? England 1540–1880.* The fact that for a century the gentry was a rank to which people belonging to different social groups could ascend and from which individuals could as easily decline was inscribed upon the English countryside:

> In the eighteenth century, upwardly mobile purchasers might change the old name of a seat, because they found it insufficiently genteel or imposing to suit their aspirations. In Hertfordshire, Pricketts became Greenhill Grove, Tillers End became Coles Park, and Cokenhatch, at least for a time, became Earlsbury Park. Such name-changing of houses is an indication of the very real degree of identification between an owner and his seat: the latter's name was meant to enhance the status of the former, which is why so many houses in the eighteenth century were called "Park" instead of the older, less grandiose, "Hall." By the nineteenth century, the close identification of the *nouveau-riche* with his small villa was an aping, lower down the social scale, of this form of proprietorial imperialism. (p. 71)

In quite literally effacing the history of the house, the turnover of country property destabilized the signs of personal identity, a historical process recorded most obviously in *Mansfield Park* but resonating throughout all of

Austen's fiction. "Since continuity of the 'house'—meaning the patrilinear family line—was the fundamental organizing principle to which these families subscribed," the Stones continue, "the prime object was to keep together the . . . component elements which made it up." Among these were not only the land, the family name, and a title, if there happened to be one, but also—and of equal importance—the household objects which preserved the family's history, "especially valuable relics such as the family archives, including the deeds and patents of nobility, portraits of ancestors, family plate and jewels, and personal gifts from kings and queens" (p. 72). If it was primarily nostalgia for the iconicity of such household objects that animated her representation of a community in crisis, we would have to place Austen with the liberal Tories of her day. But this, I feel, would be to adopt too simplistic a view of her understanding of the medium in which she thought out the dynamism of the ideal community. I am quite certain that Austen understood as well as anyone could the power of fiction to constitute things, truth, and reality. It was not the country gentry and their specific interests that she promoted as the best life for everyone to live. The ways of the town and the city and their connection with commerce abroad always hover at the borders of the elite community to remind and reassure us of its limitations. It was not this particular segment of society that she idealized, then, but rather the language that constituted the nuances of emotion and the ethical refinements that seemed to arise from within to modify the political meaning of signs, a new language of kinship relations capable of reproducing this privileged community on a personal scale within society at large. It is in this respect that Austen's writing implies the presence of a new linguistic community, a class that was neither gentry nor nobility as the eighteenth century knew them, yet one that was clearly a leisure class and thus a paradoxical configuration that can only be called a middle-class aristocracy.

Notes

1.   See my discussion of *The Compleat Servant, Being a Practical Guide to the Peculiar Duties and Business of all Descriptions of Servants* (London, 1825) in my *Desire and Domestic Fiction* (New York: Oxford University Press, 1987), 59–95.

2.   The nature of that community has been the point of a well-known disagreement. See, for example, Lionel Trilling, "*Emma*," *Encounter* 8 (1957), 45–59, and John Bayley, "The 'Irresponsibility' of Jane Austen," in *Critical Essays on Jane Austen*, ed. B.C. Southam (New York: Barnes and Noble, 1969), 9–14.

3.   Raymond Williams, *The Long Revolution* (London: Chatto and Windus, 1961), 134.

4.   Williams, 134.

5.   Brian Simon, *Studies in the History of Education 1780–1870* (London: Lawrence and Wishart, 1960), 23.

6.   Williams, 134.

7.   Williams, 126.

8.   It is testimony to her power to create the impression of a separate, yet familiar and unique, speech community that several critics discuss Jane Austen's work on the basis of some

kind of linguistic analysis. See, for example, K. C. Phillips, *Jane Austen's English* (London: Andre Deutsch, 1970); Norman Page, *The Language of Jane Austen* (Oxford: Basil Blackwell, 1972); and Mary Varanna Taylor, "The Grammar of Conduct: Speech Act Theory and the Education of Emma Woodhouse," *Style* 12 (1978), 357–71.

9. For a discussion of Austen as "the mother" of the nineteenth century novel, see Clifford Siskin, "A Formal Development; Austen, the Novel, and Romanticism," *The Centennial Review* 28/29 (1984–85), 1–28.

10. Daniel Cottom, "The Novels of Jane Austen: Attachments and Supplantments," *Novel* 14 (1981), 152–67, has discussed the power of society in terms of the power over conditions of communication in Austen's novels.

11. Jane Austen, *Emma*, ed. Stephen M. Parrish (New York: W. W. Norton, 1972), 44; citations of the text are to this edition.

12. To classify Austen's politics, Marilyn Butler places her within eighteenth century categories: "in eighteenth-century terms, she is a Tory rather than a Whig." *Jane Austen and the War of Ideas* (Oxford: Clarendon, 1975), 2. In nineteenth century political terms, I am arguing, the eighteenth century distinction between Tory and Whig no longer appears to have defined the important difference between one person's political viewpoint and another's.

13. While I would take issue with Tony Tanner's general model, which presupposes more categories—nature, culture, male, female—than it questions for historical purposes, my own understanding of the operation of language in *Emma* bears striking affinities, I think, with the relationship between community and communication that Tanner describes in his introduction: "Thus the energies of the family are ideally aimed at countering any slippage or shifting in the status quo, at resisting change, supplying lacks, filling up gaps, and denying unacceptable kinds of difference. . . . But language itself introduces gaps and lacks into conscious being, as we have seen and as a phenomenon, it is rooted in difference, change, and shifting. Thus there is a potential paradox between the speaker who is an owner (in the bourgeois sense), for speaking presages desire and change, while ownership succumbs to the logic of inertia and permanence." *Adultery in the Novel: Contract and Transgression* (Baltimore: Johns Hopkins University Press, 1979), 115.

14. Wilbur Samuel Howell, *Eighteenth-Century British Logic and Rhetoric* (Princeton: Princeton University Press, 1971), 115.

15. Howell, 115.

16. Kim Sloan, "Drawing—A 'Polite Recreation' in Eighteenth-Century England," *Studies in Eighteenth-Century Culture* 11 (1982), notes that when drawing and painting began to be taken up by the aristocracy and the upper middle-class practitioners to fill up their leisure time, mastering the rudiments of drawing and painting was considered a virtue. When, however, they became practical skills for naval personnel and tradespeople, painting and drawing had to be distinguished as leisure-time activities. It was necessary to indicate the very amateur quality of the rendering and to point out other signs that suggested this female artistic activity was not to be confused with the work of those who needed the skill for their occupation. By the end of the eighteenth century, Sloan writes, "women amateurs concerned themselves less with the ability to draw and were turning to easier artistic accommodations" (234).

17. Jeremy Bentham, *Bentham's Theory of Fictions*, ed. C. K. Ogden (New York: Harcourt, Brace and Company, 1932), 64; citations of the text are to this edition.

18. Maria Edgeworth and Robert L. Edgeworth, *Practical Education*, vol. II (London, 1801), 383–84.

"Not at All What a Man Should Be!": Remaking English Manhood in *Emma*

Claudia L. Johnson

I began this book about politics, sentimentality, and gender in late-eigh-teenth-century fiction by observing how Austen's achievement seemed to erase that of her slightly older contemporaries. For many years, it was univer-sally acknowledged that Austen defined herself negatively vis-à-vis the fig-ures I gather here, shunning the plots of Wollstonecraft's radical feminism, Radcliffe's exaggerated gothicism, and Burney's escalated melodrama, and opting instead to exercise the cameoist's meticulously understated craft. But effects are not intentions. In *Northanger Abbey,* that novel which was to have been her first published work, Austen launches into a spirited defense of her chosen genre over and against those who would decry it as "only a novel." Rather than proceed through negations, she inaugurates her career by assert-ing solidarity with a distinctively feminine tradition of novelists that devel-oped in the late eighteenth century, a tradition in which Burney and Radcliffe ranked very high. Though Wollstonecraft remained an unmentionable throughout Austen's career, there is ample evidence that she too was a figure Austen reckoned with. Indeed, in many respects *Emma* actually succeeds at Wollstonecraft's grand aim better than Wollstonecraft did: diminishing the authority of male sentimentality, and reimmasculating men and women alike with a high sense of national purpose.

This claim may sound highfalutin'. Given the lingering grip of janeism in Anglophone culture, however, virtually any large claim about Austen tends to sound excessive and desecratory.[1] Besides, no less discriminating a critic than Lionel Trilling himself advanced a similar thesis in 1957, when he declared that *Emma* "is touched—lightly but indubitably—by national feel-ing." With its tribute to "English verdure, English culture, English comfort," *Emma* tends, as Trilling put it, "to conceive of a specifically English ideal of life." As it so happens, Trilling also regards *Emma* as what I have been calling an "equivocal being": "The extraordinary thing about Emma," he argues, "is that she has a moral life as a man has a moral life." Beyond alluding to de Tocqueville now and then, however, Trilling is not interested in pondering what these assertions mean historically. By calling *Emma* an "idyll"—a genre he considers definitionally cut off from "real" history—he forecloses the possibility that *Emma* may be enmeshed in the national ideals of its period, just as he insists that Emma's manliness has no relation to eighteenth- and nineteenth-century debates about women's rights when he remarks that she possesses it not "as a special instance, as an example of a new kind of woman, which is the way George Eliot's Dorothea Brooke has her moral life, but quite as a matter of course, as a given quality of her nature."[2] For Trilling, these assertions remain at some distance from each other: there is and can be no connection between Emma's manly moral life and *Emma*'s "national feeling." By historicizing the treatment of femininity *and* masculinity in *Emma*, I will attempt in the following pages to integrate the arguments about female manliness and national feeling which Trilling keeps apart, and in the process to show that Austen engages the work of her predecessors more positively and more intricately than is generally supposed.

In part because Austen's canonization—unlike Wollstonecraft's, Radcliffe's, or Burney's—was so steady and so assured, we have had as a rule very little historical imagination about her and about our relation to her. Before considering the subjects of nationality and gender in *Emma* it will be instructive to review Austenian commentary on this subject as well. Eve Kosofsky Sedgwick's paper "Jane Austen and the Masturbating Girl" was savagely attacked in the press for having violated the monumentally self-evident truth that Austen had the good fortune to predate such indecorous sexual irregularities as homo- and autoeroticism. In her novels, the supposition runs, men are gentlemen; women are ladies; and the desires of gentlemen and ladies for each other are unproblematic, inevitable, and mutually fulfilling.[3] As any full-time Austenian knows, however, a lively and explicit interest in the sexual irregularities of Emma Woodhouse has been the stuff of "establishment" criticism for almost fifty years now. Indeed, Trilling's assertion about Emma's manliness was certainly the least original thing about his essay. For post–World War II critics writing on Austen immediately before Trilling did, Emma was as "unsexed" a female as any of the heroines I have assembled here. The difference between late eighteenth- and mid-twentieth-century notions of what it means to be "unsexed" is that discourses of deviance drawn from psychoanalysis came to occupy this category during our century so that far from signifying immodest heterosexuality, it has now meant being homosexual, manhating, and/or frigid. The sexual ambiguities of Radcliffe's and Burney's happily or unhappily equivocal heroines were, to be sure, spared commentary on their deviance by literary scholars only because no one paid attention to them at all. Wollstonecraft was not always so lucky. In *Modern Woman: The Lost Sex* (1947), Ferdinand Lundberg and Marynia Farnham maintained that modern-day "feminists" too were unsexed, and that they had Wollstonecraft to thank for their debilitatingly "severe case of penis-envy."[4]

Postwar discussions of Emma Woodhouse were rarely as clinical as that of Lundberg and Farnham, but they were fixated on Emma's lack of heterosexual feeling to such a degree that Emma's supposed coldness became the central question of the novel: was Emma responsive to men? could she ever really give herself in love, and thus give up trying to control other people's lives? would marriage "cure" her? Ever since Edmund Wilson's review essay "A Long Talk about Jane Austen" (1944), Emma was commonly charged with lesbianism. Wilson does not actually use the l-word, but his attention to Emma's lack of "interest . . . in men" and to "her infatuations with women"—along with his allusion to a certain, unspecified "Freudian formula"—makes his point clear. Pooh-poohing G. B. Stern's and Sheila Kaye-Smith's book *Speaking of Jane Austen* (1944) for treating characters as "actual people . . . and speculating on their lives beyond the story," Wilson does the same, arguing that Emma's offstage lesbianism is that "something outside the picture which is never made explicit in the story but which has to be recognized by the reader before it is possible for him to appreciate the book." In the following meditation on the conclusion, especially as it relates to Knightley's imprudent decision to move in at Hartfield, Wilson trails off into a fantasy about ménages-à-trois that threaten the domestic and erotic sovereignty to which a husband is entitled:

> Emma, who was relatively indifferent to men, was inclined to infatuations with women; and what reason is there to believe that her marriage with Knightley would prevent her from going on as she had done before: from discovering a new young lady as appealing as Harriet Smith, dominating her personality and situating her in a dream-world of Emma's own in which Emma would be able to confer on her all kinds of imaginary benefits, but which would have no connection whatever with her condition or her real possibilities. This would worry and exasperate Knightley and be hard for him to do anything about. He would be lucky if he did not presently find himself saddled, along with the other awkward features of the arrangement, with one of Emma's young protegées as an actual member of the household.[5]

Try as Wilson did to dignify his commentary by differentiating it from the merely gossipy discussions of the women critics he is reviewing, his dilatory sixth-act fantasy about Emma's extramarital infatuations with women and her autonomy from male authority is on a par not only with Miss Stern's effusions but also with Miss Bates's. And like Miss Bates's prattle, I hasten to add, Wilson's here is in its own way exceedingly sensitive to the drama represented or hinted at in the novel.

On the subject of Emma's sexual irregularity, Marvin Mudrick is Wilson's direct descendant. For him, Emma's "attention never falls so warmly upon a man" as on Harriet, whom she observes "with far more warmth than anyone else." Wilson's discussion of Emma's homosexuality, though aligned in sympathy with a husband bewildered to find himself displaced by a woman, nevertheless takes the liberal tone of a man of the world. Mudrick is more censorious: Emma's interest in women is pathological, stemming from the same defensive fear of commitment, the same detachment, and the same need to control that he diagnoses in Austen herself on virtually every page of *Irony as Defense and Discovery:* a woman's emotions ought to be passionately committed to a man, even if this means she might not, then, wish to write brilliant novels. But when Mudrick's scolding ceases, his discussion of Emma is astute: "Emma's interest in Harriet is not merely mistress-and-pupil, but quite emotional and particular: for a time, at least . . . Emma is in love with her: a love unphysical and inadmissible, even perhaps undefinable in such a society; and therefore safe."[6] Without knowing and certainly without intending it, Mudrick verges here on a theory of the closet: aware that sex and gender are not equivalent, and alert to the relation between sexuality, gender, and social power, he suggests that sexuality is a discursive practice: "inadmissible" forms of sexuality become undiscussable, "undefinable," and therefore under certain circumstances, even "safe."

Wilson's and Mudrick's essays on *Emma* had an incalculable impact on Austen studies from the 1950s through the mid-1970s. Their work is discernible, as we have already seen, in Trilling's Introduction to *Emma;* they are also behind Mark Schorer's widely reprinted "The Humiliation of Emma Woodhouse" (1959), which accepts the gothically strained love of Jane Fairfax for Frank Churchill as wholesome and normal and treats Emma's chilliness as a pathology deserving of the wondrously salubrious humiliation heralded in his title;[7] and finally they are the targets of Wayne Booth's indignation in his "Control of Distance in Jane Austen's *Emma*" (1961). This immeasurably influential essay, which links an intensely normative reading of Emma to the genre of fiction itself, attacks Mudrick and Wilson for suggesting that Emma "has not been cured of her 'infatuations with women' " and thus for doubting that "marriage to an excellent, amiable, good, and attractive man is the best thing that can happen to" her. For Booth—and a generation of Aristotelian-oriented formalists—the novel's comic structure and oral lesson are the same. Because heterosexuality is encoded teleologically onto a rhetoric of fiction, Emma's drama, her "development" and "growth" are inseparable from her learning to desire a man. Booth's rebuttal equates the perversity of women who indulge such "infatuations" with the perversity of novel critics who refuse to accept a happy ending when they see one.[8]

Clearly, a long time before feminists came along, "classic" Austenian critics considered the sex and gender transgression of Emma their business. The generation of male academics returning to American culture after the war made Emma go the way of Rosie the Riveter, and enforced imperatives of masculine dominance and feminine domesticity without examining the historical contingencies of these imperatives and their own investment in them.

Pained as I am by the cheeriness of their misogyny, I also think they were basically right about Emma: quite susceptible to the stirrings of homoerotic pleasure, Emma *is* enchanted by Harriet's "soft blue eyes" (E 23, 24); displaying all the captivating enjoyment of "a mind delighted with its own ideas" (E 24), Emma *is* highly autonomous and autoerotic; and, finally, displaying shockingly little reverence for dramas of heterosexual love, Emma's energies and desires are *not* fully contained within the grid imposed by the courtship plot. By restoring Austen to the specific social and political context I have been reconstructing throughout this book, we can examine in a more sustained and responsible way the slippages of sex and gender which post–World War II critics discussed by fits and starts.

Emma indeed pays conspicuous attention to gender definition. But whereas mid-twentieth-century critics were mostly preoccupied with Emma's waywardness as a woman, *Emma* itself evinces amazingly little anxiety on the subject. This omission itself is highly unusual, and it demands an explanation. Many late-eighteenth- and early-nineteenth-century novels responded directly to Mary Wollstonecraft and/or her "disciple" Mary Hays by introducing into their novels protofeminists who challenged the ways in which sexual difference had been defined. In the same year Austen started *Emma* she also read Burney's belated *The Wanderer* (1814), where as we have amply seen, Elinor Joddrel torments herself as well as the women and men around her with her doomed feminist mania. Austen also knew and admired Edgeworth's *Belinda* (1801), featuring the mannish Herriot Freke, who erupts into feminist diatribes. It is also likely that Austen read Charlotte Smith's *Montalbert* (1795), which includes an "Amazonian" who is (like Emma) destitute of vanity about her personal appearance and who exhibits other "symptoms of a masculine spirit" that make the proper heroine cringe with horror;[9] Elizabeth Hamilton's *Memoirs of Modern Philosophers* (1800), whose Bridgetina Botherim is a malicious spoof on Mary Hays; and Amelia Opie's more sympathetic *Adeline Mowbray* (1805), whose heroine strives not only for emancipation from specific sexual mores, particularly as these relate to the institution of marriage, but also for the autonomous, self-responsible "moral life" Trilling detects in Emma.

Considered in the context of these heroines, Austen's prediction that no one but herself would like Emma makes enormous sense. Although precedents for doing so were abundantly at hand, Austen never faults Emma's "masculine spirit." Postwar critics groove on what they are pleased to call Emma's *humiliation,* her *chastisement,* her *submission.* But *Emma* is not interested in subjecting the masculine independence of its heroine to disciplinary correctives.[10] To be sure, Emma has flawed and unattractive ideas about the class structure of her world—and unlike her feminist prototypes, she is ridiculed for being too little rather than too much of a democrat—but we are never invited to consider her infractions against "femininity" per se to be the cause of her problem as a snob. On the contrary, the narrator trots out

Emma's sister, Isabella Knightley, as a "model of right feminine happiness" (E 140), an indulgent mother and adoring spouse, as blissfully oblivious to the faults of her husband's temper as she is to the vapidity of her own conversation. Rather than pathologize Emma's deviations from "right feminine happiness," the novel introduces Isabella for the sole purpose of making Emma look better by comparison. The narrator says that Isabella's "striking inferiorities" (E 433) throw Emma's strengths into higher relief in Knightley's own mind. And when the novel explicitly describes Emma's behavior in ways that bend gender, it does so without the slightest hint of horror. As Mr. Knightley puts it, for example, taking care of Emma at Hartfield proves a sort of conjugal training camp for Miss Taylor: "You were preparing yourself to be an excellent wife all the time you were at Hartfield . . . on the very material matrimonial point of submitting your own will, and doing as you were bid" (E 38). While the strong-willed Emma here is a surrogate husband, claiming submission as marital privilege, elsewhere she comes near to usurping what Henry Tilney in *Northanger Abbey* called the exclusively male "prerogative of choice":

"Whom are you going to dance with?" asked Mr. Knightley.
[Emma] hesitated a moment, and then replied, "With you, if you will ask me."
(E 331)

It is not necessary to overstate this point. Austen's Emma Woodhouse is not Hays's Emma Courtney, who proposes marriage outright. Unlike the latter and other protofeminist characters who occupy novels by Austen's contemporaries, Emma Woodhouse stops short of transgressing at least one very important gender rule: by the end of the novel, she finds herself in the certifiably orthodox position of having possibly to wait to be proposed to. But the ending does not entirely cancel out what has come before, however it may delimit it. The novel basically accepts as attractive and as legitimate Emma's forcefulness. As Knightley says when comparing Emma's handwriting to that of others, "Emma's hand is the strongest" (E 297) and this observation is tinged with fondness rather than censure.

Where this novel *is* concerned with gender transgression, it is from the masculine, not the feminine side. What "true" masculinity is like—what a "man" is, how a man speaks and behaves, what a man really wants—is the subject of continual debate, even when characters appear to be discussing women. The following sampling is typical of the novel's tendentiousness on the ever-recurrent subject *man:*

"A man of six or seven-and-twenty can take care of himself." (E 14)
"A man always imagines a woman to be ready for anybody who asks her." "Nonsense! a man does not imagine any such thing." (E 60)
"There is one thing, Emma, which a man can always do, if he chuses, and that is, his duty." (E 146)

"I can allow for the fears of the child but not of the man." (E 148)
"General benevolence, but not general friendship made a man what
    he ought to be." (E 320)
"She has not the open temper which a man would wish for in a
    wife." (E 288)
"He is a disgrace to the name of man." (E 426)
"A man would always wish to give a woman a better home than the
    one he takes her from." (E 428)

Emma attaches no opprobrium to the manly Emma, nor does it—unlike
a novel such as *Mansfield Park*—dwell on the (contradictory) qualities typify-
ing a truly feminine woman. But it persistently asks how a *man* should behave
and what he ought to do. Committing itself to the discussion of true manhood and disparaging men who do not measure up, *Emma* demonstrates that
manhood is *not,* as Trilling supposed, "a matter of course . . . a given quality"
of a man's "nature," any more than manhood can ever be a matter of course
of a woman's nature. This is my point. "Classic" Austenian critics assumed
the constancy of feminine norms, and policed Emma's womanhood accordingly, but they sometimes cast an eye towards errant males too, even if they
once again did not imagine that masculinity could be something the novel
contests and constructs. Edmund Wilson appears to have been the first to call
Mr. Woodhouse a "silly old woman," and this epithet has proved horribly
durable. Mudrick once again follows suit when he declares that Mr. Woodhouse possesses no "masculine trait," that he is "really an old woman." Re-
fraining from the grossness of name-calling, others beheld Mr. Woodhouse's
anility with fascination or alarm. For Joseph Duffy, Mr. Woodhouse is "otiose
and androgynous" much like Lady Bertram, a judgment echoed by Trilling
years later. For Tony Tanner, on the other hand, Mr. Woodhouse is a gender-
derelict of dangerous proportions, a "moribund patriarch," the "type of male
who would bring his society—any society—to a stop," the "weak emasculate
voice of definitive negations and terminations." Mr. Woodhouse's transgressions—his "weak emasculate" qualities—would spell doom for all of society,
if it weren't for the counterexample of Knightley, whom Tanner calls the "responsible active male."[11]

    The assumption behind these readings is that there is one, continuous
mode of manliness against which Mr. Woodhouse is to be judged and found
lacking, though the assumption is at odds with their perception that manliness is already multiple and problematic. When Trilling attempted (and
chivalrously so) to defend Mr. Woodhouse from Mudrick's attacks by insisting that in the novel he is a "kind-hearted, polite old gentleman," he was
right in more ways than one: Mr. Woodhouse is both a kindly old gentleman
and an old kind of gentleman.[12] We see his old-fashionedness first in his resistance to change—his desire to keep the family circle unbroken, his wish to retain the hospitable customs of his youth, his "strong habit of regard for every

old acquaintance" (E 92); and second in his attitude towards women—as Emma puts it, Mr. Woodhouse loves "any thing that pays woman a compliment. He has the tenderest spirit of gallantry towards us all" (E 77). Historically considered, far from being an unusual, deviant, emasculated, or otherwise deficient figure, Mr. Woodhouse represents the ideal of sentimental masculinity described throughout this book. The qualities that typify him— sensitivity, tenderness, "benevolent nerves," allegiance to the good old ways, courtesies to the fair sex, endearing irrationality, and even slowness, frailty, and ineptitude itself—also typify the venerated paternal figures crowding the pages of Burney and Radcliffe, to say nothing of those of Edmund Burke.

During the 1790s, a man's "benevolent nerves" carried a national agenda; they were formed by and guaranteed the continuation of the charm, the beauty, the hospitality, and the goodness of Old England itself, which liked its gallant old ways even if they did not make sense, and which won our love, veneration, and loyalty. In a world where the "age of chivalry" was ebbing, where the courtesies of the old regime were being displaced by the cold economic calculations of the new one, a Woodhousian man of feeling held out for civility; his attachment to the old ways preserved continuity and order, while qualities such as energy, penetration, forcefulness, brusqueness, bluntness, and decision were deemed dangerous, volatile, and cold. The heroically sentimental "man of feeling" presided over his neighborhood and family by virtue of the love he inspired in others, not by virtue of the power he wielded over them; his sensitivity legitimized his authority, enabling him to rule by weakness rather than force. In Burney's *Camilla*, Sir Hugh Tyrold never holds more sway in the minds and hearts of his extended family than when he weeps and takes to his bed—which happens rather often. In Radcliffe's *Udolpho*, St. Aubert flinches when Quesnel plans to hew down "that noble chestnut, which has flourished for centuries, the glory of the estate!" (MU 13); his tears make his injunctions sacred to his daughter, just as his faintness and infirmity consolidate as well as conceal his authority, making him a fitter object of "gallantry" than a woman like Emily. And in Burke's *Reflections*, Englishmen like Mr. Woodhouse are proud members of a "dull sluggish race" (RRF 106), and are celebrated for their instinctive aversion to change, their frankly irrational attachment to prejudices because they are prejudices, and their fond love for their "little platoon," their attachment "to the subdivision" (RRF 97), to diminutive, pathos-driven units of national identity.

Emma is written after the crisis that launched the reemergence of male sentimentality had abated. In it, this tradition of sentimental masculinity is archaic, and it has become somewhat of a joke. Mr. Woodhouse is dearly beloved and fondly indulged, but his sensitivity is not revered. The novel works instead to redefine masculinity. We will miss what is distinctive about Austen's achievement if we assume that masculine self-definitions were givens rather than qualities under reconstruction. Critics commonly agree that Mr. Knightley represents an ideal, but what has *not* been adequately appreciated, I think, is the novelty of that ideal, for by representing a "humane" rather than "gallant" hero, Austen desentimentalizes and deheterosexualizes virtue, and in the process makes it accessible to women as well. Twentieth-century critics assailed Mr. Woodhouse for "effeminacy," and as unpleasant as this charge is in its blend of misogyny and homophobia, there is a good deal in *Emma* that corroborates it, although the novel is careful to spare Mr. Woodhouse the full brunt of such opprobrium and to deflect it onto Mr. Elton and Frank Churchill instead.

Knightley frequently faults men for crossing the masculine/feminine divide. It is Mr. Woodhouse who first refers to Mr. Elton as a "pretty fellow," and coming from Mr. Woodhouse, this is a compliment to Elton's dapperness. From Knightley's viewpoint, however—the viewpoint generally endorsed by the narrator—male prettiness is small, weak, and self-preening. Mr. Knightley finds the company of fellow farmers such as Robert Martin and William Larkins just as absorbing, if not more so, than the society of women; but Mr. Elton disgraces himself in his studied attentions to women. In *Emma*, gallantry—that generous loyalty to rank and sex—rather than representing the acme of manliness, is figured as an effeminating proximity with and submission to women, and as patently absurd. Unlike *Northanger Abbey* and *Mansfield Park*, *Emma* is permeated with petticoat government, and heroes here show their mettle not by standing up to men with power and authority, but rather by resisting tyrannical female rule. True: Mr. Knightley impresses Emma by his heroic rescue of Harriet-in-distress; but he also proves himself to be a man by bringing bossy women—like Mrs. Elton—up short. Indeed, when "the great Mrs. Churchill" not only henpecks her husband but also bullies Frank Churchill, Mr. Knightley complains that Frank lacks the gumption to stand up to her like a man and to do what is right by that man, his father: "If he would say so to her at once, in the tone of decision becoming a man, there would be no opposition made to his going" (E 146). As Emma says, Knightley is "not a gallant man, but he is a very humane one" (E 223), and this means not only that he resists the encroachments of female authority, but also that he does not make a big deal out of sexual difference and the benevolizing sentiments that emerge from it in sentimental culture. Implying a counterdiscourse of "true feeling," *Emma* suggests in a most unBurkean way that "humanity" and gallantry are two different things. The "gallant Mr. Elton" by contrast damns himself when he avows that it is impossible "to contradict a lady" (E 42); when he takes care "that nothing ungallant, nothing that did not create a compliment to the sex should pass his lips" (E 70), and when he "sign[s] and languish[es] and stud[ies] for compliments" (E 49). As presented here, gallantry is intrinsically nonsensical: artificial and disingenuous, taking on the very femininity it courts. No man, as the logic of this novel would have it, talks or believes such rubbish. When Mr. Elton is alone among men, as Mr. Knightley informs us, he makes it clear that he wants to marry into money and that his attentions to the fair sex are only a means to this end, that he is not really a man of feeling at all.

Knightley waxes even more magisterially censorious on the subject of Frank Churchill, rebuking his derelictions from true manliness in highly loaded terms. Before Knightley even meets Frank, he predicts that he will be a "chattering coxcomb" (E 150). Manifestly, the word "coxcomb"—like "puppy," "foppish," and "trifling," which come up later—connotes the shameful insufficiency already lambasted in Mr. Elton. But the epithet "chattering" interests me more here, *chatter* being a word reserved for feminine speech (like Miss Bates's)—excessive, undisciplined, diffuse, frivolous—and applied to a man, it is an insult. I dwell on this because *Emma* pays a lot of attention to the language of true manliness. Privileging gender over class, Austen grants to Robert Martin what Frank Churchill lacks: a manly style of writing, where manly is defined (by Emma herself) as "concise," "vigorous," "decided," and "strong" (E 51)—*strong*, of course, also being the term Knightley uses to describe the manly Emma's hand.[13] Knightley delivers an emasculating blow to Frank Churchill when he declares of his handwriting, "I do not admire it. It is too small—wants strength. It is like woman's writing" (E 297). But Mr. Knightley casts what his company terms "base aspersions" on more than the mere size of Frank Churchill's handwriting. The related style of Frank's letter also degrades him as being somehow "like a woman." Having already remarked, and more than once, on the prolixity of Frank's final letter, Knightley goes on to censure its hyperbole: "He is a very liberal thanker, with his thousands and tens of thousands." The real man, it is implied here, is a man of few words. Whereas an earlier generation of sentimental men had made a spectacle of their affect—of honorable feelings so powerful as to exceed all possibility of control, thus saturating handkerchiefs and liberally bedewing eloquent pages—the manful Mr. Knightley retreats from display, cultivating containment rather than excess, and "burying under a calmness that seemed all but indifference" (E 99) the "real attachment" he feels towards his brother and towards Emma as well. And this new, plain style of manliness is a matter of national import, constituting the *amiable*, "the true English style," as opposed of course, to the *aimable*, the artificial, the courtly, the dissembling, the servile, and (as the tradition goes) the feminized French.[14]

It is the work of *Emma* to make Mr. Knightley seem traditional. Combining as it does the patron saint of England with the knight of chivalry, his name itself conduces to his traditional-seeming status. But as I hope I have indicated, he is not a traditional and certainly not a chivalric figure, and far from embodying fixed or at the very least commonly shared notions of masculinity, there is nothing in Scott, Burney, More, Burke, Radcliffe, or Edgeworth remotely like him. On one hand, Knightley is impeccably landed, a magistrate, a gentleman of "untainted" blood and judicious temper, and as such emphatically not the impetuous, combustible masculine type Burke so feared, the mere man of talent who is dangerous precisely because he has nothing to lose. But on the other hand, Knightley avows himself a farmer and a man of business, absorbed in the figures and computations Emma considers so vulgar, a man of energy, vigor, and decision, and as such emphatically not an embodiment of the stasis unto sluggishness Burke commended in country squires. The exemplary love of this "humane" as opposed to "gallant" man is *fraternal* rather than heterosexual. If Emma has difficulty realizing that Knightley is in love with her, it is not because she is impercipient, but rather because he is highly unusual in loving a woman in the same manner he loves his brother rather than the other way around: in the ambient light of senti-mental hyperbole, such love seems "indifferent." But while Knightley is in some respects a new man, Austen also harkens back to some older ideals in creating him, looking to the chivalric pseudotraditonalism celebrated by Burke, but instead bypassing the trauma of 1790s sentimentality altogether to recover a native tradition of gentry liberty, which valued its manly inde-pendence from tyrannical rule, where that rule is figured as courtly, feminine, and feminizing (as with the absolute monarchy of Louis XIV, for example)—a tradition which the French Revolution made dangerous by fulfilling.

Emma puts pressure not on deviance from femininity, then, but on de-viance from masculinity, and it is engaged in the enterprise of purging mascu-line gender codes from the ostensible "excesses" of sentimental gallantry and "feminized" display, redefining English manhood instead as brisk, energetic, downright, "natural," unaffected, reserved, businesslike, plain-speaking; gen-tlemanly, to be sure, but not courtly. What does this reconfiguration mean for Emma? For one, it demotes the moral importance of heterosexual feeling for women. The more conventionally feminine women in the novel—one thinks of Harriet, who is willing to marry any man who asks; of Mrs. Elton, with her fulsome little love-names for her husband; or of Isabella, whose wifely devo-tion verges on sheer stupidity—give heterosexuality a rather revolting ap-pearance, against which Emma's coolness looks sane and enviable. *Emma*'s pa-tience with Emma's gender transgressions and its impatience with Mr. Elton's and Frank Churchill's are related. *Emma* disdains not only the effeminacy of men, but also the femininity of women. There appears to me as little doubt on Austen's part as there is on Mr. Knightley's that Emma's masculine strength is better than Isabella's "proper," "feminine" weakness, weaknesses that link her to her father. Here, conventional femininity is a degradation to which Emma does not submit. But it is not merely femininity that Emma's portion designedly lacks. It is effeminacy as well, as Emma's rebuke of Frank Churchill's double-dealing and trickery makes clear: "Impropriety! Oh! Mrs. Weston—it is too calm a censure. Much, much beyond impropriety!—It has sunk him, I cannot say how much it has sunk him in my opinion. So unlike what a man should be!—None of that upright integrity, that strict adherence to truth and principle, that disdain of trick and littleness, which a man should display in every transaction of his life!" (E 397).

To the extent that Emma's condemnation here reprises Mr. Knightley's—and even Emma's own—initial gender-based censure of Frank, it indicates that Emma has come back to her basically sound senses at last. But of course, the full import of Emma's censure falls not so much on Frank Churchill at this point as on Emma herself. Every bit as guilty of espionage, trick, littleness, and slack waywardness from truth and principle, Emma is convicting herself not for being unlike what a *woman* should be, but rather for being "unlike what a man should be!" And as is generally the case under the sentimental dispensation, its claims to love and protect notwithstanding, sentimental effeminacy harms other women. An effeminate man herself, the gallant Emma is gratified by Harriet Smith's infantile sweetness and malleability, just as she is even less generously invested in and fascinated by Jane Fairfax's gothicized debility, by the stalwart yet visibly wavering fortitude she tries to sustain in the face of her "female difficulty." Having magnified rather than alleviated the "wrongs of woman," Emma reproaches herself for transgressing the duty of woman to woman; this momentous duty is better honored when women too are like "what a man should be."[15]

When *Emma* was published in 1816, Mary Wollstonecraft had been dead for some twenty years; Ann Radcliffe was still alive but had not published since 1797; and Frances Burney had just published the long-awaited *The Wanderer; or Female Difficulties* (1814), which assumed that the concerns of the 1790s were still pressing, only to fall with a thud. Their careers did not survive the decade that inspired them to such magnificence. In light of this silencing, Austen's achievement in *Emma* impresses me as an act of homage; in the second decade of the nineteenth century, she is still thinking about them, still working through the problems their fiction represented, albeit in a necessarily different social context. Chivalric sentimentality was an incitement to the forces of reaction and reconsolidation, and once its success was assured, sentimentality was refeminized, and the dignity more readily accorded to women's affectivity would go on to authorize their activity in charity work, education, nursing, reform societies, and the like. But *Emma* does not look forward to Victorian visions of feminine puissance, but harkens backwards still to the norms of manly independence which Burke's paean to Marie-Antoinette interrupted.

Notes

[In this essay, these abbreviations are used for the following texts:

RFF   Edmund Burke, *Reflections on the Revolution in France*, in *The Writings and Speeches of Edmund Burke*, vol. 8, *The French Revolution 1790–1794*, ed. L. G. Mitchell (Oxford: Clarendon Press, 1989).

MU   Anne Radcliffe, *The Mysteries of Udolpho*, ed. Bonamy Dobrée (Oxford: Oxford University Press, 1970).

E   Jane Austen, *Emma*, vol. 4, *Oxford Illustrated Jane Austen*, ed. R. W. Chapman (Oxford: Oxford University Press, 1982).}

1.   For the most recent full-scale assertion of janeism, see Roger Gard, *Jane Austen's Novels: The Art of Clarity* (New Haven: Yale University Press, 1992).

2.   Lionel Trilling, "*Emma* and the Legend of Jane Austen," in *Jane Austen's Emma: A Casebook*, ed. David Lodge (London: Macmillan, 1991), pp. 130, 124. Trilling's essay was originally published as an introduction to the Riverside Edition of *Emma* (Boston: Houghton Mifflin, 1957).

3.   Sedgwick notes the virulent response to her paper in the expanded article version, "Jane Austen and the Masturbating Girl," *Critical Inquiry* 17 (1991), pp. 818–37.

4.   Ferdinand Lundberg and Marynia Farnham, *Modern Woman: The Lost Sex* (New York: Harper and Brothers, 1947), p. 43.

5.   Edmund Wilson, "A Long Talk about Jane Austen," in *Classics and Commercials: A Literary Chronicle of the Forties* (New York: Farrar & Strauss, 1950), pp. 201–3.

6.   Marvin Mudrick, *Jane Austen: Irony as Defense and Discovery* (Berkeley: University of California Press, 1952), p. 203.

7.   Mark Schorer, "The Humiliation of Emma Woodhouse," *Literary Review* 2 (1959), pp. 547–63; rpt. in *Jane Austen: A Collection of Critical Essays*, ed. Ian Watt (Englewood Cliffs: Prentice-Hall, 1963), p. 107. Helen Corsa also notes the "homosexual components" of Emma's relations with Miss Taylor and Harriet, but nevertheless concludes with Schorer that Emma's narcissism withholds her from the fullness of sexual feeling; in "A Fair But Frozen Maid," *Literature and Psychology* 19 (1969), p. 107.

8.   Wayne Booth, *A Rhetoric of Fiction* (Chicago: University of Chicago Press, 1961), pp. 243–66; rpt. in Lodge (ed.), *Casebook*, pp. 137–56.

9.   Charlotte Smith, *Montalbert* (London, 1795), p. 118.

10.   The "humiliation" school of *Emma* criticism is almost too populous to give an accounting for. Along with discussions by Booth and Schorer cited above, other notable celebrations of Emma's humiliation include C. S. Lewis, "A Note on Jane Austen," *Essays in Criticism* 4 (1954), rpt. in Watt (ed.), *Jane Austen*, pp. 25–34; Bernard Paris, *Character and Conflict in Jane Austen's Novels: A Psychological Approach* (Detroit: Wayne State University Press, 1978); and Jane Nardin, *Those Elegant Decorums: The Concept of Propriety in Jane Austen's Novels* (Albany: State University of New York Press, 1973). Eve Sedgwick's critique of the "Girl Being Taught a Lesson" mode of Austenian criticism ought, in my view, to be required reading for everyone interested in writing and reading about Austen; in Watt (ed.), *Jane Austen*, pp. 833–34.

11.   Wilson, "A Long Talk about Jane Austen," in *Classics and Commercials*, p. 201; Mudrick, *Jane Austen*, pp. 192–93; Joseph M. Duffy, "Emma: The Awakening from Innocence," *ELH* 21 (1954), p. 42; Lionel Trilling, in Lodge (ed.), *Casebook*, p. 130; Tanner, *Jane Austen* (Cambridge, Mass.: Harvard University Press, 1986), p. 180.

12.   Lionel Trilling, in Lodge (ed.), *Casebook*, p. 134.

13.   Nancy Armstrong illuminates Emma's respect for the manliness of Robert Martin's style; see *Desire and Domestic Fiction: A Political History of the Novel* (New York: Oxford University Press, 1987), pp. 146–50.

14.   For an excellent discussion of the opposition of the "impure, dishonest, dissembling, imitative, servile" French to the "moral sobriety, individual independence, and collective fellowship" of the English, see Gerald Newman, *The Rise of English Nationalism: A Cultural History 1740–1830* (New York: St. Martin's Press, 1987), pp. 230, 231ff. My discussion of the anti-French elements of *Emma* has also been informed by Stella Cottrell, "The Devil on Two Sticks: Franco-Phobia in 1803," in *Patriotism: The Making and Unmaking of British National*

Identity, ed. Raphael Samuel (London: Routledge, 1989); and Ernest Gellner, *Nationals and Nationalism* (Ithaca: Cornell University Press, 1983).

15. For a compelling study of Emma's reproduction with Harriet of the same heterosexual protocols Wollstonecraft lambastes in *Rights of Woman,* see Allison Sulloway, "Emma Woodhouse and *A Vindication of the Rights of Woman,*" *Wordsworth Circle* 7 (1976), pp. 320–32. Ruth Perry also reads *Emma* as a plea for the enlargement of female friendship; see "Interrupted Friendships in Jane Austen's *Emma,*" *Tulsa Studies in Women's Literature* 5 (1986), pp. 185–202.

[Austen's Accommodations]

Alistair M. Duckworth

> With all the chances against her of house, hall, place, park, court, and cottage,
> Northanger turned up an abbey.

So Catherine Morland exults, while wondering that her friends, the Tilneys,
are not elated by a home that surely has "long, damp passages . . . narrow
cells and ruined chapel" (*Northanger Abbey*, 141).[1] In fact, Northanger Abbey
is the *dernier cri* in modern improvements. Caring for "no furniture of a more
modern date than the fifteenth century" (*NA*, 182), Catherine is dismayed to
find "furniture in all the profusion and elegance of modern taste" (*NA*, 162),
a smoke-free Rumford fire-place, and a breakfast room with a set of Stafford-
shire china. The late Mrs. Tilney's apartment has a Bath stove, mahogany
wardrobes, and neatly painted chairs. True, the kitchen is the original kitchen
of the convent, but even here General Tilney's "improving hand had not loi-
tered . . . every modern invention to facilitate the labour of the cooks, had
been adopted within this, their spacious theatre" (*NA*, 183). Outside in the
grounds, Catherine is shown a huge kitchen garden, countless walls, a "whole
village of hot-houses," and much more. Northanger has pineapples in its
plantations and French bread in its ovens. The General is conspicuous in his
modernism, resembling Count Rumford in his inventiveness, or Pope's Timon
in the grandiosity of his conceptions.[2] Surely there is more to Jane Austen's
untypically detailed descriptions of house and grounds than the aim of deflat-
ing the heroine's "gothic" preconceptions.

General Tilney is, in fact, a modern rather than gothic tyrant, a member
of the wealthy gentry voraciously intent on extending his power and riches
through arranging an advantageous matrimonial alliance for his son. This explains his deference to Catherine at Northanger and, later, at Woodston parsonage. Woodston is a "new-built substantial stone house, with . . . semi-cir-
cular sweep and green gates" (*NA*, 212). Disappointed at Catherine's
apparent lack of enthusiasm, the General suggests a bow window as an improvement. His solicitude vanishes when he discovers that Catherine is not

From Alistair M. Duckworth, "Jane Austen's Accommodations," *Tennessee Studies in Literature* 29
(1985): 225–67. The essay has undergone minor revisions by its author since its original publication.
© 1985 by The University of Tennessee Press; reprinted by permission.

the heiress he has assumed. She is dismissed immediately from the Abbey, forced to borrow money from Eleanor, and, after a journey of seventy miles, unattended, eventually returns home to the Fullerton parsonage, a "heroine in a hack post-chaise" (NA, 232).

Within the parody of the gothic novel that is the obvious genre of Northanger Abbey, another drama is played out, the drama of an innocent girl of modest means abroad in society. That there are horrors enough in this scenario is a hidden message of the novel. Alongside the delight Jane Austen took in spoofing The Mysteries of Udolpho, and in exposing the social hypocrisies of Bath society, there are even in this buoyant early work intimations of concern for the predicament of the single woman in a materialistic world. Jane Austen was in her twenty-fourth year when she first composed the novel in 1799 and may already have seen the writing on the wall. Within two years she would be forced to leave her own parsonage home at Steventon for residence in Bath, and (despite the report of her fainting away on being abruptly told by her mother of the intended move) she is likely to have known of her father's plans to retire, relinquish his livings to his eldest son, and remove with his wife and two daughters to another place—one appropriate to a reduced income. What domestic destiny lay ahead? What were Jane Austen's own chances of "house, hall, place, park, court and cottage"? In Bath the Austens stayed first in Sidney Place and Green Park Buildings and then, after Mr. Austen's death, in smaller houses in Gay Street and Trim Street. In 1806, Mrs. Austen and her two daughters shared a house with Frank Austen and his wife in Castle Square, Southampton, and in 1809, mother and daughters took up residence in Chawton Cottage, a house recently inhabited by the Chawton Manor steward and said to have been a "posting-inn" in the past.

Jane Austen ended up in a cottage, then. For apart from visits such as those to her brother Edward in Kent and to her brother Henry in London, she would stay at Chawton for the rest of her life, revising the novels she wrote in the late 1790's—published as Sense and Sensibility (1811), Pride and Prejudice (1813), and Northanger Abbey (1818)—and composing the novels of her maturity: Mansfield Park (1814), Emma (1816), and Persuasion (1818). Her domestic destiny was to be a spinster in a cottage, sharing a bedroom with her sister Cassandra and writing her novels in the common sitting room, where, warned by a creaking door, she could slip her papers under the blotting-book before visitors discovered her at her creative work. Without a room of her own, certainly without the £500 a year that Virginia Woolf thought essential to a woman's artistic freedom, she wrote about the sorts of houses she would never be mistress of—Delaford, Pemberley, Mansfield Park, Donwell Abbey—and described women who, through good marriages, acquire comfortable domestic establishments. Three of her heroines—Catherine Morland, Elinor Dashwood, Fanny Price—find accommodation in parsonages, a destiny that I suspect Jane Austen would herself have found congenial. Another three—Marianne Dashwood, Elizabeth Bennet, Emma Woodhouse—become the mistresses of estates varying from the modest to the magnificent. To be mistress of Pemberley, Elizabeth recognizes when that possibility seems remote, would be something. When she does become mistress of the estate, with its park "ten miles round" and its income of £10,000 a year, she can fulfill her aunt Gardiner's dream of a trip around the park in "a low phaeton, with a nice little pair of ponies" (*Pride and Prejudice*, 325). Readers who recall George Stubbs's painting of *Two Cream Ponies, a Phaeton and a Stable Lad* (c. 1785) will gain a sense of the elegance and grace of Elizabeth's married situation.

The fate that Marianne Dashwood escapes, "of remaining . . . for ever with her mother, and finding her only pleasures in retirement and study" (*Sense and Sensibility*, 378), came to none of Jane Austen's heroines, then, but was reserved for herself. Her study, however, was not the study of a scholar but of a novelist unsurpassed in the observation of social manners and in the discrimination of the distinctive signs of social difference. Pushed to the margin, she obtained a lucid perspective on the center of her world, the world of the modest gentry in its relations with the wealthy gentry and with trade and the professions. The exact character of her perspective on society has divided critics for a century. Virginia Woolf believed the "chief miracle" of *Pride and Prejudice* was that it had not been adversely affected by its author's circumstances; Jane Austen wrote "without hate, without bitterness, without fear, without protest, without preaching"; like Shakespeare's, her mind had "consumed all impediments."[3] Others have disagreed, finding hatred in her novels and letters, a criticism of primogeniture, a subversion of patriarchal rule. It is true that she did not always consume impediments with the same success as in *Pride and Prejudice.* But she did effect miracles. Deprived in her life of the house she felt entitled to, afflicted by a sense of restricted social space, she gave her heroines homes ranging from the "snug" to the "commodious." In order to *give* accommodations, however, she had to *make* accommodations. Aware that happy endings are the triumph of fantasy over fact, and that in traditional novels plot is the accomplice of desire, she sought to bring her dreams into acceptable conformity with the exigencies of real life.

Her novels are subtle and complex negotiations with the facts of her social experience. Her heroines are Pamela's daughters in the sense that they marry appropriately and well, implying in the process that the "virtues" of integrity and intelligence will be "rewarded" with a fitting domestic establishment. But while she accommodates her sense of social fact to conventional Richardsonian plot structures and, in so doing, caters to the wishes of her reading public, she also puts "desire"—her own as well as her readers'—in ironical perspective. To this end, for example, she "lays bare" the mechanism of her denouement in *Northanger Abbey.* Her techniques of "desublimation" are not as patent as those later employed by Thackeray, but by foregrounding the artificiality of her conclusion, they serve similar "realistic" goals.[4]

"What probable circumstance could work upon a temper like the General's?" (*NA,* 250) is the question of the final chapter. Henry has followed Catherine to Fullerton and has proposed and been accepted by her, and by her parents, but how are his father's objections to be overcome? Jane Austen concedes that the anxiety "can hardly extend . . . to the bosom of my readers, who will see in the tell-tale compression of the pages before them, that we are all hastening together to perfect felicity" (*NA,* 250). The circumstance that removes the General's objections is the advantageous marriage of Henry's sister Eleanor to a gentleman, whose addresses to her had previously been prevented by "inferiority of situation." His "unexpected accession of title and fortune" removed *that* problem, but Jane Austen can say little else—since the rules of composition forbid the late introduction of characters—except that "this was the very gentleman whose negligent servant left behind him that collection of washing-bills . . . by which my heroine was involved in one of her most alarming adventures" (*NA,* 251). By such parodic means—worthy of Cervantes—Jane Austen brings the pleasure principle into alignment with the reality principle. If it requires such a concatenation of fortuitous events to bring about the marriage of hero and heroine, then we are in the realm of romance still, and should assess the marriage of Henry and Catherine accordingly.

Yet this is perhaps to put it too strongly. Despite the subversion of conventional novelistic endings that the final chapter displays, Jane Austen's conclusion allows "desire" a measure of triumph. Henry's marriage to Catherine finally rests on a realistic basis; the General learns, contrary to the misinformation of John Thorpe, that the Morlands are "in no sense of the word . . . necessitous or poor," that Catherine will have £3,000, and that the Fullerton estate is entirely at the disposal of its proprietor, Mr. Allen, and therefore "open to every greedy speculation" (*NA,* 252). Thus, while Catherine may not be entitled to become mistress of the Abbey, she does have a claim on Woodston parsonage. And if she does not merit "the dignity of a countess, with a long train of noble relations in their several phaetons" (*NA,* 232), then neither need she settle for a hack post-chaise. Even while bringing Catherine's expectations down to their proper (architectural) size, Jane Austen claims for Catherine and her other heroines what Othello claims for Desdemona:

> Due reference of place and exhibition
> With such accommodation and besort
> As levels with her breeding.
> (*Othello,* I.iii.237–39)

But at the back of her consciousness there is always the possibility (to allude to Shakespeare again) of the "unaccommodated" woman, reduced to bare, penurious, single existence. Such women appear, in fact, in the novels in secondary roles: Elizabeth Watson in the unfinished fragment, *The Watsons;* Miss

Bates in *Emma;* Mrs. Smith in *Persuasion;* and their fates shadow the lives of the heroines, who are all, with the exception of Emma Woodhouse, in uncertain social positions at some point in their lives.

II

What was there in Jane Austen's background to explain this sense of entitlement shadowed by apprehensions of disinheritance? As recent interpreters have shown, a key to her fictional vision is to be found in the particular circumstances of her social position.[5] On her mother's side Jane Austen was related to nobility, being a great-grandniece of the first Duke of Chandos (though by her time the Chandos peerage was extinct). Her mother was a Leigh of the Leighs of Adlestrop. Stoneleigh Abbey in Warwickshire belonged to a younger, ennobled branch of the family. A magnificent example of that mixture of architectural styles to which the eighteenth century gave the name "Sharawadgi," Stoneleigh comprises the remains of a Cistercian Abbey, an Elizabethan mansion, and a classic west range, which Smith of Warwick added on to the mansion in the years after 1714. It was the one truly imposing country house Jane Austen knew. She visited it in August 1806, shortly after it was inherited by her mother's cousin, the Rev. Thomas Leigh of Adlestrop. So vast was the house (twenty-six bedrooms in the new part alone) that Mrs. Austen humorously suggested he put up signposts. Equally interesting were the grounds, which had remained unaffected by successive waves of landscape improvements in the eighteenth century, and were thus as old-fashioned as the family itself. (Long known for their Tory and Jacobite sympathies, the Leighs had made their house available to Charles I when he was denied entry to Coventry, and they were just as willing to accommodate the Young Pretender in 1745.)

In 1806, however, the grounds at Stoneleigh were about to be improved. Impressed by the work Humphry Repton had done at Adlestrop—where his "improvements" involved the sweeping away of a seventeenth-century garden, complete with canal, fountain and alcoves—Dr. Leigh planned to invite the controversial landscape architect to redesign his newly acquired property. Undoubtedly he discussed his ideas with the Austen women and, as Mavis Batey has argued, the visit is thus the probable source of the conversation over improvements in chapter six of *Mansfield Park*. Stoneleigh—its Elizabethan parts anyway—may indeed be a model for the fictional Sotherton Court. But Repton appears in a dubious light in the novel, and it may be doubted whether Jane Austen viewed with approval the prospect of his "improvements" at Stoneleigh. How she reacted to his actual improvements is not known. (Repton removed walls, opened vistas, and altered the course of the river Avon; his Red Book [1809], detailing his plans and illustrating his proposed designs, is at Stoneleigh to this day.) In 1806, it may well be that Stoneleigh confirmed her sense of connection to a historical heritage. Jane Austen was no enemy to tasteful improvements but, as I shall argue later, her novels show a fondness for old estates that have evolved naturally over the years, without the aid of the professional improver's hand.[6]

On her father's side, Jane Austen's lineage was less distinguished. George Austen's family descended from Kentish clothiers who had become prosperous and landed, but George's father was a mere surgeon, not a respectable profession in the eighteenth century. His uncle Francis Austen, the solicitor, did become very rich, however, by virtue both of his legal work (including being the agent to the Duke of Dorset at Knole) and of his marriage to not one but two heiresses. At about the time of Jane Austen's birth in 1775, Francis Austen persuaded Lady Falkland, the godmother of his eldest son, to will his godson a legacy of lands worth £100,000.[7] Earlier he had paid his nephew's fees at Tonbridge School (whence George obtained a fellowship to St. John's College, Oxford), and had purchased for him, after he took orders, the living at Deane in Hampshire. This became vacant in 1773, providing a welcome addition to the living at nearby Steventon, which another rich relation, Thomas Knight of Godmersham in Kent, had presented to George in 1761.

Despite his combined livings, George Austen was not particularly well off during Jane Austen's childhood. Steventon was valued at £100 a year, and Deane at £110, and though tithes increased his income, he evidently found it necessary to take in pupils and farm his glebe lands. He was able to improve Steventon Rectory, however, so that it became a roomy and comfortable home, as shown in several drawings made by Jane Austen's niece, Anna Lefroy; one sketch shows a front of two stories with dormered attics above.[8] Moreover, he kept a carriage and was a kind of acting squire of Steventon. If his connections with such territorial magnates as Lord Portsmouth and Lord Dorchester were slight, those with such gentry families as the Harwoods of Deane and the Bigg-Withers of Manydown were cordial and close.

As she was growing up, Jane Austen occasionally visited great houses like Hurstbourne Park, the home of the third Lord Portsmouth, who had been for a short time a pupil at Steventon; she went there, we know, to the annual ball in November 1800, an occasion graced by the presence of her brother Lieutenant Charles Austen, of the frigate *Endymion,* home from the successful capture of the French ship *Scipio* in a heavy gale. But more usual and congenial were visits to Deane House, Ashe Park, and Manydown. These houses, though on a much smaller scale than Hurstbourne Park—or Hackwood Park, the seat of the Duke of Bolton near Basingstoke—were commodious manor houses dear to Jane Austen's heart. "To sit in idleness over a good fire in a well-proportioned room is a luxurious sensation," she wrote to Cassandra in November 1800, after a "sudden invitation" and a journey in a post-chaise had taken her to Ashe Park.[9]

This was a year before she left for Bath. A year after that removal she returned to Steventon and, while on a visit to Manydown, accepted a proposal of marriage from Harris Bigg-Wither, the son and heir, and a man six years her junior. This action, the most precipitate of her life, was almost instantly revoked (the next morning); but can we doubt that it was the appeal of house and establishment in her beloved Hampshire that prompted the acceptance, and the realization that there were certain accommodations she could not make to gain that end that prompted the change of mind? Jane Austen was almost twenty-seven when she rejected Bigg-Wither's proposal in December 1802. At the same age, Charlotte Lucas accepts the abominable Mr. Collins, a decision Elizabeth Bennet considers to lack "integrity" (*PP,* 135–36). Marriage throughout the novels is the most important "accommodation" of all, and we may be sure that, like Elizabeth, Jane Austen pondered long over "the difference in matrimonial affairs, between the mercenary and the prudent motive" (*PP,* 153), especially since the answer seemed to assume a double standard. When Elizabeth visits Charlotte at the Hunsford parsonage, she is surprised to discover how well Charlotte has fitted up her house, how successfully she has arranged the rooms so as to be as little bothered by Collins as possible. But while she gives Charlotte credit for her neat accommodations, she does not alter her view that marriage simply out of desire for an "establishment" is an unprincipled act.[10]

From such a home as the Steventon Rectory, children with the right training, a little luck, and sufficient will could expect to do well—if they were male. The careers of the Austen brothers support this view. James, the eldest, became a clergyman, succeeded his father at Steventon in 1800, and by 1808, with the aid of an allowance from James Leigh Perrot, his mother's rich brother, enjoyed a comfortable annual income of about £1,100. Of George, the second son, little is known except that he was deaf and suffered from fits. Edward, the third son, had the great good fortune of being adopted in his teens by George Austen's kinsman Thomas Knight, and of becoming the heir and eventual owner of estates in Kent (Godmersham) and Hampshire (Chawton). Henry, the fourth son, the most versatile and least dependable, became a banker; as the result of a number of factors, including the failure of wheat prices, his firm—Austen, Maunde and Tilson of London—failed in 1816, and he was declared bankrupt. Edward lost £20,000 as a result; James Leigh Perrot lost £10,000 but was nonetheless able, on his death in 1817, to leave considerable funds and property to his wife, much of which eventually came to James Austen's family. After the bankruptcy, Henry settled into the congenial role of clergyman. The younger sons, Francis and Charles, pursued highly successful careers in the Royal Navy, both ending up as admirals.

Even such a brief sketch of the brothers' careers suggests that the Austens as a family were successful, "at home" in their society, figures of varying consequence in the church, the land, and the naval profession. Aware of her lineage, particularly on her mother's side, and proud of the accomplishments of her brothers (all except Charles older than she), Jane Austen had more than sufficient cause to feel that she had a stake in her country. The origins of her fictional patriotism, expressed so overtly in the praise of "English verdure, English culture, English comfort" in *Emma* (p. 360), were familial, deep, and never—despite provocations—eradicated. The "francophobia" of her novels, too, has a family origin. Jane Austen lived through the French Revolutionary and Napoleonic wars, which touched her family directly. In 1797, Henry married his cousin Eliza, widow of the Comte de Feuillide who had been guillotined in 1794. Her brothers Frank and Charles were engaged at sea against the French. In 1800, Frank Austen was elevated to the rank of post-captain for his feat of capturing off Marseilles a French ship laden with corn for the forces in Egypt. Later his bravery and efficiency caught the eye of Nelson, but to his disappointment Frank missed the Trafalgar action in 1805. Such connections help explain Jane Austen's nationalism, the strain of cultural affirmation that is genuinely present in her novels; at the same time they put in doubt recent claims by some feminist critics that she was a severe and unremitting critic of the patriarchal system in which she lived.

Feminist criticism of the past decade, however, has valuably focused our attention on Jane Austen's predicament as a woman in her society.[11] In spite of a presumably happy childhood at Steventon—with its pleasures of reading, private theatricals, balls, and visits—she was, along with other women of her time and class, restricted as to opportunities. Her brothers' routes to power, position, money, and success were closed to her, and particularly after her removal from Steventon, her position was insecure. George Austen had very nearly £600 a year on retirement, not a rich income but enough to provide for a comfortable establishment with two maids and a manservant (*Letters*, 99). But on his death the family income from the livings at Deane and Steventon ceased, and Mrs. Austen and her daughters found themselves with a mere £210 year—and some of this came from a settlement made to Cassandra in 1797 on the death of her fiancé in the West Indies. The Austen brothers rallied round: James, Henry, and Frank each provided an allowance of £50 a year, and the considerably richer Edward came up with £100. Thus the income of the Austen women became £460 a year, a sum sufficient to provide for a fairly comfortable life and a servant. But Jane Austen had become, one suspects, a member of that significant group in English life and letters, the "distressed gentility."

She was hardly beneath the poverty line; indeed, her fictional sense of what was financially due to persons of her position was, as R. W. Chapman noted, high. Katherine Mansfield apparently agreed; in a diary entry for February 1914, her comment on the statement in *Sense and Sensibility* that neither Elinor nor Edward was "quite enough in love to imagine that £350 a year would supply them with all the comforts of life" is a simple "My God!"[12] We may be excused for forgetting how much a pound was worth right up to World War II. One study sets £300 as the lowest limit of a gentlemanly income in the eighteenth century.[13] But even in the 1930s professional women were lucky to earn £250 a year, as Virginia Woolf angrily pointed out in *Three Guineas*. Woolf also painted a sympathetic portrait of the plight of distressed gentility in Ellie Henderson in *Mrs. Dalloway* (1925), and Ellie Henderson has some features in common with the Jane Austen who was grateful to receive handouts from Edward's adoptive mother, Mrs. Knight (*Letters*, 194); who took gifts she had made herself to Godmersham on her visits (*Letters*, 190); and who was forever worrying about how she would get from place to place, or somewhat bitterly aware that until she had a "traveling-purse" of her own she must not expect to determine visits or itineraries (*Letters*, 203).

From an early age, Jane Austen had imagined the condition of the impoverished woman with social claims. The third letter of her juvenile "Collection of Letters" is entitled "From a young Lady in distres'd Circumstances to her freind." The heroine, Maria Williams, has to endure Lady Greville's questioning as she is driven in the latter's carriage to a private ball. Like Lady Catherine's in *Pride and Prejudice*, Lady Greville's aggressive questions are intended to establish the social inferiority of the heroine and her family. She is incensed that the Williamses spend money on candles and on an expensive gown for their daughter: "But I suppose you intend to make your fortune tonight," she charges (*Minor Works*, 156). Like Elizabeth later, Maria shows independence and courage in her "humiliating Situation." The heroine of reduced means abused by a vulgar aristocrat is an encounter that can be traced back at least to Pamela's experiences with Lady Davers in Richardson's novel, but in this particular "exercise," Jane Austen was comically exaggerating possibilities closer to home.

During the years following George Austen's death, Jane Austen shared her mother's expectations of increased income. As she was fond of remarking, "a Legacy is our sovereign good" (*Letters*, 199). Marriage as a means of increased income was now improbable; both Cassandra and Jane were in their thirties, well beyond the "terminal" age for marriage (twenty-seven) suggested by the novels. But there were two hopeful sources of funds. One of these was Mrs. Austen's brother, James Leigh Perrot. The Leigh Perrots were wealthy and childless; James, the eldest Austen son, was considered their natural heir, but it is clear from the letters that Mrs. Austen was in continuous expectation of a legacy from her brother. It never came—not after George Austen's death, when it would have been particularly welcome; not after the "vile compromise" (*Letters*, 316) over the Stoneleigh estate which made Leigh Perrot—who had a legal claim—richer by a sum of £24,000 and £2,000 a year; not even after Leigh Perrot's death in 1817, when there were great expectations from his will.

The other possible source of improved income was Edward Austen. Besides the allowance of £100 a year that he provided after his father's death, in 1809 he offered his mother and sisters a choice of houses on his estates at

Chawton and Godmersham. Moreover, he extended his hospitality to his sisters, who went to Godmersham for long stays. Jane Austen's biographers have generally been uncritical of Edward, noting his tendency to ill health and hypochondria but not accusing him of tightfistedness. Yet we may wonder whether he did as much for his mother and sisters as he could. He had become, through his fortunate adoption, "the master of a great gentry estate of the order of Mr. Rushworth's [Sotherton Court],"[14] as well as of Chawton Manor. We can view these estates as they appeared during or just before Jane Austen's time: engravings of W. Watts's views of Godmersham (dating from 1784–85) appear in E. Hasted's *The History and Topographical Survey of the County of Kent* (1799) and are reproduced in Chapman's edition of the *Letters* (facing pp. 168 and 330). Viewing them, we not only get an accurate sense of the setting of houses like Mansfield Park ("so well placed and well screened," Mary Crawford finds, "as to deserve to be in any collection of engravings of gentlemen's seats in the country" [*Mansfield Park*, 48]) but a sense, too, of the contrasts in Jane Austen's existence: contrasts between "rooms concise [and] rooms distended," as she expressed it in a poem written on the occasion of their moving to Chawton (*Letters*, 266), or between the "vulgar cares" of her normal existence and "the happy Indifference of East Kent wealth" that she conformed to at Godmersham (*Letters*, 336).

Godmersham was what Jane Austen would call a "modern house": that is, a house in the Palladian style, with a central block (dating from the 1730s) flanked by matching wings that were added in 1781. Watts's views show it set in a park improved in the style of Capability Brown. A winding approach skirts a smooth lawn, interspersed with "clumps" of trees; there is a rather aggressively serpentine river with a well-designed bridge; the offices and farm buildings are largely screened from view. It is "complete," as Mary Crawford would say, a visible sign of the prosperity the owner enjoyed as a result of income for agricultural rents. These must have been considerable, as may be suggested by the "Book of Maps containing the Several Estates in the County of Kent belonging to Thomas Knight of Godmersham Park, Esquire" (1789). There are seven plans of the Godmersham estate in the book, as well as detailed maps of "Great Eggerton, Little Eggerton, Pope Street Farm, East Stour, Upper Drucksted, Waltham, Eggering, Crundall Farm, Buckwell Farm," and more (some two dozen farms in all).[15]

Edward's annual income from his estates, as well as that accruing from his marriage contract with Elizabeth Bridges of Goodnestone, Kent, is not known, but at the risk of circular reasoning, it is possible to speculate. The income of the gentry in Jane Austen's fiction ranges from about £600 a year (Willoughby's before his marriage to Sofia Grey) to the noble £12,000 enjoyed by Rushworth at Sotherton. Colonel Brandon of Delaford and Mr. Bennet of Longbourn have £2,000 a year. Henry Crawford draws £4,000 a year from Everingham. The grasping John Dashwoods at Norland, despite their expensive improvements and land purchases, live within an income that may be estimated at about £5,000 or £6,000 a year.

If one assumes that Edward's income was in this range (and David Spring's comparison of Godmersham with Sotherton suggests that it may have been twice as much) then there is an intriguing question to be asked about how Edward Austen interpreted the brilliantly satirical second chapter of *Sense and Sensibility* on its publication in 1811. John Dashwood's stepmother and half-sisters leave Norland for distant Devonshire there to live in a cottage with a combined income of £500 a year (close to that of the Austen women). John Dashwood, in the meantime, has given a minimalist interpretation to his father's dying request that he look after them. Abetted by his wife, who has brought a fortune of £10,000 into the family, he progressively reduces his generosity from a gift of £1,000 to each of his three sisters to £500 each, to an annuity of £100 to their mother during her lifetime ("but then if Mrs. Dashwood should live fifteen years we shall be completely taken in," his wife points out) to occasional gifts of £50, to presents of fish and game, to a final rationalization that his stepmother and sisters will be "comfortable" on their £500 a year. It is a masterly exposure of greed and the failure of a generosity which, if not possessed innately, was obligatory in the circumstances. Could Edward have read it without qualms? It is possible. He did after all provide the annuity of £100.[16]

Chawton Manor was neither so grand nor so modern as Godmersham, nor was the style of its landscape so distinctively fashionable. It was nevertheless a place of some consequence. The Elizabethan house, with Tudor porch and mullioned windows, was set in a modestly improved park, as one may see in Prosser's print (reproduced in the *Letters,* facing p. 304). An even more charming view exists in an anonymous gouache of the house.[17] The Austen women lived, as it were, on the edge of this estate, which was not occupied by Edward during their early years there but rented to a family named Middleton—interesting in view of the family with the same name in *Sense and Sensibility.* Attempts have been made to view Chawton Cottage as "the small house at Chawton," following the example set by Trollope's *The Small House at Allington;* and it is true that the house was not called a cottage at the time and that the Austens seemed to enjoy their house and garden, in which they planted syringas, sweet williams, and columbines. Edward took steps to give the house an air of privacy and quiet. The large drawing room window was blocked up, and the garden was screened from the road by a hornbeam hedge. Even so, in terms of a scale that comprised Hurstbourne Park, Stoneleigh Abbey, Godmersham, Chawton House, and the houses of Ashe, Deane, and Manydown, Chawton Cottage was not large; its modest dimensions and marginal relation to the great house measure Jane Austen's own reduced and marginal relation to society at the time when she began to write and revise her novels.

III

Jane Austen's "distressed gentility," I suggest, is a key to the incisive social analysis of her novels. Schooled by her experience in Bath, at Godmersham, and in London, where through Henry and Eliza she came in contact with French émigrée circles (*Letters,* 271–77), she became a keen observer of the nuances of social differences, a discriminating spectator of performances in public places. She measured the ways in which money mattered, particularly in marriage—what Smollett in *Humphry Clinker* had termed "the holy bands of mattermoney." As readers have long sensed and social historians have more recently confirmed, she had an extensive and exact knowledge of incomes; she knew the value of livings and the law of entails; and she knew what fortune would capture the eldest son of a baronet or the younger son of an earl. She had an eye, too, for those "positional goods" that were the signs of, or presumptive claims to, social status.[18]

She had, for example, an eye for a carriage. Carriages were not only the appendages of money and marriage but markers of rank and financial worth. As such, they have an interest well beyond the antiquarian in her life and fiction.[19] As early as 1798, when her father laid down his carriage, she knew the "disconvenience" of not having a conveyance to neighboring balls (*Letters,* 29). What such "disconvenience" could mean is suggested by Lady Greville's remarks to Maria Williams (as Maria stands outside the coach in the wind and cold): "You young ladies who cannot often ride in a Carriage never mind what weather you trudge in, or how the wind shews your legs" (*MW,* 159).

In the instance of carriages as of houses, however, social dispossession led to possession in another—aesthetic—mode. The hero of *Memoirs of Mr. Clifford* (written before Jane was fifteen) travels to London in a "Coach and Four," but he also possesses "a Coach, a Chariot, a Chaise, a Landeau, a Landeaulet, a Phaeton, a Gig, a Whisky, an Italian Chair, a Buggy, a Curricle & a Wheelbarrow," as well as "an amazing fine stud of horses . . . six Greys, 4 Bays, eight Blacks & a poney" (*MW,* 43). Beyond the Rabelaisian parody of the "list," there is here, as in Catherine Morland's list of possible domestic destinies, a spectrum of discriminated social claims and possibilities.

The list is not complete, despite its length. It lacks the barouche-landau which Mrs. Elton recalls to boost her claims to status, and Henry Crawford's barouche, which causes so much dissension between the Bertram sisters on the trip to Sotherton. But it includes other conveyances that figure often significantly, in the novels. General Tilney, as one would expect travels in a fashionable chaise-and-four, with liveried postilions and numerous outriders (*NA,* 156). Lady Catherine travels to Longbourn in a similar state to tell Elizabeth she cannot marry Darcy (*PP,* 351). Her sickly daughter "often condescends to drive by [Mr. Collins's] humble abode in her little phaeton and ponies" (*PP,* 67). In the same novel the Bennets have a carriage, but its horses are sometimes needed on the farm. The nouveau riche Bingley has a chaise, and several characters own curricles (the curricle was a fashionable two-wheeled conveyance, drawn by a pair of horses); Darcy drives one when he brings his sister to meet Elizabeth. Henry Tilney has one, too, and when Catherine transfers from the General's chaise to Henry's curricle on the way to Woodston, she is "as happy a being as ever existed" (*NA,* 156). Willoughby drives Marianne to Allenham, unchaperoned, in a curricle (*SS,* 67) but he is, one suspects, living beyond his income. John Thorpe in *Northanger Abbey* covets a curricle but has to make do with a gig, a vehicle drawn by one horse, which is appropriate to his income, social status, and driving skills. Other characters who own gigs are the hard-up Sir Edward Denham in *Sanditon;* Mr. Collins, ever anxious to demean himself in *Pride and Prejudice;* and Admiral Croft in *Persuasion,* where the gig signifies not modest means (he is rich enough to rent Kellynch Hall) but his freedom from social vanity and his close partnership with his wife. In the same novel Anne Elliot eventually becomes "mistress of a very pretty landaulette" (*Persuasion,* 250). By contrast, in her own life at Chawton, Jane Austen became mistress of a donkey and cart (*Letters,* 475–76, 485).

As she was deprived of the house she desired, so she was deprived of a carriage adequate to her dreams. The years brought a philosophic mind. She found she could enjoy the "luxury" of riding in Henry's open barouche in the summer of 1813, while admitting that she had "naturally small right to be parading about London in a Barouche" (*Letters,* 312–13). But in her youth she had not been quite so resigned. Everywhere in the juvenilia we can sense her resentment of a world in which social competitiveness and husband-hunting are the norm. With verve and brio she exposes the rationalizations and hypocrisies of this world. Like Mary Wollstonecraft, she attacks the acquisition of accomplishments by young women of leisure, an attack that continues in the novels. She observes, somewhat obsessively, how important a fair complexion is in marriageable women, a theme that recurs in *Pride and Prejudice,* for example, where Miss Bingley considers Elizabeth "so brown and coarse," but Darcy thinks her only "rather tanned" (*PP,* 27–71). As in the later novels, she criticizes women obsessed with clothes and external appearance, and men addicted to shooting or billiards or overeating.

Again and again, her most pointed satire has to do with the importance of money in matters of marriage and position. "In Lady Williams," she writes, "every virtue met. She was a widow with a handsome Jointure & the remains of a very handsome face" (*MW,* 13). Through such non sequiturs, through zeugma, hyperbole, and mock-Johnsonian antitheses, she exposes the gap between money and morals, desire and decorum. She exaggerates her own social anxieties and for the most part laughs them out of existence. A tailor's daughter leaves her home in Wales in pursuit of a nonpareil, Charles Adams. Her journey ends when she is caught in a man-trap in his grounds. This is not, however, her main worry. Though "possessed of Youth, Beauty, Wit & Merit, & tho' the probable Heiress of [her] Aunts House & business," she

fears Charles Adams might think her "deficient in Rank" (*MW,* 21). More often the deficiency is financial. In "The Three Sisters," written when Jane
Austen was seventeen, and as brilliant an exposure of sibling competitiveness
as one could wish, the following dialogue takes place:

> "Yet how can I hope that my Sister may accept a Man, who cannot make her
> happy."
> "He cannot it is true but his Fortune, his Name, his House, his Carriage
> will." (*MW,* 61)

"He" is Mr. Watts, and his income of £3,000 a year is, as one of the sisters
says, "but six times as much as my Mother's income" (*MW,* 62). Or, we can
add, but five times as much as George Austen's probable income at the time
of the story.

No one can doubt, reading the minor works, that Jane Austen was a
critic of her society. There is a wit, a frankness, a vitality to the exposure of
mercenary conduct in the juvenilia that amply justify the attention they have
received in recent criticism. But whether they measure the depth of the
young Jane Austen's alienation from her patriarchal culture is another question.[20] Her apprehension of social dislocation gives edge to her satire but does
not leave her disaffected with her culture. The epistolary *Love and Freindship*
(1790), for example, delights in capturing the grotesque shapes that the cult
of sensibility can achieve; but it also measures the vicious consequences of
selfish individualism, disregard of propriety and of property, disobedience of
parents, and an ungrounded faith in the power of love and "elective affinities." However severely Jane Austen attacked social vices, she retained in the
juvenile pieces, as in her published fiction, a vision of ideal social modes. The
force of humor and irony, indeed, rests on an awareness of the difference between ideal and perverted forms of social conduct, as is surely evident in *Lady
Susan,* her brilliant essay in the epistolary mode, of about 1794–95. Lady Susan is a predatory widow quite without a moral sense. She enjoys London,
finding existence in a country village "insupportable" (*MW,* 245). She is a co-
quette, a manipulator, a tyrannical mother intent on forcing her daughter
into a financially rewarding match with a man she detests and, to this end,
insistent that her daughter gain "those accomplishments which are now necessary to finish a pretty Woman" (*MW,* 253). She has a regard for her brother-
in-law Charles Vernon—"he is so easily imposed on" (*MW,* 250)—but has
eyes for Reginald de Courcy, scion of a noble family, whose "insolent spirit"
she means to subdue and whose money and position she plans to acquire.
Against her the forces of conventional morality (chiefly Mrs. Charles Vernon)
are somewhat dull, as critics have argued (although Letter 12, to Reginald
from his father, warning him of his duties to himself, his parents and his
name, is sufficiently dignified and effective). Jane Austen delighted in capturing "the artifice of this unprincipled woman" (like Keats, she could imagine

an Iago as well as an Imogen), but the brilliance of her characterization does not imply her covert sympathy. Like Mary Crawford later, Lady Susan joins an amoral character to a witty command of language. But she is too clever by half, and ends up married to the man she intended for her daughter.

By indicating the moral content of the minor works, we may seek to qualify a recent tendency in Austen criticism to value the juvenilia over the published novels on the grounds of the early works' lack of "organic camouflage."[21] In this view, the formal achievements of the mature novels tend to be reduced to the status of defense mechanisms, blunting or deflecting what would otherwise be frank attacks on patriarchal oppression. Of course, there are dangers also in counterposing a "moral" Jane Austen. On some occasions, her criticism of mercenary conduct seems more like a reflex of her own reduced or threatened circumstances than a position grounded in moral principle. On other occasions, her satire works in self-protective ways. Critical of aristocrats like Lady Catherine, who appeal to decorum in order to suppress social aspirations, she can make her own appeal to tradition in order to expose "illiterate" and vulgar characters like Lady Steele and Mrs. Elton, who pose threats from below.[22] Yet she is generally successful in distinguishing the false appeal from the true, and while we may in particular instances question the motives of her appeal to traditional manners and morals, we need not—with Mr. Knightley's characterization in mind—question that Jane Austen sincerely believed in them. There is both a public and a private thrust to her search for fictional accommodations. Her "public" intention bears some resemblance to the project of Coleridge and other nineteenth-century authors, who sought to heal the breach between "cultivation" and "civilization," culture and society. Her "private" intention, unacknowledged, and sometimes unconsciously in the service of aggression or desire, was to construct a fictional society in which she could feel at home. Herself dispossessed, she sought to possess her world aesthetically. Without a comfortable income, she commanded a precisely discriminated range of incomes in her fiction. The accommodations (and carriages) she missed in life she found in her novels. Her novels are "nests," which she built with the "twigs" of characters and themes (*Letters*, 468). Her formal structures are not the same from novel to novel, and they do not always work—so that it is wrong to insist that her novels are seamless fabrics, organic wholes. Nevertheless, her resolutions are the consequence of authentic searches after accommodation and not, as is sometimes implied, capitulations to conventions, either social or fictional.

IV

Perhaps the most difficult aspect of Jane Austen's work to describe is the coexistence in her attitude of sincere conservative convictions and a woman's perspective on her society. She has no structural changes to propose in her world, and her social criticism, while it takes sharp focus from her marginal perspective, is not political in the manner of Mary Wollstonecraft. Though she shares Wollstonecraft's distaste for a society which values feminine "refinement" over intelligence, and the appearance more than the reality of chastity, she has no program for rectifying the situation (as Wollstonecraft has, for example in chapter 12 of *A Vindication of the Rights of Woman* [1792], in which she advocates a progressive and co-educational system of national schools). Nor is this merely the difference between novelist and polemical writer; Jane Austen could find accommodation for her ideals within existing structures, as Mary Wollstonecraft could not; accommodations were not always easy to find, as the "dark" lives of Jane Fairfax in *Emma* and Mrs. Smith in *Persuasion* show; but though she occasionally resembles Wollstonecraft in her awareness of women's "enslavement," she shows no signs of advocating alternative roles for women (e.g., those of physicians or businesswomen), as Wollstonecraft does in chapter 9 of *Rights of Woman*. As she seeks homes for her heroines, so, with varying degrees of success, and with some qualifications necessary in a discussion of *Persuasion*, she seeks to invigorate an old society rather than to inaugurate a new.[23]

What was her society, and from what perspective did she criticize it? David Spring has rightly argued that she belonged to "a capitalist money culture" and lived at a time when improving landowners were transforming English agriculture; in the process, they "put an end to a traditional and communal agriculture and a backward, truly reactionary peasantry, thereby promoting the forces of economic individualism in the rural community."[24] But did Jane Austen see it this way? The economic individualism John Dashwood shows in enclosing the Norland common and engrossing East Kingham Farm (*SS*, 225) is evidence of his selfish and mercenary character. In *Emma*, Mr. Knightley provides a better example of an agricultural improver: he shows concern for his sheep, is continually closeted with his steward William Larkins over estate questions, and when his lawyer brother visits, discusses with him questions of drainage, fencing, tree-felling, "and the destination of every acre for wheat, turnips, or spring corn" (*E*, 100). Yet however committed to the improvement of the land, Knightley is opposed to fashionable landscape improvements. Donwell Abbey is unfashionably "low and sheltered"; the house is "rambling and irregular"; the ample gardens stretch down to "meadows washed by a stream, of which the Abbey, with all the old neglect of prospect had scarcely a sight"; there is an "abundance of timber in rows and avenues, which neither fashion nor extravagance had rooted up" (*E*, 358).

All the notations here—the situation and style of the house, the unimproved grounds—are coded signifiers of traditional values. Emma Woodhouse is our observer in this scene, and what she sees is a proleptic expression of the values she will embrace when she marries Knightley. Included in her view is the Abbey-Mill farm, "with all its appendages of prosperity and beauty, its rich pastures, spreading flocks, orchard in blossom, and light column of smoke ascending" (*Emma*, 360). The Abbey-Mill farm, however, is also the home of Knightley's tenant farmer, Robert Martin, whom Emma will come to recognize as a worthy husband for her protégée, Harriet Smith. Mr. Knightley may well participate in an agrarian capitalist economy, but as his name implies and his actions confirm, he holds to the paternalist values of what E. B. Thompson and others have termed a "moral economy." And in this, it seems to me, he is backed by his author, who, conscious of her maternal ancestry and of her links to an estate like Stoneleigh Abbey, felt an allegiance to the old society.

What is Tory in her outlook is nowhere more evident than in the ideal settings she envisages through much of her fiction as the final accommodations of her heroines. Delaford, the married home of both Dashwood sisters in *Sense and Sensibility,* is one example of this ideal community:

> Delaford is . . . a nice old fashioned place, full of comforts and conveniences; quite shut in with great garden walls that are covered with the best fruit-trees in the country; and such a mulberry tree in one corner! . . . Then there is a dove-cote, some delightful stewponds, and a very pretty canal; and every thing in short, that one could wish for . . . it is close to the church . . . A butcher hard by in the village, and the parsonage-house within a stone's throw. To my fancy, a thousand times prettier than Barton Park, where they are forced to send three miles for their meat. (*SS,* 196–97)

Through the garrulity of Mrs. Jennings's description appear certain codes of representation, found elsewhere in Jane Austen's work and in the eighteenth-century novel. Apparently lost in the flow of the discourse, these codes—the enclosing garden walls, fruit-trees, church, parsonage—imply traditional cultural values of continuity, growth, and the interdependence of church and land. One notation, the contrast between Delaford and Barton Park, has classical provenance. The Middletons at Barton Park, who are forced to send three miles for their meat, join a long line of characters from Martial's Bassus ("*Baiana nostri villa, Basse, Faustini*") onward, who have forsaken the ideal of the self-subsistent community. In contrast, Delaford is an organic social community of the kind Pope admired in "To Bethel" or Smollett in *Humphry Clinker* or, for that matter, Henry James in *English Hours.*[25]

Like Donwell Abbey, Allenham, Sotherton Court, and the Great House at Uppercross, Delaford has escaped the attentions of professional improvers like Kent, Capability Brown, and Humphry Repton. Such places are old-fashioned, and though this is not an invariable virtue (Sotherton Court obviously needs "modern dress," if not of the kind Henry Crawford proposes), an old-fashioned condition usually signifies value in the fiction. Thornton Lacey, the home of Fanny Price before she moves to the Mansfield parsonage, is old-fashioned. "I was suddenly," says Henry Crawford, "in the midst of a retired little village between gently rising hills; a small stream before me to be forded, a church standing on a sort of knoll to my right . . . the Parsonage, within a stone's throw of the said knoll and church" (*MP,* 241). His proposed "improvements" entail the clearing away of the farmyard, the screening of the blacksmith's shop, the reorientation of the house, the creation of a new garden, the damming of the stream: in short, the total transformation of the parsonage into the home of a family "spending from two to three thousand a year" (*MP,* 243). But here he is being impractical, for the living brings in no more than £700. Like his plans for an improved liturgy or improved delivery of sermons (*MP,* 341) Crawford's modernizing plans at Thornton Lacey pose threats to the continuity of a morally grounded traditional society.[26] His sister's response is equally suspect. Disappointed that Edmund Bertram intends to be a resident clergyman at Thornton Lacey, Mary Crawford is "no longer able, in the picture she had been forming of a future Thornton, to shut out the church, sink the clergyman, and see only the respectable, elegant, modernized, and occasional residence of a man of independent fortune" (*MP,* 248). Mary, we recall, had responded to the news of the cessation of prayers in the Sotherton chapel with the remark, "Every generation has its improvements" and had also declared "a clergyman is nothing" (*MP,* 86, 92).

The threats posed by the Crawfords and other materialists and improvers in Jane Austen's fiction are threats to an organic social heritage, grounded in religion: a heritage in which, as Edmund Bertram suggests (*MP,* 92), religious principles, morals, and manners exist in relations of mutual reciprocity. There is no need to be sentimental about this. Jane Austen's values, like those of other conservative writers, are class-based and, like the ideal communities she envisioned, ultimately dependent on money. As has been argued, the distinction between country virtue and urban vice is, in historical terms, false, and the ideal of an organic rural community innocent of fiscal "speculation" (and usually set in the past) a mythic reification.[27] Farm rents generally rose in the period, on the estates of improvers and traditionalists alike.[28] We need not seek to elevate Jane Austen's criticism of economic individualism to a set of universal values, but neither need we deny the sincerity of her traditional commitments. Aware of the prosperity resulting from, among other factors, agricultural improvements and increased rents, she criticized the absence of matching moral behavior among the prosperous.

V

In the instance of her unfinished work *The Watsons,* Jane Austen's criticism is bitter. The fissured society she depicts; the exact notation of social backgrounds, incomes, idiolects; the discrimination among the manners of different sets; the general sense of oppression throughout—all these accord with the date of composition, 1804–5, a period when Jane Austen's fate as a distressed gentlewoman was clearly written (her father died in January 1805). Our point of view on this society is Emma Watson, who (in the words of her brother, the Croydon attorney) has found herself "instead of heiress of 8 or 9,000£, sent back a weight upon [her] family, without a sixpence" (*MW*, 352). Emma's father is a sickly country vicar, too poor to afford a carriage. Her elder sister Elizabeth is twenty-eight years old (Jane Austen's age in 1804) and a pathetic husband-hunting woman: "I think I could like any good humoured Man with a comfortable Income," she admits, while lamenting that "my Father cannot provide for us, & it is very bad to grow old & be poor & laughed at" (*MW*, 318, 317). Emma's brother Sam is "only a Surgeon" (like Jane Austen's paternal grandfather), a fact that militates against his suit with the Edwards' only daughter, who "will have at least ten thousand pounds" (*MW*, 321). Her other brother, Robert, has been luckier, having married the daughter of the attorney to whom he had been clerk; she (a vicious piece of goods) has a fortune of £6,000 and can therefore look on Emma with "Triumphant Compassion" (*MW*, 349). Emma's other sister, Margaret, also unmarried, has become a sycophant to those with money and is fretful and querulous with members of her family. Elizabeth believes that "if Margt had had a thousand or fifteen hundred pounds, there was a young man who wd have thought of her" (*MW*, 353).

By what mechanisms of plot and theme was *The Watsons* to transcend its gloomy analysis of the economic calculus at work? At the ball, Emma finds herself, "she knew not how, seated amongst the Osborne set," and when Miss Osborne reneges on her promise to dance with Master Blake, "Emma did not think, or reflect;—she felt and acted" (*MW*, 330). Like Mr. Knightley's act of dancing with Harriet Smith (*E*, 328), Emma's action bespeaks not only excellent manners but a good heart, and it gains her the attention of Lord Osborne, Tom Musgrave, and Mr. Howard, the clergyman at Osborne Castle. Had the fragment been finished, Emma would surely have married Mr. Howard (whose worth is signified, briefly, by the excellence of his sermon delivery), after rejecting Lord Osborne and, perhaps Tom Musgrave. Lord Osborne is a patrician hero whose pride, unlike that of Darcy, is too ingrained to be improved; and Musgrave, like Willoughby and Wickham, is an attractive false hero whose social aspirations overcome his attraction to a heroine without a dowry.

Since the plot of *The Watsons* is clear enough, one may suggest that the fragment was left unfinished not merely because the heroine was too "low,"[29] but because the task of closing the social rifts so bitterly represented was too great. The emphasis is oppressively on the plight of distressed gentility, and society as a possible arena of values does not substantially appear through the agencies of character or setting.

There is a bitterness and oppression present, too, in her first published work, *Sense and Sensibility* (1811). Like *Pride and Prejudice* (1813), this novel seeks to define an ideal relation between the individual and society through the accommodation of opposed terms. Behind both works (completed in early versions in the 1790s)[30] is a century of debate over whether man is naturally selfish, as Hobbes and Mandeville had argued, or naturally social and benevolent, as the Third Earl of Shaftesbury had suggested when he posited an innate moral sentiment. Jane Austen was hardly the first to see that—in the world as given—sense, prudence, circumspection, even a touch of *astutia serpentis* were needful (in this general sense she follows the example of Fielding). Her attitudes were formed in the context of anti-Jacobin polemic, however, and she had greater inducements than earlier novelists to express a conservative suspicion of idealistic conceptions of human nature.[31]

The success with which these early novels accommodate individual and social claims is by no means equal. Whereas *Pride and Prejudice* (like *Emma*) largely contains its criticisms within an affirmation of cultural heritage, *Sense and Sensibility* (like *Mansfield Park*) leaves many readers with a sense of a discordance between meaning and form. As in *The Watsons,* there is a bitter indictment of a world vitiated by economic individualism and—despite its completed plot—a failure to dramatize a convincing moral alternative to this world. The marriages of Marianne to Colonel Brandon, and of Elinor to Edward Ferrars, with both sisters "accommodated" at Delaford (in house and parsonage respectively) are not convincing. The heroes in particular do not carry the weight of moral authority she successfully invests in Darcy and Knightley. But the heroines pose problems, too. Elinor, the exemplar of "sense" in its best forms, the advocate of traditional values, and the upholder of manners as an expression of such values is successful to some extent; hers is the consciousness the reader has continual access to, and her solitary courage in maintaining integrity in a world of moral corruption connects her with Fanny Price and Anne Elliot, who in later novels find themselves similarly placed. Yet Elinor's characterization is not always perfectly pitched, and her hewing to traditional ways can seem on occasions brittle and formulaic, even insincere. Her sister, Marianne, is the vulnerable spokeswoman for "sensibility," that misguided belief in the holiness of the heart's affections, which leads her (at the age of seventeen) to voice her criticisms tactlessly in public, to disregard decorum (as in her correspondence with Willoughby, to whom she is not engaged), to act insensitively (as on her unchaperoned trip to Allenham), and to endanger her own life by so pledging herself to Willoughby ("I felt myself . . . to be as solemnly engaged to him, as if the strictest legal covenant had bound us to each other" [*SS*, 188]) that when he rejects her in pursuit of an heiress, she finds no reason to live.

As regards Marianne, Jane Austen's rhetoric is clear: sensibility as a program of living is false. Yet to read the novel mainly as an exposure of Rousseauist sentimentalism seems somehow beside the point. Marianne's outbursts, as the testimony of many readers confirms, are sometimes admirable expressions of sincerity (perhaps in spite of her author's rhetoric); in some instances—as in her spirited defense of Elinor's "very pretty pair of screens" against the curt, dismissive praise of Mr. Ferrars (*SS,* 235)—Marianne's protests serve as a safety valve for the reader's own pent-up disgust. Moreover, Marianne's sensibility is not what endangers the world depicted in the novel; her sensibility endangers no one so much as herself. What endangers the world of *Sense and Sensibility* is "sense," semantically debased from its associations with the Christian humanist virtue of prudence and now too often descriptive of attitudes of venal self-interest.

In chapter 11 of the second volume, Elinor, on a mission to sell her mother's jewels, meets her brother in Gray's of Sackville Street. Everything in the dialogues that follow confirms the deep-dyed materialism of the man. Mistakenly believing Colonel Brandon to be in love with his sister, John Dashwood tells Elinor he wishes that Brandon's income (£2,000) were twice as much for her sake. (His own income from Norland is £4,000 a year.) When Elinor denies Colonel Brandon's interest in her, he counsels a policy of "sense": "the smallness of your fortune may make him hang back; his friends may all advise him against it. But some of those little attentions and encouragements which ladies can so easily give, will fix him, in spite of himself" (*SS,* 223). He tells of an alliance between Edward Ferrars and the Hon. Miss Morton with £30,000. To make this an "equal alliance," Mrs. Ferrars promises to settle on Edward a thousand a year. He laments his own expenses caused by enclosures, land purchases, and improvements. Elinor keeps her "concern and censure to herself." In his conduct traditional obligations have been eradicated as surely as the old walnut trees at Norland during his improvements. We are in the world of Goldsmith's Traveller, where

> As nature's ties decay,
> As duty, love and honour fail to sway,
> Fictitious bonds, the bonds of wealth and law
> Still gather strength, and force unwilling awe.
> (*The Traveller,* 349–52)

Impervious to Elinor's irony, John Dashwood persists in valuing people in proportion to the extent of their income. Like the Steele sisters, he knows the price of everything. Like his wife, he has the mind of an actuary. Having seen Marianne looking pale and sickly—the consequence of Willoughby's repudiation—he questions "whether Marianne *now,* will marry a man worth more than five or six hundred a-year at the utmost" (*SS,* 227).

Yet Marianne, in the end, finds herself "in a new home, a wife, the mistress of a family, and the patroness of a village" (*SS,* 379). Like the journey of Catherine Morland from the Fullerton parsonage to the Woodston parsonage by way of Bath and Northanger, the journey of the Dashwood sisters takes them from one enclosure of values at Norland to another at Delaford by way of London. But in her illness Marianne had begged that her mother not "go round by London . . . I shall never see her if she goes by London" (*SS*, 311), and for many readers the "London" habits of the novel, like the "Croydon" habits in *The Watsons,* have been so forcefully described that the happy conclusion does not convince. Against all the odds (to adopt the "betting" language characteristic of the speech of the John Dashwoods, of Willoughby, of Lucy Steele), Marianne through her marriage gains the "competence" she had ingenuously estimated (£2,000 a year), while Elinor through her marriage gains rather less than her practical estimate of "wealth" (£1,000 a year) (*SS*, 91).[32]

VI

Pride and Prejudice succeeds where *Sense and Sensibility* fails. As mistress of Pemberley, Elizabeth Bennet is the most lavishly rewarded of Jane Austen's heroines, and the novel she so delightfully inhabits is the happiest of her author's works. How are we to explain this? Did Jane Austen achieve her affirmative vision through ignoring, for once, the mercenary and competitive character of her society? By no means. The financial and social registers are as precise here as ever. Fitzwilliam Darcy has £10,000 a year, a beautifully improved estate, a London house, and influence at court. His friend Bingley has inherited a fortune of nearly £100,000, but the money was made in trade; he rents rather than owns Netherfield, and his social roots—as Jane Bennet discovers to her dismay—are shallow. Mr. Bennet is landed and has a considerable income of £2,000 a year; but he has saved nothing over the years, his estate is entailed on Mr. Collins, and the five Bennet daughters can look forward to little more than £50 a year each from their share of the settlement of £5,000 made on Mrs. Bennet at marriage. Mr. Bennet is a gentleman, as Elizabeth will proudly remind Lady Catherine. Mrs. Bennet's origins and relations are less well established. Her father was an attorney, who left her £4,000; her sister is married to a Meryton attorney; and her brother is engaged in trade in London, where he lives in unfashionable Gracechurch Street. The Bennets' neighbor, Sir William Lucas, had been "formerly in trade" also, his knighthood the result of an address made to the king while mayor of Meryton. Sir William is not rich, which explains his daughter's prudential decision to marry that ogre, Mr. Collins. One consequence of the marriage is that Charlotte will eventually be mistress of Longbourn, a fact that leads her mother, Lady Lucas, "to calculate with more *interest* than . . . before, how many years longer Mr. Bennet was likely to live" (*PP,* 122, italics added).

In one way, *Pride and Prejudice* is closer to home than any of the novels, the mixed social claims of the Bennet parents bearing a reverse relationship to those of Jane Austen's own, and the representation of a family in danger of "degradation" having some relevance to Jane Austen's own apprehensions of a déclassé state. Yet as Virginia Woolf suggested, the novel is raised to a level of comic power where humor, wit, and intelligence triumph over social obstacles and pettiness. Elizabeth and Darcy are kin to Beatrice and Benedick (particularly in their witty conversations at Netherfield). Elizabeth, to test Virginia Woolf's comparison to *Antony and Cleopatra,* is kin to Cleopatra. When her sister Jane is ill, Elizabeth walks to Netherfield, "crossing field after field at a quick pace, jumping over stiles and springing over puddles with impatient activity, and finding herself at last within view of the house, with weary ancles, dirty stockings, and a face glowing with the warmth of exercise" (*PP,* 32). Did Virginia Woolf recall Enobarbus's memory of Cleopatra?

> I saw her once
> Hop forty paces through the public street;
> And having lost her breath, she spoke, and panted
> That she did make defect perfection,
> And breathless, power breathe forth.[33]

Jane Austen confessed that she considered Elizabeth "as delightful a creature as ever appeared in print" (*Letters,* 297); but even the obnoxious characters are delightful in this novel. The Rev. Mr. Collins descends from a line of moralizing clerics like Dr. Bartlett in *Sir Charles Grandison,* of whose piety he is a splendid parody.[34] Lady Catherine, too, is a type (the grande dame) but perhaps the best compliment we can pay to her characterization is to suggest that without her, Oscar Wilde could not have created Lady Bracknell. The danger the critic faces is that he will weigh down this superbly comic novel with ponderous analysis; yet the alternative—a sense of wonder before the book's comic power—is empty praise. For Jane Austen's comedy not only serves and rests on a confident moral vision but emerges from an aesthetic intelligence unequaled in the English novel.

The novel's formal excellence does not disguise its social criticism but includes it within a vision of a worthy society. The plot works first to humble Darcy's patrician pride and then to chasten Elizabeth's antisocial prejudices. In the process a most satisfying structural balance is achieved: if Elizabeth suffers at the beginning from her mother's vulgar behavior at Netherfield, Darcy is later embarrassed by his aunt's rudeness at Rosings. Ill manners are not peculiar to one social level. Nor for that matter is poor taste, as Rosings, the "gaudy" opposite of the "elegant" Pemberley, reveals. Nor, finally, is sexual immorality. Elizabeth's hopes are dashed by the news of her sister Lydia's elopement with Wickham; but in bringing this affair to a successful resolution, Darcy is guiltily aware that he has suppressed the fact of his own sister's earlier elopement with Wickham. Thus Elizabeth's hypothetical definition of "connubial felicity" (*PP,* 312) will, in fact, be fulfilled. By "her ease and liveliness," Darcy's "mind" will be "softened, his manners improved"; and from "his judgment, information, and knowledge of the world," she will receive "benefit of greater importance" (*PP,* 312).

In achieving its *concordia discors* the union of Darcy and Elizabeth defines what is absent from the other marriages in the novel. Mr. and Mrs. Bennet are incompatible opposites, a cause of humor and (increasingly for Elizabeth) of regret. Lydia and Wickham are alike in their appetites, irresponsibility, and rashness. Collins and Charlotte are alike in their prudent, self-serving acceptance of a marriage of convenience. Jane and Bingley are alike in a better sense; yet, though pleasant and unsuspicious by nature, they would never have married if left to themselves. Only in the marriage of Darcy and Elizabeth do we have a vital union that gives assurance that the gap between debased "sense" and morality can be crossed. Such a union is absent from *Sense and Sensibility*. We need not deny that their marriage fulfills the fantasy of sexual compatibility across social and economic divisions. Elizabeth, too, is an offspring of Pamela (or of Harriet Byron). What disarms the charge of fantasy fulfillment, however, is the moral authority the novel gains through its continual moral discriminations.

Jane Austen loads every rift with ore. Her dialogues, summaries, descriptions all carry thematic supercargo. Reading, writing, smiles, laughter, music, art, running, walking, silence, noise: these are only some of the apparently "anodyne data" that pepper the novel's discourse, permitting the author to distinguish between moral and immoral behavior, to measure attitudinal extreme, and to define accommodative norms.[35]

Consider, again, the visit to Netherfield. Elizabeth's instinctive response to her sister's illness is, of course, admirable, a demonstration of her selfless concern as well as of her superior moral character among the Bennets: her mother's scheming is the cause of Jane's cold in the first place; her father's disengagement is no help; her sisters, Kitty and Lydia, agree to accompany her on the walk, but only "as far as Meryton," where they hope to meet the officers. Yet it is not quite enough to admire Elizabeth's action. We can discount, of course, the jealous criticisms of the Bingley sisters, who object to her "wild" appearance, her "petticoat, six inches deep in mud," and the very idea of her "scampering about the country" (*PP*, 35–36). And we surely prefer Bingley's response to the episode: he has not noticed the dirty petticoat and excuses Elizabeth's actions on the grounds of her affection for Jane. But we have also to assess Darcy's divided response: he admits he would not wish to see his sister "make such an exhibition," and yet, to the disappointment of Miss Bingley, his admiration of Elizabeth's "fine eyes . . . brightened by the exercise" has increased.

We are asked to read the episode both realistically, in terms of its psychological disclosure, and thematically, as a means of normative definition. Both Bingley and his sisters are "prejudiced" here, their positive and negative interpretations preceding a true judgment of the event; only Darcy (whose uncle was a judge) is judicious. This is not to say that his criticism exposes Elizabeth's behavior; because it is morally motivated, her vigorous, instinctive, socially unconventional action is, on this occasion, censureproof. Yet

Miss Bingley's charge that Elizabeth has shown a "sort of conceited independence, a most country town indifference to decorum" (*PP,* 36), does more than reveal her jealous resentment. Other "independent" characters—like Elizabeth's sister Lydia, given to instinctive self-gratification, "wild" behavior, noisy laughter, indecorous "scampering" here and here—*are* open to censure. Even Elizabeth herself, when she prejudicially accepts Wickham's version of the history of his relationship with Darcy, can culpably ignore the "rules" of decorum even as she exhibits a misguided reliance on "first impressions."

In the Netherfield episode Elizabeth's "primitive" behavior is obviously preferable to the "civilized" rectitude of the Bingley sisters; and elsewhere in the novel, in Mary Bennet's bookish erudition, in Collins's formulaic pedantry, in Darcy's own grave insistence on punctilio and rules (all these characters go by the book, we might say), the uses of "civilization" to suppress spontaneity and exclude individual aspirations are laughed out of court. But *Pride and Prejudice* is, in the end, a very civilized novel. It calls for a worthy "marriage" of individual behavior and social conventions; it asks that the rules be informed by individual commitment; it requires the continuous exercise of active and intelligent (rather than formulaic) judgment. Darcy's admiration of Elizabeth's fine eyes represents his accessibility to what is worthy in her individualist position; she will learn that inherited social and moral principles are worthy of her commitment. The thematic marriage repeatedly implied from the beginning is confirmed by the marriage of the sexes at the end; and, by a superb accommodation of theme, Jane Austen justifies Elizabeth's final accommodations at Pemberley.

VII

Mansfield Park, the first of the Chawton novels, composed between February 1811 and June 1813, is not an accommodative novel in the manner of *Pride and Prejudice,* nor can its heroine, Fanny Price—timid, unassertive, physically weak—be said to invigorate her adoptive culture when she becomes mistress of the Mansfield parsonage. In this novel vigor describes not the heroine, as in *Pride and Prejudice* and *Emma,* but the anti-heroine, Mary Crawford, whose "London" values are finally expelled from the park. Lionel Trilling recognized the affront Fanny poses to many modern readers but went on to argue that the "almost perverse rejection of Mary Crawford's vitality in favor of Fanny's debility lies at the very heart of the novel's intention."[36]

Trilling's view of the novel's rhetoric is surely right. Jane Austen consistently exposes the danger of any union with the Crawfords. Especially in the beautifully choreographed sequences in the first volume (the visit to Sotherton and the theatricals episode), her serious, even Christian, intention is conveyed through dialogue and setting. Walking through the grounds of Sotherton, the Bertrams and the Crawfords leave accustomed "paths"; enter a moral "wilderness"; follow "winding," "serpentine," and "circuitous" ways; and break social bounds. Acting in *Lovers' Vows,* they impersonate dramatic roles that prefigure their future errors, while failing to fulfill the responsibilities of their given or chosen roles (elder son, clergyman, affianced woman). In turning "house" ("my father's house") into "theatre," they endanger the moral fabric of their inheritance as surely as Maria Bertram risks tearing her gown, when—"so far from the house already"—she squeezes past the gate and crosses the ha-ha with Henry Crawford rather than wait for her fiancé, who is "so long fetching [the] key" (*MP,* 97). None of the other novels reaches quite the same level of symbolic resonance, or the same command of double entendre in description and dialogue; none more successfully foreshadows its conclusion; and with Tom Bertram chastened by illness, Maria exiled following her adultery and divorce, and the Crawfords banished, no conclusion is less accommodating.

Yet running beneath rhetorical "intention" there is a stream of fantasy in *Mansfield Park,* which may partly account for its perennial ability to offend readers, especially those who have a Nietzschean suspicion of the Christian ethic. At the still center of the moving world sits Fanny Price, the Christian heroine, the meek woman who inherits the Mansfield earth, "the lowest and the last" (*MP,* 221) who becomes first, the object of charity who—Sir Thomas finally recognizes—is "the daughter that he wanted" (*MP,* 472). The fantasy fulfilled in *Mansfield Park* is not erotic but social and oral, the fantasy of a society saved from corruption by the fidelity of its least powerful, most marginal figure. As usual, Jane Austen seeks to "desublimate" her final union (*MP,* 470) and, as at the end of *Sense and Sensibility,* to concede that her fictional distribution of rewards and punishments achieves patterns of unrealistic neatness (*MP,* 468–69). But social fantasy persists in the novel, along with social anxieties that are, as usual, expressed in descriptions of accommodations and interiors. At every stage, Fanny's social options are defined and limited by the physical space she inhabits. On arrival at Mansfield as a child of ten, she is "placed" (in more than one sense) "in the little white attic . . . so near Miss Lee [the governess], and not far from the girls, and close by the housemaids" (*MP,* 910). By age eighteen, she has "artlessly" annexed the East Room, thus making up for "the deficiency of space and accommodation" in the attic (*MP,* 151). In the East Room, Fanny's position is still marginal, but she has more than Jane Austen had in Chawton Cottage: space for privacy and withdrawal, "a room of her own" where she can pursue her interests in plants and works of charity, read Crabbe and Johnson, and hang her transparencies of Tintern Abbey and the Lake District. Fanny in the East Room represents the kind of life Jane Austen might have led had Edward taken her into the household at Godmersham; her existence surely also mirrors that of many single women in the period, with "good" connections and reduced means. But in *Mansfield Park,* Jane Austen imagines social possibilities both better and worse than the East Room. Fanny's journey to the better possibility (the Mansfield parsonage) involves a trip to the worse (her old home in Portsmouth).

The Portsmouth episode (*MP,* 375–447) is the single most problematic sequence in Jane Austen. Like Emma Watson, Fanny returns home and, out of a consciousness formed in a spacious and elegant adoptive environment, finds her home not only deficient in decorum but a cause of disgust: "She sat in a blaze of oppressive heat, in a cloud of moving dust; and her eyes could only wander from the walls marked by her father's head, to the table cut and knotched by her brothers, where stood the tea-board never thoroughly cleaned, the cups and saucers wiped in streaks, the milk a mixture of motes floating in thin blue, and the bread and butter growing every minute more greasy than even Rebecca's hands had first produced it" (*MP,* 439).

In having Fanny repudiate her noisy, disordered home (here "felicity" is defined as escaping from the "evil" of Henry Crawford's having to dine in her father's house), Jane Austen serves up a dish that is harder to swallow, for many readers, than "Rebecca's puddings and Rebecca's hashes" (*MP,* 413). In having her discover in her sister Susan an "innate" taste for "the genteel and the well-appointed" (*MP,* 419), she strikes a false note. And in allowing her "a review of the two houses," she provides a nostalgic retrospect in which the moral anarchy of Mansfield, and Fanny's sufferings there, are largely suppressed in an unconvincing picture of elegance, propriety, and regularity (*MP,* 391–92).

The rhetorical intention of the episode is to reveal the collapse of the Mansfield society during Fanny's banishment; in Portsmouth she becomes the absent center of reference and values, the confidante—through letters—of Lady Bertram, Edmund and Mary Crawford. But as the descriptions of the Price household reveal, the rhetorical and structural ironies of the episode accompany, perhaps cover, a nightmare vision of claustrophobia, oppression, and dirt. The subtext of Fanny's Portsmouth experience is a living-through of the possibility of real social distress, glimpsed elsewhere in Miss Bates's dark and narrow staircase in *Emma,* and described in fuller and more threatening detail in Mrs. Smith's restricted accommodations, noisy parlor, and dark bedroom in *Persuasion.*[37] In having Fanny experience the horror (however temporary) of this fate, Jane Austen complicates her heroine's role, which is otherwise to be the rock and guardian of traditional values. Fanny's double role is perhaps at the heart of *Mansfield Park*'s problem. In its "public" intention, the novel brilliantly imagines the dangers posed to inherited cultural structures (an estate, the Anglican liturgy, the English language itself) by the irresponsibility and materialism of its heirs. But in its "private" apprehensions, it takes a rather too "masochistic" interest in Fanny's weakness and suffering.

This dimension of the novel is evident throughout in the character of Mrs. Norris, who warrants comparison with Snow White's stepmother, the scheming and sadistic Queen.[38] Mrs. Norris's enmity to Fanny is constant:

she opposes her getting a horse, visiting Sotherton, dining out; she ensures that there is no fire for her in the East Room; she tries to prevent the ball in her honor; and she is incensed when Crawford proposes to her. Her bitter opposition to Fanny's rise, however, is not simply a fairytale given; it originates in her sense of insulted ambition. As eldest of the three Ward sisters, she has seen a younger sister marry a baronet, her fortune of £7,000 being "at least three thousand pounds short of any equitable claim" (*MP,* 31). Some six years later, she herself marries the Rev. Mr. Norris, who, "with scarcely any private fortune," is given the Mansfield living. Mr. and Mrs. Norris begin "their career of conjugal felicity with very little less than a thousand a year" (*MP,* 3). (This is a comfortable income in Jane Austen's scale, close to that enjoyed by Jane Austen's brother James, before Leigh Perrot's will made him richer.) But when Fanny is fifteen, Mr. Norris dies, and the Mansfield living devolves on Dr. Grant. Her income reduced, Mrs. Norris moves to the White House, refusing to take Fanny with her on the grounds that she has "barely enough to support [herself] in the rank of gentlewoman" (*MP,* 29). Once again the financial details are precise, allowing us to estimate what Mrs. Norris sets as a minimum income for a gentlewoman, as well as the income lost to Edmund as a result of his elder brother's extravagance.[39]

Mrs. Norris is a brilliant portrait of a woman, embittered in her own social experience, who seeks to prevent the "encroachments" of her indigent niece and others who reveal the "folly" of "stepping out of their rank" (*MP,* 221). Her own rise blocked, she compensates by associating with those, like Maria, whose position and prospects are splendid. By economizing over the years, she almost doubles her principal; by "sponging," she increases her stock. We can understand her attraction for feminist critics. She is the most energetic of Jane Austen's villains—arranging, contriving, directing, dictating, managing, projecting, promoting, planting, improving, walking, and so on, throughout the novel. Jane Austen observes that she would have managed nine children on a small income better than her sister, Mrs. Price. But it is misguided to view her sympathetically. While her strategies are understandable, they are hardly admirable. Jane Austen imagines her psychology brilliantly, not to sympathize with her but to expose the selfishness of her schemes and "spirit of activity."

VIII

With a fortune of £30,000, the heroine of *Emma* (1816) lacks Mrs. Norris's motives for displaying a "spirit of activity" and pursuing schemes and promotions. Emma is richer than Mary Crawford, who considers her £20,000 more than enough to catch the eldest son of a baronet, and far richer than Anne Elliot, daughter of a spendthrift baronet, who will be lucky to receive her portion of £10,000. Financially secure, Emma nevertheless bears a superficial resemblance to Mrs. Norris, who loves to manage and direct. Like Mrs. Norris, she is a matchmaker, taking credit for the marriage of her governess, Miss Taylor, to Mr. Weston and promoting matches for her friend Harriet Smith with, successively, Mr. Elton, Frank Churchill, and an "unnamed" gentleman who turns out (to her chagrin) to be Mr. Knightley. She exaggerates the social claims of Harriet (who becomes a kind of surrogate for herself in search of a husband), at the same time depressing the social claims of Robert Martin, the worthy tenant farmer and proper suitor for Harriet's hand. She also opposes the encroachments of the aspiring Eltons and Coles. Her snobbery in these instances aligns her with Mrs. Norris, but in spite of such resemblances, she is no real kin to that "officious" character. Her activity poses no final danger to her society; like Elizabeth Bennet, she chooses to accommodate her energies within social bounds. Her self-limitation is not, any more than Elizabeth's, abject or conformist; in accepting her culture, she invigorates and improves it.

The community in which Emma finds accommodations for her wit and vitality is a traditional community, ideally characterized by its members' adherence to public structures of manners and morals. The consistent exemplar of this community is Mr. Knightley, whose Donwell Abbey, as we have seen, is a metonym for a moral economy operating according to unwritten rules and inherited obligations. Throughout the novel Mr. Knightley the gentleman is opposed to Frank Churchill the gallant. At the end of the first volume, the terms of their opposition appear in Knightley's response to Churchill's "letter of excuse" for yet another failure to pay a promised visit to his father and his father's new bride. In Knightley's view, Churchill has failed to do his "duty," which "a man can always do, if he chuses . . . not by manoeuvring and finessing, but by vigour and resolution" (E, 146). Knightley's judgments are uncompromising, but not seriously flawed by his incipient jealousy of a possible rival. "Your amiable young man," he tells Emma, "can be amiable only in French, not in English. He may be very 'aimable,' have very good manners, and be very agreeable; but he can have no English delicacy towards the feelings of other people; nothing really amiable about him" (E, 149).

Endorsing Mr. Knightley's code of conduct, Jane Austen extends and complicates the contrast between Knightley's "open" world of work, truth, and social obligation and Churchill's "closed" world of games, duplicity, and selfishness. Though the tone of *Emma* remains comic, something of *Mansfield Park*'s seriousness is communicated by the vocabulary of secrecy, deceit, hypocrisy, double-dealing, mystery, finesse, equivocation and even "espionage" (E, 399) that attaches to Churchill's games and maneuvers. Trivial and amusing as his "whims" and "freaks" may seem, they carry implications of cultural treachery. Secretly engaged to Jane Fairfax, he has presented himself as "disengaged." Greatly given to talk, he has misled and deceived. By misusing "communication," he has endangered "community."[40]

As social and moral norm, Knightley is not to everyone's taste, and in recent years a number of critics have sought to deny or qualify readings of *Emma* as a novel about the heroine's moral education.[41] Certainly, *Emma* is more than this, but to the considerable extent that it describes Emma's change of attitude—a change described in a vocabulary of "penance" (*E*, 141, 182) and "mortification" (*E*, 376)—the novel expresses Jane Austen's commitment to a traditional morality. As an heiress, Emma does not at first consider the problems of distressed gentlewomen to be of much concern. She airily informs Harriet that "a single woman, with a very narrow income, must be a ridiculous, disagreeable old maid! the proper sport of boys and girls" (*E*, 85). And on Box Hill she fulfills her prophecy by indeed making Miss Bates the object of her "sport" (*E*, 370). But Emma's insult is neither "proper" nor "amiable"; caught up in Churchill's world of games, she fails to observe that "English delicacy towards the feelings of other people," which Knightley had earlier found to be lacking in Churchill's behavior.

The Box Hill episode suggests that Jane Austen's "solution" to the predicament of the poor single woman is a traditional appeal to the gentry's sense of social obligation. Such a solution would not have satisfied Mary Wollstonecraft, and—for many readers—does not accommodate the difficulties presented by Jane Fairfax's situation. Jane's difficulties are partly the consequence of her having placed herself beyond the reach of traditional forms of help. Trapped in her clandestine engagement to Churchill, never securely confident that he will fulfill his promise, Jane contemplates with horror a future in which she must seek employment at "offices for the sale—not quite of human flesh—but of human intellect" (*E*, 300). At such moments, the shadow of another story darkens the summer romance of *Emma*, but the substance of that story had to await Charlotte Bronte's telling in *Jane Eyre* and *Villette*.

Jane Fairfax's story allows for the exploration of other difficulties in *Emma*—the difficulty, for example, of accommodating nouveau riche aspirations in a settled community. Waiting for Churchill's decision, Jane has to endure the insufferable and often officious intermeddling in her affairs of Mrs. Elton, née Augusta Hawkins, the younger of two daughters of a Bristol merchant. In Emma's infuriated responses to Mrs. Elton's "pert pretension and under-bred finery" (*E*, 279), a good deal of the novel's humor resides. Her anger is expelled in a flurry of plosives directed against Mrs. Elton's "pique and pretension" (*E*, 182), her "pic-nic Parade" (*E*, 352), which suggest that her antagonism results not so much from a moral position as from a sense of her own insulted priority in Highbury. A moral opposition there is to Mrs. Elton, however, in Knightley, who here as elsewhere bears the burden of Jane Austen's trust in a gentry version of noblesse oblige. Bringing his gifts of apples to the Bates household, thoughtfully providing his carriage for their conveyance, Mr. Knightley "naturally" exemplifies both the form and spirit of the gentry life, which (as Jane Austen believes) an *arriviste* like Mrs. Elton can only "artificially" and unsuccessfully imitate. Even as we recognize the ideological assumptions here, we delight in the counterpoint achieved between Mr. Knightley's manners and Mrs. Elton's ill-breeding—as for example during the absurd alfresco strawberry party that Mrs. Elton takes it upon herself to "manage" at Donwell Abbey (*E*, III, ch. 6).

Emma may contain yet another kind of accommodation: the accommodation of the creative artist in a communal society. Emma is an "imaginist" (*E*, 335), who seeks to improve upon the actual, as in her portrait of Harriet (*E*, 47–48), or who uses her creative imagination to invest an everyday view, like the street scene visible from Ford's, with aesthetic order and meaning (*E*, 233). Adept at word games and puzzles, she is also a superb mimic, capable of imitating (with cruel accuracy) the scattered thoughts and uncoordinated syntax of Miss Bates (*E*, 225). As Jane Austen was well aware, verbal wit can endanger communal values—this is the lesson of Box Hill. Even earlier, Emma had resolved on "repressing imagination all the rest of her life," following the fiasco of her scheme to have Harriet marry Elton (*E*, 142). She does not keep her resolve, of course, for if she were to do so she would impugn her author's own vocation. Jane Austen's task in *Emma* is to marry Emma's "wit" to Knightley's "wisdom," not to eradicate her wit—to distinguish and expose the false uses of the imagination while affirming society's hospitality to the true. To this end she involves herself in a curious paradox: while exposing the social dangers of Churchill's duplicity, as author she creates a duplicitous discourse. *Emma* is a good example of Roland Barthes's classic plot, in which the reader (at least on a first reading) is prevented from discovering the "hermeneutic" secret (here Churchill's engagement to Jane) by a series of false or partial clues, dissimulations, snares, and delays.[42] Churchill's equivocations with Emma and other characters parallel Jane Austen's equivocations with the reader. Indeed, as readers we have yet to sound all the depths of her tricks, secrets, and double-dealing in the novel. In pursuing this paradox, we can find in *Emma* an interest beyond its affirmative social and moral meanings, but we need not argue that the paradox introduces a fissure between her aesthetic and moral commitments. Even Mr. Knightley, "open" as he is, can (as we are amused to observe) adopt a measure of art in promoting, directing, and arranging the marriage of Harriet and Robert Martin, which confirms in this novel the viability of an organic community. In something of the same way, Jane Austen's art in *Emma* works in the service of her social ideals.

IX

The success with which *Emma* accommodates its imaginative heroine in a traditional community invites us to read Jane Austen's conservative commitment as a sincere response rather than a conventional cover or camouflage. Unlike *Emma*, however, *Persuasion* (1818) does not bring its heroine to a defined social place and role; and in the last novel the attitude to social heritage differs subtly, if not in the end radically, from that communicated in the earlier novels. Though Anne Elliot becomes the wife of Captain Wentworth and the delighted mistress of a "very pretty landaulette," she has (as her status-obsessed sister Mary observes with satisfaction) "no Uppercross-hall before her, no landed estate, no headship of a family" (*P,* 250), *Persuasion* marks a new direction in Jane Austen's search for accommodations. Her deliberate decision not to provide Anne with abbey, house, hall, place, park, or cottage on her marriage to a man who has gained a fortune of £25,000 from prize money does not indicate—as the failure to finish *The Watsons* did—an oppressed sense of insurmountable difficulties to be overcome. The nature of the problem has changed, as has the kind of accommodation sought.

One way to describe the new direction of *Persuasion* is to compare Anne Elliot's role with that of Fanny Price. Like Fanny, Anne is often made aware of her "own nothingness" (*P,* 42). Fanny, however, becomes involved despite herself in issues of social importance at Sotherton, Mansfield, and Thornton Lacey, defending traditional "grounds" from the injuries of selfish improvements, innovative behavior, and materialistic ways. When she becomes the mistress of the Mansfield parsonage, she redeems her society. In *Persuasion,* by contrast, "place" is no longer there to be defended, since Sir Walter Elliot, the "foolish spendthrift baronet, who had not had principle or sense enough to maintain himself in the situation in which Providence had placed him" (*P,* 248), has rented his ancestral home and moved to Bath, where, to Anne's sorrow, he feels "no degradation in his change" (*P,* 138). Kellynch Hall will never be Anne's to "improve," nor is she to find a home like Uppercross (of which she could have been mistress one day, had she accepted Charles Musgrove's proposal of marriage).

Uppercross mansion, with "its high walls, great gates, and old trees, substantial and unmodernized" (*P,* 36), exists at the heart of the kind of organic community Jane Austen had described in her positive pictures of places like Delaford and Thornton Lacey. But in *Persuasion* the viability of its "old English style" is put in some question. Charles Musgrove, heir to the estate, has introduced improvements in the community in the form of a farmhouse "elevated into a cottage," complete with "veranda, French windows, and other prettinesses" (*P*, 36). Meanwhile, within the great house the Musgrove girls have created an air of confusion in the old-fashioned, wainscoted parlor, by furnishing it with a pianoforte, harp, flower stands, and "little tables placed in every direction" (*P,* 40). The ancestral portraits seem "to be staring in astonishment" at "such an overthrow of all order and neatness" (*P,* 40). Yet despite her exposure of the selfishness of the younger generation, Jane Austen does not adopt a censorious attitude. In this respect, *Persuasion* differs from earlier works in which the desire of Mary Crawford to new-furnish Mansfield (*MP,* 48) or of Marianne Dashwood to new-furnish Allenham (*SS,* 69) were suspect signs of "modern manners" to be repudiated by the reader.

Anne's task in *Persuasion* is not, then, to reclaim Kellynch (debased beyond Anne's powers of recovery by her father's extravagance, otiosity, and absurd pride in rank) but to discover new possibilities of accommodation for herself. Thus in conversation with Mr. Elliot, her false suitor, she proclaims herself "too proud to enjoy a welcome which depends so entirely upon place" (*P,* 151) while later she assures Wentworth that "every fresh place would be interesting to me" (*P,* 184). The novel provides Anne with a number of "fresh" possibilities of accommodation, which are associated not with the stabilities of the land (Winthrop, the future home of Henrietta Musgrove, is significantly described as an "indifferent" place, "without beauty and without dignity" [*P,* 85]) but with the risks and uncertainties of life at sea or among sailors. Mrs. Croft knows "nothing superior to the accommodations of a man of war," having lived with her husband Admiral Croft in no fewer than five ships, crossed the Atlantic four times, and been once to the East Indies (*P,* 68–70).[43] Ashore, the Crofts are tenants of Kellynch, where their improvements include the removal of a number of large looking glasses from Sir Walter's dressing room. They drive an unfashionable gig and, while in Bath, live in lodgings that are none the worse, as the Admiral tells Anne, "for putting us in mind of those we first had at North Yarmouth. The wind blows through one of the cupboards just in the same way" (*P,* 170). Described as "generally out of doors together . . . dawdling about in a way not endurable to a third person" (*P,* 73), the Crofts are the most successful portrait of seasoned "connubial felicity" in Jane Austen's work. Their partnership in life, no less than in their style of driving the gig (*P,* 92), provides Anne with a model of marriage, an exemplary way of responding to an existence in which the waters are not always smooth.

A second naval family, the Harvilles, provides another positive example. Anne meets Captain Harville in Lyme shortly before Louisa Musgrove's disastrous leap from the steps on the Cobb calls into question the nature of her "fortitude." Suffering from a severe wound, Harville reveals a more estimable form of fortitude in his modest house near the Cobb. Its rooms are so small that Anne is at first astonished that he can think them "capable of accommodating so many." But her astonishment gives way to pleasure deriving from "all the ingenious contrivances and nice arrangements of Captain Harville, to turn the actual space to the best possible account, to supply the deficiencies of lodging-house furniture, and defend the windows and doors against the winter storms to be expected" (*P,* 98). In his illness, Captain Harville has at least set his house in order; and we are surely asked to discover in his usefulness, active employment, and positive outlook an exemplary response to reduced social expectations. Like Mrs. Smith in her even worse circumstances in Westgate Buildings, Harville responds not only with resolution and independence but with "elasticity of mind" (*P,* 154). Without fortune or carriage or spacious accommodations, Harville extends an "uncommon" degree of hospitality to the visitors in Lyme, whereas the Elliots in Bath, in sycophantic pursuit of their aristocratic relations and guiltily aware of their own reduced style of living, have altogether abandoned "old fashioned notions" of "country hospitality" (P, 219).

So consistent is the contrast between the landed and the naval characters in *Persuasion,* and so consistent the preference for the latter, that critics (myself included) have been led to make excessive historical claims concerning the new directions of the novel. We should not see the renting of Kellynch Hall as a doom-laden portent of the decline of the landed order; nor should we see in the energy and initiative of the naval characters implications as to the arrival on the social scene of a new, perhaps "bourgeois," class.[44] As Jane Austen's own family showed, a modest but well-connected gentry family could more than adequately fill both landed and naval roles in the period. Nor should we see *Persuasion*'s new directions as a contradiction of the traditional values embodied in the character of Mr. Knightley. It is true that in her last completed novel, Jane Austen reexamines both the idea of the gentleman and the role of manners. But in repudiating Sir Walter's definition of the gentleman—which excludes sailors on the grounds that they are without property, have to work, and are exposed to inclement weather that ravages their looks—she does not abandon her trust in gentlemanly behavior; and in consistently presenting the hypocritical Mr. Elliot as a man of "polished" manners, she does not renounce her faith in morally informed manners as a medium of social intercourse.

The contrast between land and sea in *Persuasion* works not to announce a new social leadership but rather to open new possibilities of accommodation for the marginal woman. What if our hopes of landed entitlement are disappointed—is this the end of the world? "Desire" is, of course, fulfilled in the marriage of Anne to Wentworth, but the dependence on marriage for the closure of the novel's plot is not escapist, in view of the positive examples of the Crofts, the Harvilles, Mrs. Smith, and Anne herself, who in the lonely period before her rapprochement with Wentworth showed stoicism, self-reliance, and above all "usefulness" in her social relations.

Even the most interesting of *Persuasion*'s new directions, its new attitude to nature, needs careful description. Sister of a great landowner, Jane Austen had always shown (like Fanny on her trip to Sotherton) a proprietary interest in "the appearance of the country, the bearings of the roads, the difference of soil, the state of the harvest, the cottages, the cattle" (*MP,* 80). In her last works, however, nature begins to express states of consciousness, as her heroines respond to atmospheric conditions and seasonal moods.[45] On the walk to Winthrop, for example, Anne's "autumnal" feelings of loss and loneliness find consolation in "the view of the last smiles of the year upon the tawny leaves and withered hedges" (P, 84). But such "romanticism" is closer to that expressed in the sonnets of Charlotte Smith (1784) and William Lisle Bowles (1789) than to that of Wordsworth or Coleridge, and unlike Captain Benwick's romantic attitudes, it is never allowed to become self-indulgent. Even so, Anne's feelings for the natural scene mark a new emphasis in Jane Austen's response to the land, which is no longer viewed mainly as a place to be inhabited by the heroine in a responsible social role but as a possible source of alternative emotional consolation.

Like *Persuasion,* Jane Austen's unfinished fragment *Sanditon,* written in the winter before her death on 18 July 1817, also shows signs of a more private interest in nature. *Sanditon* describes with remarkable brio the transformation of an old village into a seaside resort for valetudinarians. Mr. Parker and Lady Denham are partners in this speculative enterprise, which brilliantly captures aspects of the rootless, fashion-seeking Regency era.[46] Mr. Parker makes of his inheritance "his Mine, his Lottery, his Speculation & his Hobby Horse" (*MW,* 372). He moves from his old house—like Donwell Abbey, unfashionably low and sheltered but "rich in . . . Garden, Orchard & Meadows"—to a new house, to which he gives the topical name of Trafalgar House. Trafalgar House lacks a kitchen garden and shade trees, is exposed to winter storms, and is built near a cliff "on the most elevated spot on the Down" (*MW,* 379, 384). Jane Austen's satire is in the eighteenth-century tradition of Horace Walpole, who, in a letter to Montagu (15 June 1768), wrote: "How our ancestors would laugh at us, who knew there was no being comfortable, unless you had a high hill before your nose, and a thick warm wood at your back! Taste is too freezing a commodity for us, and depend upon it will go out of fashion again."[47] It seems clear that the lofty and precarious location of Mr. Parker's new house was intended to prefigure the crash of his speculative ventures, but what is remarkable about *Sanditon* is Jane Austen's *sang-froid* in face of the "improvements" she describes. Here, after all, is the theme of *Mansfield Park,* but *Sanditon's* heroine is unlikely to play Fanny's role of social redeemer, or even of social conscience. Like *Emma,* she responds aesthetically to the external scene, finding "amusement enough in standing at her ample Venetian window, & looking over the miscellaneous foreground of unfinished Building, waving Linen, & tops of Houses, to the Sea, dancing & sparkling in Sunshine & Freshness" (*MW,* 384). Charlotte Heywood is like previous heroines in terms of her emerging from a traditional rural home into the glare of a materialistic world, but her accommodation to this world is more detached, more self-contained; she finds the Sanditon scene "very striking—and very amusing—or very melancholy, just as Satire or Morality might prevail" (*MW,* 396). And rather than being critical of Sanditon's "modern" developments, she views them "with the calmness of amused curiosity" (*MW,* 384). *Sanditon* is a remarkable work by a woman about to move into her last accommodations in College Street, Winchester. In its satire of hypochondria, it announces itself to be on the side of life and health; and in its presentation of the heroine, it arouses our curiosity. Like Mr. Knightley in his early concern for Emma, we "wonder what will become of her" (*E,* 40). More than in her future husband, we are interested in the home she would have found.[48]

Notes

1. All page references to Jane Austen's fiction are to *The Novels of Jane Austen,* ed. R. W. Chapman, 3rd ed., 5 vols. (London: Oxford Univ. Press, 1932–34), or to *The Works of Jane Austen: Minor Works,* ed. R. W. Chapman, rev. B. C. Southam (London: Oxford Univ. Press, 1954, rev. 1969). Where appropriate, novels will be indicated by the initial letters of their titles; *MW* stands for *Minor Works.*

2. Brian Southam, *"Sanditon:* The Seventh Novel," in *Jane Austen's Achievement,* ed. Juliet McMaster (London: Macmillan, 1976), 12–16; Christopher Kent, " 'Real Solemn History' and Social History," in *Jane Austen in a Social Context,* ed. David Monaghan (Totowa, N.J.: Barnes & Noble, 1981), 98–99.

3. *A Room of One's Own* (1929; rpt. New York: Harcourt Brace, 1957), 71.

4. For an analysis of Jane Austen's denouements, see Lloyd W. Brown, *Bits of Ivory: Narrative Technique in Jane Austen's Fiction* (Baton Rouge: Louisiana State Univ. Press, 1973), 199–235; for a consideration of the dialectic played out between realism and desire in *Northanger Abbey,* see George Levine, *The Realistic Imagination* (Chicago: Univ. of Chicago Press, 1981), 61–80.

5. Brigid Brophy, "Jane Austen and the Stuarts," in *Critical Essays on Jane Austen,* ed. B. C. Southam (London: Routledge & Kegan Paul, 1968), 21–38; David Spring, "Interpreters of Jane Austen's Social World," in *Jane Austen: New Perspectives,* ed. Janet Todd (New York: Holmes & Meier, 1983); 53–72. For biographical details I am mainly indebted to R. W. Chapman, *Facts and Problems* (Oxford: Clarendon Press, 1948); George Holbert Tucker, *A Goodly Heritage: A History of Jane Austen's Family* (Manchester: Carcanet New Press, 1983); and John Halperin, *The Life of Jane Austen* (Brighton: Harvester Press, 1984; Baltimore: Johns Hopkins Univ. Press, 1984).

6. Mavis Batey, "Jane Austen at Stoneleigh Abbey," *Country Life* 160 (30 December 1976), 1974–75. Jane Austen's negative use of Repton in *Mansfield Park* troubles scholars who consider his philosophy of tasteful improvement to be close to hers. Along with such predecessors as Dryden, Cowper, and Burke, however, she had a conservative distrust of "improvements," which may explain her (perhaps unfair) treatment of Repton; see Alistair M. Duckworth, "Improvements," in *The Jane Austen Companion,* ed. A. Walton Litz et al. (New York: Macmillan, 1986), pp. 223–27. It is also possible, as Tucker suggests, that she disliked what she saw of Repton's work at Adlestrop (*Goodly Heritage,* 58).

7. David Waldron Smithers, *Jane Austen in Kent* (Westerham, Kent: Hurtwood Publications, 1981), 17.

8. Two sketches of Steventon Rectory are included in F. B. Pinion's valuable *Jane Austen Companion* (London: Macmillan, 1973), facing p. 18.

9. *Jane Austen's Letters to her Sister Cassandra and Others,* ed. R. W. Chapman, 2d ed. (London: Oxford Univ. Press, 1964), 84. Subsequent page references to the letters are given in the text.

10. For an excellent treatment of the question, see Stuart M. Tave, *Some Words of Jane Austen* (Chicago: Univ. of Chicago Press, 1973), 131–41.

11. The liveliest expression of the vigorous recent movement of feminist criticism of Jane Austen's fiction may be found in Sandra M. Gilbert and Susan Gubar, *The Madwoman in the Attic: The Woman Writer and the Nineteenth-Century Literary Imagination* (New Haven, Conn.: Yale Univ. Press, 1979).

12. *Journal of Katherine Mansfield,* ed. John Middleton Murray (New York: McGraw-Hill, 1927), 5.

13. G. E. Mingay, *English Landed Society in the Eighteenth Century* (London: Routledge &. Kegan Paul, 1963).

14. Spring, "Interpreters," 63.

15. *Godmersham Park Sale Catalogue* (London: Christie, 1983), II: 7, item 003.

16. It should be added that little resentment toward Edward Austen or Mrs. Knight appears in the letters, whereas there is a good deal of resentment expressed toward James Austen and his wife, Mary. Not only had they usurped Jane Austen's childhood home; they seem to have been parsimonious as well. There is also no cause to question Edward's generosity after 1814, when a lawsuit over the ownership of Chawton, followed by Henry's bankruptcy (in 1816) severely depleted his funds.

17. Reproduced in Marghanita Laski, *Jane Austen and Her World* (London: Thames and Hudson, 1969), 72–73. The same work includes contemporary views of Stoneleigh Abbey, Godmersham, and Manydown.

18. Spring, "Interpreters," 61.

19. Readers with antiquarian interests will delight in Chapman's copious illustrations of carriages in *The Oxford Illustrated Jane Austen;* F. B. Pinion has a more critical interest, to which I am indebted; see *A Jane Austen Companion,* 28–29.

20. Gilbert and Gubar, *Madwoman,* 117.

21. Ibid., 153.

22. For Jane Austen's defense of the gentry against pressures from above and below, see David Monaghan, *Jane Austen: Structure and Social Vision* (Totowa, N.J.: Barnes & Noble, 1980), 7, and elsewhere.

23. For a different view of Jane Austen in relation to Mary Wollstonecraft, see Margaret Kirkham, *Jane Austen, Feminism and Fiction* (Brighton: Harvester Press, 1983).

24. Spring, "Interpreters," 64–65.

25. Proposing that "the walk to church from a beautiful country-house, of a lovely summer afternoon, may be the prettiest possible adventure," Henry James also described the Warwickshire countryside as expressing "imperturbable British Toryism." The fact that this was a conservative county, he said, was "written in the hedgerows. . . . Of course the owners of these things were conservative; of course they were stubbornly unwilling to see the harmonious edifice of their constituted, convenient world the least bit shaken" (*English Hours,* ed. Leon Edel [Oxford: Oxford Univ. Press, 1981], 117, 120; "In Warwickshire" was written in 1877).

26. Alistair M. Duckworth, *The Improvement of the Estate: A Study of Jane Austen's Novels* (Baltimore: Johns Hopkins Univ. Press, 1974), 38–54.

27. Raymond Williams, *The Country and the City* (London: Oxford Univ. Press, 1973).

28. Terry Lovell, "Jane Austen and Gentry Society," in *Literature, Society and the Sociology of Literature,* ed. Francis Barker et al. (Colchester: Univ. of Essex, 1977), 120.

29. James Edward Austen-Leigh's opinion, in *A Memoir of Jane Austen* (London: R. Bentley, 1870).

30. According to Cassandra's memorandum, *First Impressions* (the original of *Pride and Prejudice*) was begun October 1796 and ended August 1797; *Sense and Sensibility* was begun November 1797.

31. Marilyn Butler, *Jane Austen and the War of Ideas* (Oxford: Clarendon Press, 1975).

32. Even with Colonel Brandon's generous gift of the Delaford living, worth £200 a year, Edward and Elinor face the prospect of beginning married life on £350 a year—the living plus income from his £2,000 and her £1,000. Mr. Ferrars eventually gives Edward £10,000 which brings their income up to a comfortable but certainly not wealthy £750 a year. This sum would suffice only for *"menus plaisirs"* in the worldly London life of the Crawfords (*MP,* 226). I suspect that Jane Austen's own youthful anticipations may have hovered between "a competence" of £1,000 a year and "wealth" of £2,000 a year; the income of Edmund and Fanny at the end of *Mansfield Park* is between these limits.

33. *Antony and Cleopatra,* II.ii.236–240. When Mr. Gardiner's letter describing the resolution of the Lydia-Wickham affair arrives at Longbourn, Elizabeth runs across the lawn to her father and, "*panting* for breath," eagerly asks, "What news?" (*PP,* 301, italics added).

34. Henrietta Ten Harmsel, *Jane Austen: A Study in Fictional Conventions* (The Hague: Mouton, 1964), 83.

35. For a discussion of the thematic use of "anodyne data" in classic fiction, see Roland Barthes, *S/Z*, trans. Richard Miller (New York: Hill and Wang, 1974), 22–23.

36. Lionel Trilling, "*Mansfield Park,*" in *The Opposing Self* (1955); reprinted in *Jane Austen: A Collection of Critical Essays,* ed. Ian Watt (Englewood Cliffs, N.J.: Prentice-Hall, 1963), 18.

37. Sidney Ives has suggested that the squalor of the Price household owes its origin to Jane Leigh Perrot's experiences (and her epistolary description of the same) in the Scaddings household, Ilchester. She was held there, at her own expense, in the autumn and winter of 1799–1800, while awaiting trial on the charge of shoplifting (of which she was acquitted). See *The Trial of Mrs. Leigh Perrot* (Boston: Club of Odd Volumes, 1980), 13–15, 29–32.

38. Gilbert and Gubar, *Madwoman,* 172.

39. If we assume that, like her sister Lady Bertram, Mrs. Norris has a fortune of £7,000, or £350 a year, then by subtracting this from "very little less than a thousand a year," we can estimate the Mansfield living as bringing in about £600 a year (since Mr. Norris has "scarcely any private fortune"). After Mr. Norris's death, however, his widow will have, according to Sir Thomas, £600 a year (*MP,* 29). This means that she has raised her principal to £12,000, which suggests in turn that over her married life of roughly twenty years, she must have saved something like £200 a year. These details not only illuminate Mrs. Norris's character as an "economist" ("I must live within my income, or I shall be miserable" [*MP,* 30]) but also allow for a retrospective criticism of Mr. Bennet in *Pride and Prejudice,* who is unable to save anything from his £2,000 a year.

40. Alistair M. Duckworth, " 'Spillikins, Paper Ships, Riddles, Conundrums, and Cards': Games in Jane Austen's Life and Fiction," in *Jane Austen: Bicentenary Essays,* ed. John Halperin (London: Cambridge Univ. Press, 1975), 292–96.

41. Recent critics who dispute moral interpretations of *Emma* include Julia Prewitt Brown, *Jane Austen's Novels: Social Change and Literary Form* (Cambridge, Mass.: Harvard Univ. Press, 1979), who finds "the drive toward cooperation" in Jane Austen to be dictated by "anthropological" rather than by moral imperatives; Susan Morgan, *In the Meantime: Character and Perception in Jane Austen's Fiction* (Chicago: Univ. of Chicago Press, 1980), who values the perceptual and the epistemological dimensions of Emma over the ethical; and Bernard J. Paris, *Character and Conflict in Jane Austen's Novels: A Psychological Approach* (Detroit: Wayne State Univ. Press, 1978), who proposes that Emma's education may be viewed, in Horneyan terms, as Jane Austen's glorification of self-effacement as a strategy of living.

42. Barthes, *S/Z,* 75–76 and passim.

43. One wonders whether the eight hundred sailors crammed between decks in Nelson's *Victory* would agree with Mrs. Croft's opinion respecting the superiority of a man-of-war's accommodations.

44. For David Spring's strictures, see "Interpreters," 65–66.

45. A. Walton Litz, *Jane Austen: A Study of Her Artistic Development* (London: Chatto and Windus, 1965), 150–69.

46. Southam, "*Sanditon,*" 1–26.

47. Horace Walpole's *Correspondence with George Montagu,* ed. W. S. Lewis and Ralph S. Brown, Jr. (New Haven: Yale Univ. Press, 1941), II, 262.

48. I wish to thank John Fain, John Halperin, Sidney Homan, Sidney Ives, Donald Justice, and Bernard J. Paris for their helpful comments.

Traveling to the Self:
Comic and Spatial Openness in Jane Austen's Novels

LAURA MOONEYHAM WHITE

A boundary is not that at which something stops, but as the Greeks recognized, the boundary is that from which something *begins its presencing.*[1]
—Heidegger, *Poetry Language Thought*

To dwell between heaven and earth means to "settle" in the "multifarious in-between," that is, to concretize the general situation as a [humanly]-made place. The word "settle" here does not mean a mere economical relationship; it is rather an existential concept which denotes the ability to symbolize meanings. When the [humanly]-made environment is meaningful, [we] are "at home".... From the beginning of time [human beings] have recognized that to create a place means to express the essence of being.[2]
—Norberg-Schulz, *Existence, Space, and Architecture*

If the task of novelists is to express the essence of being—and so it is—then we should read the geography, architecture, and interior design of a novel's world as if we were reading its values. What a novelist wishes the reader to accept as "home" tells us what the novelist wishes the reader to accept existentially. This is particularly true in comic narratives, in which our pleasure at identifying with the protagonists' happy close is yoked to our pleasure in their placement in an ideal place. Perhaps the most important British comic novelist is Jane Austen, and to read the places of her world in order to understand her comic values is the task of the present essay.

Traveling in Jane Austen's world takes one from the most miniature of enclosed spaces, such as the mysterious Gothic trunk of *Northanger Abbey,* to the unseen but epic arenas—Antigua in the midst of a slave revolt, for instance, or the war-torn Mediterranean.[3] Everywhere in Austen's novels, scale and place measure human limitations, which not only protect but restrict,

This essay was written specifically for this volume and is published for the first time by permission of the author.

and human freedom, which releases but may also injure. The most serious injury in Austen occurs when the headstrong Louisa Musgrove of *Persuasion* insists on being jumped down the steep steps at Lyme by her male admirer, Captain Wentworth. "The sensation was delightful to her," we are told.[4] Despite its "delight," its sense of liberation, this escape from the dullness of usual and measured movement has its dangers; by a second's error, Louisa propels herself not into the gentleman's hands but onto the stone below. The boundaries of space and time maintain their habitual obduracy. But enclosed, restricted space can be deadly too, as we may judge from the catatonic example set by Lady Bertram of *Mansfield Park,* who cocoons herself in a deathlike but genteel inertia, the horizons of her world delineated by the two ends of her sofa. Where then, in accommodations large or small, are Austen's heroines to place themselves? Where are they to find what Alistair Duckworth terms their "grounds of being"?[5]

From both ends of the scale, from four-cornered sanctuary to open air, the metaphorical status of place functions as a Janus figure, scanning both safety and danger, bondage and liberation. This essential ambiguity of either enclosed or open space in Austen, however, operates on two levels. In her works, spatial representation uses a double logic, standing for social values on the one hand and psychological values on the other. In the social arena, we find space embodies Austen's conservative sense of fixed rights and wrongs. Because enclosed space is both shelter and prison, it exists as an emblem for both the coherency and the restrictions of society. Open space, on the other hand, when it stands for social values, represents pure freedom and equally pure anarchy. When place represents society, then, both its order and the suffocation such order may entail, the level of representation is primarily moral and cultural. As Alistair Duckworth has argued in his *Improvement of the Estate,* the central symbol of Austen's spatial imagination, the estate, should be viewed as the focus of Austen's conservative impulse. He suggests that the estate represents a reactionary solution to threats of social change and that the dissolution of the estate, a threat implicit or explicit in each of Austen's novels, stands for the disintegration of social order. The estate when upheld, however, symbolizes cohesion and stable social values.[6]

But space by no means operates only on the scale of cultural value. Space also represents the self and its quest for identity. It is true that the social dimensions of spatial representation in Austen's novels work by a more self-evident and less complex logic because Austen's social values are relatively rock-ribbed. Spatial symbology of the self follows a more ambiguous pattern because Austen's understanding of psychological realities shuns the sort of monolithic certainty we find in her social vision. In general, however, when space operates as a metaphor for the self, it follows a pattern: enclosed space tends to represent either the achievement of identity or the prisonhood of self. Likewise, open space has potentially benign or malign significance; it may stand for either transcendence or the dissolution of selfhood.

Importantly, when the self is represented spatially, the issues at hand are generally less moral than existential.[7] Certainly in Austen's fiction we find what Lionel Trilling refers to as her "militant categorical certitude," that is, her clear belief in moral imperatives, working in concert with an almost equally apparent sense of the self's essential disunity (Trilling, 79). Repeatedly, we find that Austen's knowledge of the multilayered nature of human personality tempers her moral absolutism. For example, there is perhaps no statement more naive in Austen's work than that which she gives Marianne Dashwood in *Sense and Sensibility:* "We always know when we are acting wrong."[8] This claim for the wholeness and self-sufficiency of moral judgment is devastated by the subsequent events in the novel, which prove Marianne to have been acting amid a throng of self-delusions. That Marianne more than any other character in Austen's fiction seeks open air and transcendence with nature indicates her threatened disintegration of self. It is no accident that Marianne almost dies of fever after roaming "where there was something more of wildness . . . where the trees were the oldest, and the grass the longest and wettest" (*SS*, 258). Moral absolutism tends to be suspect in Austen when brought into the realm either of subjective value or of social necessity. For instance, untruth is a wrong, but Austen's sympathies clearly lie with Elinor rather than with Marianne when Marianne refuses to say the appropriate polite nothings in response to Lucy's effusions: "Marianne was silent; it was impossible for her to say what she did not feel, however trivial the occasion; and upon Elinor therefore the whole task of telling lies when politeness required it, always fell" (*SS*, 104). We find a corresponding diminishment of moral absolutism in the face of subjective interpretation; for example, when Mr. Knightley in *Emma* wonders if his ready dislike of Frank Churchill and his condemnation of Frank's double-dealing may have their origins in personal bias, and if his suspicions are rather a case of "Myself creating what I saw."[9]

Nonetheless the complexity and multilayered nature of consciousness itself is not to be shunned; after all, refusing to recognize the multiple properties of the self solves nothing. Because the self perceives itself, identity is a necessarily dual condition. Recognition of the self's disjunction is crucial, but suturing the wound through such awareness may be the best remedy. It is true that before Elizabeth Bennet may have Darcy and Pemberley, she must cry out: "Till this moment, I never knew myself."[10] It is also true that before Emma may have Mr. Knightley, she must perceive her own blindness; whether sitting or standing, in her own room or in the shrubbery, she finds "in every place, every posture . . . that she had been imposing on herself" (*E*, 266), a dislocation of place and self conjoined. Such epiphanies of moral judgment and clarity of inner vision seem to imply that clear vision will prevail thereafter. But never does complete self-knowledge and a resultant wholeness of being follow such moments of insight. Elizabeth Bennet and Emma both must make further calibrations of identity: Emma even has still to plot a match between the Westons' baby girl and the John Knightleys' youngest son, a *ricorso* in miniature to the errors that brought the whole of the previous narrative into being. The goal of the comic dilemma is a recognition and acceptance of our own doubleness; the self-perceiver must further perceive his or her act of self-perception. Austen seems to recognize this paradox. We have, for instance, Mr. Knightley's assertion that his beloved and newly affianced Emma is "faultless in spite of all her faults" (*E,* 269); that is, she is entirely herself and simultaneously not so. Her "faultlessness" arises as a condition of her ability to know not only her failings but also her seemingly unlimited potential for error and self-deception. Emma's knowledge of her own disunity is her greatest triumph, and her humility in the face of her repeatedly demonstrated fallibility seems the only morally adequate stance.

The ultimate goal for each of Austen's heroines is to find a home in herself, for only then may she be rewarded with the idealized physical space that represents this inner integration. All of Austen's heroines learn two related lessons. First, they come to understand that personal identity may be threatened or even annihilated as one moves away from customary surroundings into alien territory. As Anne Elliot of *Persuasion* proclaims, her proficiency is at "the art of knowing our own nothingness beyond our own circle" (*P,* 28). Such an art is mastered by each of Austen's heroines as one by one they are expelled from the quasi-Edenic home front into a larger, more demanding, and increasingly hostile society. Elizabeth Bennet, for instance, need not confront the apparent self-serving illogic of her aversion to Darcy and her admiration of Wickham while she remains in her own home. But the movement outward to visit the newlywed Collinses results in a necessary reassessment of identity. Here she must defend herself and her social position against the assaults of Lady Catherine de Bourgh. She is situated for the home truths Darcy's letter contains only when she is in fact not at home; here she can exclaim, "Till this moment, I never knew myself" (*PP,* 237). A more complete readjustment of Elizabeth's understanding must wait for the even greater spatial dislocation to Pemberley, Darcy's territory, where Elizabeth's presence is embarrassing and equivocal.

Catherine Morland of *Northanger Abbey* likewise learns to doubt her absolutist notions about human morality only after she has traveled to Bath; she questions her romanticized notions about human morality only after she has visited Northanger Abbey. In Bath she learns that people can lie. In Northanger Abbey she learns that books too can "lie," that is, tell stories only loosely related to real human experience. Such lessons threaten Catherine's sense of self and leave her at one crisis point mortified, self-murdered with shame: "she hated herself more than she could express."[11] Emma's expulsion from the home front where identity remains unchallenged, where she is perfect in her father's eyes and in her own, takes her no further than the beauty spot of Box Hill, seven miles distant, or to Donwell Abbey, which is but a mile from Hartfield but which has remained unvisited by Emma for several years. The more cloistered the sense of identity, the less the distance needed to disrupt and discompose old structures of selfhood. In *Sense and Sensibility,* Elinor and Marianne are expelled twice, first from the stability of Norland and then from their adopted home. Only away are there the necessary assaults on the self, assaults that bring necessary change. Anne's expulsion in *Persuasion* is probably the most brutal endured by an Austen heroine; at the Musgroves' she learns that everyone is wrapped up in insular concerns and that they adjudge as peripheral Anne's loss of home. Anne's proficiency (at "the art of knowing our own nothingness beyond our own circle") is at the art that brings self-knowledge. The threatened self in comic plots is the self that adapts and reasserts personal integrity, a remade selfhood to be carried to the new home of the comic close where personal identity has been redefined.

But there is a truth corollary to Anne's observation that is equally if more subtly demonstrated through the whole of Austen's work: the certainty that we must learn our own nothingness *within* our own circle as well. From Catherine Morland to Anne Elliot, the protagonists learn that home is not home. Austen is not content to identify home with asylum and the outside world with unalloyed jeopardy. The womb is, after all, a safe place only for gestation, a lesson such heroines as Fanny Price and Emma Woodhouse learn to their sorrow. And Catherine Morland's return to the home front and her ordinary family life leaves her extraordinarily dissatisfied. Her mother's platitudes are now revealed as insufficient wisdom for the larger problems to which Catherine has been exposed while away. She has learned all she is capable of learning by this point in the plot and waits for the turn of external events to bring her to the new home of the hero, a turn that will signal her comic achievement of self; a return to the Morland home would constitute a tragic close. Catherine learns the lesson reserved for all of Austen's heroines: there is a threat in *both* places, home and away, because everywhere one finds one's self and its divisions.

An awareness of consciousness as divided is of course central to the duality of place we have considered thus far. This duality is a phenomenon of the increasingly privatized sense of being that began in the Renaissance and that almost certainly caused or, at least, accompanied the accelerated use of private accommodations in domestic interiors of the same period. Lionel Trilling contrasts an individual's sense of place before and after the historical development of a private self:

> Certain things he did not have or do until he [*sic*] became an individual. He did not have an awareness of . . . internal space. He did not . . . imagine himself in more than one role, standing outside or above his own personality. . . . It is when he becomes an individual that man lives more and more in private rooms; whether the privacy makes the individuality or the individuality requires the privacy the historians do not say. (24–25)

As a historical development, Trilling tells us, that sense of the individual as inauthentic, multiple, and fragmented reaches its zenith in the early nineteenth century.[12]

The literary use of spatial symbology seems to confirm that thesis. In the novel of the early and middle eighteenth century, the use of place is still largely either incidental or allegorical.[13] For example, in *Tom Jones* Allworthy's estate stands for the comic reward but has little in its description that aids in our understanding of Allworthy's character, beyond its allegorical function as the well-run estate of the virtuous man. But as place comes increasingly to represent the self, it cannot surprise that by the time we reach Austen, the sense of place in the novel is necessarily marked by doubleness and ambiguity. The "hut dreams" Gaston Bachelard proposes in his *Poetics of Space,* what he terms "well-determined centers of revery" (Bachelard, 31), are ever present in this period's literature as ideals of unity and integration.[14] "Hut dreams" are the primal form the human imagination gives to its desire for refuge and enclosure; as Bachelard tells us,

> the dreamer of refuges dreams of a hut, of a nest, or of nooks and corners in which he would like to hide away, like an animal in its hole. . . . The hut appears to be the tap-root of the function of inhabitation. Indeed it is so simple that it no longer belongs to our memories . . . but to legend; it is a center of legend. When we are lost in darkness and see a distant glimmer of light, who does not dream of a thatched cottage, or, to go more deeply still into legend, of a hermit's hut? (Bachelard, 30–31)

This archetypal yearning for huts makes itself felt in narrative by such devices as the protagonist's settling into a privileged space at the narrative close. A related and ubiquitous narrative pattern in the early novels of the eighteenth century features a lost heir who is restored to his inheritance (again, as in *Tom Jones*). Such narrative patterns remind us of Heidegger's statement: "dwelling is the essential property of existence" (qtd. in Norberg-Schulz, 12).

But such dreams of a safe retreat for the self are continually challenged at the close of the eighteenth century by the age's increasing sense that such nests of comfort and wholeness—and the wholeness of being living in them promises—are mythic goals only. The deepening mimetic tradition in fiction makes necessary a transformation of the romantic place of the end (the bower, the estate, the half of a kingdom) into a realistic place that one might know and recognize. However, the change in spatial meaning is not merely one from romanticized, idealized function to one that serves the demands of social realism. Enclosed space comes to represent danger and suffocation, the self closed in upon itself. The hut dream is reimagined darkly, particularly by the Romantics, for whom, as Nina Auerbach explains, "closed-in space [becomes] the spirit's most appropriate, if most bitter, home."[15] As Keats tells us in

"Lamia," "Love in a hut, with water and a crust, / Is—Love forgive us!—cinders, ashes, dust."[16] We also find Jane Austen, the greatest English novelist of this pivotal period and an anti-Romantic, according ambiguity to even the most privileged and idealized of her dwellings.

The simplest and most infantile of Austen's "hut dreams," that longing for a reclaimed idyllic home, occurs in *Mansfield Park* as Fanny Price and her brother William fantasize about the perfect harmony of a "little cottage . . . in which [they are] to pass all their middle and latter life together."[17] Austen does not propose this endogamous solution seriously, though Fanny does end by marrying not her brother but her first cousin. William and Fanny are to have destinies beyond this dream of quasi-incestuous seclusion. They formulate this fantasy, in fact, on their journey to Portsmouth, Fanny's first home and the center of her desire for reciprocal love. That dream too is revealed as doomed by the shoddy reality of Portsmouth. Space here is entirely too narrow, crowded, and comfortless:

> [Fanny] was . . . taken into a parlour, so small that her first conviction was of its being only a passage-room to something better, . . . but . . . she saw there was no other door; . . . Fanny was almost stunned. The smallness of the house, and the thinness of the walls brought every thing so close to her, that . . . she hardly knew how to bear it. (*MP,* 342, 347–48)

Literally and figuratively, there is little room there for Fanny. She remains on the periphery, alone and disregarded.[18] Even on her first welcome, William must remind Fanny's mother of her daughter's presence: "Here's Fanny in the parlour, and why should we stay in the passage?" (*MP,* 344).

As Frances Hart has shown, space constricts around Fanny throughout the novel, and in response she is forced to retreat into the privacy of the self to "compose or collect" herself, to reconstitute what in her being is threatened by outside forces. This process of reordering one's self postulates the existence of an authentic, whole inner being that can be restored by an act of meditation and withdrawal, by the willed creation of the intimate space (Hart, 310). But although composing or collecting oneself is in the largest sense the goal of every fictive event, it does not follow that absolute inner unity is ever *accomplished* in the body of any narrative. That accomplishment is signaled, *represented,* by the act of comic closure, but nowhere concretely achieved. As D. A. Miller argues in *Narrative and Its Discontents,* narrative closure always necessitates the working out of a structure of readerly identity that requires the reading of another narrative to reaffirm the quest; closure, illusory though it may be, nonetheless provides the impetus to drive our search for identity and our way through the text.[19] Peter Brooks's psychodynamic model of narrative, a model explicated in his 1984 *Reading for the Plot,* likewise describes closure as the psychical equivalent of readerly identity and plot as the history of the quest for that identity:

The deviance and error of plot may necessarily result from the interplay of desire in its history with the narrative insistence on explanatory form: the desire to wrest beginnings and ends from the uninterrupted flow of middles, from temporality itself; the search for that significant closure that would illuminate the sense of an existence, the meaning of life. The desire for meaning is ultimately the reader's.[20]

Such an understanding of plot requires a model that

structures ends (death, quiescence, nonnarratability) against beginnings (Eros, stimulation into tension, the desire of narrative) in a manner that necessitates the middle as detour. . . . The model proposes that we live in order to die, hence that the intentionality of plot lies in its orientation toward the end even while the end must be achieved only through detour. (Brooks, 108)

This orientation toward the end is impelled by a desire for identity, acted out by the protagonist and felt by the reader. What Northrop Frye claims about this quest for identity in romance applies with equal force to the comic romances of Jane Austen: "Identity means a good many things, but all its meanings in romance have some connection with a state of existence in which there is nothing to write about. It is existence before 'once upon a time' and subsequent to 'and they lived happily ever after.' "[21] In the comic romance, identity is the state before and after plot, the realm of nonnarratability, where nothing remains, seemingly, worth the writing.

In "Misrecognizing Shakespeare," Barbara Freedman quotes Heidegger on the illusory nature of this textual quest for identity; self-identity, Heidegger says, is

a *Sich-Verhoren,* a word that in German denotes at one and the same time our attempt to know the truth by taking the self into custody and interrogating it, and the failure of that attempt, since a mishearing or mistaking of what has been said is inevitable. Language gives the lie to the ego's capture of a specular identity just as it gives the lie to itself. . . . The most art can do, as a mirror of language, is to burn through, in its own cold way, the desire for self-definition . . . to expose the desire to own one's own name.[22]

Comedy finds its own "cold way" by decentering the final achievement of identity; this decentering is effected by a partial undoing of the symbols by which identity is represented. In comedy, as Freedman has demonstrated, one's identification with a given place is always illusory; we are always decentered from our longed-for place of solidity.[23] We partake of this promised stability and idealized placement without entirely being fulfilled—because ending the story makes impossible a rendering of the perfection promised to hero and heroine.

Everywhere in Austen the emphasis falls on the quest for integration and the stations of its attainment; once the self has been humbled into a recognition of its own disorder and multiplicity, the potent symbols of integrated consciousness, marriage and the estate, embody integration but do not extend beyond a strictly symbolic function. We never see more than the merest glimpse of married life or of the estate under its new management by the newlyweds. Each heroine is indeed simply rewarded with both hero and estate, except Anne Elliot, who is rewarded merely with hero and landau (a special case I will discuss later). We are at the same time placed and not placed at the end of each of Austen's novels. Radical spatial disjunction is conquered at each close, and the heroines at that point enjoy an apparent stability of place. But these places of rest maintain a curious opacity; they are not to be known fully. This condition of unknowability does not extend to the intermediate spaces of the text, either the other estates or cities that provide negative examples, or the gardens, walks, and outdoor holiday settings that constitute what we may perceive—if hazily—as Austen's green world. The binary threat of comedy—peril at home and peril in the midst of foreigners—can be resolved only by confronting the foreign before returning to a redesigned and reconstituted place of the self, and it is characteristic of comedy that the ideal places of the end are thus sparsely designed in contrast to the fuller rendering of the places of transition.[24] Thus we learn far more of the Miltonic wanderings that take place at Sotherton in *Mansfield Park* or at Box Hill in *Emma* than we do of Mansfield Park or Hartfield, the closing estates of each novel. And we learn that transition must take place in alien territory, such as the resorts of Bath or Lyme, that education is stymied on the home front itself. It cannot be accidental that no proposal of marriage made indoors in Austen is ever successful (among these we must account Mr. Elton's tipsy wooing in the spatially ambiguous setting of a carriage), whereas all those made outdoors are fruitful and lead directly to the comic resolution.[25]

These comic resolutions are achieved in places that seem absolute and central but that also incorporate elements of openness and decentering. Delaford, the home-to-be of the heroines in *Sense and Sensibility*, is idealized but never rendered scenically. Our only report comes from a relatively minor character, the vulgar Mrs. Jennings, and she herself has visited there but once; she terms it "every thing . . . that one could wish for" (*SS*, 68). Two months after Elinor and Edward marry, they are planning improvements to the small estate, working to "project shrubberies, and invent a sweep" (*SS*, 318). The place will be extended and broadened even as it contains the promised perfection of an ideal marriage. Visiting the couple, Mrs. Jennings finds in "Elinor and her husband . . . one of the happiest couples in the world. They had, in fact, nothing to wish for but the marriage of Colonel Brandon and Marianne, and rather better pasturage for their cows" (*SS*, 318). As this sentence reveals, even the most ideal of marriages has room for expectations, even if they are only comically low expectations of improved spaces for livestock.

The final home in *Northanger Abbey* is the parsonage at Woodston, again an idealized place but one that we see most vividly through the corrupt and mercenary eyes of General Tilney. It is he who describes the place, emphasizing its material comforts so as to interest the heiress he believes Catherine to be. There is one brief scene at Woodston in which Catherine is enchanted with all she sees, but the scene functions primarily to set Catherine's simple delight in the place against the mercenary calculations of Henry's father. For Catherine it is enough that Woodston is Henry Tilney's. In the first room she enters, her "mind was too full . . . for her either to observe or to say a good deal; and till called on by the General for her opinion of it, she had very little idea of [it]"; nonetheless, she terms the room "the prettiest I ever saw; the prettiest room in the world" (*NA,* 171–72). Woodston's perfections lie in part in its views, "pleasant, though only over green meadows" (172). The one view particularly remarked occasions yet another expression for "hut dreams"; Catherine notes, "what a sweet little cottage there is among the trees—apple trees too! It is the prettiest cottage!" (173). But even this movement toward a fantasy habitat is truncated, for the General immediately commends her approval of the cottage by contravening his earlier order to have it torn down: "You like it—you approve it as an object;—it is enough. Henry, remember that Robinson is spoken to about it. The cottage remains" (173). There is no scene set at Woodston beyond the romantic resolution; we are merely told that it is where the protagonists will live. Austen is particularly offhand in her disposal of heroine to hero in this novel; she alerts her reader to the "tell-tale compression . . . of pages" that signals the "hastening together to perfect felicity" (203); and a page or so later claims "perfect happiness" for her protagonist, dictating ideality without describing it.

We see *Pride and Prejudice*'s Pemberley most fully (Elizabeth tours the estate of her future husband, with her aunt and uncle, midway through the novel), so openness in this novel must be maintained despite the completeness of narrative rendering. Pemberley remains open because all the virtuous and potentially virtuous characters are allowed within its gates after Elizabeth and Darcy's marriage, and because the relationship between Pemberley's man and wife is flexible, admitting both wisdom and wit. Spatial openness is maintained as well, because spatially Pemberley is described primarily through views, either views from inside to out or from one prospect of the landscape to another:

> The dining parlour . . . was a large, well-proportioned room, handsomely fitted up. Elizabeth . . . went to a window to enjoy its prospect. The hill, crowned with wood, . . . receiving increased abruptness from the distance, was a beautiful object. Every disposition of the ground was good; and she looked on the whole scene, the river, the trees scattered on its banks, and the winding of the valley, as far as she could trace it, with delight. As they passed into other rooms, these objects were taking different positions; but from every window there were beauties to be seen.

She saw and admired every remarkable spot and point of view. They gradually ascended for half a mile, and then found themselves at the top of a considerable eminence, where the wood ceased, and the eye was instantly caught by Pemberley House, situated on the opposite side of a valley, into which the road with some abruptness wound.

They entered the woods, and bidding adieu to the river for a while, ascended some of the higher grounds; whence, in spots where the opening of the trees gave the eye power to wander, were many charming views of the valley, the opposite hills, with the long range of woods overspreading many, and occasionally part of the stream. (*PP*, 267–74)

Perspectives—human and visual—are never closed at Pemberley once Elizabeth has become its chatelaine; there the eye is given "power to wander."

A similar resistance to closure attends the closing places of *Emma*. Emma's Hartfield is not the Great Good Place of the novel; that distinction falls to Donwell Abbey, Mr. Knightley's estate. Donwell, "larger than Hartfield, and totally unlike it . . . was just as it ought to be, and it looked what it was," an estate of a prosperous and hardworking landowner (*E*, 230). When Emma visits Donwell late in the novel, she congratulates herself on the "honest pride and complacency" her familial relationship with the Abbey and its many virtues makes possible; what she does not at that point recognize is that "her alliance with the present . . . proprietor [Knightley]" will become the crucial relationship of her life and will inevitably expand the nature of her own proprietary view. However, because Emma's father cannot be left alone at Hartfield, Mr. Knightley must begin his married career by moving to Emma's home and leaving Donwell uninhabited. Mr. Woodhouse will die (Austen told her family that his death occurs two years after the novel's close), but this needful event does not take place within the action of *Emma* itself. So though the newlyweds will ultimately move to the idealized placement of Donwell, ideality is postponed.[26]

Persuasion alone of Austen's novels ends with heroine and hero in doubt of their home. The concept of estate has become so corrupt, ambiguous, and threatening by this stage in Austen's development that to place Anne and Wentworth spatially would be to limit them. As Duckworth has shown, the estate at this point for Austen has lost its force as a symbol of tradition, though tradition itself is no less valued (Duckworth, 199–203). Duckworth stresses that although "the dissociation of the heroine from her estate is . . . the most significant of *Persuasion*'s departures from the norms of Jane Austen's fiction. . . . these departures do not mean that . . . Austen rejects or abandons a social morality" (Duckworth, 203–4). The ideal home in this novel becomes a "home on the sea," a floating estate constituted by mutual love alone, openness as complete as one could wish and yet safe because we have Mrs. Croft's earlier assurances that there is no better home than a cozy sea cabin: a marine version of Bachelard's "hut dream."[27]

The connection between the idealized and undefined placement of the heroine at novel's close, on the one hand, and the desire for identity, on the other, is of particular interest in *Mansfield Park* because Fanny, the novel's heroine, attempts throughout the whole of the narration to achieve identity through a militant vigilance. Yet even the most rigorously controlled self defies its own self-imposed unity and must find its proper home in a space both enclosed and open, a space that more adequately confirms the necessary disjunctions of selfhood. As Ruth Yeazell has explained, Fanny's preferred method of seeking self-integration is through the purgation of all morally tainted thoughts and outside influences. Fanny prowls what she herself terms "the confines of her imagination" (*MP,* 239), playing "mental housekeeper."[28] Consciousness remains pure, Fanny thinks, by shutting things out. But clearly the path to unified being lies through inclusion not exclusion, and such inclusion becomes the track of Fanny's unwilling education. Noxious realities are thrust at her every turn, even in the behavior of her beloved Edmund, and only when Fanny can actively face and combat these ills can she grow.

A sign that Fanny has progressed beyond an entirely locked system of self occurs toward the close of the novel as she rides back from exile in Portsmouth to Mansfield Park. It is spring, and the grounds of the estate seem to Fanny, we are told, "in that delightful state . . . when, while much is actually given to the sight, more yet remains for the imagination" (*MP,* 407). Here landscape embodies a delight in openness. If, as gardenist commentators have suggested, a landscape is a dramatic poem and "its major character the perceiver who puts the parts together," then Fanny here recognizes that in a landscape full closure may be, paradoxically, the emptier state; the scene's legibility is enhanced by its openness.[29] This lesson applies with equal force to the landscape of consciousness, but is a lesson Fanny learns only partially in the novel as a whole.

Spatially too the novel ends in ambiguity.[30] Edmund and Fanny move into the Parsonage, a place Fanny has dreaded the whole of the story for its connections, first with the vile Mrs. Norris and later with the immoral Crawfords. But the Parsonage also lies on the boundary of Mansfield Park itself, another Jamesian "Great Good Place." Edmund and Fanny are not heirs to the estate, of course, any more than is Mr. Collins to Lady Catherine's Rosings in *Pride and Prejudice.*[31] But they are the place's spiritual heirs; that Fanny displays some form of integrative consciousness of both spatial and moral dimensions is made evident by the last lines of the novel: "the parsonage . . . which under each of its two former owners, Fanny had never been able to approach but with some painful sensation . . . soon grew as dear to her heart, and as thoroughly perfect in her eyes, as everything else, within the view and patronage of Mansfield Park, had long been" (*MP,* 432). This sense of appropriation is to be preferred over Fanny's prior urge to expunge those persons and thoughts she deemed impure. At any rate, despite the novel's seeming closing of ranks at the end, *Mansfield Park* does not end, either spatially or existentially, in a fully closed box, nor is the unity consciousness seeks entirely gained. Fanny ends her story placed both at the spatial center and at its periphery, ends by not only excluding all moral taint but also including a more open understanding of the self's compound essence.

Place in Austen thus has two important functions: in terms of its relationship to society's structure and received morality, place is an emblem of Austen's allegiance to the same. The estates all her heroines but Anne Elliot achieve in the final pages are uniformly ideal in this sense. They are symbols of traditional morality, unimproved by the rampaging "improvers" of her day, bastions against the polluters, who are ejected to a man (and woman, if we think of Mary Crawford). The mistake would be to confuse Austen's endorsement of social and moral tradition with a like endorsement of the possibility of absolute psychological integration. The same vehicles—marriage and the estate—that represent the achievement of social and moral order also embody at the very same time a mythic (and in that sense an imposed) solution to an insoluble dilemma of being: the self's war with itself. In this sense, the settling into an estate that ends all but one of the novels creates "grounds of being" (Duckworth, 184), emblems for the self and its attainments. It is for this reason that the estates play an ambiguous role, first, because all containers for the self both protect and imprison, and, second—and more importantly—because there is no final integrating symbol possible for the self, final integration being itself impossible, unless we follow Clarissa into the grave.

But there we are not in the realm of the comic. The plots of comedies are games played within the context of the unstable self and are fueled by that energy that desires integration, union, closure. But because such a goal is illusory, the protagonists of comedy and we ourselves are perpetually situated as is Peter Quince in his prologue in act 5 of *A Midsummer Night's Dream:* "All for your delight / We are not here."[32] Spatially, comedy depends on an acceptance of displacement and decentering. A comedy that ends, finally and absolutely, in the enclosed space has failed. In comedy, we *seem* to achieve integration through the power of wedding bells and the happy hearth, but as fiction's primary function is to focus on the self's quest for a stable identity, to show how to hold a self together, then to close a story is in essence a fait accompli. Comedy, Austen's only genre, does not grieve at this paradox of openness within closure but instead accepts the condition of our disunity. We strive for psychic order and the marriages and estates that give it representation, but we do not follow the newlyweds home, at least not until the novel of the mid-nineteenth century; and there again, with such works as *The Odd Women* and *Jude the Obscure,* we have left comedy behind. We do not ever, nor should we, test the validity of Kingsley Amis's assertion that no one would lightly undertake an evening at home with the Edmund Bertrams of *Mansfield Park.*[33] Placement must be both ideal and untested, for to test is to destroy ideality. Narrative closure within the comic is an unconditional promise, for in a sense it is bad faith to surmise beyond a comic end. One should instead begin another comedy, and once again start the unceasing quest for integration.

Notes

1. Martin Heidegger, *Poetry Language Thought*, trans. Albert Hofstadter (New York: Harper, 1975), 154; emphasis in original.

2. Christian Norberg-Schulz, *Existence, Space, and Architecture* (New York: Praeger Publishers, 1971), 50; hereafter cited in text.

3. See Barbara Hardy, *A Reading of Jane Austen* (New York: New York University Press, 1975), 106–48; and Stuart Tave, *Some Words of Jane Austen* (Chicago: University of Chicago Press, 1973), chap. 1, on the relation between scale and setting in the novels.

4. Jane Austen, *Persuasion*, ed. Patricia Meyer Spacks (New York: W. W. Norton, 1995), 73; hereafter cited in text as *P.*

5. Alistair Duckworth, *The Improvement of the Estate* (Baltimore: Johns Hopkins University Press, 1971), 184; hereafter cited in text.

6. See also R. F. Brissendon, "*Mansfield Park:* Freedom and the Family," in *Bicentenary Essays: Jane Austen*, ed. John Halperin (Cambridge: Cambridge University Press, 1975), 156–71, who continues Duckworth's argument in terms of *Mansfield Park* by suggesting that the quasi-incestuous romance between hero and heroine in this novel is allied to the theme of estate as cloister for received values.

7. The most comprehensive survey of Austen's manipulation of space to represent psychological states can be found in Frances Hart's "The Spaces of Privacy: Jane Austen," *Nineteenth Century Fiction* 30 (1975): 305–33; hereafter cited in text. Hart first surveys Lionel Trilling's argument about the privatization of space in *Sincerity and Authenticity* (Cambridge: Harvard University Press, 1973); hereafter cited in text; she then follows the phenomenology of Gaston Bachelard as set out in his text *The Poetics of Space* (New York: Orion Press, 1964); also hereafter cited in text. As Hart surveys the novels' properties of expansion and constriction, she pays particular attention to the principle of exclusion—that of shutting out morally corrupt characters—a principle she sees as crucial to the ideality of the placement accorded Austen's heroines at their narrative ends.

8. Jane Austen, *Sense and Sensibility*, ed. Ros Ballaster (New York: Penguin, 1995), 60; hereafter cited in text as *SS.*

9. Jane Austen, *Emma*, ed. Stephen M. Parrish, 2d ed. (New York: W. W. Norton, 1993), 221; hereafter cited in text as *E.*

10. Jane Austen, *Pride and Prejudice*, ed. Tony Tanner (New York: Penguin, 1972), 237; hereafter cited in text as *PP.*

11. Jane Austen, *Northanger Abbey*, ed. John Davie (New York: Oxford University Press, 1990), 160; hereafter cited in text as *NA.*

12. See Trilling, 24–25, and Hart, 301–8, for further explications of the historical development of the concept of privacy and its relationship to space. See also Orest Ranum, "The Refuges of Intimacy," trans. Arthur Goldhammer, in *The History of Private Life*, ed. Phillipe Aries and Georges Duby, (Cambridge, Mass.: Belknap Press, 1989), 3:207–63, who concentrates on the growing presence of private apartments (bedrooms, closets, chambers, etc.) in the West from the fourteenth through the nineteenth centuries.

13. David Jackel, "Moral Geography in Jane Austen," *University of Toronto Quarterly* 47 (1977–1978): 2.

14. Leland S. Person Jr. offers a fine appraisal of Austen's own "hut dreams" in his "Playing House: Jane Austen's Fabulous Space," *Philological Quarterly* 59 (1980): 62–75. Like

Hart, Person finds exclusiveness to be an essential ingredient of the near-fantasy establishment each heroine, with the exception of Anne Elliot, achieves at novel's end. He documents in Austen's life a "corresponding preference for secretive, exclusive places" (63) and concludes that "the most valuable places for her heroines . . . become symbols of the withdrawn and liberated self. Whatever their physical size, they allow their tenants an expansive exercise of imagination and support the heroines' desire to project a fabulous internal order on their surroundings" (62). Person derides these achievements, however, calling them mere wish fulfillments; I would argue in opposition that no wish is more important than our desire to achieve identity, a wish granted temporarily for the reader and (in imagination) permanently for the heroine by the comic close and its spatial settlement.

15.   Nina Auerbach, "Jane Austen and Romantic Imprisonment," in *Jane Austen in a Social Context,* ed. David Monaghan (Totowa, N.J.: Barnes & Noble, 1981), 11.

16.   John Keats, "Lamia," *Keats: Poetical Works,* ed. H. W. Garrod (Oxford: Oxford University Press, 1978), 171.

17.   Jane Austen, *Mansfield Park,* ed. James Kinsley (Oxford: Oxford University Press, 1990), 341; hereafter cited in text as *MP.*

18.   Kenneth Moler, "Miss Price All Alone: Metaphors of Distance in *Mansfield Park,*" *Studies in the Novel* 17 (1985): 191.

19.   D. A. Miller, *Narrative and Its Discontents* (Cambridge: Harvard University Press, 1981).

20.   Peter Brooks, *Reading for the Plot* (New York: Knopf, 1984), 140; hereafter cited in text.

21.   Northrop Frye, *The Secular Scripture: A Study of the Structure of Romance* (Cambridge: Harvard University Press, 1975), 54.

22.   Heidegger, quoted in Barbara Freedman, "Misrecognizing Shakespeare," in *Shakespeare's Personality,* ed. Norman Holland, Sidney Homan, and Bernard Paris (Berkeley: University of California Press, 1989), 254.

23.   Barbara Freedman, "The Construction of Subjectivity in Shakespeare: A Lacanian Analysis of the Comedies" (paper presented at the annual meeting of the Shakespeare Association of America, Seattle, April 3, 1987).

24.   Bachelard (12–13) suggests that to describe is (paradoxically) to destroy intimacy: "To describe [these ideal houses] would be like showing them to visitors," and Hart (311) expands this argument to consider the ironic or artificial character of touring a house in Austen's fiction.

25.   Catherine Searle, "Outdoor Scenes in Jane Austen's Novels," *Thought* 59 (1984): 421.

26.   See Paul Fry, "Georgic Comedy: The Fictive Territory of Jane Austen's *Emma,*" *Studies in the Novel* 11 (1979): 129–46. Unlike Paul Fry, I would maintain that this postponed spatial ideality, for which "perfect happiness" is promised, operates on the psychological as well as the social level (*E,* 313). Fry's reading of *Emma* as Georgic idyll is persuasive; he finds at the novel's close that the "unsituated 'Garden of England' is transformed by Jane Austen into a *rus conclusus*[a closed rustic estate], and enclosed farmland ample enough in range, . . . but firmly immured against outlying fictions" (Fry, 142). I would disagree, however, with his contention that, "like her ethics and her politics, Jane Austen's territory is determinate and fixed" (143). Her social territory is generally indeed as strictly mapped as the Donwell estate, but her comic territory, where identity comes to its putative fulfillment, remains to some essential degree undefined, terra incognita.

27.   Mrs. Croft explains the virtues of naval housekeeping as follows: "I do assure you, ma'am, . . . that nothing can exceed the accommodations of a man of war. . . . I can safely say, that the happiest part of my life has been spent on board a ship. While we were together, you know, there was nothing to be feared" (*P,* 47–48).

28.   Ruth Yeazell, "The Boundaries of *Mansfield Park,*" *Representations* 7 (1984): 144.

29.   Christina Marsden Gillis, "Garden, Sermon, and Novel in *Mansfield Park:* Exercises in Legibility," *Novel* 18 (1985): 124.

30.   Of the novels, *Mansfield Park* has garnered the most attention in terms of its symbolic use of space. Beyond Duckworth's thorough treatment of the subject in *The Improvement of the Estate,* chap. 1, one might see Barbara Hardy's "The Objects in *Mansfield Park,*" in *Bicentenary Essays,* ed. John Halperin (Cambridge: Cambridge University Press, 1975), 180–96; and Ann Banfield's "The Moral Landscape of *Mansfield Park,*" *Nineteenth Century Fiction* 26 (1971): 1–24. Vladimir Nabokov gives a formalist rendering of place in the novel and provides handdrawn maps of such crucial topoi as Sotherton Court and the rooms for the theatricals in "*Mansfield Park,*" in *Lectures on Literature,* ed. Fredric Bowson (New York: HarcourtBraceJovanovich, 1980), 7–61.

31.   On the peripheral nature of Fanny and Edmund's position, see F. T. Flahiff, "Place and Replacement in *Mansfield Park,*" *University of Toronto Quarterly* 54 (1984–1985): 225.

32.   William Shakespeare, *A Midsummer Night's Dream,* ed. R. A. Foakes, *New Cambridge Shakespeare* (Cambridge: Cambridge University Press, 1984), 537.

33.   Kingsley Amis, "What Became of Jane Austen?" *Spectator* 199 (1957): 440.

Jane Austen's Anti-Romantic Fragment:
Some Notes on *Sanditon*

John Halperin

On 27 January 1817, six months before her death, Jane Austen began a novel. She called it "The Brothers." The manuscript commenced "in her usual firm and neat hand," the family tells us, "but some of the latter pages were first traced in pencil—probably, when she was too ill to sit long at a desk—and afterwards written over in ink."[1] Less than two months later, on 18 March, she abruptly stopped writing "The Brothers," and, except for half a dozen (surviving) letters composed over the next four months, laid down her pen forever. "The Brothers," then, was her last piece of sustained fiction-writing and may tell us something about her creative impulses and interests during the period just before her death.

Jane Austen's brother Henry, who was her literary executor, gave the fragment the posthumous title by which it has come down to posterity: *Sanditon*. What survives is only a first draft, and heavily corrected. Twelve chapters were completed between January and March 1817; there are no paragraph divisions, and much is abbreviated—the whole thing having the air, as one critic has noted, of being written fast to keep pace with the speed of composition[2]—as if, that is, the writer, puffing and breathless, could not get it all down fast enough. This suggests both mental vivacity and physical decline and such terms indeed seem applicable to Jane Austen during the early months of 1817. From February on, her illness, adrenal insufficiency brought on by tuberculosis which perhaps had been in remission for some months, attacked her again with renewed vigor.

What we have, then, is about 25,000 words—a fragment roughly one-quarter the length of the two shortest completed novels, *Northanger Abbey* and *Persuasion*. Critics in the main have tended to ignore *Sanditon;* only a few have discussed it at any length or taken it seriously, and many of these (most notably E. M. Forster) have dismissed it as the last gasp of a dying woman. But "there is no evidence here of mental fatigue or loss of ideas," as Joan Rees ob-

John Halperin, "Jane Austen's Anti-Romantic Fragment: Some Notes on *Sanditon*," *Tulsa Studies in Women's Literature* 2 (1983): 183–91. © 1983 by *Tulsa Studies in Women's Literature*; reprinted by permission.

serves, or that the novelist's art had "reached the end of its trajectory," as Alistair M. Duckworth rightly says—quite the contrary. Brian Southam calls it "the most vigorous of all Jane Austen's writing. There is not the least sign of fatigue in its style, invention, or design." He goes on, in both of his long essays on the fragment, to emphasize the similarities (and the differences) between *Sanditon* and the rest of the fiction.[3]

Even in its unfinished form—the manuscript did not have a contemporary editor to regularize spelling and punctuation or smooth out diction—*Sanditon* is recognizably a Jane Austen performance. At the center of it, as so often in her stories, is the question of appearance and reality, true and false moral values, true and false ways of *seeing*. Before she encounters them, *Sanditon*'s heroine, Charlotte Heywood (the novelist once said she had always wanted to have a heroine named Charlotte), is told a great many things about Sanditon and its inhabitants. Like Elizabeth Bennet, she must discover the truth of what she has been told—the actual nature of things and people in the world she inhabits—for and by herself. What she hears about Lady Denham, and how she ultimately perceives her, is only one case in point. Southam is surely right to suggest that *Sanditon* could well have been sub-titled "Delusion and Reality."[4]

Sanditon is also a familiar performance in its savage attack on "improvers" and "developers," and in its anti-urban bias. Could any breed of man be more calculated to incur the wrath of a Jane Austen than that which seeks to turn unspoiled countryside into urban sprawl? Anticipating such later nineteenth-century attacks on "developers" and their new methods of "advertising" as those contained in Gissing's *Demos* and *In the Year of Jubilee*, Jane Austen in *Sanditon* condemns people who feel the need to bring "civilization" to country villages. Here is part of her description of what Lady Denham and her partner Mr. Parker have done to Sanditon:

> A very few years ago . . . it had been a quiet Village of no pretensions; but some natural advantages in its position & some accidental circumstances have suggested to [Mr. Parker], & the other principal Land Holder [Lady Denham], the probability of it's [sic] becoming a profitable Speculation, they had engaged in it, & planned & built, & praised & puffed, & raised it to a something of young Renown.[5]

Marilyn Butler has written brilliantly of this theme in *Sanditon:*

> the point is Sanditon's perversion from its earlier natural role as fishing village and agricultural community, a place where children are born and vegetable gardens flourish. Its new smart terraces are an artificial engraftment, created by an oversophisticated society's obsession with its bodily health, and by the economic opportunism of characters like Mr. Parker and Lady Denham. The people who flock to Sanditon are of the type of gentry Jane Austen always censures: urban, rootless, irresponsible, self-indulgent.[6]

Everyone in such places, the novelist declares, must " 'move in a circle,'—to the prevalence of which rototory Motion, is perhaps to be attributed to Giddiness & false steps of many" (p. 422). The "society" of fashionable towns Jane Austen always regarded with abhorrence.

Sanditon is a spa. Like Bath, Brighton, and Cheltenham, it caters primarily to invalids, though it may be modeled on Worthing, then a new development. There are references in Jane Austen's letters of 1805 to a proposed visit to Worthing, along with cryptic reference to a competing visit to Sandling, in Kent. The latter name is inevitably suggestive; so is Sandgate, an even more likely possibility.[7] Indeed, "Never was there a place more palpably designed by Nature for the resort of the Invalid—the very Spot which Thousands seemed in need of," declares Mr. Parker (p. 369). *Sanditon* extends this theme to satirize hypochondria. The novelist suffered at close quarters from her mother's hypochondria during much of her adult life. In all likelihood she started to work off some of the results of that particular form of suffering in the character of Mr. Woodhouse in *Emma;* in *Sanditon* the attack on hypochondriacs is less gentle, and less subtle.

The sea and air of Sanditon are said to be "a match for every Disorder. . . . They were anti-spasmodic, anti-pulmonary, anti-sceptic, anti-bilious & anti-rheumatic" (p. 373). The fragment bulges with invalids and hypochondriacs of various species (one of them cannot eat toast without huge amounts of butter—otherwise it acts on his stomach like a nutmeg-grater), each of whom is able to demonstrate astonishing strength and blinding energy on selected (and usually private and selfish) occasions. Mr. Parker's description of his sister Susan shows Jane Austen writing in a vein approaching something like black comedy:

> She has been suffering much from the Headache and Six Leaches a day for 10 days together relieved [sic] her so little that we thought it right to change our measures—and being convinced on examination that much of the Evil lay in her Gum, I persuaded her to attack the disorder there. She has accordingly had 3 Teeth drawn, & is decidedly better, but her Nerves are a good deal deranged. She can only speak in a whisper—and fainted away twice this morning on poor Arthur's trying to suppress a cough (p. 387).

Charlotte sees the Parkers and their relations for what they are:

> It was impossible for Charlotte not to suspect a good deal of fancy in such an extraordinary state of health.—Disorders & Recoveries so very much out of the common way, seemed more like the amusement of eager Minds in want of employment than of actual afflictions & relief. The Parkers, were no doubt a family of Imagination & quick feeling . . . an unfortunate turn for Medecine [sic], especially quack Medecine, had given them an early tendency at various times, to various Disorders;—the rest of their sufferings was from Fancy, the love of Distinction & the love of the Wonderful.

"There was Vanity in all they did, as well as in all they endured," Charlotte concludes (pp. 412–13).

The theme of excessive "Fancy," "the love of the Wonderful," and "the amusement of eager Minds" in otherwise unimaginative people is part of the novelist's continuing attack on "romance" and the excesses of sentimentality. Coming into Willingden, Mr. Parker sees a cottage "romantically situated among wood on a high Eminence at some little Distance," and waxes fanciful about it (p. 364); later he discovers that it is inhabited by Mr. Heywood's shepherd and three old ladies. Sir Edward Denham, one of Jane Austen's most brilliant creations, speaks of nature as if he were a Romantic poet on temporary leave from a lunatic asylum:

> He began, in a tone of great Taste & Feeling, to talk of the Sea & the Sea shore—& ran with Energy through all the usual Phrases employed in praise of their Sublimity, & descriptive of the *undescribable* Emotions they excite the Mind of Sensibility.—The terrific Grandeur of the Ocean in a Storm, its glassy surface in a calm, it's [sic] Gulls and its Samphire [a maritime plant; but Denham may be remembering the hackneyed "Dover cliffs" scene in *King Lear*, Act III, scene vi, where the word occurs: "gathering samphire, dreadful trade"], & the deep fathoms of it's Abysses, it's quick vicissitudes, it's direful Deceptions, it's Mariners tempting it in Sunshine & overwhelmed by the sudden Tempest. All were eagerly & fluently touched (p. 396).

Surely the novelist had been reading the *Lyrical Ballads*—or Byron. When Sir Edward goes on to speak extravagantly of Burns, the following colloquy takes place between himself and Charlotte:

> Sir Edward: Burns is always on fire.—His soul was the Altar in which lovely Woman sat enshrined, his Spirit truly breathed the immortal Incence [sic] which is her Due.
>
> Charlotte: I have read several of Burn's [sic] poems with great delight . . . but I am not poetic enough to separate a Man's Poetry entirely from his Character;—& poor Burns's known Irregularities greatly interrupt my enjoyment of his Lines.—I have difficulty in depending on the *Truth* of his feelings as a Lover. I have not faith in the *sincerity* of the affections of a Man of his Description. He felt & he wrote & he forgot.
>
> Sir Edward: Oh! no no . . . He was all ardour & Truth!—His Genius & his Susceptibilities might lead him into some Aberrations—But who is perfect?— It were Hyper-criticism, it were Pseudo-philosophy to expect from the soul of high toned Genius, the grovellings of a common mind.—The Coruscations of Talent . . . are perhaps incompatible with some of the prosaic Decencies of Life (pp. 397–98).

Besides suggesting that the novelist had adopted the standard early nineteenth-century view of Burns (which was also Wordsworth's) as a man of genius but of irregular habits and undependable temperament (amply documented in Currie's "Life," appended to the first edition of the poet's works published in 1800 and in several subsequent editions thereafter[8]), this exchange may be seen in many ways as characteristic of Jane Austen. It is all there—man's tendency to "forget" before woman does (a theme of *Persuasion*), the belief in "*Truth*" and "*sincerity*" as the cornerstone of art (rather than "Sensibility"), the conviction that the artist is no less obligated than the ordinary mortal to lead an exemplary life.

Charlotte ultimately discovers Sir Edward to be "downright silly . . . why he sh[d] talk so much Nonsense, unless he could do no better, was unintelligible.—He seemed very sentimental, very full of some Feelings or other, & very much addicted to all the newest-fashioned hard words—had not a very clear Brain she presumed, & talked a good deal by rote" (p. 398).

In fact, Sir Edward has been driven nearly mad by his reading of sentimental and romantic literature. Written on the heels of *Persuasion,* which also takes an anti-romantic line, *Sanditon* gives another clear indication of what Jane Austen thought of sentimental literature and its readers. This perspective is not unusual in her work. We encounter it not only in *Persuasion,* but also in *Emma,* more forcefully in *Northanger Abbey* and *Sense and Sensibility,* in the Juvenilia and even in the letters (March 1814: "I have read the Corsair, mended my petticoat, & have nothing else to do"[9]). Sir Edward's taste in novels is described in particular detail and with obvious relish; it provides a good example of the age's predilection for the sort of "highly seasoned" fiction referred to by *Blackwood*'s the following year in its review of the posthumous *Northanger Abbey* and *Persuasion.* Sir Edward says:

> The Novels which I approve are such as display Human Nature with Grandeur—such as shew her in the Sublimities of intense Feeling—such as exhibit the progress of strong Passion from the first Germ of incipient Susceptibility to the Utmost Energies of Reason half-dethroned,—where we see the strong spark of Woman's Captivations elicit such Fire in the Soul of Man as leads him—(though at the risk of some Aberration from the strict line of Primitive Obligations)—to hazard all, dare all, atchieve [sic] all, to obtain her.— Such are the Works which I peruse with delight, & I hope I may say, with amelioration. They hold forth the most splendid Portraitures of high Conceptions, Unbounded Views, illimitable Ardour, indomptible [sic] Decision—and even when the Event is mainly anti-prosperous to the high-toned Machinations of the prime Character, the potent, pervading Hero of the Story, it leaves us full of Generous Emotions for him;—our Hearts are paralized [sic]—. T'wer Pseudo-Philosophy to assert that we do not feel more enwraped [sic] by the brilliancy of his Career, than by the tranquil & morbid Virtues of any opposing Character. Our approbation of the Latter is but Eleemosynary [charitable].—These are the Novels which enlarge the primitive Capabilities of the Heart, & which it cannot impugn the Sense or be any Dereliction of the character, of the most anti-puerile Man, to be conversant with (pp. 403–04).

Here is Jane Austen's version of How Not To Do It—a definition of the kind of novel she had spent a lifetime working to expunge from public taste, described in language which, one feels, she found equally repugnant. "If I understand you aright," Charlotte replies succinctly to this long speech, "our taste in Novels is not at all the same."

The author of *Sense and Sensibility* and *Northanger Abbey* goes on in her own voice to attack the literary taste of Sir Edward Denham.

> The Truth was that Sir Edw: whom circumstances had confined very much to one spot had read more sentimental Novels than agreed with him. His fancy had been early caught by all the impassioned, & most exceptional parts of Richardsons [sic]; & such Authors as have since appeared to tread in Richardson's steps, so far as Man's determined pursuit of Woman in defiance of every opposition of feeling & convenience is concerned, had since occupied the greater part of his literary hours, & formed his Character.—With a perversity of Judgement, which must be attributed to his not having by Nature a very strong head, the Graces, the Spirit, the Sagacity, & the perseverance, of the Villain of the Story outweighed all his absurdities & all his Atrocities with Sir Edward. With him, such Conduct was Genius, Fire & Feeling.—It interested & inflamed him; & he was always more anxious for its Success & mourned over its Discomfitures with more Tenderness that c^d ever have been contemplated by the Authors (p. 404).

Thus Jane Austen continues the assault, begun years earlier in her Juvenilia, on inept imitators of her favorite Richardson who turn out nothing but false sentiment. As in her preceding works, the excesses of "fancy" are specially singled out for excoriation and associated with lack of insight.

The novelist's attack here on sentimental and romantic fiction concludes with a hilarious account of the result, morally speaking, of Sir Edward's reading of trashy novels. They have not made him merely fanciful; they have made him deranged.

> Sir Edw.'s great object in life was to be seductive.—With such personal advantages as he knew himself to possess, & such Talents as he did also give himself credit for, he regarded it as his Duty.—He felt that he was formed to be a dangerous Man—quite in the line of the Lovelaces.—The very name of Sir Edward he thought, carried some degree of fascination with it.—To be generally gallant & assiduous about the fair, to make fine speeches to every pretty Girl, was but the inferior part of the Character he had to play (p. 405).

Looking around for someone appropriate to seduce and carry off with him, Sir Edward settles on Clara Brereton: "Her Situation in every way called for it. She was . . . young, lovely & dependant [sic]." Even Charlotte—"perhaps . . . owing to her having just issued from a Circulating Library"—sees Clara as, in every way, "a complete Heroine . . . She seemed placed on purpose to be ill-used. Such Poverty & Dependance joined to such Beauty & Merit seemed to leave no choice in the business" (p. 391). Making allowances for the novelist's irony, one might conclude that Sir Edward's disease could be contagious—especially among the users of circulating libraries. Sir Edward has in mind no ordinary escapade: he wishes to do something spectacular in the seduction line—"to strike out something new, to exceed those who had gone before him." He has a problem, however: he cannot afford anything extravagant. "Prudence," Jane Austen comments here, "obliged him to prefer the quietest sort of ruin & disgrace to the more renowned" (pp. 405–06). Poor Sir Edward: *quiet* ruin and disgrace do not coincide with his concept of duty in these circumstances.

Well, here is no seducer; here is no Wickham, no Willoughby, no William Elliot. Instead, here is a deeply interesting and amusing psychological study of a type; here is one of Jane Austen's most superb human portraits. Her marvelous account of the character of Sir Edward Denham even by itself must make us bitterly regret the catastrophic illness which put a stop to the writing of *Sanditon*. It promised to be one of her greatest achievements; her critics and students ignore it at their peril. Elizabeth Jenkins is one of the few readers of *Sanditon* to see the true significance of Sir Edward Denham:

> The character breaks new ground; because though Willoughby had a very ugly story in his past, and Wickham thought nothing of eloping with a girl who threw herself at his head, and Henry Crawford was so loose-living that he couldn't resist an affair even in circumstances when it was bound to cost him the engagement he was really anxious to secure; Edward Denham, the young man who had read too many novels and fancied himself as a Lovelace, approached the matter from a different angle, and his attitude is defined with an outspokenness unprecedented even in Jane Austen's workmanlike frankness, and with an almost weary cynicism.[10]

Sir Edward is not the only character in *Sanditon* lacking a true education. There is another of Jane Austen's attacks here on inept female "education" and the false values it may implant. The Miss Beauforts, for example, are "very accomplished & very Ignorant," their intellectual efforts being expended chiefly on matters of dress—"the object of all they do being to captivate some Man of much better fortune than their own" (p. 421). The connection between false values, insufficient education, and plain cupidity is centered chiefly in the character of Lady Denham, another portrait one regrets Jane Austen left unfinished. Lady Denham's "faults," it is said, "may be entirely imputed to her want of Education" (p. 376). She is surrounded by people whose sole object is to get their hands on her money; her sole object is to keep them from succeeding. Lady Denham's ideas of what constitutes Sanditon's greatest need is revealing:

> And if we c^d but get a young Heiress to [Sanditon]! But Heiresses are monstrous scarce! I do not think we have had an Heiress here, or even a Co—since

Sanditon has been a public place. Families come after Families, but as far as I can learn, it is not one in an hundred of them that have any real Property, Landed or Funded.—An Income perhaps, but no Property. Clergymen may be, or Lawyers from Town, or Half pay officers, or Widows with only a Jointure. And what good can such people do anybody? (p. 401)

This might comfortably fit into one of the early burlesques: Jane Austen had come full circle from the Juvenilia. If in *Sanditon* she had been planning to go more deeply into the human psyche than ever before, this last work, had it been completed, might have been her most savagely cynical performance (Miss Jenkins, half a century ago, certainly thought so).

As might be expected, there are also one or two autobiographical resonances here. Charlotte's parents are pointedly praised for doing as much as they can in the small village in which the Heywoods live to enable their daughters to come in the way of husbands. After all, in *Sanditon*, "young Ladies that have no Money are very much to be pitied!" (p. 401)—husbands must be found for them. Though her intelligence and her powers of discernment are acute, Charlotte, as long as we know her, manages to avoid overt censoriousness. She sees much, but says little—though, "There is someone in most families privileged by superior abilities or spirits to say anything" (p. 382). Surely we hear the voice of the novelist here.

No account of *Sanditon* was given out until 1871. In the second edition of the *Memoir* of his aunt, J. E. Austen-Leigh provided a description of what he called her "last work," and quoted some things from it. The whole did not see the light of day until 1925, when it was published in Chapman's edition of the *Minor Works*. To this day, in a sense, *Sanditon* has yet to be reviewed.

Notes

1. See J. E. Austen-Leigh, *A Memoir of Jane Austen* (London: Bentley, 1870; 1871), and William and Richard Arthur Austen-Leigh, *Jane Austen: Her Life and Letters* (London: John Murray, 1913), p. 382.

2. Joan Rees, *Jane Austen: Woman and Writer* (London: Robert Hale; and New York: St. Martin's Press, 1976), p. 184.

3. See Rees, p. 184; Alistair M. Duckworth, *The Improvement of the Estate: A Study of Jane Austen's Novels* (Baltimore and London: The Johns Hopkins University Press, 1971), p. 210; B. C. Southam, *Jane Austen's Literary Manuscripts: A Study of the Novelist's Development through the Surviving Papers* (Oxford: Oxford University Press, 1964), p. 102; and Southam, "*Sanditon*: The Seventh Novel," in *Jane Austen's Achievement*, ed. Juliet McMaster (London: Macmillan, 1975), p. 2. This essay also includes an interesting discussion of some possible connections between *Sanditon* and Peacock's *Headlong Hall* (1815).

4. Southam, *Jane Austen's Literary Manuscripts*, p. 115.

5. *The Novels of Jane Austen*, ed. R. W. Chapman, Vol. VI: *Minor Works* (London: Oxford University Press, 1954; rpt. 1958; rev. eds., 1963, 1965), p. 371. All subsequent quotations from *Sanditon* are taken from this edition; page references are given in the text.

6. Marilyn Butler, *Jane Austen and the War of Ideas* (Oxford: Oxford University Press, 1975), p. 286.

7. I am grateful to Professor Donald Greene for calling my attention to Sandling as a possible model for Sanditon, and to Dr. Clyde Binfield for suggesting Sandgate.

8. I should like to thank Professor Peter Manning for helping me to gloss the exchange between Charlotte Heywood and Sir Edward Denham on Burns.

9. *Jane Austen's Letters to Her Sister Cassandra and Others*, ed. R. W. Chapman (London: Oxford University Press, 1932; 2nd ed., 1952; rpt. 1959, 1964, 1969), p. 379. The letter (5 March 1814) is to Cassandra Austen.

10. Elizabeth Jenkins, *Jane Austen* (London: Pellegrini & Cudahy, 1938; 1949), pp. 386–87.

The Late Jane Austen

D. A. MILLER

> In the midst of this disorder, La Zambinella remained thoughtful, as though terrorstruck. She refused to drink, perhaps she ate a bit too much.
> —Balzac, "Sarrasine"

For many years after I first left home, whenever I got sufficiently sick with a cold or flu to need to "take to bed," I would take Jane Austen there with me. In the two or three days it took me to finish reading whichever one of her novels chance might choose for me, it never failed to happen that my health would be completely restored, or at least my convalescence essentially secured. Whichever novel, I say, but my indifference admitted one exception. I never dreamt at such times (more truly, I *only* dreamt, once and uneasily) of reading *Sanditon*, the novel satirizing hypochondria that Jane Austen, unfeignedly ill, died before completing. Barring *Sanditon*, Jane Austen's novels nursed me as effectively, I still like to think, as Miss Taylor nursed little Emma, who grew up into "the complete picture of grown up health": as effectively, as my own mother—who first invited me to read them and who of course was no longer appropriate to expect in attendance on my sickbed—might have done. So strongly did I thus learn to associate the promise of health with the various (comic, maternal) assurances borne in Austen's fiction that the link became a superstition. "Mansfield shall cure you." Jane Austen's novels did more than accompany my return to health; they accomplished it, I felt, in providing the *story* of recovery (albeit recovery different in kind) that was just as necessary to working my cure as the abundance of fluids with which I washed that story down. If I am like many other readers in having a fundamentally elegiac relation to Jane Austen, what I mourn is not a historical period (the so-called quiet England about to disappear in the noisy business of the Industrial Revolution) or a cultural ideal (a community whose leisure bore fruit in an ethics of civility and an esthetics of elegance), but an even more patently utopian fantasy about the body in a morbid state, a body

D. A. Miller, "The Late Jane Austen," *Raritan* 16 (1990): 55–75. © 1990 by *Raritan;* reprinted by permission.

that can't help displaying the same sanative logic as one of Austen's novels, with initially alarming symptoms of a disorder whose vicissitudes could nonetheless be plotted with precision from the vantage of eventual "improvement" and "amendment." What Jane Austen means to *me* (my Janeism) comes down to a childish notion that is easy to refute—or that would be if, after a certain age (or during an epidemic), the very ease of refutation didn't become poignant with its own kind of pain: the notion that while you may sometimes fall sick, you can always get better.

The fantasy might begin to be chastened (or carried through) in the less personal terms of a literary criticism that would notice how regularly in Austen an elementary medical diction, whose keyword is "cure," licenses various narrative and thematic crossovers between moral or psychological conditions and physical or medicable ones. In one direction, a state of desire may sometimes come to be hysterically converted into a question of health. Making Jane Fairfax unhappy, Frank Churchill finally makes her ill; Jane's recovery follows on her reconciliation with him, whom Mrs. Elton archly, but aptly, refers to as "a certain young physician from Windsor." Likewise, no one fails to remark that all the symptoms of Marianne Dashwood's nearly mortal illness—the nervous headache, the heavy cold, the infection, and the fever—result from the disappointment and depression she is suffering in the wake of her attachment to Willoughby; the sensible Elinor herself "felt all the reasonableness of the idea." In the opposite direction, health may be suggested to determine a moral-psychological state rather than resulting from it. This is the case with Emma Woodhouse, whose own good health is so abundantly signified: she has "a bloom of full health"; she is "the complete picture of grown-up health"; "she hardly knew what indisposition was"; her very home, Highbury, is reckoned "a particularly healthy spot." It is only a matter of time, we are thus made to feel, before the health that is "not only in her bloom, but in her air, her head, her glance" exuberantly reaches to absorb those "little faults" of her character, whose implied corrigibility assimilates them, as so many cases of moral measles, to "the various illnesses of childhood" already successfully got over. Sometimes, unable to decide whether the mind or the body be given priority, we can note only correlations: between Fanny Price's headaches, say, and her jealousy of Mary Crawford, or between Anne Elliot's renewed proximity to Captain Wentworth and the "second spring of youth and beauty" she comes to enjoy.

Insofar as the body in sickness and health is thus heaped high—in the language of murder and menus, one might say smothered—with moral and psychological meanings, it might seem to attest to its own virtual evanescence, which Austen has been accused of engineering by proponents of realism, who are puzzled not to know what her characters look like, and by advocates of "sexuality," who cannot discover the body except in flagrante delicto. Yet such semiotic pressure is too fierce to bespeak a body altogether devalorized, and too constant to presuppose a body wholly denied. On the contrary, one must argue that the body thus targeted plays a crucial, even supreme role in the construction of Jane Austen's "ideology." For if Austen feels obliged to somatize a psychological condition, or a moral judgment, or a delicate conflation of the two, this is not to dismiss the body's materiality as a mere echo chamber for meaning, so much as to exploit the body's felt self-evidence in the interests of anchoring within it an ideology that will therefore seem less arbitrarily imposed. All the deployments of the "bio-power" that characterizes our modernity depend on the supposition that the most effective take on the subject is rooted in its body, insinuated within this body's "natural given" imperatives. Metaphorizing the body begins and ends with literalizing the meanings the body is thus made to bear. Only by virtue of being felt to remain refractorily itself, for instance, is illness *worth* making mean something besides itself. At critical junctures, therefore, the anxiously large moral stakes of Austen's fiction come to ride on a representation of the body whose physical health and sickness will ground the propositions about mental states most needful of corroboration.

The most extreme example is furnished by Marianne Dashwood during her recovery: "My own feelings had prepared my sufferings and my want of fortitude under them had almost led me to the grave. My illness, I well knew, had been entirely brought on by myself, by such negligence of my own health as I had felt even at the time to be wrong. Had I died, it would have been self-destruction." On hearing this, Elinor, "too honest to flatter, gave her instantly that praise and support which her frankness and her contrition so well deserved." Poor Marianne: it is not enough that the novel continually censures her for the feelings and behaviors of her "sensibility"; it is not even enough that the novel chides her for getting sick. Finally, she must herself be brought forward to exonerate the sadism of all this unrelenting reprobation by pleading guilty to every charge. Just as, under torture, the most brutal means of coercion are employed in the paradoxical interest of securing a "voluntary" confession, similarly, Marianne must be taken to death's door so that she can say she traveled there of her own volition. The considerable modernity of this proceeding (which—pace Foucault—the analogy to torture hardly gainsays) might well be appreciated by many of the authors of our self-help books, who, themselves the Higher Power to whom they often recommend surrendering, swaddle the bodies of their actual "cases" in similarly structured recovery narratives; appreciated, too, rather more wryly, by the gay men who, if they would escape the full severity of social stigmatization that currently claims to find its natural justification in AIDS, are invited to confess the errors of a "meaningless promiscuity" and to celebrate the ways in which AIDS has mutilated their persons, and decimated their communities, as a new postadolescent maturity. The extent to which Marianne's recovery depends on her acceptance of so thoroughgoing a moralization of her body might seem extravagant, did not the intrinsic instability of moral rationalization in Jane Austen make the task of establishing a "just" proportion of requisite discipline impossible. For insofar as a major effort of Jane Austen's fiction is to provide rational and moral terms for a process that, deemed neither necessarily rational nor particularly moral, is not exactly felt to lend itself to such regulation—namely, what Austen calls the "transient, varying, unsteady nature of love" and could be more broadly recognized as the course of desire's many and various impulsions into configurations of which love is only one example—then the moral of the story, not to mention the morale of the storyteller and of all those to whom her narration is proffered, will always be in need of the confirmation that, taken in sickness and in health, *by* the marriage plot as well as in it, the heroine's body may be thought to provide.

It bears repeating that even a strong ideological use of the body grants the body's autonomy, its authority *never to be wrong* about its own responses: this is why, when the body can be made to second the motions of ideology, as with Marianne Dashwood, its support is so powerful. But this is also why the body can equally be used to counter that kind of correctness with the unimpeachability of its own exigencies. One recalls how the laughter that incessantly convulses Lydia Bennet's hyperactive body makes her entirely deaf to the voices that seek to moralize her as "untamed, unabashed, wild, noisy, and fearless"; or how Lady Bertram's low metabolism (sometimes condemned as indolence, but other times characterized as "the picture of health") protects her from all worry about her family, prevents her from ever having to entertain such anxious-making issues of love and right conduct as engross the other characters at Mansfield Park. Sometimes, even Emma's abundance of good health seems less a guarantor of good conduct than a Nietzschean bounty, responsible not exactly for what is good in Emma, or even for what is bad, but finally for what seems, in principle, to be neither: a spontaneous energy of will that doesn't bother to count the cost of its blissful assertion, whether that cost be defrayed by others, who may be hurt (Miss Bates) or virtually annihilated ("Harriet was nothing, she was everything herself"), or by Emma herself, whose desire is overbearing enough to welcome a self-inflicted wound ("it darted through her, with the speed of an arrow, that Mr. Knightley must marry no one but herself"). Of a certain necessity, then, Austen satirizes the figure of what one may call the semantically uncooperative body. By insisting on its status as sheer corporal mass, this body takes meaning with the exasperating indifference of a particularly cunning (or thoroughly obtuse) child taking a beating; and having taken meaning (any meaning whatsoever, as every meaning is equally beside the mark, equally unfair) will not *render it,* will not do it the justice of recognizing it as at all its own. The purest instance of this body—the fat body of Mrs. Musgrove, who in conversation with Captain Wentworth gets sentimental over the memory of her dead son—drives Austen to untypical distraction:

> [Anne and Wentworth] were actually on the same sofa, for Mrs. Musgrove had most readily made room for him—they were divided only by Mrs. Musgrove.

It was no insignificant barrier indeed. Mrs. Musgrove was of comfortable substantial size, infinitely more fitted by nature to express good cheer and good humor than tenderness and sentiment; and while the agitations of Anne's slender form, and pensive face, may be considered as very completely screened, Captain Wentworth should be allowed some credit for the self-command with which he attended to her large fat sighings over the destiny of a son whom alive nobody had cared for.

Personal size and mental sorrow have certainly no necessary proportions. A large bulky figure has as good a right to be in deep affliction as the most graceful set of limbs in the world; but fair or not fair, there are unbecoming conjunctions, which reason will patronize in vain—which taste cannot tolerate—which ridicule will seize.

We might expect this ridicule from Sir Walter Elliot, whose more than skin-deep obsession with personal beauty makes the prevailing variant of the socially prescribed body a first priority; we might expect the defense of this ridicule from Emma Woodhouse at her worst—on Box Hill, where she excuses her rudeness to Miss Bates in similar terms ("I know there is not a better creature in the world; but you must allow, that what is good and what is ridiculous are most unfortunately blended in her"). We don't expect it in a novelist whose compulsion to inflict mortification is usually better masked (if not less indulged) not just by being assigned to characters or embedded in plot, but also, with far greater thoroughness, by mortifying itself in the ironic, unobtrusive, *disciplined* narrative voice. The lapse—of technique as well as of what Austen would call moral taste—is hardly recovered from in the recognition that "personal size and mental sorrow have certainly no necessary proportions." The text has already established the very proportion between personal size and mental suffering whose necessity the example of Mrs. Musgrove supposedly makes doubtful: her sighings for a son whom alive nobody had cared for are themselves "fat," as inflated beyond proper scale as the large body which has been thus analogously taken to discredit them. In any case, the novelist seems to advance her ethical perspective ("certainly") the better a sentence later ("but fair or not fair") to prevent it from interfering with a battery that may now proceed in good conscience: rather like the obesity researcher who, having conclusively disproven the notion that obesity results from eating too much, but remaining nonetheless unable to resist, or unwilling to relinquish, the disciplinary opportunities in which this notion has long proven rich as a forbidden foodstuff in calories, must once more enjoin the obese to watch—as compulsively as he does—what they eat.

The fat body, even in the abuse it here receives, figures a body whose materiality is most clearly irreducible to whatever it may be made to mean— the body most likely to baffle the operations of semiotic liposuction into bearing witness to the violent mutilation that is their truth. The fat body matters, so to speak, but it doesn't signify; it matters *because* it doesn't signify, and vice versa. Even when Mrs. Musgrove most readily makes room for Wentworth, therefore, her body will seem not to have budged: not to have surrendered an inch of its space on the sofa, where, evidently as comfortable as it is big, it erects the barrier of its bulk, and so blocks the passage of eventual communication, which *Persuasion* has made essential, between Anne and Captain Wentworth. Perhaps if Mrs. Musgrove's consciousness had been shaped by a more recent fat discourse, which would exact tribute to the norm she must-not-but-can't-not depart from in the coin of self-abjecting diets, the socio-semiotic problem she poses—of the excess of the signifier over the signified—might have been resolved, through being by all parties acknowledged as *her* problem. For it is one thing that, held to the verisimilitude of a fat-phobic culture, this body is ill qualified (unlike Anne's "slender form") to signify anything so refined and un-Falstaffian as affliction. But it is another, and worse, when this body doesn't seem *to know enough* to apologize for this unfitness. This obliviousness—so unlike, one must add, the actual situation of most fat people in Western countries, who find it a far less easy achievement to suspend, or transcend, a sense of their oppression—compounds the resistance that Mrs. Musgrove's body offers to the prescriptions of a certain social legibility. In light of the high premium Jane Austen puts on a well-ordered signification and on its coinciding with right social dispositions, one readily sees why her taste cannot tolerate those unbecoming conjunctions which ridicule will seize *only after and because* reason has patronized them in vain. Perhaps there only remains to remark how the semiotic outrage or despair, which the fat body provokes in the novelist, turns her abuse of it into a projective version of what is being abused—a point that might least amply be put by noting that, with no damage to our understanding of *Persuasion,* the passage might have been trimmed. But even when thus turned against the text here, why should its valorization of the "slender form" remain ours? Why not instead maintain stoutly, if only to illustrate that body language can cut—be cutting—two ways, that the passage, in so exiguous a relation to the plot characters, and themes of *Persuasion,* is discursively "thin"?

One reason why not is to avoid seconding the aggression that the diminutive woman suffers in Austen no less than the large: consider another Anne, Miss de Bourgh in *Pride and Prejudice,* and Elizabeth Bennet's astonishment at her "being so thin and so small" and at her "insignificant" features. Insofar as it is the text's own ego-ideal, therefore, the slender form is not a question of starting small, but of making smaller. The exquisite economy, not to say parsimony, practiced on the "little piece (two inches wide) of ivory" entails fierce gestures of refusal. Here, from *Sense and Sensibility,* are typical examples of Austen's use of the word *enough:* "It is enough; to say that he is unlike Fanny is enough. It implies everything amiable. I love him already" (Mrs. Dashwood about Edward Ferrars); "This specimen of the Miss Steeles was enough. . . . [Elinor] left the house without any wish of knowing them better"; "Marianne gave one glance around the apartment as she entered; it was enough, *he* was not there—and she sat down, equally ill-disposed to receive or communicate pleasure"; "Marianne heard enough. In one moment her imagination placed before her a letter from Willoughby, full of tenderness and contrition, explanatory of all that had passed, satisfactory, convincing, and instantly followed by Willoughby himself"; "I happened to drop in for ten minutes, and I saw quite enough of her. The merest awkward country girl, without style or elegance, almost without beauty" (Robert Ferrars about Lucy Steele); "His coming for me, as he did, with such active, such ready friendship, is enough to prove him one of the worthiest of men" (Mrs. Dashwood about Colonel Brandon).

Whether the word betrays the eagerness of prejudice (Marianne's or Mrs. Dashwood's) or compliments an unusual quickness of comprehension (Elinor's), *enough* in these contexts uniformly bears a nuance of meaning *less than enough*. As such, it does not mark a point of actual satiety or sufficiency, so much as the site of a preemptive strike against redundancy and excess. The narrator is hardly exempt from this fear of flap—for example, "To give the feelings or the language of Mrs. Dashwood on receiving and answering Elinor's letter would be only to give a repetition of what her daughters had already felt and said." Except for its finer (but less minced) expression, the mechanism at work is not greatly dissimilar from that recommended by the Thin Within Program, where on Day 5 "we learn when to begin [eating] (when we're hungry) and when to stop (when we've had 'just enough')." Let Austen's lovers feast on the food of love ("between *them*, no subject is finished, no communication is even made, till it has been made at least twenty times over") or her chatterboxes, no less shamelessly fixated at the oral phase, binge on their blahblah; her narrator (anerotic and anorectic, truly "an old maid at last,") will never cease invigilating over *what she puts into her mouth.*

The auctorial violence that "breaks" Marianne's body, so that it conforms to a moral truth, or breaks against Mrs. Musgrove's, because it does not so conform, no doubt betrays how important a rectitude of the body is to that instruction in good conduct which makes so large a part of the project of the so-called novel of manners. Yet when Austen marches Marianne and Mrs. Musgrove to the woodhouse (Emma's? the same school, at any rate, where Emma imagines teaching the presuming Coles *some manners*), the humbling blows hardly strike what we like to think of as her characteristic note. For Austen's famous irony, in performing its essential work of transcoding one account (a character's, the world's) into another (the narrator's) capable of reading the blind spots in the first, necessitates no fewer discursive instances than two; whereas the body in question here remains as silent as the population-object of a poll, its autonomy restricted to the small number of positions it may take on the meaning that confronts it from the outside: yes, no, no opinion. However received, meaning thus remains the body's other, fabricated elsewhere on a different foundation. In any *typical* fashion, therefore, the body can only enter Austen's fiction when it has a voice of its own, or provides the basis for an alternative semiosis—and so, as it were, justifies getting hit with meaning by talking back. One begins to understand why, as it happens, the password that confers the right to such access is hypochondria. For unlike the sentimentalized sick, whose defenses are so far down that they may be ventriloquized into saying whatever morality needs to hear, or the savaged fat, whose supposed deaf-mutism deserves only to be shouted and gestured at, the *ironizable* hypochondriacal truly discourse: nothing is more dependent on language—to incite, express, distend it—than their imaginary malady. As intensely committed to sense-making as the novelist or any of her heroines, but basing it on medical rather than moral principles, hypochondriacs provide Austen with that odd compatibility we call a congenial target.

It is not just Mr. Woodhouse, "a valetudinarian all his life," who believes that "where health is at stake, nothing else should be considered." The generally uncontested priority of the right to health in Austen is precisely what allows his hypochondria to invoke it to blunt or relieve the pressure of those other considerations that, far from simply being trivial or irrelevant, as he is pleased to get to claim, are so overpowering that they seem to determine the very desire to advance such a claim. Tellingly, the only other notable trait to characterize Mr. Woodhouse, besides a preoccupation with health, is an equally extravagant and obsessive respect for the dues of civility. In the economy of his character, the two traits are versions, conversions, of one another: only appeals to civility seem to make any inroads on the empire of his *imaginaire malade,* which alone in turn gives promise of abridging the endless ceremony in which he believes he must stand. Thus, adducing the necessity of his exercise, he delegates his duties as Mr. Knightley's host to Emma ("we invalids think we are privileged people"); but "the scruples of his own civility" require that even so minor a dereliction be made the object of endless apology ("if you will excuse me, Mr. Knightley, if you will not consider me as doing a very rude thing"; "I leave an excellent substitute in my daughter"; "I would ask for the pleasure of your company, but I am a very slow walker, and besides—"). Hypochondria thus appears as a solution to the problem posed by an excessive sensitivity to what is owed to society—of which, as the text aptly notes, "Mr. Woodhouse was fond in his own way." "Unfit for any acquaintance, but such as would visit him on his own terms," he is released from the responsibilities of etiquette that, the first to feel, he would otherwise be compelled into accepting. To this extent, the appeal of hypochondria lies in a promised exemption from the wages of socialization: a suspension of the various social and moral nomenclatures ready to saturate, and aiming to constrain, a subject who instead is sheltered under the privileged jurisdiction of health.

As such, hypochondria betokens a response to what without exaggeration may be called the tyranny of the social: for the social order imagined by hypochondria (in its unconscious, as it were) is so intractably oppressive that resistance can only take the form of an equally total and nonnegotiable negation. It comes as no surprise, therefore, that hypochondria can only differentiate itself from the tyranny of the social by establishing a tyranny of its own. "The great Mrs. Churchill," the "capricious woman," "as impatient as the black gentleman," whose "illnesses never occurred but for her own convenience," offers the most striking example of the despotic character assumed by the hypochondriac: she "governed her husband"—and by implication everyone else around her—"entirely." Others are Mary Musgrove in *Persuasion*, "always fancying herself ill" as a way of compelling attention and having her way; Diana Parker in *Sanditon*, an imaginary invalid of "unaccountable officiousness"; and Mr. Woodhouse himself, whose amiable temper better colors an egocentrism that must be "consulted in everything" by Emma and her friends. So complete a tyranny hardly spares the tyrant, and precisely to the extent that Mrs. Churchill "is ordered, or has ordered herself" from Enscombe, which is too cold for her, to London, and then from London, which is too noisy for her, to Richmond, her caprices have her coming and going as much as anyone in her entourage. Likewise, the intricacies of etiquette from which Mr. Woodhouse's hypochondria somewhat disentangles him get refigured in his quasi-Levitical culinary observances regarding gruel, boiled eggs, and baked apples. And while Arthur Parker in *Sanditon* may avoid the social injunction to have a profession by "fancying himself too sickly for any"—while he may also thus avoid the necessity even more comprehensively impending on single men in Austen's novels, being "in want of a wife"—he does not escape the rigors of the *régime* (as the French like to call a diet) enforced by his sisters: indeed, during what the text calls tea (but when, "by no means so fond of being starved as they could desire," he in fact prefers to coddle and cook a fine, dark-colored cocoa), the amazing sleight-of-hand responsible for his sneaking an extra "great dab" of butter onto his toast yields nothing in pathos to the smooth efficiency with which, between the work left in town and the domesticity attendant in the suburbs, certain businessmen interpose the pleasure obtainable in the roadside venues not dissimilarly misnamed tea-rooms.

All this affines hypochondria to the social, which therefore remains capable of reappropriating it without effort or loss. Arthur, for instance, is said to adopt illness "principally for the indulgence of an indolent temper,—and to be determined on having no disorders but such as called for warm rooms and good nourishments." Wherever hypochondria has attempted to erase socio-moral nominations of conduct, Austen's irony consists of simply writing them back in, as the first and last word: accordingly, just as Arthur is more indolent than ill, so Mrs. Churchill and Mary Musgrove are not sickly so much as selfish, and Diana Parker, though she may often seek to appear moribund, is only meddlesome. This game of hide-and-seek turns on a double instrumentalization of health, first by the hypochondriac to conceal the right moral terms for his behavior, then by the novelist to educe them once more and so reaffirm their universal application. However basic the theme of health may be in Jane Austen, therefore, extending even to the frequent no-tation of the weather (whose mutability might prevent daily exercise or bring on a cold), its primary figuration as hypochondria keeps it an ancillary theme, in a docile relation to the traditional social order on which the novel is respectfully based. The theme merely affords us the pleasure—as paradox-ical as the pleasure of doing the police in different voices, of doing cops *tout court*—of rediscovering dominance: the dominance of the socio-moral pre-scriptions from which the theme promised relief. (In the same way, much of our fun and even our competence in reading Dickens's *Little Dorrit* depends on our ability to recognize, again and again, in countless new guises and dis-guises, the same old prison.)

The vulgar construction of hypochondria—"but nothing is really the matter"—invites us to consider the general absence of serious illness from an oeuvre whose additional failure to represent the deathbed—the great *scene à faire* for the Victorians—makes it absolutely unique in nineteenth-century fic-tion. Major characters in Austen do not die; barring a couple of regulative ex-ceptions (Marianne's fever, Louisa Musgrove's fall), they scarcely suffer less derisory maladies than a sore throat. Evidence of a body that distaste, protec-tiveness, indifference would eclipse? But the body is not dismissed thus, so much as held in reserve for other more productive uses: for the blushing, the blooming, the dancing—for all the comportments, in short, entailed on it by the marriage plot. "Oh! that he had sprained his ankle in the first dance," Mr. Bennet pretends to wish of Mr. Bingley at the beginning of *Pride and Preju-dice,* antithetically setting out the physical requirements for this plot, which so completely and compulsively engrosses Austen's novels, that her charac-ters—though idle and well off, here resembling workaholics and the poor—simply *can't afford* to be ailing.

Emma, the best developed example, has an unhappy state of health for the child of such a man as Mr. Woodhouse, "for she hardly knew what indis-position was, and if he did not invent illnesses for her, she could make no fig-ure in a message." Yet the text is not drawing a contrast between health and illness (since Mr. Woodhouse is inventing illnesses for himself as much as for Emma), but between two, more and less strong modes of being well. While Emma manifests her health through the sheer silence she keeps about a body so radiantly well functioning that everything about it may be taken for granted, Mr. Woodhouse affirms his own by garrulously fabricating an infi-nite series of worries and dangers that make health all the more precious for seeming precarious. The two modes cooperate in the proper ("healthy") func-tioning of the traditional form of the novel Austen writes. Health either goes without saying as the necessary condition of the socially productive, repro-ductive body, or only speaks to utter the discourse of hypochondria, which in turn gets ironized into reinforcing the socio-moral code that, among not so many other things, instructs this body in the right ways to realize its nubility.

Sanditon imagines the radical refiguring of the relationship between health and the social. If the status of hypochondria now expands from an eighteenth-century *humor* to a twentieth-century *life style* (Mr. Woodhouse calls himself an invalid; in *Sanditon,* Austen speaks of invalidism), the chief reason is that the eponymous bathing place offers hypochondria a "support system" in social organization. In *Emma,* the distribution of hypochondria allotted no more than one hypochondriac per given world: Mr. Woodhouse at Highbury, Mrs. Churchill at Enscombe, Isabella Woodhouse in London. These demographics are overthrown in Sanditon, which is home to not just one hypochondriac, whose singularity might have been marginalized accordingly, but a whole family of them—a family, moreover, comprising much and many more than its immediate circle. Mr. Parker is the "projector," or developer, of Sanditon itself: he is obsessed, if not with health, like his sisters, who though spinsters, nonetheless take on the quasi-reproductive task of multiplying the species, busily assist him in the enterprise by recruiting other persons and families to populate this space. Generalized to a family that is in turn generalized to a community, hypochondria no longer stands in even superficial opposition to the social (as, for instance, a refuge from its demands). On the contrary, this individual, individualizing disorder has become newly sociable, to the point where the very term *hypochondria*—either as medical diagnosis or moral trait, a personal property—ceases to be a useful designation for a concern with health that is too productive (of bodily mutilation and pain—think of Susan Parker, who when "six leeches a day" bring her no relief from headache, resorts to having three teeth drawn—no less than of goods, services, and what developers, perhaps taking the metaphor from oncology, call "growth") to be just in someone's head—or at any rate, it is now in the head of almost everybody. The justification for an openly anachronistic reading of *Sanditon*—one that would ride the "chamber horse" right into the Nautilus club; distill "asses' milk" into wheat grass, and get wind of aroma therapy in the "saline air"; even refuse to acknowledge any difference between the various herb teas drunk at the Parkers (where there were "almost as many teapots as there were persons in company") and our own—lies in the interest of dramatizing the text's own modernity as it grasps the emergence, and frames the essential practice, of what we had better call *a culture of morbidity.*

In the growth of this culture, "health"-oriented discourses, perceptions, and practices are floated broadly across the social space and sunk deeply within the subject. No longer may health be signified by a body whose silence on the subject merely crowns its boast of perfect well-being. Health now includes as a major component of its meaning talking, caring, worrying, at all events *doing something,* about health. Charlotte Heywood, the heroine of *Sanditon,* has no less "excellent health" than Emma Woodhouse, and no more to say about it; but this fact, far from making her the splendid physical specimen that everyone admires, makes her more recessive a presence in a world where the sign of health has passed from one's enviable ability to take health for granted to one's imperative self-inscription in health discourses and health practices. Just as *cuisine* only earns its name when it affords other pleasures than satisfying hunger, and *couture* designates those aspects of clothing that cannot be reduced to functions of decency or protection, so in morbidity culture, health-care exceeds an order of utility to become a *practice of perversion,* "the exercise of a desire which serves no purpose," Roland Barthes reminds us, like "the exercise of the body which gives itself up to love with no intention of procreation."

A stranger to morbidity culture, Charlotte Heywood naively assumes that you consult medical authority *because* you are not well ("in any illness, I should be so anxious for professional advice"); Austen, more at home in Sanditon, knows that it is their "turn for medicine" no less than "some natural delicacy of constitution" that gives the Parker sisters their tendency "at various times, to various disorders." In the novel's opening incident, allegorical of how little morbidity owes to commonsensical notions of illness, health, or the mediation by medicine between the two, it is the simple desire for a doctor that precipitates an occasion for his services. As their carriage toils up a rough lane to the presumed dwelling of an "advertising surgeon," Mr. and Mrs. Parker are overturned, and Mr. Parker badly sprains his ankle. "It could not have happened in a better place," he comforts himself, with the prospect of nearby medical relief, and offers in the next breath a still more sanguine account of his injury as "the very thing perhaps to be wished for." Well might he so cheerfully regard the irony of his situation, even without "an intention of breaking his ankle, or doing himself any other injury for the good of [the] surgeon." For he had originally wanted this surgeon not on his own account, but for the sake of Sanditon, where "the advantage of a medical man at hand would very materially promote the rise and prosperity of the place—would in fact tend to bring a prodigious influx." In principle, therefore, his happy fall confirms his speculation on the precedence of the doctor over disorders that are only summoned into being consequently. Such a doctor, it is already implied, would not be primarily occupied in curing sickness, but rather in the manufacture and management of morbidity, initiating the clients conjured by his sheer presence into the jargons, technologies, and practices of modern "health care," and generally helping to mark middle-income bodies with signs of their appurtenance to a system run—like the gadgets of the modern home (or, for that matter, to anticipate Austen's own association, of the modern hospital)—without necessary reference or responsibility to criteria of use.

When it comes to the proof, however, Mr. Parker has mistaken the address (there are two Willingdens, and his advertisement refers to the other), and no doctor is in the house. "But we shall do very well without him," dares say Mr. Heywood, who arrives on the scene to offer Mr. Parker the "hospitality," as the text repeatedly has it, of a family "well stocked with all the common remedies for bruises and sprains," not to mention daughters to wait on and nurse him. The inceptive desire for the doctor is balked, but being balked, engenders and even legitimates the transfer of his authority to a whole population of paramedics. Morbidity culture is thus founded in precise relation to the doctor figure, whom it first negates, or at least sets at a distance, and then sublates in the "habit of self-doctoring" required to produce a morbid subject. Diana Parker, as good an example as promoter and manager of this subject, articulates the double move thus: "We have entirely done with the whole medical tribe. We have consulted physician after physician in vain, till we are quite convinced that they can do nothing for us and that we must trust to our own knowledge of our own wretched constitutions for any relief." Dear and despised, felt now to facilitate, now to foil the habit of self-doctoring and the ensuing formation of the doctoring self, the medical man haunts morbidity culture as the great phantom of its operation: wherein he is at once nowhere, all desire for him frustrated or repudiated, and everywhere, his expertise usurped and exceeded, pulverized as finely as one of the powders he might in times past have prescribed (or nowadays snort) and undislodgeably ground into the whole social fabric—how good for the rug is still to determine. The desire for the doctor, in other words, is eventually explicated as a desire to be one—one's own.

Accordingly, we best make out the distinctiveness of morbidity culture where we see it parasitizing traditional attitudes toward the doctor (independence, mistrust, worshipful fidelity to his "orders") that it therefore, by the way, has no need to replace. Thus, for instance, if Austen is able to draft the Heywoods' self-sufficiency at Willingden into an inductive parable of Sanditon and its very different ways, this attests to the hegemony, of signification as much as of style, that morbidity exercises over the remotest sphere: Mr. Parker's recovery dilates to "a whole fortnight," time enough to recruit Charlotte Heywood, "with excellent health, to bathe and be better if she could" at Sanditon. Within Sanditon, a similar self-reliance, become crabbed and superstitious, is bespoken by Mr. Parker's "colleague in speculation," Lady Denham. With "a fine healthy frame for a woman of seventy," Lady Denham hasn't taken physic "above twice," "never saw the face of a doctor in all her life," and believes that if her late husband "had never seen one neither, he would have been alive now." Yet though unwilling to be morbid herself, she is well prepared to help others become so. As she wishfully converts the absence of a doctor into a demand for the sea, the downs, her late husband's chamber horse, and above all her own milch asses, her apparent rejection of morbidity culture proves merely to entertain it on a more modest scale. In the form of those very milch asses, Mrs. Griffith, on behalf of the "sickly and rich" Miss Lambe in her charge, rejects morbidity culture on opposite grounds: "Miss Lambe was under the constant care of an experienced physician;—and his prescriptions must be their rule." But this rule, too, never to deviate from "the strict medicinal page," requires the corroboration of a "morbid" exception—"some tonic pills, which a cousin of hers had property in."

As these examples suggest, morbidity is always linked to an economic incentive, as the health that variously makes and is made by wealth. With no interest in "encouraging . . . servants and the poor to fancy themselves ill," morbidity instantiates the privilege of a middle class whose income permits indulgence in "symptoms of the gout and a winter at Bath." Its perverse practices—in this respect not perverse enough—motivate the implantation of a consumer economy that, like the library at Sanditon, thrives on the circulation of "all the useless things in the world that could not be done without." So intimately knit are the economy and the culture that the discursive dilation of the morbid symptom characteristic of the superstructure metaphorically matches, and metonymically makes way for, the no less programmatic increase of prices, profits, and property values that must, for the speculation to succeed, occur in the base. Superstructure and base are together caught up in a general inflation of the sign: a destabilization of the connection between sign and meaning, or between sign and referent, that would encompass, in addition to the morbid symptom and the price rise, "the bewilderment of some of [the] sentences" of Sir Edward Denham, who is "very much addicted to all the newest-fashioned hard words" and "talk[s] a good deal by rote," and the equally inconsistent communication of Diana Parker, who appears to lack "the slightest recollection" of what she wrote under a week ago, and—like her brother contracting two Willingdens into one—expands the itinerary of a single family into the expectation at Sanditon of two: but "the family from Surrey and the family from Camberwell were one and the same."

Yet morbidity makes more difference in *Sanditon,* and between this text and Austen's previous six novels, than as a figure of a consumer economy or even of a general problematic of the sign. After all, the prospect of consumerism is not that threatening to a novelist who has always taken pride in her somewhat snide knowledge of economic determinants and whose text in any case aspires to nothing better than a place among the rings and brooches in the circulating library. As a reading focus, the semiotic problematic likewise risks merely assimilating *Sanditon* to the rest of Austen's oeuvre, where the volatility of the sign is posed as part of a project of its eventual restabilization; from this perspective, though *Sanditon* happened to be unfinished, the anticipated lines of its closure might easily be drawn. In regrounding the social in a body perversely valorized for its own sake, however, morbidity effects such mutations on the narrative that the usual working out is no longer plausible, is perhaps not even possible. The most text-specific meanings of morbidity in *Sanditon* warrant nothing less eventful than the disintegration of the very plot defining what we call the Jane Austen novel.

The typical, that is to say, eighteenth-century, watering place portrayed by Smollett (in *Humphry Clinker*), Scott (in *St. Ronan's Well*), and Austen herself (in *Persuasion*) supplied a scene for middle-class encounters whose modalities—visits, dinners, outings, balls—and finalities—the display of status, the reaffirmation of social norms, the distribution of wealth, above all the business of marriage—hardly differed from what they would have been elsewhere, in the more formal town or the less dense country. Even here, considerations of health, while they might preoccupy humor characters, so little interfered with the generic circuitry of middle-class space that in the same breath Mrs. Elton—formerly "a Miss Hawkins of Bath"—could recommend her native spa to Mr. Woodhouse, for the waters, and to Emma, for those "advantages to the young" which, she said, were "pretty generally understood." But if the socialization of hypochondria at Sanditon changes its status, the resultant culture of morbidity in turn transfigures the elements and operations of social space, whose ethos can no longer be epitomized, indeed may not even be at all tenable, by the marriage plot that in Austen's other novels never relaxes the rigor of its grip on every episode.

Let Miss Lambe, a "young woman, sickly and rich," exemplify the torsion to which morbidity culture submits the elements out of which Austen's marriage plot would ordinarily be made. As "a young West Indian of large fortune," Miss Lambe is unexceptionably entitled to play at the marriage game (if only, like the heiresses in *Mansfield Park* and *Pride and Prejudice*, as the heroine's vanquished rival), and Lady Denham seems already to have marked her out for Sir Edward, who she insists "*must* marry for money." But Miss Lambe is also, uniquely in Austen, a person of color, or what, engaging in the self-contradictory attempt to calculate and control the damage, which thereby becomes all the more immitigable, the text must more precisely call "half mulatto." How can such a character enter a marriage plot that tolerates class difference only when a middle-class woman, such as Elizabeth Bennet or Maria Ward, has "the good luck to captivate" a man of the aristocracy and could hardly admit racial difference except by severing its reliance on the class decorums to which its very identity is owing? Yet exactly what will most likely make Miss Lambe unusable to the marriage plot puts morbidity culture at no loss for ways of articulating her within the horizon of its characteristic concerns. The very presence of a "half mulatto" in the text probably encodes Jane Austen's concern with her own changed looks—"black & white & every wrong colour," as she complained to her niece only a few days after her illness (likely Addison's disease, with its darkening of the skin on the face)—and compelled Austen to abandon *Sanditon* for good. In the manuscript's unfinished state, the characterization of Miss Lambe is never more than begun, but what there is of it already suffices to pathologize her mixed race as a possible cofactor of her "delicate health," alongside the "hot climate" that Diana Parker holds responsible for helplessness and indolence. Via the word *mulatto* itself (from the Latin *mulus*, mule), Miss Lambe is linked with the salubrious milch asses that Lady Denham dreams of leasing her and with those accident-prone horses which, just before the Parkers' carriage is overturned, its proto-Dostoevskian driver inconsistently "pitie[s] and cut[s]," as though he cut them precisely not to pity them, or himself, and in explanation of the text's own mannered sarcasm when it finds Miss Lambe "chilly and tender": referring doubtless to her attenuated blood, but rehearing just as surely thereby the discoloring causticity of tone whose more than customary emphasis in *Sanditon* might have everything to do with its being proffered as a fantasy of the author's own corrected and hence uncompromised body.

In contrast to Miss Lambe, or to those "excellent . . . women," as Barbara Pym might, and Jane Austen does, denominate the Parker sisters, at an age that puts them in those "years of danger" when though marriageableness may no longer be presumed, spinsterhood has not yet been confirmed, Charlotte Heywood is unambiguously tracked for matrimony. Yet not unlike the baffled Goldilocks portrayed by many a contemporary self-help book, who going in search of a husband "just right" for her finds nothing but prepotent papa bears with an aspiration to date-rape or too-close-to-mama bears ready to launch her career in faghagging, Charlotte only meets male heterosexual desire at either of two equally unacceptable "extremes": in the excessive form of Sir Edward Denham, whose "great object in life was to be a seducer . . . quite in the line of the Lovelaces," plotting "ruin and disgrace for the object of his affections," and in the defective condition of Arthur Parker, whose sissy-boy syndrome is already stimulative of Mr. and Mrs. Parker's worries—if only his sisters would leave him "more alone"—that he is not the marrying kind.

Accordingly, with Miss Lambe proving the plurality of an ostensibly universal and unified culture, and with Arthur and Sir Edward manifesting how irreconcilably male desire differs from wanting women or from what women want, as though all the good men had been taken by earlier Austen heroines, the norm of couple formation that governed *their* marriages becomes here hard to imagine, unless by assuming with unimaginable frankness the violence of its requisite (racist) exclusions and (heterosexist) oppressions. And if a couple were to form in Sanditon, what could be its prospects? The figurations of what usually passes for the normal family make it anomalous not to say monstrous: leaving aside "the whole Parker race," a phrase that brings them into suspect association with Miss Lambe on the one hand and "the whole medical tribe" on the other, there remain only the Heywoods, whose progeny of fourteen has outstripped what the text considers the "reasonable limits" of their class. Besides, *Sanditon* also calls *families* those alternative social groupings not based on conjugality, such as Mrs. Griffith's girls' boarding school, which suggests (among less euphoric possibilities) that certain desiderata connected with "familiality" could be and in fact have already been detached from the bourgeois insistence on a nuclear family that in any event, the Heywoods' case illustrates, is as likely as any other nuclear technology to explode.

Yet for all that the world of *Sanditon* may be thought of as postconjugal, the novel dutifully carries on its predecessors' business (as though it knew no other) of escorting a nubile heroine through a gradated series of encounters with the single men whose suitability and intentions she must minutely assess. Nor, having engaged the marriage plot, does Austen show the slightest interest in dramatizing its failure or in developing a critique of it, as might the Victorian novelists. George Elliot's disappointment with this plot and Thomas Hardy's rage against it alike presuppose cathecting it; whereas in *Sanditon,* from a plot whose motions merely she continues to perform, Austen simply and fatally *withdraws affect.* As with some necessary, but not especially pleasant or even interesting domestic chore, her boredom takes alternate forms of procrastination and dispatch, putting off the marriage plot and getting it over. Putting it off: though we have almost twelve full chapters of *Sanditon,* we are as uncertain of who will ultimately win the heroine's affections—if indeed he has yet been introduced—as in *Emma* or *Pride and Prejudice,* after far fewer chapters, we feel sure of him; if most readers fill in the blank with Sidney Parker, this is mainly because he alone of the eligible men enjoys the recommendation of not having been enough exhibited to disqualify himself. Getting it over: the heroine's usual long education in the limited appeal of the Agreeable Young Man (Willoughby, say, or Wickham) is here impatiently abridged to the "half-hour's fever" that attacks Charlotte on her first pleased observation of Sir Edward ("she liked him"), drops considerably in the next paragraph ("perhaps there was a good deal in his air and address and his title did him no harm"), and has passed altogether by the next page ("she began to think him downright silly. . . . she felt that she had had quite enough").

Now while a woman in Austen's world *must* marry for reasons (of status, security, social obligation) that have nothing to do with love, it is no less true that she *must not* marry for those reasons, or for them alone. "How wretched, and how unpardonable, how hopeless and how wicked it was, to marry without affection" is Fanny Price's pious, but otherwise unexceptionable thought. The compelling objective necessity of getting married never by itself amounts to an acceptable subjective reason for doing so. Instead, a woman who marries must feel she is determining her destiny and discovering her desire, albeit under the same patriarchal dispensation that alienates the one and the other. Accordingly, she must solicit that mental state most propitious for reconciling whatever she may want to do with what she has little choice about doing in any case—in a word, she needs to try and fall in love. In the consummate form that Fanny calls affection, affect is the means through which the social pressure to marry may seem to originate in the subject's will, and culminate in her fulfillment. Austen's distinctive contribution to ideology lies not in her insistence on producing or even featuring a marriage plot (an obsession that few English novels fail to share), but in the unprecedented concentration of romantic feeling in which she imbues this plot, whose outcome becomes not simply inevitable, but also supremely desirable, to readers as well as characters. For here is a novelist as bent on internalizing the marriage obligation as any of her heroines, and the unmistakable artfulness that invests her arrangement of the marriage plot bears more manifest witness to her famous control than to what is likewise the case, the control of such control by the social prescriptions that readers are palatably, even deliciously made to swallow in the process. Into the Jane Austen novel that thus aims at redeeming the external social necessity of marriage, at rendering it an emotionally rich realization of both the heroine's personal satisfaction and, in the different registers appertaining to them, the novelist's and reader's as well—into this novel, therefore, the no worse than perfunctory treatment of the marriage plot in *Sanditon* must introduce an irreparable malfunction. (*Here the manuscript breaks off.*)

Index

◆

The Volume Editor

Laura Mooneyham White is visiting associate professor of English and assistant dean of the College of Arts and Sciences at the University of Nebraska–Lincoln. She received her B.A. in English at Yale University, and her M.A. and Ph.D. at Vanderbilt University. She is the author of *Romance, Language, and Education in Jane Austen's Novels* (Macmillan, 1988) and numerous essays on nineteenth- and twentieth-century British literature.

The General Editor

Zack Bowen is professor of English at the University of Miami. He holds degrees from the University of Pennsylvania (B.A.), Temple University (M.A.), and the State University of New York at Buffalo (Ph.D.). In addition to being general editor of this G. K. Hall series, he is editor of the James Joyce series for the University of Florida Press and the *James Joyce Literary Supplement*. He is the author and editor of numerous books on modern British, Irish, and American literature. He has also published more than one hundred monographs, essays, scholarly reviews, and recordings related to literature. He is past president of the James Joyce Society (1977–1986), former chair of the Modern Language Association Lowell Prize Committee, and current president of the International James Joyce Foundation.

ISBN 0-7838-0093-2

90000

9 780783 800936